ANNUAL REGISTER OF INDIAN AFFAIRS

THE ANNUAL REGISTER OF INDIAN AFFAIRS

In the Western (or Indian) Territory

1835 - 1838

by

Isaac McCoy

Particular Baptist Press

Springfield, Missouri

Facsimile Reprint

1998

Particular Baptist Press
2766 W. Weaver Rd.
Springfield, Missouri 65810

This edition has been enlarged
20% to facilitate reading

ISBN   1-888514-12-4

© Copyright 2000

Reproduced from the originals
in the collections of the
American Baptist Historical Society
Rochester, New York

and

The Franklin Trask Library
Andover-Newton Theological Seminary
Newton Centre, Mass.

Second Edition - Illustrated & Indexed
Printed on Acid -Free Paper

PREFACE

Isaac McCoy (1784-1846) has been justly ranked with John Eliot and David Brainerd as apostles to the American Indians, furnishing "one of the most thrilling chapters in the history of missions."[1]

In a desire to raise public awareness and support of Indian Missions, McCoy conceived the idea of publishing what he entitled "The Annual Register of Indian Affairs Within the Indian Territory." The first issue of this work "was published in the fore part of January, 1835," McCoy wrote later.[2]

> The first number was prepared under circumstances extremely disadvantageous. I was at the time attending the deathbed of a daughter, and could seldom find as much time as an hour without interruption, to prepare my materials or to write; and, moreover, most of the work was performed in the midst of company. The anxieties occasioned by our deep afflictions, and the difficulties which attended writing, were sometimes exceedingly discouraging, and at one time I had almost concluded to relinquish the undertaking. But believing that the interest of our missions, and of the work of Indian reform generally, imperiously required such a work, it was prepared. I published it at my own cost, and circulated it gratuitously. One was sent to each member of Congress, and to each principal man in the executive departments of Government.
>
> I requested the board to allow it to be printed on their press, and published without cost to me, upon the same principle upon which they printed other missionary matters prepared by other missionaries; but this they declined. I therefore purchased the paper, and paid Mr. Meeker for printing. It is but just, however, to state that the charges were more reasonable by about twenty dollars, in the whole, than if the work had been performed at another printing office. But had it been otherwise, I should have preferred publishing at this, on account of its location being in the *Indian territory*, and the partiality which also grew out of the agency which it had been my happiness to employ in its establishment, and without which, it was probable, a printing press would not have been in operation in the Indian country. Nevertheless, finding it difficult at times to support my family from what I earned, when in the employment of Government, it would have been gratifying if the cost of this and of some other printing I had done about the same time, all of course on Indian matters, had not devolved upon myself. This, too, was a time of poverty, with us, particularly oppressive. My commission under Government had expired about the 1st of August, 1831, and from that time until the 1st of October, 1835, more than one year, I had no public business by which I earned anything, and before the printing of the Register, my funds were nearly exhausted.[3]

---

1 Routh, E. C. *The Story of Oklahoma Baptists.* Oklahoma City: Baptist General Convention. 1932, p. 20.

2 McCoy, Isaac. *History of Baptist Indian Missions.* Washington, D. C.: William H. Morrison. 1840, p. 481.

3 *Ibid.,* pp. 481-482.

The second Annual Register was published in December of 1835, with the expense being defrayed by the Baptist Board of Missions.[4] The third number was issued "about the 1st of July, 1837."[5] These first three numbers of the annual Register were printed at the Shawanoe Mission Station by McCoy's co-workers, Jotham Meeker and John Gill Pratt. The Shawanoe Mission was located at what is now the intersection of Interstate 35 and Route 10, Kansas City, Kansas. It was a significant outpost and training center for Baptist missionaries in the west.[6]

The fourth number of the annual Register, "was executed in Washington, which made its distribution in the various parts of the United States convenient. It was published at my own cost, and, like all the preceding numbers, issued gratuitously," McCoy related.[7]

These four Registers of 1835 to 1838 were all that were issued, and are of great historical value. McCoy, who was also a skillful surveyor, provides us with precise locations of mission stations, forts, Indian agencies and settlements.

In short, McCoy's Annual Registers are a wealth of primary source material to not only students of Christian missions among the Indians, but to any who are interested in Western history and settlement.

To the uninitiated, some of the geographical references of the time can be confusing. The "Western" or "Indian Territory," which one naturally has come to identify with Oklahoma, actually embraced both Kansas and Oklahoma. The "Arkansas Territory" or "Arkansas Country" in the 1830's was sometimes used to designate the Western Cherokee country which included eastern Oklahoma, where the early Cherokee capital at Piney, in Adair County, was located from 1824-1828.

We are honored to be able to make these very rare Registers available again in a convenient one-volume format. We hope this republication will help rekindle an interest in the courageous life and work of Isaac McCoy.

Terry Wolever
January 16, 1998

---

[4] *Ibid.*, p. 492.

[5] *Ibid.*, p. 524.

[6] Brackney, William H. *A Traveler's Guide to American Baptist Historical Sites.* Rochester, New York: American Baptist Historical Society. 1982, p. 61.

[7] McCoy, Isaac. *History of Baptist Indian Missions*, pp. 555-556.

Biographical Sketch

Rev. Isaac McCoy, the great apostle to the American Indians, was born in Fayette Co., Pennsylvania., June 13, 1784. He came with his father to Kentucky in 1790. In 1801 he was converted and joined the Buck Creek Baptist church. In 1803 he was married to Christiana Polk, daughter of Capt. Polk, whose wife and several children were captured by the Ottowas. Mr. McCoy and his wife were afterwards missionaries to that tribe.

In 1804 he came to Vincennes, Indiana, and in 1805 removed to Clarke County. He had a marked influence upon the churches and Associations of that part of the State. He was licensed to preach by the mother of all Indiana Baptist churches,—Silver Creek. In 1810 he was ordained by the Maria Creek church. In 1817 he received an appointment as missionary to the Indians of Indiana and Illinois. After his departure for his work the influence of Daniel Parker grew rapidly in the southwestern part of Indiana, and the missionary spirit waned. Mr. McCoy was appointed for one year, but had no thought that he should cease to labor for the red man at the expiration of that time; his plans embraced many years. After spending some time in western Indiana, it occurred to him that he should move to Fort Wayne and establish a mission. He labored there till 1822, when he established a mission about one mile west of where Niles (Michigan) now is. He named it Carey, after the English missionary. Deprivations, sicknesses, and sorrows such as but few mortals know were not strangers to them. Mr. McCoy rode hundreds of miles through the wilderness, and swam the swollen streams, lying on the wet ground at night, for the sake of carrying forward his missions. He went on horseback to Washington several times to interest Congress in measures beneficial to the Indian. Many months would be occupied in these journeys. One of the severest trials that Mr. McCoy was called to bear was that during his absence from home, sickness and sometimes death would visit his family. Five of his children were called by death at different times while he was absent from home. Persons of narrow selfish views would readily call him cruel and indifferent, but men who could rise to his plane of devotion to the work that he believed God had given him can see that his loyalty to the Master was superior even to parental affection. No man loved his wife and children more than he.

Many conversions occurred at the Carey mission. The hymns composed by him on the occasion of the first baptism at Fort Wayne and at Carey are expressive at once of his great joy and his great hope of what would yet be done for the Indian.

He records that the greatest obstacle by far that he was obliged to meet in his labors for the conversion of the Indians was the introduction of whisky among them by white men. So great were his annoyances at one time that he decided to send several of his Indian pupils East to be educated, so that they might become teachers for their own people. They found a ready welcome at Hamilton, New York.

His labors at Washington were to secure a territory for the Indians into which the white man might not intrude his wicked commerce. This he regarded as the only sure hope for the Christianization or civilization of the red man. He lived to see some of the tribes settled on their own territory, industrious and happy. In his labors for the passage of such acts as he recommended to Congress he speaks of the sympathy and co-operation afforded him by Spencer H. Cone, William Colgate, and others of his brethren.

October 9, 1825, Mr. McCoy preached the first sermon in English ever delivered in Chicago or near its site. In 1826 he gave up the personal superintendence of the Carey mission for the purpose of selecting lands for the Indians farther West. He made surveys west of the Mississippi River, and several times went to Washington to communicate facts to Congress and to lay his plans before that body. In 1840 he published his "History of Indian Affairs," a volume of 600 octavo pages, and full of interest. In 1842 the American Indian Mission Association was formed, and he was made secretary, with headquarters at Louisville, Kentucky.

In June, 1846, as he was returning from Jeffersonville, where he had preached, he was caught in a rain-storm, from the effects of which he died in a few days at his home in Louisville.

"His life and labors were truly the connecting link between barbarism and civilization in this region of the country and over a large portion of the West. His perseverance and devotion were morally and heroically sublime. For nearly thirty years he was the apostle to the Indians of the West." His last words were, "Tell the brethren, never to let the Indian mission decline."

Illustrations

Isaac McCoy	6
Ben Perryman (Creek)	146
Jotham Meeker	148
Chief Clermont (Osage)	226
Dr. Johnston Lykins	231
Non-on-da-gon (Delaware)	232
Christiana McCoy	322

Contents

County Map of Eastern Oklahoma..4

I. ANNUAL REGISTER OF INDIAN AFFAIRS
    FOR 1835
    Printed by Jotham Meeker
    Shawanoe Baptist Mission, Indian Territory......................5

II. ANNUAL REGISTER OF INDIAN AFFAIRS
    FOR 1836
    Printed by Jotham Meeker
    Shawanoe Baptist Mission, Indian Territory....................57

III. ANNUAL REGISTER OF INDIAN AFFAIRS
    FOR 1837
    Printed by John Gill Pratt
    Shawanoe Baptist Mission, Indian Territory..................145

IV. ANNUAL REGISTER OF INDIAN AFFAIRS
    FOR 1838
    Printed by Peter Force
    Washington, D. C..227

V. APPENDIX A
    Articles of Faith of the Baptist Mission at
    Fort Wayne, Indiana Territory................................323

    APPENDIX B
    Early Particular Baptist Churches of Oklahoma.......325

    APPENDIX C
    General Rules for the Fort Wayne Mission
    Family...327

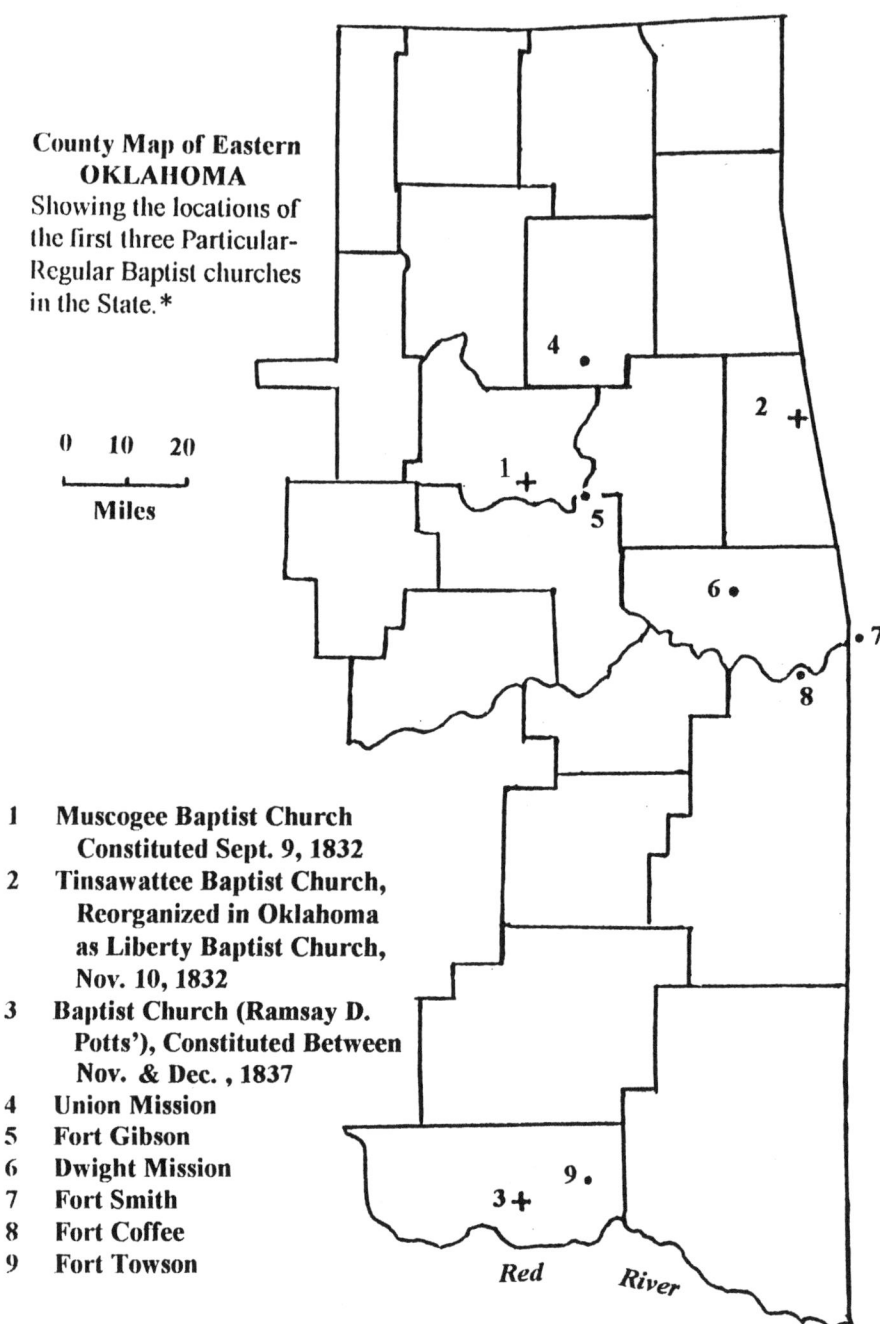

THE   No. 1.

ANNUAL REGISTER

OF

INDIAN AFFAIRS

WITHIN

THE INDIAN (OR WESTERN) TERRITORY.

PUBLISHED BY

ISAAC M'COY.

SHAWANOE BAPTIST MISSION HOUSE, IND. TER.

JANUARY 1, 1835.

SHAWANOE MISSION,
J. MEEKER, PRINTER.
1835.

Isaac McCoy
Courtesy of The Kansas State Historical Society
Topeka, Kansas

The following Prospectus is in circulation. The paper will appear so soon as the subscription list shall justify the publishers in encountering the expense of its publication.

It is hoped that the necessity which exists for such a periodical, especially at the present *crisis* in Indian affairs, will be so obvious to an enquiring community as to recommend it to ample patronage.

PROPOSALS

For publishing, on the Kauzau river, within the Indian Territory, west of the state of Missouri, and three hundred miles west of St. Louis, a semi-monthly periodical, to be entitled

THE INDIAN ADVOCATE.

Devoted chiefly to Indian Affairs.

A residence in the Indian country, and an acquaintance with Indian affairs for more than sixteen years, have convinced the publishers, that the character and condition of the Aborigines of America, have not been well understood. They have been censured for acts for which they were not blameable, and have been commended when they have not merited praise.—Their predilection for war, and their attachment to the hunters' life, have been over-rated. Their religious ceremonies have been misapprehended; and too much reliance has been placed upon their tradi-

(*See 3d page of Cover.*)

(*From 2d page of Cover.*)

tions. Many things, both seriously and in romance, have been said respecting their habits and modes of thinking, which are not in accordance with Indian character. The names of tribes, and the Indian names of places, in many instances, have been so altered as scarcely to resemble the original.

To furnish correct historical sketches of the past, and information respecting their present condition, and their future prospects, together with the earliest notices of important events which shall transpire within the Indian country, and of the transactions of Government and benevolent societies, among the Indians, will be the design, principally, of the work under consideration.

The Publishers believe that, in times past, even the distresses of war have sometimes occurred for want of a correct knowledge of Indian circumstances; and expensive measures have been adopted without utility; the benevolent have bestowed upon them money and labor disadvantageously, and with limited rewards of success; and the Indians have diminished in number, and sunk deeper in misery.

They also believe that, even now, it is not too late to rescue from ruin, the scattered remnants of this noble race of men; and that, in doing this, the interests of the United States will be promoted, equally with those of the Aborigines, with the exception of the dearer interests of *life* and *hope* of the latter, which the subject involves.

The design of giving the Indians a permanent residence, and of constituting them citizens of the United States, has increased the importance of Indian affairs;—and as those measures, by which their relation to one another, and to the U. States, is to be changed, are now in actual progress, such a print as is here proposed is the more necessary.

It is hoped that the work will prove a mean of enabling the government, and the benevolent, to act understandingly in Indian matters. It will be devoted to subjects alike interesting to all parts of our country, and it will not be made the instrument of any political party.

As Christians, the Publishers belong to the Regular Baptist communion; nevertheless, they hope that nothing sectarian in its character, will ever render their labors less acceptable to other denominations of Christians than to that to which they belong; and that the work will be a vehicle of communication, of which the officers of our government, and the missionaries within the Indian Territory, indiscriminately, will be happy to avail themselves.

The Indian Advocate will be printed on new types, upon a super-royal sheet, in quarto form, suitable for binding.

A portion of it will contain the most interesting news of the day, for the benefit of readers within, and near to, the Indian Territory. The greater portion of it will consist of original articles, or such selections from documents, not in common use, as will occasion much labor.

The first number will be issued so soon as the subscription list shall justify it. The remote location of the office will unavoidably occasion a delay of a few months in hearing from distant subscribers.

The price to subscribers will be two dollars per annum, in advance; or $2 50 at the end of the year.

Any person forwarding $10 in advance will be entitled to six copies for one year.

Communications will be made to the undersigned, (who is associated with others,) addressed to Westport, Jackson county, Missouri.

☞ It is respectfully requested that the Post Office of each subscriber be distinctly stated, and that a return of the names be made as early as practicable.

ISAAC M'COY.

August, 1834.

☞ They who are favorable to the design of the above Prospectus, will confer a favor by procuring subscribers, and forwarding their names.

ADVERTISEMENT.

PREPARATION was making to issue this number of the Register some six months since; when, first, some changes in the Indian department, and, secondly, some personal engagements of the author, occasioned a delay. In the mean time, other changes have probably occurred, of which he has not been able to obtain correct information.

While he bespeaks the indulgence of the readers of this number, he would express the hope that the next (to be issued one year hence) will be less imperfect.

He will be thankful to have the errors of this number pointed out, and additional matter furnished for the next, by any who may feel interested in the publication.

His Post Office is, Westport, Jackson county, Missouri.

ANNUAL REGISTER,

By the Indian Territory is meant the country within the following limits; viz.—Beginning on Red river, east of the Mexican boundary, and as far west of Arkansas Territory as the country is habitable: thence down Red river eastwardly to Arkansas Territory; thence northwardly along the line of Ark. Ter. to the state of Missouri; thence north, along its western line, to Missouri river; thence up Missouri river to Puncah river; thence westwardly as far as the country is habitable; thence southwardly to the beginning.

The scarcity of wood renders the remoter regions towards the Rocky mountains uninhabitable. It is supposed that the quantity of timber within the Territory is sufficient to admit of settlement, an average width, from east to west, of two hundred miles, and the country, as described above, is, from north to south, about six hundred miles.

There is a striking similarity between all parts of the Territory. In its general character it is high and undulating, rather level than hilly, though small portions partly deserve the latter appellation. The soil is generally very fertile. It is thought that in no part of the world so extensive a region of rich soil has been discovered as in this, of which the Indian Territory is a central portion. It is watered by numerous rivers, creeks and rivulets. Its waters pass through it eastwardly, none of which are favorable to navigation. There is less marshy land and stagnant water in it than is usual in the western country. The atmosphere is salubrious, and the climate precisely such as is desirable, being about the same as that inhabited by the Indians on the east of Mississippi. It contains much mineral coal and salt water, some lead, and some iron ore. Timber is too scarce, and this is a serious defect, but one which time will remedy, as has been demonstrated by the rapid growth of timber in prairie countries which have been settled, where the grazing of stock, by diminishing the quantity of grass, renders the annual fires less destructive to the growth of wood. The prairie (i. e. land destitute of wood) is covered with grass, much of which is of suitable length for the scythe.

The Choctaws, Creeks, Cherokees, Osages, Kauzaus and Delawares, are entitled to land westward, some, as far as the U. S. Territories extend, and others, as far as the Rocky Mountains. But we choose to limit our description of all to 200 miles, because the average width of habitable country cannot be greater.

EXPLANATORY REMARKS.

By a law of the last session of Congress, there can be no more than two Indian Agencies within the Western (or Indian) Territory.

A Sub-Agent, in the Territory, is not an officer subordinate to an Agent. The duties and responsibilities of the two are precisely the same. The only difference is that the compensation of an Agent is $1500 per ann. and the compensation of a Sub-Agent $750 per ann.

All the tribes south of the Osages have been placed under the superintendency of Col. F. W. Armstrong, the Agent for the Choctaws.

The Osages, and all north of them, are under the superintendency of Gen. William Clark, who resides in St. Louis.

INDIGENOUS TRIBES.

Osage,	about	5,510	Pawnee,	about	10,000
Kauzau,	"	1,500	Puncah,	"	800
Otoe & Omaha		3,000			
				In all	20,810

EMIGRANT TRIBES.

Choctaw, about	15,000	Ottawa,	about	75
Cherokee, "	4,000	Delaware,	"	800
Creek, "	3,000	Kickapoo,	"	575
Seneca & Shawanoe of Neosho,	462	Putawatomic,	"	250
Wea & Piankesha,	400	Emigrants,	"	25,452
Peoria & Kaskaskia,	140	Indigenous,	"	20,810
Shawanoe, of Kauzau river,	750	In all		46,262

CHOCTAWS.

The southern boundary of the Choctaw country is Red river, south of which is the province of Texas. On the east they adjoin Arkansas Territory, are bounded north by Arkansas and Canadian rivers, and on the west by the almost woodless prairie regions.

The extent of their country from north to south is about 150 miles; and from east to west, 200 miles. It is expected that the Chickasaws will obtain a residence with the Choctaws.

Their country is supposed to embrace three districts; one of which adjoins Arkansas river, and the other two extend to Red river. None reside in villages. The greater part of the tribe fence and cultivate land, raise cattle, hogs and sheep; employ upon their farms horses and oxen, waggons and plows; manufacture cloths, &c.

They are far advanced in civilization. Being in

A 2

the act of *settling* in their country, society and business have not yet acquired that order which would correspond with the improved character of the people. Among them are favorable openings for schools, and for other aids to improvement.

AGENCY.

Their Agency is south of Arkansas, and 14 miles west of Fort Smith.
Francis W. Armstrong, Agent, comp'n. $1500 pr. ann.
David M'Clelland, Sub-Agent,   " $750   "
R. W. Jones, Interpreter,   " $300   "
  Post Office at the Agency.

PRESBYTERIAN MISSIONS.

Under the direction of the American B. C. F. M.
  BETHABARA STATION.—On Mountain Fork of Little river, which is a branch of Red river. Commenced in 1830.
  Missionaries.—Rev. Loring S. Williams, Mrs. Williams, Miss Clough.
  1st School, 30 scholars, taught by Miss Clough,
  2nd "   30   "   "   " a Choctaw,
  3rd "   25   "   "   "   "
The scholars are supported by their parents. The missionary society pays the teachers.
  Church.—Organized Aug. 19, 1832.
    Native Church members, 136,
    White persons,   5, 143.
    Black persons,   2,
  WHEELOCK STATION.—On Little river. Commenced in 1832.
  Missionaries.—Rev. Alfred Wright, Mrs. Wright, Samuel Moulton, Mrs. Moulton, Miss Burnham.
  School of 25 scholars. The parents board and clothe the scholars, and generally furnish books.
  Books in the Choctaw language, written upon the common principles of English orthography, and

printed upon our English types, have been well received among them, and many of these books are used in schools.

A Church was organized Dec. 1832. Number of members 37.

The Choctaws have erected two log houses on the waters of Red river, for places of worship. They have three Sabbath Schools, taught chiefly by Choctaws; and under the superintendence of Rev. Mr. Williams.

Rev. Mr. Hotchkin and Mrs. Hotchkin, are locating near Wheelock.

Rev. Henry R. Wilson is preparing to labor among the Choctaws.

METHODIST MISSION.

One station near Fort Towson, originated in 1831.
Missionaries—Rev. Mr. Tally, M. D. Mrs. Tally, Rev. Mr. Myers, Mrs. Myers.
Church members, in all, 300.

BAPTIST MISSIONS.

1st Station, at the Choctaw Agency, on Arkansas river. Under the patronage of the Baptist General Convention. Commenced in June, 1833, by Rev. Charles E. Wilson. Three missionaries, who will also teach schools, are preparing to labor at this place. Post Office, Choctaw Agency, Arkansas.

2nd Station. Rev. Sampson Burch, a native Choctaw, is located on Red river, at which place he arrived in the summer of 1833.

CHEROKEES.

The Cherokee country is bounded as follows; beginning on the north bank of Arkansas river, where the western line of Arkansas territory crosses the river; thence northwardly along the line of Arkansas territory, to the S. W. corner of the state of Missouri; thence north along the line of Missouri, 8 miles, to Seneca river, thence west along the south boundary of the Senecas, to Neosho river, thence up said river to the Osage lands; thence west with the southern boundary of Osage lands as far as the country is habitable; thence south to the Creek lands; and east along the northern line of the Creeks to a point about 43 miles west of the territory of Arkansas, and 25 miles north of Arkansas river; thence to Virdigris river, and down Arkansas river, to the mouth of Neosho river; thence southwardly to the junction of the North fork and Canadian rivers; and thence down Canadian and Arkansas rivers to the beginning.

The treaty of 1828 secures to the Cherokees, 7,000,000 of acres, and then in the same article adds, lands westward as far as the U. S. territories extend.

They own numerous salt springs, four of which are worked by Cherokees. The amount of salt manufactured at the whole, is probably about 100 bushels per day.

They also own two lead mines. Their salt works and their lead mines are in an eastern portion of their country, and all the settlements yet formed are within this eastern portion, which embraces about two and a half millions of acres.

Politically, this eastern portion of their country embraces four districts, viz:—Lee's creek Dist. Flint Dist. Illinois Dist. and Neosho Dist.

Principal Chiefs are Maj. John Jolly, and Black Coat. Col. Walter Webber was another, but he died within the last year.

It may properly be said that the Cherokees have adopted the habits of civilized man. There is not one village in their country; they are, generally, agriculturalists; a few are mechanics and salt manufacturers. The late Col. Webber was a merchant who was doing a respectable business. At present, John Drew, John Brown, and Ellis F. Phillips, are merchants in good business. It is supposed that the Cherokees own 2500 horses, 10,000 horned cattle, 10,000 hogs and 300 sheep; 100 waggons; a plow, and often several plows to each farm, several hundred spinning wheels and 100 looms.

They raise corn, beans, peas, pumpkins, cabbage, turnips and potatoes, in great abundance, and some have commenced the growing of wheat.

Their fields are enclosed with rail fences. They have, generally, good log dwellings, (for a new country) many of which have stone chimneys to them, with plank floors, all erected by themselves. Their houses are furnished with plain tables, chairs, bedsteads, and with table and kitchen furniture, nearly or quite equal to the dwellings of white people in new countries.

They have one grist mill and two saw mills, erected at their own cost.

Their form of civil government resembles that of one of our states. Their Legislature consists of upper and lower house. Each of which has a President and a Secretary; meets annually in autumn, and may be convened at other times by order of the principal Chiefs.

Each district has two Judges, and also two *light-horse-men*, (sheriffs) who are prompt in the discharge of the duties of their trust.

AGENCY.

Within the last year their Agency has been denominated a *Sub-Agency*. This office is filled by Capt. George Vashon, their late Agent, whose salary is $750 pr. ann. His Post Office is Fort Gibson, Arkansas river.

PRESBYTERIAN MISSIONS.

Under the patronage of Am. B. Com. For. Mis.

DWIGHT STATION.—20 miles west of Arkansas territory, and 12 miles north of Arkansas river. Commenced in 1829. Has 30 buildings, consisting of dwellings, school houses, dining hall, store, barn, carpenters' and blacksmiths' shop, &c.

Missionaries.—James Orr, Mrs. Orr, Rev. Cephas Washburn, Mrs. Washburn, Mrs. Lockwood, Asa Hitchcock, Mrs. Hitchcock, Jacob Hitchcock, Aaron Grey, Mrs. Sophia M. Joslyn, Miss Cynthya Thrall.

Schools.—The male school consists of 44 scholars, 5 of whom are Creeks, 4 board at their homes. The residue are supported gratuitously by the mission.

The female school consists of 30 scholars, 7 of whom are Creeks, and one is Osage.

The infant school contains 14 scholars, two of whom are Indian, and 12 are white children.

The *Cherokee Mission Church* was organized at old Dwight in Ark. Ter. It embraces all of Presbyterian order, within the Cherokee country.

Members who are full Indian, 50,
" " of mixed blood, 38, } 106.
" " white, 18,

FAIRFIELD STATION.—On Salisaw creek, 15 miles N. W. of Dwight. Commenced in 1829.

Missionaries.—Rev. Marcus Palmer, M. D. Mrs. Palmer, Miss Jerusha Johnson.

School.—40 scholars, 30 of whom are boarded at the cost of the U. States, according to a treaty provision, and 10 are boarded at the expense of the mission.

UNION MISSION STATION is within the Cherokee country. Operations there were discontinued in 1833.

METHODIST MISSION.

Commenced in 1831, under the Tennessee Conference. Is at present under the patronage of the Missouri Conference.

Rev. Burnell Lee, travelling preacher. Preaches at 17 places.

Church members, in all, about 230; native Class leaders, 6; native exhorters, 4, two of whom speak in Cherokee; native Interpreters, 2.

Schools.—No. 1. Begun Nov. 15, 1832. Scholars 30. Mr. John Harral, teacher.

No. 2. Begun July 1, 1833. 25 scholars.

No. 3. Begun 1833. 42 Scholars. John W. Hunton, teacher.

BAPTIST MISSION.

Cherokee Missionary Station. Under the patronage of the Baptist General Missionary Convention, within Flint Dist. near the eastern boundary of the Cherokee country. Commenced Nov. 10, 1832.

Missionaries.—Rev. Duncan O'Briant, Mrs. O'Briant. Within the last year Mr. O'Briant deceased. Rev. Mr. Rollin, Mrs Rollin, and Miss Colbourn, are on their way to that place, with a view of taking charge of the Mission.

Post Office. Vineyard, Washington county, Arkansas Territory.

School.—40 scholars, taught gratuitously, but supported by their parents.

Church.—Liberty Baptist Church was constituted in the Cherokee nation within the state of Georgia. Emigrated to Arkansas in 1832.

Native Church members, 7,
Black   "   "   6, } 23,
White   "   "   10,

CREEKS. (properly Muskogees.*)

The country of the Muskogees joins Canadian river and the lands of the Choctaws on the south, and

---

*Accent the second syllable, and sound g hard.

the Cherokee lands on the east and north. Their eastern limit is about 45 miles from N. to S. thence their country extends westward as far as the quantity of wood will admit of habitation.

They own salt springs west of their settlements, not yet worked. The celebrated salt rock, on the Red fork of Arkansas, where, from time immemorial, the natives have collected salt, will likely prove to be near the line, from east to west, between the Creeks and Cherokees.

The settlements which they have formed are on Arkansas and Canadian rivers, on the eastern portion of their lands. None reside in villages. Their fields are invariably enclosed with rail fences. They cultivate corn extensively, so that within their settlements there have been fifty or sixty thousand bushels more than they needed for home consumption. They cultivate the variety of culinary vegetables common among the whites, and raise wheat and highland rice in small quantities.

They spin, weave, sew, knit, and follow other pursuits of industry common in the west.

Their dwellings are composed of logs, erected by themselves, and resembling those of their frontier white neighbors; and many of them are furnished with plain, decent furniture, such as farmers generally own.

They have one grist mill erected at the expense of the owner.

They own horses, cattle, hogs, plows, and cotton spinning wheels, enough to answer their domestic purposes with common convenience. Also, some sheep, waggons and looms, but these three kinds of articles are scarce.

Principal Chiefs.—Rolly M'Intosh, 1st.—Benjamin Perryman, 2nd.—Few-hat-che-mi-co, Commanding General of the Militia,—Chilly M'Intosh and Jacob Derrisaw, Judges.

There are chiefs and head men in every settlement,

who severally manage their local affairs.

The Muscogees are governed by *written laws*, In spirit resembling laws of the United States. These laws are enacted by a general council of the nation, which convenes as often as circumstances require.

Their Sheriffs, who execute the decisions of the Council, and of the Judges, are termed *Light-horsemen*, and are exceedingly prompt in the discharge of their duties.

The Creeks are remarkable for the respectful and dignified attention which they bestow upon matters submitted to their consideration by officers of the government of the United States, and by those who are employed in labors of benevolence among them.

There are favorable openings for benevolent efforts for aiding them in their promising career of improvement, in the western settlements, on the north of Arkansas river, and in the southern settlements upon Canadian river.

Their late Agency was near the mouth of Virdigris river. Gen. John Campbell was Agent. During the last year the Agency was discontinued, and the Creeks were placed under the superintendency of Col. Armstrong, the Agent for Choctaws.

BAPTIST MISSIONS;

Under the management of the Baptist Gen. Miss. Con.

1st STATION.—North of Arkansas river, and four miles west of the late Agency. Missionary labors were commenced in Oct. 1829, by John Davis, a native Muscogee. The station was regularly organized in Oct. 1832.

Missionaries.—Rev. David Lewis. Rev. Mr. Aldrich also is on his way to this station.

School.—35 scholars, taught gratuitously, but supported by their parents. They have a good log dwelling, school house, &c.

B

Church.—Muscogee Baptist Church was constituted Sept. 9, 1832.

Native Church members, 18,⎫
Black   "   "   58,⎬ 80.
White   "   "   4,⎭

The Church worships in the school house at 12 o'clock on Sabbaths; at 3, P. M. a sermon is preached at a neighboring place, and at night a sermon is preached at a third place.

2D. STATION.—8 miles west of the first.

Missionaries.—Rev. John Davis, Mrs. Davis. Miss Mary Rice is on her way to join one of these stations.

Mr. Davis began to labor separately in Feb. 1834. He has three regular places of preaching.

The Post Office for all within the Creek country, is Fort Gibson, Arkansas.

PRESBYTERIAN MISSION,

Under the direction of American B. Com. For. Miss.
Six miles west of the late Agency.
Missionaries.—Rev. John Fleming, Mrs. Fleming.
Church.—Organized in 1830.

Native Church members, 8,⎫
Black   "   "   7,⎬ 17.
White   "   "   2,⎭

Sunday School of 15 scholars; bible class 10.

METHODIST MISSION,

Under the patronage of Missouri Conference.
Missionary labors commenced in 1831.
Schools.—No. 1, Rev L. B. Stateler, ⎫
 No. 2, Rev. J. N. Hamil,   ⎬ In all, 70
 No. 3, Mr. P. Berryhill, native, ⎭ Scholars.

Their three school houses are used for places of public worship.

Church.—Members on the list in 1833, 360, including natives, black persons and white persons; of whom two are ordained ministers, four are exhorters, and seven are class leaders.

22

SENECAS, &c.

These consist of three bands, viz:
Senecas, 200,
Senecas and Shawanoes, 211, } 461.
Mohawks, 50,

Their lands on the east adjoin the state of Missouri; on the south the Cherokee lands; on the west Neosho river is the boundary between them and the Cherokees. Their lands extend north between Neosho river and the state of Missouri so far as to include about 127,500 acres.

Seneca Chiefs.—Geo. Curley Eye, 1st Civil Chief,
Comstick, 2d " "
Capt. Good Hunter, 1st War Chief,
Seneca Steel, 2d " "
Small Cloud Spicer,
Thomas Brant, } Head men.
Tall Chief,

Seneca and Shawanoe Chiefs.—Civil John, 1st Civil Chief; Pe-wy-ha, 2d do. Skil-lo-wa, 3d do.
Onondaqua Isaac, and Capt. Reed, Head men.

Mohawk Chiefs.—Isaac White, Principal Chief—George Heron, 2d. Chief.

They are within the Cherokee Agency.
James Pool, Blacksmith, pd. by U. S. $480 pr. ann.
A. Holcomb, Miller, " " $500 "

As a people they are partly civilized. Most of them can speak English. All cultivate land for support, and grow potatoes and other garden vegetables, and corn sufficient to support them and their live stock. Their fields are enclosed with rail fences. None reside in villages. They own about 800 horses, 1200 cattle, 13 yoke of oxen, 200 hogs, 5 waggons, and 67 plows.

They have one tailor, and one cooper, and many of them can use edged tools.

Their dwellings are neat hewed log cabins, erected by themselves. Within them are bedsteads, chairs, and tables of their own manufacturing.

They own one grist and saw mill, erected at the cost of the U. States. One of their number, Mr. John Brown, is a merchant.

They are, generally, favorably disposed towards civilized habits, and evince a desire to improve their condition, except in the matter of education. They have no school, and desire none.

About 36 persons can read in the Mohawk language, the book of Common Prayer, and the gospel of St. Mark, translated into Mohawk by Captain Joseph Brant in 1787, which contains 505 octavo pages. Also, they read the gospel by St. Luke, translated by H. A. Hill, and printed in 1827, by the American Bible Society.

Among them is a Church of 50 members, denominating themselves Episcopalians. Capt. Bowless, who is about 60 years of age, officiates as minister every Sabbath. In this service they read portions of the Book of Common Prayer, sing, &c. They have no house of public worship.

Capt. Bowless says that he was taught to read by educated Indians, and that he has never enjoyed an intimate acquaintance with any missionary.

Their condition calls for the early attention of missionary societies.

OSAGES. (properly Wos-sosh-e.*)

The country of the Osages lies north of the western portion of the Cherokee lands, commencing 25 miles west of the state of Missouri, and thence in a width of 50 miles, extends west as far as the country can be inhabited.

---

*O as in not, accent the second syllable.

About one half of the tribe reside on the eastern portion of their lands. The residue are in the Cherokee country. The latter form three villages, the two larger of which are on Virdigris river, and the smaller on Neosho river.

The small band upon Neosho have made some advances towards civilized life. They have fenced small quantities of land with rail fences. A few have erected very ordinary log cabins, and keep a small number of cattle and hogs, and occasionally have used the plow.

The residue of the tribe have made no improvement.* Their fields are small, say one acre or less to a family, and enclosed by the insertion of stakes in the earth, to which a line, or two lines of small poles are fastened horizontally with the bark of trees.

Their huts are constructed by inserting small poles in the ground, the smaller ends of which are bent over the room and united, so as to produce the form of a cone, some eight or nine feet high. On the outside is fastened, either broad pieces of bark, which forms a kind of weather-boarding, or a mat of flags or of bulrushes, sewed together with threads of bark. The fire is placed in the centre, the smoke of which escapes through an aperture in the top. Many of these houses are oblong, and contain two or three fire places, and a greater number of families. All the Osages live in villages, in which their houses are crowded close together without order.

Some of their shelters are covered with buffalo or elk skins; and these, as well as those covered with flags, are portable.

Their villages are merely *summer* residences. In winter they change encampments, as the prospect of grazing for their horses suggests.

Within their houses are neither tables, chairs, nor

---

*The most barbarous tribes keep horses and dogs, and cultivate a small quantity of corn and other vegetables. So that these things are not an indication of improvement.

B 2

bedsteads, unless we fancy an exception in a platform raised about two feet high, upon stakes set in the earth. This platform extends along the side of the hut, and may serve for a seat, a table, or a bedstead. This, however, is generally dispensed with.

The leggings, and the mockasins for the feet, are seldom worn, except in cold weather, or when travelling in the grass. Excepting these, and the temporary garments fastened about the waist, and extending downward, neither the males nor the married females have any covering for the body except a buffaloe skin, or a blanket, thrown loosely around them. This robe is their garment by day, and their bed at night.

The younger females usually wear a plain strip of cloth, eight or nine inches broad, resting upon one shoulder, and passing over the breast, and under the opposite arm.

The Osages are not fierce and warlike, as has been generally represented: on the contrary, they are uncommonly servile and manageable.

Whilst the condition of depraved man, unimproved, is pitiable in the extreme, there is something noble to be admired in these pupils of nature.

Three framed dwellings, for as many chiefs, have been erected by the U. States at a cost of about $2000 each.

Also, about 70 acres of prairie land have been fenced, and plowed for them by the government.

Game near them is exceedingly scarce. They go upwards of one hundred miles before they find buffaloe, and then they are frequently either frighted, or whipped back empty by their enemies. They suffer much for want of food and raiment, and they are *wretched in the extreme.*

Favorable openings for benevolent efforts for the improvement of their condition, present themselves in, at least, four places.

Cleremont is principal chief. Subordinate chiefs:

are Mo-ne-push-ee, Tow-un-ma-kee, Sho-ba-shing-a, Nung-e-wash-e, O-wau-sau-be, Ne-she-mo-ne, Mau-shau-ke-tau.

Their Agency house is among the villages of the north eastern part of their lands. Within the last year their Agency was made a Sub-Agency, which office is held by their late Agent, P. S. Choteau, with a salary of $750 per ann. The Interpreter receives $300 dollars per annum.

They have a blacksmith with a salary of $480 pr. ann. and a striker with a salary of $240.

PRESBYTERIAN MISSION,

Under the direction of the Am. Bd. Com. For. Miss.

HOPEFIELD STATION.—In the improving band of Osages on lower Neosho. Commenced Sept. 22, 1823. William C. Requa, missionary.

BOUDINOT STATION.—In the vicinity of the Osage villages upon upper Neosho. Located in 1830.

Missionaries.—Rev. Mr. Dodge, Mrs. Dodge.

PUTAWATOMIES.

By treaty at Chicago, in 1833, the Putawatomies agreed to remove westward, and accepted an extensive and valuable tract of country on the N. E. side of Missouri river, above the state of Missouri.

Within the last year a delegation of Putawatomies, conducted by Col. Pepper, visited the unappropriated tract of country, on the upper branches of the Osage river, south of, and adjoining their allies, the Ottawas, and their old neighbors, the Weas, Peorias, and others, and chose that as the most desirable place for their future residence. It is expected that the tribe will accept of this country in lieu of the one first offered them.

This change will be advantageous, both to the United States and to the Indians. To the latter, because they will be along side of their former neighbors, in a central portion of the Indian Territory, and where the permanency of their location cannot be suspected.

Col. Pepper is appointed "*Removing Agent*," and Anthony L. Davis is appointed "*Emigrating Agent*," to take care of them as they arrive.

250 Putawatomies have arrived in this country, and at present mingle with the Kickapoos upon the lands of the latter. Their Chief is Qua-qua-taw.

BAPTIST MISSION.
Under the patronage of the Bap. Gen. Miss. Con.

CAREY MISSIONARY STATION, in Michigan Territory, was among the Putawatomies. The treaty of Sept. 20, 1828, includes an article favorable to the removal of the establishment to the west of Mississippi. In accordance with which, matters are held in readiness to resume the operations of the institution as soon as the Putawatomies shall become settled.

Since the suspension of labors at Carey, some of the missionaries who belonged to that station, have been employed for the benefit of other tribes. In the mean time those matters have been in charge of Mr. Robert Simerwell and Mrs. Simerwell, missionaries; who are, at present, at the Shawanoe Mission house, awaiting the location of the Putawatomies.— On resuming labors at their permanent station they will be reinforced.

Mr. Simerwell has written a small book upon the new system, which has been printed in Putawatomie. He visits that part of the tribe which lives with the Kickapoos, and teaches upon the new system.

WEAS & PIANKESHAS.

These are bands of Miamies. Their country is north of the unappropriated tract in which it is expected the Putawatomies will settle, adjoins the state of Missouri on the east, the Shawanoes on the north, and the Peorias and Kaskaskias on the west. It embraces 160,000 acres.

These people cultivate little over an acre of land to a family. Some of their fields are fenced with rails, and some are enclosed with poles only, like those of the Osages. Some of their dwellings are of logs, and others are of bark. They own a few cattle and hogs.

In compliance with treaty stipulations the U. S. government has lately furnished them with cattle to the value of $500, and have fenced and plowed fields to the amount of 74 acres.

Principal Chiefs are Negro legs and Swan.

Their Sub-Agent is Gen. Maston G. Clark, compensation $750 per annum.
Interpreter, Charles Shane, a Shawanoe, comp. $300.
Blacksmith, William Carlisle,   " $480
Ass't. blacksmith, —— ——,   " $240

PRESBYTERIAN MISSION,

Under the management of the Western For. Mis. Soc.

Commenced in April, 1834.

Missionaries—Rev. Joseph Kerr, Mrs. Kerr, Mr. Henry Bradley, Miss Nancy Henderson.

The Post Office for all connected with this tribe, is Westport, Jackson Co. Missouri.

Peorias & Kaskaskias.

The land of these bands lies immediately west of the Weas, adjoins the Shawanoes on the north, and the Ottawas on the west. They own 96,000 acres.

The fields which they have made themselves are small, though they are generally enclosed with rail fences. The number of their cattle and swine is greater than of those of their neighbors, the Weas. Some of their dwellings are composed of logs, and others are of bark.

In conformity with treaty stipulations, government has recently fenced and plowed for them 25 acres of land, and has erected three log houses, worth $400.

Chiefs.—White skin, Peoria Jim, and Gemasah.
Sub-Agent.—M. G. Clark.

METHODIST MISSION,

Under the management of the Missouri Conference.
Commenced in 1832.
Missionaries.—Rev. N. M. Talbot, Mrs. Talbot.
School of 18 scholars.

The Post Office of all connected with these bands, is Westport, Jackson Co. Mo.

OTTAWAS.

This band owns 36,000 acres of land immediately west of the Peorias and Kaskaskias, and south of the Shawanoes. They are at present in the act of settling upon their lands. Their condition, as it respects civilization, is similar to that of the Weas.

Chiefs.—Ok-wun-ox-e and She-kauk.
Sub-Agent.—M. G. Clark.

BAPTIST MISSION.

Missionaries.—Jotham Meeker, Mrs. Meeker.—At present at the Shawanoe Mission House. Expect to be on the ground as soon as the Ottawas shall be settled, early in the ensuing spring.

The Post Office for all connected with this band, is Westport, Jackson Co. Mo.

SHAWANOES.

Immediately on the north of the Weas and Piankeshas, the Peorias and Kaskaskias, and the Ottawas, lies the country of the Shawanoes, extending along the line of the state of Missouri north 28 miles to Missouri river, at its junction with Kauzau river;—thence up Kauzau river to a point 60 miles on a direct course, to the lands of the Kauzau Indians;—thence south on the Kauzau line 6 miles, thence west with a width of about 19 miles to a north and south line 120 miles west of the state of Missouri. Their tract embraces 1,600,000 acres.

The Shawanoes reside in the north eastern corner of their country, near the line of Missouri, and near the Kauzau river.

Generally, their dwellings are neat hewed log cabins, erected with their own hands; and within them is a small amount of furniture. Their fields are enclosed with rail fences, and are sufficiently large to yield them corn and culinary vegetables plentifully. They keep cattle and swine, work oxen, and use horses for draught; and own some plows, waggons, and carts.

Principal Chiefs.—John Perry and William Perry.
Other Chiefs.—Capt. Black feather, Little Fox, Henry Clay, Letho.
Sub-Agent.—M. G. Clark.
Interpreter.—Charles Shane.
Blacksmith.—L. Jones, compensation, $480 pr. an.
Striker.— —— ——   " $240 "

METHODIST MISSION,
Under the direction of the Missouri Conference.

Missionaries.—Rev. Thomas Johnson, Mrs. Johnson, Rev. William Johnson, Mrs. Johnson.

School.—Number of scholars, 27; supported in part by the Mission, and in part by their parents.

The *Church* worships in the school house.
Hopeful native converts in the Church, 40,
Other natives " " 34, } 78.
White persons " " 4,

BAPTIST MISSION,

Under the direction of the Bap. Gen. Miss. Con.

Commenced in 1831.
Missionaries—Johnston Lykins, Mrs. Lykins. Robert Simerwell, Mrs. Simerwell, Jotham Meeker and Mrs. Meeker, are temporarily here.

The *Church* worships in the school house.

Native Church members, 8, viz. 1 Shawanoe, 1 Chippewa, 1 Osage, and 5 Delawares. White persons, 12. In all, 20.

At the Shawanoe station is a printing press in operation, under the management of Jotham Meeker, Missionary for the Ottawas.

Mr. Meeker has invented a plan of writing (not like that of Mr. Guess, the Cherokee,) by which, Indians of any tribe may learn to read in their own language in a few days. The first experiment was made with a sprightly Chippewa boy, wholly ignorant of letters, and of the English language. He studied three hours each day for nine days; at the expiration of which time there was put into his hands a writing of about twenty lines, of the contents of which he had no knowledge. After looking over it a few minutes, without the aid of an instructer, the boy read off the writing to the unspeakable satisfaction of the teacher.

Upon this plan elementary school books have been prepared, and printed, viz.—In Delaware, two; in Shawanoe, two; in Putawatomie, one; and two in Otoe, besides a considerable number of Hymns, &c. The design succeeds well.

The English school taught at the mission house has been suspended for the present, and the missionaries impart instruction upon the new system, by meeting schools at different places, on appointed days and hours, and to such as call on them at their residence. Circumstances do not admit of a more convenient method.

The interest which the natives take in learning to read their own language, upon this easy plan, has increased their calls for instruction, both for adults and youth, beyond what the missionaries can supply.

Fifty are receiving instruction. Some of these attend school on sabbaths. 25 can read, and 16 can also write.

The Post Office for all connected with the Shawanoes is Westport, Jackson Co. Mo.

DELAWARES. (properly Lin-nop-pe.)

The lands of the Delawares lie north of the Shawanoes, and in the forks of Kauzau and Missouri rivers, extending up the former to the Kauzau lands; thence north 24 miles to the N. E. corner of the Kauzau survey. It extends up the Missouri river to Cantonment Leavenworth, a distance of about 23 miles on a direct course; thence with a line westward to a point 10 miles north of the N. E. corner of the Kauzau lands, and then, in a slip only 10 miles wide, it extends west along the northern boundary of the Kauzaus, to the distance of 208 miles from the state of Missouri.

The Delawares reside on the eastern portion of their country, not far from the junction of the Missouri and Kauzau rivers. They generally occupy good hewed log cabins, and have some furniture within them. They enclose their fields with rail fences, keep cattle and hogs, apply horses to draft, and use oxen and plows. They cultivate corn and garden vegetables sufficient for their use, and have commenced the culture of wheat.

C

In compliance with treaty stipulations, the United States have erected for the Delawares a grist and saw mill, worth about $2950; have fenced and plowed 105 acres of land, and have erected a school house and buildings attached thereto worth $278 50, and have furnished them cattle worth $2000.

Principal Chiefs.—Capt. Patterson, Capt. Nah-ko-mul, and Capt. Catch'im.

Agent.—Richard W. Cummins. Resides at present, at the former Agency among the Shawanoes.—Compensation, $1500 pr. ann.

Interpreter.—James Conner, Comp. $150 "
Blacksmith.—Robert Dunlap, " $480 "
Ass't. Smith— —— —— " $240 "

U. S. School Teacher.—Rev Henry Rennick, Cumberland Presbyterian. Compensation, $400 per ann. No school as yet.

A miller to attend the mills, compensation, $400.

METHODIST MISSION.

Directed by the Missouri Conference.

Begun in 1831.

Missionaries.—Rev. E. T. Peery, Mrs. Peery.

School.—25 scholars. Taught gratuitously. Three are supported in the mission family. The residue dine at the cost of the mission, and also receive some clothing. The remainder of their support they derive from their parents.

"There are, belonging to the Church, 50 natives, about half of whom give evidence of a change of heart, and are regular in their attendance to the gospel, and are uniform in their habits of life."

Also, 7 white Church members.—In all, 57.

BAPTIST MISSION.

Under the management of the Bap. Gen. Miss. Con.

Commenced in 1832. This mission is under the superintendence of Mr. Lykins, missionary among the Shawanoes. Other missionaries at the Shawannoe station also visit this. The converts here are members of the Church which meets at Shawanoe mission house.

School.—Ira D. Blanchard, teacher. Formerly imparted instruction, in English, to a few youths at their houses. Recently, arrangements have been made for the erection of a school house, and for a regular school in English.

A small comfortable dwelling has been erected for the residence of the teacher. Besides those who occasionally attend to receive instruction at his residence, Mr. Blanchard attends at three other places, and gives lessons. His instructions, at present, are in the Delaware language, upon Meeker's new system. Number of scholars, 44; many of whom are adults. Twenty can read tolerably well, and two can also write.

The circumstances of these people, as well as of the Shawanoes, are such that attention to study, especially among adults, can seldom be obtained more than two or three days in a week, and then, only two or three hours in the day. Often the students are absent on hunting excursions for days and weeks.—Moreover, the writing of books, and the discharge of their other duties, have filled up so much of the time of the missionaries, that little has been left for instruction in letters.

The Post Office for all connected with the Delawares, is Westport, Jackson Co. Mo.

KAUZAUS.*

The country of this tribe lies on the Kauzau river, commencing 60 miles west of the state of Missouri;

---

*Different persons have, at various times, written the name of this tribe differently, as suited the fancy of each. We have chosen to ad-

thence in a width of 30 miles it extends west as far as the country can be inhabited.

About one third of the tribe reside in a village on the north bank of Kauzau river, within three miles of their eastern boundary; one third a few miles higher up, upon the south bank; and one third on the north bank, about 40 miles from their eastern boundary.

Their language, habits, and condition in life, are in effect, the same as those of the Osages. In matters of peace and war, the interests of the two tribes are blended; and they are, virtually, one people.

Like the Osages, the Kauzaus are ignorant, poor, and wretched in the extreme; and are as uncommonly servile and easily controlled by white men who mingle with them.

All live in villages, where their huts are crowded closely, without order in their arrangement. Besides their houses of bark and of flags, constructed like those of the Osages, they have a few of earth. These are circular, and in form of a cone, the wall of which is about two feet in thickness, and is sustained by wooden pillars within. Like their other huts, they have no floor except the earth. The fire is in the centre, and the smoke escapes directly above. The door is low and narrow, so that, in entering, a person must half crawl. The door, as in their other huts, is closed by a skin of some animal suspended therein.

Principal Chief is Nam-pa-war-rah, or, White Plume.

Other Chiefs are Ka-hi-ga-wa-ta-ni-ga, Whin-ra-shu-ga, Ka-hi-ge-wa-chi-chi, Min-gar-na-chi, Ka-hi-ga-shing-ga.

---

here to the pronunciation of the natives themselves, which is Kau-zau. We have been the more inclined to do this from the supposition that its near resemblance to the name of the southern tribe (supposed to have been exterminated) from which Arkansas river derived its name, the proper pronunciation of which is Ah-kau-zau, might lead to a developement of facts relative to the origin of these people, which would be a benefit to the future historian.

At the lower village the Gov't. of the U. S. has fenced 20 acres of land, and plowed 10 acres; and has erected for the principal Chief a good hewed log house.

Agent.—Richard W. Cummins.
Interpreter.—Joseph James, Comp'n. $150 pr. ann.
Blacksmith.— ——— ———, " $480 "
Ass't. Blacksmith. ——— ———, " $240 "

Their Smithery, their Agency house, and their house for the residence of one to aid them in agriculture, are all within the Delaware country, 23 miles east of the Kauzau lands.

The wretched condition of the Kauzaus prefers strong claims upon the sympathies of a Christian public, and the prospect of success holds out great encouragement to benevolent efforts, for the amelioration of their condition.

KICKAPOOS.

The country of the Kickapoos lies north of the Delawares, extending up Missouri river to a point 30 miles direct; thence westward about 46 miles; and thence south 20 miles to the Delaware line.— Including 768,000 acres.

They live on the south eastern extremity of their lands, near Cantonment Leavenworth.

In regard to civilization, their condition is similar to that of the Weas.

Principal Chiefs.—Pos-sa-che-haw and Ka-luk-uk.
Agent.—Richard W. Cummins.
Blacksmith, paid by U. S. $480 per annum.
Ass't. Smith, " " $240 "

The United States have erected for them a school house and other buildings attached thereto, worth $300.

C 2

METHODIST MISSION,

Under the management of the Missouri Conference.
Commenced in 1833.

Missionaries.—Rev. J. C. Berryman, Mrs. Berryman, Rev. Mr. Monroe.

School.—40 Scholars. Taught gratuitously. All dine at the mission house on school days; and eight of them are supported by the mission.

The Post Office for all connected with the Kickapoos, excepting the Agent, is Fort Leavenworth, Western Ter.

KICKAPOO RELIGIOUS SOCIETY.

Kalukuk, or, the Kickapoo Prophet, one of the Kickapoo Chiefs, is a professed preacher, of an order which he himself originated some years ago.— His adherents are about 400 in number; some of whom are small boys and girls.

He teaches abstinence from the use of ardent spirits, and some other good morals. He appears to have little knowledge of the doctrines of Christianity, only as his dogmas happen to agree with them.

Congregational worship is performed daily, and lasts from one to three hours. It consists of a kind of prayer, expressed in broken sentences, often repeated, in a monotonous sing-song tone, equalling about two measures of a common psalm tune. All, in unison, engage in this; and, in order to preserve harmony in words, each holds in his or her hand, a small board about an inch and a half broad, and 8 or 10 inches long, upon which is engraved arbitrary characters, which they follow up with the finger, until the last character admonishes them that they have completed the prayer.

Polygamy is allowed. Kalukuk, the leader, has two wives.

Whipping with a rod, is one article of their creed, and is submitted to as an atonement for sin. The offender, whose crime may be known only to himself, applies to one of the four or five persons who are authorised to use the rod, and states that he has committed an offence for which he desires the whipper to inflict a given number of stripes upon his bare back. Having received the flagellation, which frequently brings the blood, the penitent immediately shakes hands with the executioner and others near, returning thanks for the favor conferred upon him, and declaring that he feels himself relieved from a heavy burthen.

OTOES & OMAHAS.

These tribes are united in their interests. Their country lies along the south side of the great Platte river, and adjoins Missouri river on the east.

By treaty a tract has been assigned to such of them as are related to the whites, commencing at the Little Nemaha river, about 15 miles north of the Kickapoos, and extending up Missouri about 20 miles to the Great Nemaha river, and thence west between the two Nemahas, ten miles. None reside on this tract.

The condition of these people is similar to that of the Osages and Kauzaus. They take the buffaloe with less difficulty and danger than the former, and, consequently, suffer less with hunger.

Principal Chiefs.—Ietan and Big Elk. On several occasions these Chiefs have evinced a discriminating judgment and sound discretion.

Their Agency is on the S. W. bank of the Missouri, 6 miles above its junction with the Great Platte.

Agent.—Maj. John Dougherty, comp. $1500 pr. an.
Blacksmith.— ——— ———,   " $480   "
Ass't. do.— ——— ———,   " $240   "

BAPTIST MISSION;

Under the management of the Baptist Gen. Miss. Con.

At the Agency. Commenced, Oct. 1833.

Missionaries.—Rev. Moses Merrill, Mrs. Merrill, Miss Cynthia Brown.

Schools.—10 scholars. Taught gratuitously, but supported by their parents.

These tribes are in want of more missionaries.

PAWNEES.

The country of the Pawnees is westward of the Otoes and Omahas. Their boundaries are not definite. Their villages are, chiefly, upon the Great Platte, and its waters. A few live on the north fork of Kauzau river.

In their habits and condition they are farther removed from those of civilized man than any tribe which we have noticed. Some of their huts are of earth, like those spoken of among the Kauzaus. In some instances they continue to cultivate the earth with the shoulder bone of the buffaloe. This being tied to a stick for a handle, serves the purposes of a spade or shovel. They obtain buffaloe with less difficulty than others, excepting the Otoes and Omahas, between whom and themselves there is an intimate connexion.

Agent.—John Dougherty.

BAPTIST MISSION.

The mission to the Otoes and Omahas was undertaken with reference to the Pawnees also; and this design is still maintained.

PRESBYTERIAN MISSION,

Under the direction of American B. Com. For. Miss.

Begun in 1834.

Missionaries.—Rev. John Dunbar, Mr. Allis. Not yet located.

Among the Pawnees is an inviting field for four Missionary establishments.

PUNCAHS.

The Puncah is a small band on the Missouri, in the northern extremity of the country spoken of as the Indian territory. Their circumstances are similar to those of the Pawnees. They have no missionaries.

Other Baptist Missionaries.

The author of this publication and his wife, have been missionaries to what is now termed the Indian territory, since August, 1828. Their circumstances differ from those of other missionaries of the Baptist General Missionary Convention, inasmuch as their labors have not been located to a particular tribe; but they have been extended to places and matters generally; and they have supported themselves without cost to the Missionary Convention.

Missionaries in general.

Excepting the missionaries noticed in the last article, all others of every denomination of Christians, are supported by the societies which patronize them severally; but they receive no more than a bare support. The amount allowed varies according to the expensiveness of living at each station, and is fixed by the missionary societies, so as barely to cover the necessary current expenditures of the several missionaries. None of them, therefore, receive any compensation which they can lay up as their own personal property. By this means, the voluntary surrender of the missionary to labors of benevolence for the benefit of the Indians, places him beyond the influence of temptation to acquire property. He does not receive even a promise of support for his family, should they out-live him; but, he trusts all to Providence.

Missionary Societies, are voluntary associations of members of the several Christian Churches in the U. States.

The Office of the American Board of Commissioners for Foreign Missions, is in Boston, Mass.

The Office of the Board of Managers of the Baptist General Missionary Convention, is also in Boston, Mass.

The Office of the Western Foreign Missionary Society, is in Pittsburgh, Pa.

The Missouri Methodist Conference convenes at such places within the state as are most convenient.

Want of Missionaries.

More than 20 male missionaries, besides females, could, at this time, find inviting situations for usefulness, within the Indian territory.

Preaching is not an essential qualification for missionaries. They should be men of good sense, ardent piety, persevering disposition, conciliating manners, contented with their own business without meddling with the business of others, industrious, frugal, and economical, ready to enlist for life, and willing to labor through life without laying up a dollar for those of their families who may outlive them.

Provisions of the Government of the U. S. for the education of the Indians within the Indian Territory, and their improvement in civilization generally.

Besides the annual appropriation of $10,000 for education purposes, a portion of which is applied within the Territory, and besides the schools which receive support from Government already mentioned, the following provisions have been made, viz:— for the

OSAGES.

The treaty of 1825 provides that the President of the U. S. "shall employ such persons to aid the Osages in their agricultural pursuits, as to him may seem expedient."

According to the action of Government upon this article, we are required to estimate the allowance at $1200 per annum.

Until recently the Osages have delighted in hunting. Now the buffaloe are far from them, and are procured at the risk of coming in contact with enemies. If government should hereafter apply the annuity of $1200 for agricultural purposes, in preparing fields for them to cultivate with their own hands, then a field of fifty acres in prairie could be well fenced with rails, and plowed, and put in order to receive seed, for $400. The annuity of $1200 dollars applied in this way, would prepare three fields of 50 acres each, yearly, until they should need no more.

The same treaty of 1825 requires that "54 sections of land be laid off under the direction of the President of the U. S. and sold," and the proceeds "applied to the support of schools for the education of the Osage children."

These lands have not yet been selected. The number of acres thus provided, is 34,560, the value of which, if sold at the minimum price of U. S. land, would be $43,200.

The cost of feeding, clothing, lodging, and instructing an Indian youth, if applied in conjunction with benevolent institutions within the Indian country, may be kept within $50 per ann. At this rate the proceeds of the Osage lands would keep 100 children in school eight years and a half.

Should the scholars be supported by their parents, in that case, a school house, books and teacher for 40 scholars, could be furnished for $500 per annum. At this rate their education fund, to wit, $43,200 would keep 400 children in school more than eight years and a half.

DELAWARES.

The treaty with the Delawares of Sept. 1829 provides that 36 sections of the *best* land within the district at that time ceded to the U. States, be selected and sold, and the proceeds applied to the support of schools for the education of Delaware children.

These lands have not yet been selected. The quantity of acres is 23,040; the value of which at the minimum price of Government land, would be $28,800. According to our calculation for the Osages, this sum would feed, clothe and educate 50 youths 11 years; or, if they should be supported by their parents, it would keep 200 children in school eleven years.

KAUZAUS.

By treaty of 1825, 36 sections of *good* land were to be selected and sold, and the proceeds applied to the education of Kauzau children *within* their country. The quantity of this land is the same as of that provided for the Delawares, and would in like manner support in a boarding school 50 children eleven years. Or, if they should be supported by their parents, it would keep 200 children in school 11 years.

By the same treaty of 1825, provision was made for the application of $600 pr. ann. to aid them in agriculture.

The difficulty with which this tribe can now procure subsistence by hunting, being similar to that of the Osages; if Government should hereafter apply this annuity to the fencing and plowing of land for them, 75 acres could be prepared for seed every year, until they were supplied.

PUTAWATOMIES.

By the treaty of 1833, the Putawatomies are allowed the sum of $70,000 dollars for purposes of education. This sum, if applied according to the plan upon which we have based our calculations, would support, in a boarding school, 100 scholars 14 years. Or, if they should be supported by their parents, it would keep in school 400 scholars for the term of 14 years.

KICKAPOOS.

The treaty of Oct. 24, 1832, provides that the U. S. shall pay $500 pr. ann. for ten successive years for the support of a school, purchase of books, &c. for the benefit of the Kickapoo tribe, upon their own lands.

The school house and teacher which have been furnished them, have been in conformity with this stipulation.

The same treaty provides $4,000 for labor and improvements on the Kickapoo lands. If the sum of $4,000 should be applied in fencing and plowing

D

prairie land, it would prepare for receiving seed, 12 fields of forty acres each. But, it is probable, that for the Kickapoos, it would be desirable to make some of their fields in wood lands, where the cost of preparing them would be greater than in prairie.

OTOES AND OMAHAS.

The treaty of July, 1830, secures to sundry tribes mentioned therein, $3,000 annually for ten years, for the education of their children. Of this sum the Otoes and Omahas are entitled to $1,000 annually.

A subsequent treaty provides for the Otoes $500 annuity for five years, to be expended in their own country.

PAWNEES.

The treaty of 1833 provides for the Pawnees an annuity of $1,000 for education, for the term of 10 years.

CHEROKEES.

It is stipulated in the treaty of the 6th of May, 1828, that "the U. S. will pay $2,000 annually to the Cherokees, for ten years, to be expended under the direction of the President of the U. S. in the education of their children *in their own country*, in letters and the mechanic arts. Also, $1,000 towards the purchase of a printing press and types."

CREEKS.

The treaty with the Creeks of March 24, 1832, stipulates that "$3,000, to be expended as the President may direct, shall be allowed for the term of 20 years for teaching their children." This sum will support 60 scholars in a boarding school; or, give education in a common school, to 240 scholars, 20 years;

CHOCTAWS.

The treaty of Sept. 1830, provides for keeping 40 Choctaw youths at school, under the direction of the President of the U. States, 20 years. Also, the sum of $2,500 is to be applied to the support of three teachers of schools, for the Choctaws, 20 years.

There is also a balance of a provision of a former treaty with Choctaws, applicable to education purposes, amounting to $ for the term of   years.

MILITARY POSTS,
Within the Indian Territory.

FORT TOWSON.

In about N. Lat. 34 deg. and W. Long. from Washington, 19 deg. It is within the Choctaw country, six miles north of Red river, and six miles west of Kiamisha river, about 45 miles west of the eastern boundary of the Choctaws, 238 miles from Little Rock, Ark. Ter. 280 miles from Natchitoches, La. and 120 miles from Fort Smith, on Ark. river.

The erection of the Fort, at present occupied, was begun in the autumn of 1831. The situation of the Fort is pleasant, the water is good, and the place is esteemed healthy. Four Companies of the 3d Infantry, compose the garrison.

OFFICERS.—Lieut. Col. J. H. Vose, *Commanding.*

Ass't. Surgeons.—C. S. Triplin, B. R. Hagen.

Captains.—J. S. Nelson, J. B. Clark, J. Dean, L. N. Morris.

1st Lieut's.—H. Bainbridge, E. P. Alexander, Ass't. Qr. Mr. N. S. Harris, John Archer.

2d. Lieut's.—A. G. Baldwin, S. K. Cobb, J. H. Taylor.

FORT SMITH.

Fort Smith is situated on the south bank of Arkansas river. The eastern precincts of the Fort adjoin the line between the Ark. Ter. and the Choctaw country, so that it is barely within the latter.

The garrison consists of Co. C, of the 7th Infantry. Capt. Stewart, Commanding.

2nd *Lieut's.*—I. P. Davis, *Act'g.* Ass't. Qr. Mr., R. Dix.

FORT GIBSON.

Fort Gibson is on the east bank of Neosho river, two miles north of Arkansas river, and two and a half miles below the junction of Arkansas and Virdigris rivers. It is within the country of the Cherokees, and about 43 miles west of their eastern boundary, about 55 miles on a direct course from Fort Smith, and about 140 miles north of Fort Towson.

It was established in 1823, by removal from Fort Smith.

Fort Gibson, or the mouth of Virdigris river, may be considered the head of Steam Boat navigation.

The Garrison consists of nine companies of the 7th Infantry.

OFFICERS.

Col. M. Arbuckle, *Cammanding*,
Brvt. Lieut. Col. Burbank,
1st Lieut. D. I. Miles, *Adj't.*
2nd Lieut. L. F. Carter, *Act. Com. Sub.*
Dr. Zina Pitcher, *Surgeon,*
Dr. J. J. B. Bright, *Ass't. Surgeon,*
Capt. E. S. Hawkins, *Com. Co. H,*
Capt. J. L. Dawson,   "   " F,
1st Lieut. Tho's. Johnson," -   "   I, and *Act. Asst. Qr. Mr.*
2d Lieut. Stephen Moore, *Com. Co.* K,
"   N. S. Holmes,   "   "   B,

2d Lieut. James West, " " D,
" R. H. Ross, " " A,
" Samuel Kinney, " " G,
Brevt. Lieut. R. C. Gatlin, " " E.

Three Companies of Dragoons are stationed at Fort Gibson.

OFFICERS.

Maj. R. B. Mason, *Commanding*,
Capt. E. Trayner, *Com. Co.* F,
Capt. Jesse Bean, on furlough, *Com. Co.* K,
Capt. David Perkins, *Com. Co.* E,
1st Lieut. Jefferson Davies, *Co.* E,
" James F. Izard, *Co.* K,
" Simonton, *Co.* K, *Extra Duty Ind. Dep.*
2d Lieut. J. H. K. Burgoyne,
" L. B. Northop,
" —— Eustis,
Brevet 2, James W. Bowman.

FORT LEAVENWORTH.

Fort Leavenworth is on the S. W. bank of Missouri river, 25 miles above the mouth of Kauzau river, and about 20 miles west of the state of Missouri. It was established in 1827.

Two Companies of Infantry, commanded by Maj. Bennet Riley, have recently been removed to Jefferson Barracks. The Post is, at present, head quarters of the U. States Dragoons.

OFFICERS.

Col. H. Dodge, *Commanding*,
Dr. B. F. Fellows, *Surg.*
Capt. C. Wharton, *Com. Co.* A,
Capt. D. Hunter, *Com. Co.* D,
Capt. Z. Ford, *Com. Co.* G,
Capt. M. Duncan, *Com. Co.* E,
1st Lieut. Philip St. George Cook, *Com. Co.* G,
1st Lieut. L. P. Lupton, *Com. Co.* A,
1st Lieut. Thomas Swords, *Act. Ass't. Qr. Mr.*

1st Lieut. T. B. Whelock, *Company C*,
1st Lieut. James W. Hamilton, *Adjutant*,
1st Lieut. Benjamin D. Moore, *Company* D,
2d Lieut. John Van Deveer, *Company* C,
2d Lieut. E. Steen, *Co.* D, *Act. Ass't. Commissary*,
2d Lieut. John Watson, *Co.* A,
2d Lieut. Burdet A. Terret, *Co.* G,
Brevet Lieut. G. B. Kingsbury, *Co.* C,
Brevet Lieut. Asbury Ury, *Co.* D.

Trading Posts.

Among the Creeks, A. P. Chouteau, and Seaborn Hill, have each a trading establishment.

The American Fur Company have a trading house near the Osage Agency, one among the Weas and their neighbors, one among the Shawanoes and their neighbors, one among the Kickapoos and Putawatomies, one among the Kauzaus, and one on Missouri above the mouth of the Platte river, in the vicinity of the Otoes, Omahas, Pawnees, and others.

Affinity of Languages.

The language spoken by the Osages, Quapaws, and Kauzaus, is the same. Between this and the dialects spoken by the Otoes, Omahas and Winebagoes, there is a near affinity.

Chickasaw and Choctaw are dialects of one language.

Putawatomies, Ottawas, and Chippewas speak the same language.

War.

All the tribes in the Territory excepting the Pawnees, Otoes, Omahas and Puncahs, are liable to insult and injury from remote tribes, especially those towards the S. West; and even the Pawnees and their allies have their enemies in the *far-west*.

A portion of the Pawnees reside in the south, upon Red river. Until lately, warriors from the Pawnees of the south, and of the north, united with Camanches of the remoter S. West, and formed war parties, which annoyed traders to Santa Fee, and were particularly inimical to the Osages and Kauzaus, as well as troublesome to many hunting parties of the emigrant tribes.

In 1833 treaties of peace were concluded between the northern Pawnees and all the other tribes within the Territory, and *all smoked the pipe of peace.*

In 1834 negotiations of peace and friendship were held with the southern Pawnees. Thus far, all parties have been faithful to the pledges of friendship which have been mutually exchanged. Delawares, who, in 1833, retaliated with some severity upon the Pawnees, have, in 1834, passed through their country, have called at the encampments of Pawnees, and have been received with warm expressions of friendship.

Government.

Most of the tribes within the Territory have expressed a desire to become united in one civil compact, and to be governed by laws similar to those of the United States.

Should the U. States provide for them a form of civil government, suited to their circumstances, a few among each of the emigrant tribes, and many among some of those tribes, would be found capable of filling responsible offices in the transaction of the affairs of their government.

Remarks.

Roger Williams, the founder of the state of Rhode Island, was perhaps the first civilized man in authority, who admitted the original ownership of the Aborigines of America, of the soil they inhabited; and few, since his day, have ventured to propagate his doctrine. It has been denied by all civilized nations which have come in contact with the Indians, including the government of the U. States.

They have been denied a political existence distinctively, and circumstances have debarred them from a participation in the interests and character of those who possessed themselves of their country.— *Here,* and not in any peculiar trait of character, or custom, may be found the true cause of their decline, and of the prolongation of their miseries.

Struggling under the peculiar disabilities which civilized nations, by common consent, had placed them under, many tribes sunk, and disappeared, and others were rapidly hurried after them, by the wasting influence of the same causes.

A few tribes gathered strength, and sought, with noble pride, the political character, which had been denied to all red men. The justness of their plea in defence of their rights, was easily appreciated by men tenacious of their own. But, now it was found to be too late to correct an error, begun three hundred years before. The U. States numbers her millions—admit the original ownership of soil to be in the original occupants, and our whole country is surrendered to the few red men who remain among us. The people of the United States have felt that they owed the Indians *much*—it could not be paid in *kind,* and an equivalent has been offered.

Now, for the first time, a government—the government of the United States, declares that the Aborigines can, and ought to have claims to soil as fully as patents to her own citizens secures to them their titles. The offer is made to the Indians, either to remain within existing states on an equal footing with her own citizens, or, to enjoy the privileges of citizenship within a population exclusively their own, where, unembarrassed by the long cherished prejudices of those who had been accustomed to look *down* upon them, they might improve in all that is profitable, and aspire to the highest felicity of citizenship in the most favored nation upon earth.

It is no more surprising that the Indians should have hesitated to compromise their rights, than that they should accept the overtures, when they perceived that their interests required it as the alternative upon which depended their future existence and prosperity.

They go to the country which, by common consent, is becoming theirs, not to remain hunters, but to become a component part of the community of the United States.

No inference unfavorable to future improvement can be made from former disappointments, because we are now entering upon an experiment never before tried. If it be sound logic to suppose that like causes will produce like effects, then, the Indians, when placed in circumstances which are essential to our prosperity, and under which we have been prosperous, will be equally prosperous with ourselves.— Rather, it is proposed to make them a part of ourselves.

Even from this hasty sketch of Indian affairs, may be inferred the facility with which they can be organized into a civil government, and the disposition of the U. States thus to organize them. Equally obvious are the uncommon facilities for doing them good which invite the efforts of the philanthropist and the Christian.

The outcasts *are* returning to the land of their *rest.* There let the arm of our government secure their political interests, science make them wise, the arts make them comfortable, and Christianity guide them to the land of *eternal Rest.*

Indians not within the Ind. Territory.

Tribes East of Mississippi.

Indians in N. England & N. York,	4,715
Indians from New York, at Green Bay,	725
Wyandots in Ohio and Michigan,	623
Miamies,	1,200
Winnebagoes,	4,591
Chippewas,	6,793
Ottawas and Chippewas of Lake Michigan,	5,300
Chippewas, Ottawas and Putawatomies,	8,000
Putawatomies,	1,400
Menominees,	4,200
Creeks,	22,668
Cherokees,	10,000
Chickasaws,	5,429
Choctaws,	3,500
Seminoles,	2,420
Appalachicolas,	340

Tribes west of Mississippi river.

Sioux,	27,500	Camanches,	7,000
Iowas,	1,200	Crows,	4,500
Sauks of Missouri,	500	Arrepahas, Kiawas,	
Sauks and Foxes,	6,400	&c.	1,400
Assinaboines,	8,000	Quapaws,	450
Crees,	3,000	Caddoes,	800
Gros ventres,	3,000	Snake and other	
Arrekaras,	3,000	tribes within the	
Cheyennes,	2,000	Rocky Mt's.	20,000
Minatarees,	1,500	Tribes west of the	
Mandans,	1,500	R. Mountains,	80,000
Black feet,	30,000		

Throughout all the vast uncultivated regions north and south of the western territories of the United States, are Indians. The population becomes more sparse as we proceed northward, to a climate less accommodated to the comforts of uncivilized man, and becomes more dense as we proceed southward to a more genial clime, where subsistence is more easily obtained.

Miscellaneous Observations.

Various conjectures have been indulged relative to the origin of the Aborigines of America. But research has left us precisely where we were—knowing nothing more than that they belong to the family of *man*, and that they have long inhabited this quarter of the world.

The arguments in favor of their being *Israelites* are founded chiefly upon the supposed similarity between some of their customs and those of Jacob's seed, but those which are most relied on for proof appear to be the natural result of Indian circumstances.

They are the pupils of nature. Hence the similarity between all the tribes, of their modes of thinking, of their common customs, and of their religious ceremonies.

All believe in the existence of the Great and Good Spirit, and acknowledge his superintending providence; and all believe in the existence of the principal Evil Spirit. They believe in future rewards and punishments, and perform various ceremonies for the purpose of propitiating the Deity.

Their principal religious festivals occur in the spring, when they assemble at their villages for the purpose of planting seed; in the summer, when they begin to eat of the fruit of their fields, and in the autumn, when they separate upon hunting excursions, and to seek more eligible winter quarters.

Their original ceremonies have disappeared in proportion to their intercourse with the whites; nor does it appear that they ever possessed more of civil order, or of religious ceremony, than would be natural to rational beings who felt a conscious accountability to God.

That they have long inhabited this continent is evident from the ancient mounds, fortifications, &c. which are discovered; all, or partly all of which bear the marks of uncivilized man.

Their fondness for war is not greater than would be that of any other people placed in similar circumstances; nor is their attachment to the hunters' life stronger than that of the white man brought up among them.

No mistake could be greater than the supposition that Indians cannot be civilized. Hundreds of them are civilized, and are qualified to fill, with credit to themselves, and usefulness to others, various spheres in a civil, and in a religious community. No heathen people upon earth ever presented so few obstacles to the introduction of christianity, useful customs, and righteous laws, as the Aborigines in their native condition. The absence of a constituted mythology, left their minds partly as a blank, on which to write the precepts of the gospel; their poverty prepared them for the admission of better customs in common life, and the equality which prevailed among all men, prepared them for the adoption of laws securing the rights of all.

In days past, educated Indians have frequently returned to savage life. What could be more natural? Our prejudices denied them admission into our society—they returned to their wilder kindred, who without any common bond of society, were all, with the exception of slight restraints, left to follow their own inclinations, and they became assimilated.—Give them opportunities which are essential to the improvement of white men, and philosophy and fact decide in their favor.—Shall we be innocent if they perish?

A new era in their history has arrived—less embarrassed opportunities for helping them present themselves, while many of them have become inspired with courage to make a last struggle to arise.—Reflection upon the past, the present, and the future, urge us to fly to their assistance, and obtain the "blessing of the poor," the quiet of our own conscience, and the approval of a righteous God.

THE   No. 2.

ANNUAL REGISTER

OF

INDIAN AFFAIRS

WITHIN

THE INDIAN (OR WESTERN) TERRITORY.

—◆—

PUBLISHED BY

ISAAC M'COY.

—◆—

SHAWANOE BAPTIST MISSION HOUSE, INDIAN TERRITORY,

JANUARY 1, 1836.

———✳———

SHAWANOE BAPTIST MISSION, IND. TER.

J. MEEKER, PRINTER.

1836.

This number of the Register is presented to the public with such alterations in the statistical portions of the work as have been rendered necessary by the changes which have taken place in Indian Affairs the preceding year. It is much larger than the former number, and it is hoped that succeeding numbers will be still more enlarged.

While our chief attention will be directed to matters within what we term the Western (or Indian) Territory, the tribes more remote, and those upon our northern frontiers, and those within the U. States, will be noticed so far as our limits will allow.

The work is issued gratuitously. Our desire is to benefit a suffering remnant of a noble, and once numerous race of men; and to contribute somewhat towards relieving our government from unnecessary difficulties which have ever hung upon the subject of Indian affairs.

We believe that, generally, this subject has not been well understood; and that the consequence has been, much injury to the Indians, and unnecessary cost and vexation to the U.S. We also believe that if their true character and condition were understood, the remedy for these evils would be apparent.

The respectful attention with which the first number of the Register has been received by the public, encourages us to hope that we shall not labor in vain.

Doubtful matter will not be inserted. We shall spare no pains to have our statements correct, so far as they extend. Should inaccuracies be detected by any, we shall be thankful to receive notice of them. Arguments and comments shall be such as appear to be unquestionably suggested by the facts stated. Our method is such as we have supposed would afford most information, with the least labor to the reader.

ANNUAL REGISTER.

By the Indian Territory is meant the country within the following limits; viz.—Beginning on Red river, on the Mexican boundary, and as far west of Arkansas Territory as the country is habitable; thence down Red river eastwardly along the Mexican boundary to Ark. Ter. thence northwardly along the line of Ark. Ter. to the state of Missouri; thence north along its western line, to Missouri river; thence up Missouri river to Puncah river; thence westwardly as far as the country is habitable; thence southwardly to the beginning.

The scarcity of wood renders the remoter regions towards the Rocky mountains uninhabitable. It is supposed that the quantity of timber within the Territory is sufficient to admit of settlement, an average width, from east to west, of two hundred miles, and the country, as described above, is, from north to south, about six hundred miles.

There is a striking similarity between all parts of the Territory. In its general character it is high and undulating, rather level than hilly; though small portions partly deserve the latter appellation. The soil is generally very fertile. It is thought that in no part of the world so extensive a region of rich soil has been discoverd as in this, of which the Indian Territory is a central portion. It is watered by numerous rivers, creeks and rivulets. Its waters pass through it eastwardly, none of which are favorable to navigation. There is less marshy land and stagnant water in it than is usual in the western country. The atmosphere is salubrious, and the climate precisely such as is desirable, being about the same as that inhabited by the Indians on the east of Mississippi. It contains much mineral coal and salt water, some lead, and some iron ore. Timber is too scarce, and this is a serious defect, but one which time will remedy, as has been demonstrated by the rapid growth of timber in prairie countries which have been settled, where the grazing of stock, by diminishing the quantity of grass, renders the annual fires less destructive to the growth of wood. The prairie (i. e. land destitute of wood) is covered with grass, much of which is of suitable length for the scythe.

The Choctaws, Creeks, Cherokees, Osages, Kauzaus, and Delawares, are entitled to lands westward, some as far as the U. S. Territories extend, others as far as the Rocky Mountains. But we choose to limit our description of the lands of all to 200 miles, because the average width of habitable country cannot be greater.

EXPLANATORY REMARKS.

By a late law of Congress, there can be no more than two Indian Agencies within the Western (or Indian) Territory.

A Sub-Agent, in the Territory, is not an officer subordinate to an Agent. The duties and responsibilities of the two are precisely the same. The only difference is that the compensation of an Agent is $1500 per ann. and the compensation of a Sub-Agent is $750 per ann.

All the tribes south of the Osages are under the superintendency of Capt. William Armstrong, who has recently been appointed to fill the vacancy occasioned by the decease of Col. F. W. Armstrong.

The Osages, and all north of them, are under the superintendency of Gen. William Clark, who resides in St. Louis, about three hundred miles east of the Indian Territory.

INDIGENOUS TRIBES.

Osage, about	5,510	Pawnee, about		10,000
Kauzau, "	1,684	Puncah, "		800
Otoe & Missouria,	1,600	Quapau, "		450
Omaha,	1,400			
		In all		21,444

EMIGRANT TRIBES.

*Choctaw, about	15,000	Shawanoe of Kauzau riv.		764
†Cherokee, "	4,000	Delaware,		856
‡Creek, "	3,600	Kickapoo,		603
Seneca & Shawanoe of Neosho,	462	Putawatomie,		444
Wea,	225	Emigrant,		26,289
Piankasha,	119	Indigenous,		21,444
Peoria, & Kaskaskias,	135			
Ottawa,	81	Total		47,733

*This estimate includes about 400 negro slaves.
†Including about 500 slaves.   ‡Including about 450 slaves.

CHOCTAWS.

The southern boundary of the Choctaw country is Red river, south of which is the province of Texas. On the east they adjoin Arkansas Ter. are bounded north by Arkansas and Canadian rivers, and on the west by the almost woodless prairie regions.

The extent of their country from north to south is about 150 miles; and from east to west, 200 miles. It is expected that the Chikasaws will obtain a residence with the Choctaws.

Their country is supplied with numerous springs of salt water, at two of which the natives are preparing to manufacture salt.

Their settlements are divided, politically, into three districts, viz.—1st. Arkansas district on the north. 2d. Poshemataha district on the south east, adjoining Red river on the south, and Arkansas territory on the east. 3d. Oglafliah, or, Red river district on the south west, adjoining Red river.

About three or four thousand of the tribe have not yet settled in their new country; some of whom are in the country which they formerly inhabited; others are dispersed in the adjoining states, and some in the province of Texas. The latter are in a wretched condition.

None of the settled emigrants reside in villages. They have suffered much by sickness. Not less than 2000 have died since emigration commenced. This mortality, however, is not attributable to the unhealthiness of the country generally, but to such causes as have usually produced similar distresses in the formation of settlements in wilderness countries.

Notwithstanding their afflictions, and the discouraging losses of property incident to early settlers, a growing spirit of improvement is widely prevalent. Their houses and fields indicate a good degree of industry. They own a considerable number of horses, cattle, sheep and hogs, waggons, plows, spinning wheels and looms. From present appearances, the growing of cotton, and the manufacturing of cloth for their own use, will soon be carried on extensively. Their corn crops of the past year will prove ample for home consumption.

In Red river district are two sets of mills, one of which is a flouring mill, and the other a flouring and saw mill. The latter cost about 1500 dollars. Both belong to natives.

Three of the natives are merchants. One of them has a capital of about $2000, and the other two a capital of $8000 each. A considerable number of them are mechanics in wood and in iron.

For their government they have adopted a written constitution upon republican principles, with slight exceptions. It provides for a general Council, or, Legislative body, to consist of the three principal Chiefs, and thirty counsellors chosen annually by the people. The Legislative Council meets once a year.

They have enacted some wholesome laws relative to the crimes of murder, theft, &c. and also respecting lost property, fences, widows and orphans, witchcraft, &c. Legal counsel and trial by jury are allowed to all. Severe laws have been enacted against the introduction of ardent spirits, and these laws are enforced with becoming zeal, so that the evil of intemperance, which is so awfully destructive to Indians generally, is now little known in the Choctaw country.

The English mode of dress has been adopted to a considerable extent, especially among the females, and is daily becoming more common. Many of the Choctaws may properly be classed with civilized men, while a large portion of the residue are little inferior to them in point of improvement.

There are favorable openings for religious teachers in some parts of their country which have heretofore been very destitute.

Each district has its principal chief. These chiefs are elected by the people for the term of four years.

PRINCIPAL CHIEFS.

Arkansas District, Joseph Kincaid;.
Poshemataha do. Nitahachi,
Red river do. Thomas Leflore..

AGENCY, &C.

Their Agency is south of, and near to Arkansas river, and fourteen miles west of the eastern Choctaw boundary.

Agent, Capt. W. Armstrong. Com. $1500 per ann.
R. W. Jones, U. S. Interpreter.

Israel Dodge, U. S. Blacksmith, for the benefit of the Choctaws. } Arkansas district.
———, Assistant do.
Post Office is at the Agency.
Christian Spring, U. S. Blacksmith, } Poshemataha district.
———, Assistant do.
——— Wallace, U. S. Blacksmith, } Red river district.
———, Ass't. do.

Capt. Jacob Brown, of the U. S. Army, is paymaster to deliver to the Choctaws the annuities due them from the U. States.

PRESBYTERIAN MISSION,
Under the direction of the A. B. C. F. M.

1st. BETHABARA STATION.—On Mountain fork of Little River, Poshemataha district. Commenced in 1832.

Missionaries.—Rev. Loring S. Williams, Mrs. Williams, Miss Clough.

A school of 30 scholars taught by John Quincy Adams, a native Choctaw. Instruction is imparted in both English and Choctaw. The scholars are supported by their parents. The teacher is supported by a Youths' Missionary society in Philadelphia.

An English school of 30 scholars, taught half the year by Miss Clough and Miss L. M. Williams. Scholars supported by their parents.

Two Sabbath schools, embracing about 60 scholars.

A school house has been erected by the U. S. in conformity with treaty provisions, not yet occupied. An increasing desire to obtain the benefits of schools is manifest in the vicinity of this station.

Church.—Organized Aug. 19, 1832.

Native Church members, 115,
White do. 5, } In all 123.
Black do. 3,

Since the organization of the Church 30 have died, apparently in the faith of the gospel, and 19 have been dismissed to form another Church.

2d. WHEELOCK STATION.—On Little river, Poshemataha district. Begun in 1832.

Missionaries.—Rev. Alfred Wright, Mrs. Wright.

School of 30 scholars, supported by their parents. Also, a flourishing Sabbath school.

Church.—Organized December 9, 1832.

Native Church members, 62, } In all 67.
White do. 5,

A considerable number of Church members have died, who exhibited evidences of genuine piety.

3d. CLEAR CREEK STATION.—Near Red river, Poshemataha district. Commenced in 1833.

Missionaries.—Rev. Ebenezer Hotchkin, Mrs. Hotchkin, Miss Ann Burnham.

School of 30 scholars, six of whom are instructed in English. The residue in Choctaw. All supported by their parents. Also, two small schools recently commenced. Two Sabbath schools.

Post Office for all the above stations is Eagletown, Arkansas Territory.

4th. BETHEL STATION.—Six miles west of Wheelock St.

Missionaries.—Mr. Samuel Moulton, Mrs. Moulton. Begun in 1834.

School of 40 scholars, some instructed in Choctaw, and some in English. Supported by their parents. Also, a Sabbath school.

5th. LUKFOATA STATION.—Ten miles west of Bethabara Station. Commenced in 1834.

Missionary.—Rev. Henry R. Wilson, M. D. (Mrs. Wilson has died.)

School.—8 miles west of the station. 25 scholars. Supported by their parents. Both English and Choctaw taught, by Allen Carney, a native.

Another small school has been taught by a native near to this station.

Church.—Bok Tuklo Church, organized May 18, 1834.

Native members, 18,} 19.
Black   do.   1,}

Six members of this Church have died in the faith.

Two Sabbath schools.

6th. PINE RIDGE STATION.—Two miles west of Fort Towson, Poshemataha district.

Missionaries.—Rev. Joel Wood, Mrs. Wood. Commenced in 1835.

Post Office for the three latter stations is Fort Towson, Western Territory.

Books in the Choctaw language, written upon the common principles of English orthography, and printed upon our English types, have been well received among them; and many of these books are used in schools. In all cases tuition is without cost to the natives, and in most cases, books also.

METHODIST MISSION.

On Little river, 11 miles eastwardly from Fort Towson. Originated in 1831.

Missionaries.—Rev. Moses Perry, Rev. Cha's. J. Carney, itinerant preacher. They have 10 Sunday schools, 5 native preachers on trial, 1 exhorter, 18 class leaders, and between 800 and 900 members in Society.

Post Office, Fort Towson, Western Territory.

BAPTIST MISSIONS.

Connected with the Baptist General Missionary Convention.

1st Station.—Canadian river, 30 miles west of the Choctaw Agency, Arkansas district, commenced in June, 1833.

Rev. Mr. Smedley, Mrs. Smedley. Mr. S. is under appointment and pay of the U. S. as school teacher, in conformity with treaty stipulations.

Post Office, Choctaw Agency, Western Territory.

2d Station.—About twelve miles westward of Fort Towson, and six miles north of Red river, in Red river district.

Mr. Ramsay D. Potts, Mrs. Potts. Mr. P. is also under appointment and pay of the U. S. as Teacher, according to treaty provisions.

An elementary school book, in the Choctaw language, upon the *new system* of writing Indian, (see an explanation of it under head of Shawanoe Mission,) has, the last year, been compiled and printed at the Shawanoe Baptist Mission House, and forwarded to the Choctaw country for use.

CHEROKEES.

The Cherokee country is bounded as follows; beginning on the north bank of Arkansas river, where the western line of Arkansas territory crosses the river; thence northwardly along the line of Arkansas Ter. to the S. W. corner of the state of Missouri; thence north along the line of Missouri, 8 miles, to Seneca river; thence west along the south boundary of the Senecas, to Neosho river; thence up said river to the Osage lands; thence west with the southern boundary of Osage lands as far as the country is habitable; thence south to the Creek lands; and east along the northern line of the Creeks to a point about 43 miles west of the territory of Arkansas, and 25 miles north of Arkansas river; thence to Virdigris river, and down Arkansas river, to the mouth of Neosho river; thence southwardly to the junction of the North fork and Canadian rivers; and thence down Canadian and Arkansas rivers to the biginning.

The treaty of 1828 secures to the Cherokees, 7,000,000 of acres, and then, in the same article, adds lands westward as far as the U. S. territories extend.

They own numerous salt springs, two of which are worked by Cherokees. The amount of salt manufactured at both is probably about 100 bushels per day.

They also own two lead mines. Their salt works and their lead mines are in an eastern portion of their country; and all the settlements yet formed are within this eastern portion, which embraces about two and a half millions of acres.

Politically, this eastern portion of their country is divided into four districts, viz:—Lee's creek Dist. Flint Dist. Illinois Dist. and Neosho Dist.

It may properly be said that the Cherokees have adopted the habits of civilized man. There is not one village in their country; they are, generally, agriculturalists; a few are mechanics, salt manufacturers, merchants, &c.

They probably own 3,000 horses, 11,000 horned cattle, 15,500 hogs, 600 sheep, 110 waggons, a plow and often several plows to each farm, several hundred spinning wheels, and 100 looms.

They cultivate all kinds of culinary vegetables common to the western country, raise corn in abundance, and have commenced the growing of wheat. Their fields are enclosed with rail fences. They have, generally, good log dwellings, (for a new country,) many of which have stone chimneys to them, with plank floors, all erected by themselves. Their houses are furnished with plain tables, chairs and bedsteads, and with table and kitchen furniture, nearly, or quite, equal to the dwellings of white people in new countries.

Charles Rogers and David Milton each own a grist mill, A. Brown owns a grist and saw mill, Dr. John Thornton owns a saw mill, and is erecting a grist mill; cost of both when completed will be $2000; John Drew owns a saw mill, and is building a grist mill.

Their form of civil government resembles that of one of our states. Their Legislature consists of upper and lower houses, each of which has a President and a Secretary, meets annually in autumn, and may be convened at other times by order of the principal Chiefs.

Each district has two Judges, and also two light-horse-men, (Sheriffs,) who are prompt in the discharge of the duties of their trust.

PRINCIPAL CHIEFS.

1st, Major John Jolly—2d, Joseph Vann—3d, James Rogers. Their Post Office is Fort Gibson.

NATIVE MERCHANTS.

David Webber, capital $14000—Lewis Rogers, capital $5000—Lura, Price & Paine, capital $5000.

Dr. John Thornton is a native Physician, who received a medical education in the United States.

AGENCY, &C.

Their Sub-Agency is at the junction of Illinois and Arkansas rivers, 30 miles south eastwardly from Fort Gibson.

Sub-Agent, Capt. George Vashon. Compensation $750. His Post Office is Fort Gibson, West. Ter.

Capt. Jacob Brown, of the U. S. Army, pays to the Cherokees the annuities due them from the U. States.

Lieut. J. Van Horn is disbursing Agent for Cherokee removal.

Jack Spear, Interpreter. Compensation $300 per ann.
Henry Freshown, ⎫ Blacksmiths employed by the U. S.
A. Holdridge, ⎬ according to treaty provisions. Compensation of each $480 per ann.
Samuel Crosland, ⎭

Four assistant Smiths. Comp. of each, $240 per ann.
Austin Copeland, U. S. Waggon maker. Comp. $600.
James A. Hart, U. S. Wheelwright. Comp. $
W. A. Shaw, ——— Bean, Blacksmiths employed by the Cherokees.

PRESBYTERIAN MISSIONS.

Under the patronage of the Am. Bd. Com. For. Mis.

1st. DWIGHT STATION.—20 miles west of Arkansas Territory, and 12 miles north of Arkansas river. Commenced in 1829. Has 30 buildings, consisting of dwellings, school house, dining hall, store, barn, Carpenter's and Blacksmith's shops, &c.

Missionaries.—Rev. Cephas Washburn, Mrs. Washburn, James Orr, Mrs Orr, Asa Hitchcock, Mrs. Hitchcock, Jacob Hitchcock, Mrs. Hitchcock, Aaron Gray, Miss Stetson, Miss Esther Smith.

Rev. S. A. Worcester and Mrs. Worcester are temporarily at this station. They expect shortly to put into operation a printing press.

Schools.—The male school consists of 37 scholars; 30 of whom are boarded at the cost of the mission, and 7 board at their homes.

One half of the scholars are instructed in the Cherokee language, and the other half in English.

The female school embraces 32 scholars; 30 of whom are

boarded by the mission, and two by their parents.

A small school is taught by Miss Smith several miles west of the station. Commenced in 1835.

The Cherokee Mission Church was organized at old Dwight, in Arkansas territory.

Native Church members, 43,
Black   "   "   3, } In all 60.
White   "   "   14.

2d. FAIRFIELD STATION.—On Salisaw Creek, 15 miles N. West of Dwight. Originated in 1829.

Missionaries.—Rev. Marcus Palmer, M. D. Mrs. Palmer, Miss Jerusha Johnson.

School.—50 scholars, taught by Miss Johnson, some in English and some in Cherokee; 30 of whom are supported by the U. States, and boarded in a Cherokee family; 9 are supported by the mission, and the residue by their parents.

Church.—Native Church members, 41,
Black   "   "   4, } In all 50.
White   "   "   5.

3d. FORKS OF ILLINOIS STATION. Begun in 1830.

Missionaries.—Samuel Newton, Mrs. Newton.

The School which contained 20 scholars, who were supported by their parents, but taught gratuitously, has been suspended on account of some changes being made in the immediate site of the station.

Instruction in the Cherokee language, as given at the above mentioned stations, is upon the syllabic system, invented by Mr. Guess, a native Cherokee.

The Post Office for the three latter stations, is Ft. Gibson.

METHODIST MISSION.

Under the patronage of the Missouri Conference.

Originated in 1831. Jeremiah Horn itinerating preacher. Preaches at 17 places.

Church members in all 245. Native preacher, Young Wolf. Native exhorters, William M'Intosh (who is also Interpreter,) Samuel Wolf, Titus Grapevine.

School, No. 1, taught by Rev. Burnell Lee. Scholars, 25.
No. 2,   "   Mr. Buttolf.   "   15.
No. 3,   "   John W. Hunton.   "   .

All the schools are instructed in English, and taught gratuitously.

The scholars are supported by their parents.

BAPTIST MISSION.

Under the patronage of the Baptist General Miss. Convention.

Near the eastern boundary of the Cherokee country. Commenced Nov. 10, 1832.

Missionaries.—Rev. S. Aldrich. Rev. Chandler Curtis is temporarily at this station.

School.—20 scholars, instructed in English, supported by their parents, and taught gratuitously.

The church was established in the Cherokee nation within the state of Georgia, and emigrated to Arkansas in 1832.

Native church members, 7
Black   "   "   6   } In all 23.
White   "   "   10

Post Office, Vineyard, Washington Co. Mo.

CREEKS.—(Properly MUS-CO-GEES.*)

The country of the Muscogees joins Canadian river and the lands of the Choctaws on the south, and the Cherokee lands on the east and north. Their eastern limit is about 45 miles from N. to S. thence their country extends westward as far as the quantity of wood will admit of habitation.

They own salt springs west of their settlements, not yet worked. The celebrated salt rock, on the Red fork of Arkansas, where from time immemorial, the natives have collected salt, will likely prove to be near the line from east to west, between the Creeks and Cherokees.

The settlements which they have formed are on Arkansas and Canadian rivers, on the eastern portion of their lands. None reside in villages. Their fields are invariably enclosed with rail fences. They cultivate corn extensively, so that within their settlements there have been fifty or sixty thousand bushels more than they needed for home consumption. They cultivate the variety of culinary vegetables common among the whites, and raise wheat and highland rice in small quantities.

They spin, weave, sew, knit, and follow other pursuits of industry common in the west.

Their dwellings are composed of logs, erected by themselves, and resembling those of their frontier white neighbors, and many of them are furnished with plain, decent furni-

---

*Accent the second syllable, and sound g hard.

ture, such as farmers generally own.

They have one grist mill erected at the expense of the owner.

They own horses, cattle, hogs, plows, and cotton spinning wheels, enough to answer their domestic purposes with common convenience. Also, sheep, waggons and looms, but these three kinds of articles are scarce.

The Muscogees are governed by *written laws*, in spirit resembling laws of the United States. These laws are enacted by a general council of the nation, which convenes as often as circumstances require.

Their Sheriffs, who execute the decisions of the Council, and of the Judges, are termed *Light-horse-men*, and are exceedingly prompt in the discharge of their duties.

The Creeks are remarkable for the respectful and dignified attention which they bestow upon matters submitted to their consideration by officers of the government of the U. States, and by those who are employed in labours of benevolence among them. There are favorable openings for benevolent efforts for aiding them in their promising career of improvement, in the western settlements, on the north of Arkansas river, and in the southern settlements upon Canadian river.

600 Creek emigrants from the east of Mississippi arrived at the settlements on Arkansas, in March 1835, headed by their chief U-fa-la-ha-cho.

Principal Chiefs.—Rolly M'Intosh, (Benj. Perryman, late 2d chief, is dead,) Tus-hat-che-me-ko, commanding general of the militia, Chilly M'Intosh, and Jacob Derrisaw, judges.

There are chiefs and head men in every settlement, who severally manage their local affairs, these form the general council of the nation which enacts laws, &c.

R. A. Macabe, U. S. Sub-Agent, north of Arkansas river, and 2 miles west of Verdigris river. Compensation $750 per annum.

BAPTIST MISSIONS.

Under the management of the Bap. Gen. Mis. Con.

1st STATION,—North of Arkansas river, and four miles west of Verdigris river : Missionary labors were commenced in Oct. 1829, by John Davis, a native Muscogee. The station was regularly organized in Oct. 1832:

Missionaries.—Rev. D. B. Rollin, Mrs. Rollin, Miss M. Rice.

An English school is taught gratuitously : The scholars are supported by their parents.

Church.—Muscogee Baptist Church was constituted Sept. 9, 1832.

Native Church Members,	18,	
Black " "	58,	80.
White " "	4,	

The Church worships in the school house.

2D STATION.—8 miles west of the first.

Missionaries.—Rev. John Davis, Mrs. Davis, both natives. Miss Mary Ann Colbourn.

Mr. Davis began to labor separately in Feb. 1834. He has 3 regular places of preaching.

School.—Taught by Miss Colbourn, originated in 1835, 20 scholars instructed in English, gratuitously, and supported by their parents.

An elementary school book of 32 pages, and the gospel by John, both upon the new system of writing Indian, have been printed, the past year, in the Muscogee language, at the Shawanoe Baptist Mission House. This service required Mr. Davis to spend about three months with the missionaries at the Shawanoe station. In the preparation of these books Mr. D. labored in conjunction with the missionaries at that place.

The Post Office for all within the Creek country is Fort Gibson, Arkansas.

PRESBYTERIAN MISSION.

Under the direction of Am. Bd. Com. For. Mis.

Six miles west of the late Agency.

Missionaries.—Rev. John Fleming, Mrs. Fleming.

Church.—Organized in 1830,

Native Church members,	8,	
Black, " "	7,	17.
White, " "	2,	

Mr. Fleming has compiled, and had printed, an elementary school book, in the Creek language, written upon the common principles of English orthography.

METHODIST MISSION.

Under the patronage of the Missouri Conference.

Missionary labors commenced in 1831.

Missionaries.—Rev. J. N. Hamil, Mr. John Harral, two schools. Church members 360.

SENECAS, &c.

These consist of three bands, viz:
Senecas, 200,
Senecas and Shawanoes, 211, } 461.
Mohawks, 50,

Their lands on the east adjoin the state of Missouri; on the south the Cherokee lands; on the west Neosho river is the boundary between them and the Cherokees. Their lands extend north between Neosho river and the state of Missouri so far as to include about 127,500 acres.

Seneca Chiefs.—Geo. Curley Eye, 1st Civil Chief.
    Comstick, 2d do. do.
    Capt. Good Hunter, 1st War Chief,
    Seneca Steel, 2d do. do.
    Small Cloud Spicer,
    Thos. Brant, } Head Men.
    Tall Chief,

Seneca and Shawanoe Chiefs.—Civil John, 1st Civil Chief; Pe-wy-ha, 2d do. Skillowa, 3d do.

Onondaqua Isaac, and Capt. Read, Head Men.

Mohawk Chiefs.—Isaac White, Principal Chief.—George Heron, 2d Chief.

They are within the Cherokee Sub-Agency.

James Pool, Blacksmith, pd. by the U. S. $480 per an.
Thos. M'Causland, Miller. Comp. $500 do. do.

As a people they are in some measure civilized. Most of them can speak English. All cultivate land for support, and grow potatoes and other garden vegetables, and corn sufficient to support them and their live stock. Their fields are enclosed with rail fences. None reside in villages. They own about 800 horses, 1200 cattle, 13 yoke of oxen, 200 hogs, 5 waggons, and 67 ploughs.

They have one tailor, and one cooper; and many of them can use edged tools.

Their dwellings are neat hewed log cabins, erected by themselves. Within them are bedsteads, chairs, and tables of their own manufacturing.

They own one grist and saw mill, erected at the cost of the U. States. One of their number, Mr. John Brown, is a merchant.

They are generally, favorably disposed towards civilized habits, and evince a desire to improve their condition, except in the matter of education. They have no school, and desire none.

About 36 persons can read in the Mohawk language. The book of Common Prayer, and the gospel by St. Mark, translated into Mohawk by Captain Joseph Brant in 1787, which contains 505 octavo pages. Also, they read the gospel by St. Luke, translated by H. A. Hill, and printed in 1827, by the American Bible Society.

Among them is a Church of 50 members, denominating themselves Episcopalians. Captain Bowless, who is about 60 years of age, officiates as minister every Sabbath. In this service they read portions of the Book of Common Prayer, sing, &c. They have no house of public worship.

Capt. Bowless says that he was taught to read by educated Indians, and that he has never enjoyed an intimate acquaintance with any missionary.

Their condition calls for the early attention of missionary societies.

OSAGES, (Properly WOS-SOSH-E.*)

The country of the Osages lies north of the western portion of the Cherokee lands, commencing 25 miles west of the state of Missouri, and thence in a width of 50 miles, extends west as far as the country can be inhabited.

About one half of the tribe reside on the eastern portion of their lands. The residue are in the Cherokee country. The latter form three villages, the two larger of which are on Verdigris river, and the smaller on Neosho river. The small band upon Neosho have made some advances towards civilized life. They have fenced small quantities of land with rail fences. A few have erected very ordinary log cabins, and keep a small number of cattle and hogs, and occasionally have used the plough.

The residue of the tribe have made no improvement.† Their fields are small, say one acre or less to a family, and enclosed by the insertion of stakes in the earth, to which a line, or two lines of small poles are fastened horizontally with the bark of trees.

Their huts are constructed by inserting small poles in the ground, the smaller ends of which are bent over the room

---

*O as in not, accent the second syllable.

†The most barbarous tribes keep horses and dogs, and cultivate a small quantity of corn and other vegetables. So that these things are not an indication of improvement.

B 2

and united, so as to produce the form of a cone, some eight or nine feet high. On the outside is fastened, either broad pieces of bark, which forms a kind of weather-boarding, or a mat of flags or of bulrushes, sewed together with threads of bark. The fire is placed in the centre, the smoke of which escapes through an aperture in the top. Many of these houses are oblong, and contain two or three fire places, and a greater number of families. All the Osages live in villages, in which their houses are crowded close together without order.

Some of their shelters are covered with Buffalo or elk skins; and these, as well as those covered with flags, are portable.

Their villages are merely *summer* residences. In winter they change encampments, as the prospect of grazing for their horses suggests.

Within their houses are neither tables, chairs, nor bedsteads, unless we fancy an exception in a platform raised about two feet high, upon stakes set in the earth. This platform extends along the side of the hut, and may serve for a seat, a table or a bedstead. This, however, is generally dispensed with.

The leggings and the mockasins for the feet, are seldom worn, except in cold weather, or when travelling in the grass. Excepting these and the temporary garments fastened about the waist, and extending downward, neither the males nor the married females have any covering for the body, except a buffalo skin, or a blanket, thrown loosely around them. This robe is their garment by day, and their bed at night.

The younger females usually wear a plain strip of cloth, eight or nine inches broad, resting upon one shoulder, and passing over the breast, and under the opposite arm.

The Osages are not fierce and warlike, as has been generally represented, on the contrary they are uncommonly servile and manageable.

Whilst the condition of depraved man, unimproved, is pitiable in the extreme, there is something noble to be admired in these pupils of nature.

Three framed dwellings, for as many chiefs, have been erected by the United States, at a cost of about $2000 each.

Also, about 70 acres of prairie land have been fenced, and plowed for them by the government.

Game near them is exceedingly scarce. They go upwards of one hundred miles before they find buffalo, and then they are frequently either frighted, or whipped back empty by their enemies. They suffer much for want of food and raiment, and they *are wretched in the extreme.*

Favorable openings for benevolent efforts for the improvement of their condition, present themselves in at least four places.

Cleremont is principal chief. Subordinate chiefs are Mo-ne-push-ee, Tow-un-ma-kee, Sho-ba-shing-a, Nung-e-wash-e, O-wau-sau-be, Ne-she-mo-ne, Mau-shau-ke-tau.

Their Agency house is among the villages of the north eastern part of their lands.

Sub-Agent, P. S. Chotcau, salary $750 per ann. The interpreter receives $300 per ann.

They have a blacksmith with a salary of $480 per ann. and a striker with a salary of $240.

PRESBYTERIAN MISSION.

Under the direction of the Am. Bd. Com For. Miss.

HOPEFIELD STATION.—In the improving band of Osages on lower Neosho. Commenced Sept. 22, 1823. William C. Requa, missionary.

BOUDINOT STATION.—In the vicinity of the Osage villages, upon Upper Neosho. Located in 1830.

Missionaries.—Rev. Mr. Dodge, Mrs. Dodge.

QUAPAWS.

The band of Quapaws was originally connected with the Osages. Some years they resided within the territory of Arkansas; within the last year, they removed to the Indian territory.

Their lands adjoin the State of Missouri, immediately north of the Senecas and Shawanoes of Neosho, extending westward from the State of Missouri about 15 miles to Neosho river. They are Southeast of, and near to the Osages.

Early in the spring of 1835, they expressed a desire that their lands should be surveyed, so that they could form their settlements with the greater certainty; this not having been done they have remained unsettled.

Their habits are somewhat more improved, and their circumstances more comfortable than those of their kindred, the Osages.

They are in charge of the Cherokee Sub-Agent, Capt. G. Vashon. S. B. Bright, Agriculturalist, appointed by virtue of treaty stipulations.

They are destitute of religious and literary teachers, and ought to be supplied without delay.

PUTAWATOMIES.

By treaty of Chicago, in 1833, the Putawatomies agreed to remove westward, and accepted an extensive and valuable tract of country on the N. E. side of Missouri river, above the state of Missouri.

In 1834, a delegation, of Putawatomies, conducted by Col. Pepper, visited the unappropriated tract of country on the upper branches of the Osage river, south of, and adjoining their allies, the Ottawas, and their old neighbors, the Weas, Peorias, and others, and chose that as the most desirable place for their future residence.

In 1835, another delegation conducted by Mr. Gordon, visited the country which had been assigned to them on the N. E. of Missouri river.

500 Putawatomie emigrants are expected to arrive about this time, and a contract has been closed for furnishing them with a years supply of food, on their land, on the N. E. of Missouri river.

444 Putawatomies are mingling with the Kickapoos on the lands of the latter, on the South west side of Missouri.

These are exceedingly averse to settling in their new country, they would greatly prefer a location on the lands chosen by the former delegation.

The country assigned to the Putawatomies is more remote than they at first apprehended. They fear that they will find unkind neighbors among the Sioux, Pawnees, and other tribes of the upper Missouri. It is believed that they will not remain contented in that country, and that they will request the government to allow them to occupy the country on the Osage river, in lieu of that which has become theirs by treaty.

This change would doubtless be advantageous, both to the government of the U. States and to the Indians. The latter would be placed alongside of their former neighbors, in a central portion of the Indian territory, and where the permanency of their location could not be doubted.

Principal Chief of the former emigrants, Qua-qua-taw.

Subordinate Chiefs, Wau-pu-nim, or, white dog, Mich-e-ke-kau-ba, or bad boy, and Nosha-kum.

BAPTIST MISSION.
Under the patronage of the Baptist General Miss. Convention.

CAREY MISSIONARY STATION, in Michigan Territory, was among the Putawatomies. The treaty of Sept. 20, 1828, includes an article favorable to the removal of the establishment to the west of Mississippi. In accordance with which, matters are held in readiness to resume the operations of the institution as soon as the Putawatomies shall become settled.

Since the suspension of labors at Carey, some of the Missionaries who belonged to that station, have been employed for the benefit of other tribes. In the mean time those matters have been in charge of Mr. Robert Simerwell and Mrs. Simerwell, missionaries; who are, at present, at the Shawanoe Mission house, awaiting the location of the Putawatomies. On resuming labors at their permanent station, they will be reinforced. Mr. Simerwell has written three small books, upon the new system, which have been printed in Putawatomie. He visits that part of the tribe which lives with the Kickapoos, and teaches upon the new system.

WEAS & PIANKESHAS.

These are bands of Miamies. Their country is north of the unappropriated tract in which it is expected the Putawatomies will ultimately settle, adjoins the state of Missouri on the east, the Shawanoes on the north, and the Peorias and Kaskaskias on the west. It embraces 160,000 acres.

These people cultivate little over an acre of land to a family. Some of their fields are fenced with rails, and some are enclosed with poles only, like those of the Osages. Some of their dwellings are of logs, and others are of bark. They own a few cattle and hogs.

In compliance with treaty stipulations the U. S. government has lately furnished them with cattle to the value of $500, and have fenced and plowed fields to the amount of 74 acres.

Also, in 1835, oxen and other cattle, carts and other farming implements were furnished the Piankesha band, to the value of $500 dollars.

Principal Chief, Swan.

Their late principal chief, Negro legs, is dead.

Agent, Maj. Richard W. Cummins, entitled agent for the Northern Indian Agency. Compensation, $1500 per ann. Agency House, on the Shawanoe lands, near the line of the State of Missouri, and seven miles south of Missouri river.

Interpreter, Joseph Parks, a Shawanoe, Comp. $300 per ann. who also interprets for all the tribes within the northern agency, except the Kauzau.

Blacksmith, William Carlisle, Comp. $180 per ann. who also labors for the Peorias and Kaskaskias.

Assistant do.— —— ——. Comp. $240, per ann.

Presbyterian Mission—Under the management of the western For. Mis. So. Commenced April, 1834.

Missionaries.—Rev. Joseph Kerr, Mrs. Kerr, Mr. Henry Bradley, Miss Nancy Henderson, Mr. Lindsey, Mrs. Lindsey.

Shcool.—Attended in the Indian village. Instructed gratuitously in English. Scholars supported by their parents.

Post Office, for all connected with this tribe, is Westport, Jackson county, Missouri.

PEORIAS AND KASKASKIAS.

These are also bands of Miamies. Their land lies immediately west of the Weas, adjoins the Shawanoes on the north, and the Ottawas on the west. They own 96,000 acres.

The fields which they have made themselves are small, though they are generally enclosed with rail fences. The number of their cattle and swine is greater than those of their neighbors, the Weas. Some of their dwellings are composed of logs, and others are of bark.

In conformity with treaty stipulations, government has recently fenced and plowed for them 25 acres of land, and has erected three log houses, worth $400.

Chiefs.—White Skin, Peoria Jim, Paschal, and Gemasah.

Agent.—R. W. Cummins.

METHODIST MISSION.

Under the management of the Miss. Society of the M. E. Church. Commenced in 1832.

Missionaries.—Rev. N. M. Talbot, Mrs. Talbot, Mr. Groves.

School.—16 Scholars, instructed in English, and supported by their parents, excepting one meal a day furnished at the Mission House.

Church.—Native Church Members, 26 } In all 28.
White   "   "   2 }

The Post Office of all connected with these bands is Westport, Jackson Co. Mo.

OTTAWAS

This band owns 36,000 acres of land immediately west of the Peorias and Kaskaskias, and South of the Shawanoes.

They have recently settled upon their lands, have made rail-fences, and in other respects commenced in a manner that indicates a disposition to improve their condition. Others of this tribe are soon expected to emigrate and join them. Their condition, as it regards civilization, is similar to that of the Peorias.

Chiefs.—Ok-wun-ox-e and She-kauk.
Agent.—R. W. Cummins.

BAPTIST MISSION.

Missionaries.—Jotham Meeker, Mrs. Meeker.

They reside at present at the Shawanoe Mission House. Mr. M. occasionally visits the Ottawas, and expects to locate permanently among them as soon as his services in the Printing Office at the Shawanoe Mission House can be dispensed with.

The Post Office for all connected with this band is Westport, Jackson Co. Mo.

SHAWANOES.

Immediately on the north of the Weas and Piankeshas, the Peorias and Kaskaskias, and the Ottawas, lies the country of the Shawanoes, extending along the line of the state of Missouri north 28 miles to Missouri river, at its junction with Kauzau river; thence up Kauzau river to a point 60 miles on a direct course, to the lands of the Kauzau Indians; thence south on the Kauzau line six miles; thence west with a width of about 19 miles to a north and south line 120 miles west of the state of Missouri. Their tract embraces 1,600,000 acres.

The Shawanoes reside in the north eastern corner of their country, near the line of Missouri, and near the Kauzau river.

Generally, their dwellings are neat hewed log cabins, erected with their own hands; and within them is a small amount of furniture. Their fields are enclosed with rail fences, and are sufficiently large to yield them corn and culinary vegetables plentifully. They keep cattle and swine, work oxen, and use horses for draught; and own some plows, waggons and carts.

In conformity with treaty stipulations, government is erecting for them a saw and grist mill, to be completed April 1, 1836; the cost of which will be about $8000.

Principal Chiefs. John Perry, and William Perry.

Other Chiefs. Black Feather, Sa-mau-kau, Little Fox, Le-tho, Wa-wá-la-pea, Black Hoof, and Cornstalk.

Agent. R. W. Cummins.
1st Blacksmith. Lewis Jones. Comp'n. $480 per ann.
Ass't. do. ———— ————. " $240 " "
2d Blacksmith. William Donelson. " $480 " "
Ass't. do. ———— ————. " $240 " "

METHODIST MISSION.

Under the patronage of the Miss. Soc. of the M. E. Ch. Originated in 1830.

Missionaries.—Rev. William Ketron, Mrs. Ketron, Mrs. Miller, Rev David G. Gregory, Mrs. Gregory.

School.—34 scholars. Instructed in English gratuitously. 19 are supported by the mission, and live in the mission family. The residue receive one meal a day at the mission house, and otherwise are supported by their parents. Five of them are learning the Cabinet making business, and two are learning the business of Shoe making.

The missionaries have instructed some of the Shawanoes to read in their native language; and some of these have become teachers of others. Instruction in Indian is systematically placed under the immediate notice of native Class leaders of the Church.

A small book in the Shawanoe language, on religious subjects, embracing some hymns, has been published by the missionaries, and introduced among the people of their charge with good effect.

Church.—Native Church members, 105, } In all, 110.
  White   "   "   5, }

Among these native Church members are some who take an active part in the performance of public religious exercises, pray in their families, &c.

BAPTIST MISSION.
Under the direction of the Bap. Gen. Mis. Con.
Commenced in 1831.
Missionaries.—Johnston Lykins, Mrs. Lykins.
Robert Simerwell, Mrs. Simerwell, Jotham Meeker, and Mrs. Meeker, are temporarily here.

Native Church members, 6, viz. 1 Shawanoe, 1 Chippewa, 1 Osage, and 3 Delawares. White persons, 11, in all, 17.

Two native members have died, who gave evidence of genuine piety.

At the Shawanoe Station is a printing press, under the management of Jotham Meeker, missionary for the Ottawas.

Since the establishment of the printing press, there have been printed in the Delaware language, two small elementary school books; in Shawanoe, two, of a larger size for the Baptists, and one for the Methodists; in Putawatomie, three; in Otoe, three, all small; selections from which have been re-printed for the benefit of the Presbyterian missionaries among the Ioways; in Choctaw, one; in Muscogee, one elementary school book, and the gospel by John; and in Wea, one school book for the Presbyterians. Also, a considerable number of hymns have been printed in various Indian languages. Besides which, there is issued from the press, a small monthly periodical, edited by Mr. Lykins, entitled "*Sauwaunowe Kesauthwau,*"—Shawanoe Sun.

In this periodical, such of the Shawanoes as have learned to read in their own language take a deep interest. Some of them have furnished matter for the work from their own pens.

All of the above prints are upon the *new system* of writing Indian, with a slight exception which occurred in the Wea book. In this system the common types are used, but not for the purpose of *spelling*. That is to say, the learner is *not* required to repeat the names of two, three, or more letters, from the combination of which he derives the sound of a syllable, and, when he has obtained the requisite syllables, to unite them, and form a word. Vowel sounds are denoted

C

by letters which never vary their several uses. Each of the other letters indicate the position of the organs of speech, preceeding or following vowels, with the exception of two or three, as, for instance, S, denotes merely the *hissing*, in which consists the real value of that letter in the word *see*, e. g. this character T, directs the reader to place the end of the tongue to the upper part of the mouth with a slight pressure from within, the voice opens on O, and he necessarily pronounces TO, transpose the characters, and adhere to the same principles, and he necessarily pronounces OT. In like manner all other characters are used, none of which vary their uses.

Hence, when the learner has acquired a knowledge of the use of each character, or in other words, when he has learned the alphabet, he is at once capable of reading.

Indian habits render them averse to study. The labour of becoming familiar with certain sounds, as is necessary in the process of spelling, is, in general, exceedingly irksome, and vastly more so when learning to read English. Upon the new system one may begin to read in a few days, or in a few weeks at farthest, and understanding what he reads, he finds amusement in the exercise.

The first experiment was made with a sprightly Chippewa boy. He studied three hours each day for nine days. At the expiration of which time, a writing of about 20 lines was put into his hands, of the contents of which he was ignorant. After looking over it a few minutes without the aid of an instructor, he read off the writing to the unspeakable satisfaction of his teacher.

Upon the new system, what we term *bad spelling*, cannot happen. A word is necessarily written precisely as it is pronounced, because each letter is the invariable sign either of a certain vowel sound, or of a certain position of the organs of speech.

The imperious demands of other duties have allowed little time to the few missionaries to attend to teaching the natives to read upon the new plan. Nevertheless, between one and two hundred of the Shawanoes, Delawares, and Putawatomies have become capable of reading, and some of them can write; a large portion of them are adults, who never would have learned to read English, and some of them old men, who use spectacles. Never since the education of the aborigines was first attempted, have so many learned to read with so little labor and cost, as in the cases under consideration, and this is the more remarkable for this reason, that they are chiefly adults.

Such is the simplicity of the system, that as soon as one begins to read, he is capable of teaching others, and many of the Shawanoes, have thus learned to read from their associates, without the knowledge of the missionaries.

The discovery of this system is a favorable indication of Providence which promises much benefit to the Indians. Could an ample supply of missionaries be brought to the work, all the tribes in the vast wilderness inhabited by them might shortly be taught to read religious tracts, &c. A revolution among them might speedily be effected, the benefit of which to our country, as such, would be great, and the advantages to them *infinite*.

The English school taught at the mission has been suspended for the present, and the missionaries impart instruction upon the new system to schools which they meet at different places, on appointed days and hours, and to such as call on them at their residence. Circumstances do not admit of a more convenient method.

A Sabbath School has been sustained the past year, attendance on which has not been very good. It would have been much better had not the poverty of the Indians denied the scholars decent apparel, in which they would have been willing to appear on such occasions.

These remarks will apply to other cases also, and we would here recommend to the various religious denominations to furnish their missionaries with some articles of clothing, with books, and in some instances, with the means of procuring a small amount of food for the benefit of Sunday schools, as well as of others, to be applied as rewards of merit, &c.

One male and two female Indian youths live in the mission family, the former of whom is an apprentice to the printing business.

The Post Office for all connected with the Shawanoes is Westport, Jackson Co. Mo.

DELAWARES. (PROPERLY LIN-NOP-PE.)

The lands of the Delawares lie North of the Shawanoes, and in the Forks of the Kauzau and Missouri rivers, extending up the former to the Kauzau lands; thence north 24 miles to the N. E. corner of the Kauzau survey. It extends up the Missouri river to Cantonment Leavenworth, a distance of about 23 miles on a direct course; thence with a line westward to a point 10 miles north of the N. E. corner of the Kauzau lands, and then in a slip only 10 miles wide, it extends west along the northern boundary of the Kauzaus, to the distance of 208 miles from the state of Missouri.

The Delawares reside on the eastern portion of their country, not far from the junction of the Missouri and Kauzau rivers. They generally occupy good hewed log cabins, and have some furniture within them. They enclose their fields with rail fences, keep cattle and hogs, apply horses to draft, and use oxen and plows. They cultivate corn and garden vegetables sufficient for their use, and have commenced the culture of wheat.

In compliance with treaty stipulations, the United States have erected for the Delawares a grist and saw mill, worth about $2950; have fenced and plowed 105 acres of land, and have erected a school house and buildings attached thereto worth $278 50, and have furnished them cattle worth $2000.

Principal Chiefs, Capt. Nah-ko-mul, Capt. Catch-him, and Non-non-da-gon. The late principal chief, Capt. Patterson, is dead.

Agent.—R. W. Cummins.
Blacksmith.—Robt. Dunlap. Compensation, $480 per an.
Asst " ——— ———,   " $240 "
U. S. School Teacher, Rev. Henry Rennick, Cumberland Presbyterian. Teaches at present at the Methodist Mission House. Scholars 19. Compensation, $480 per ann.

A miller to attend the mills and keep them in repair. Compensation, $500 per ann.

METHODIST MISSION.
Directed by the Mis. Soc. M. E. C.

Begun, in 1831.
Missionaries.—Rev. E. T. Peery, Mrs. Peery.
This Mission supports three of Mr. Rennick's scholars, and gives one meal a day, some clothing, &c. to the residue; the remainder of support they derive from their parents.

Native Church Members 70 } 77.
White   "   "   7 }

BAPTIST MISSION.

Under the management of the Bap. Gen. Mis. Con.

Commenced in 1832. This mission is under the superintendence of Mr. Lykins, missionary among the Shawanoes. Other missionaries at the Shawanoe station also visit this. The converts here are members of the Church which meet at the Shawanoe Mission House.

School.—Ira D. Blanchard and Mrs. Blanchard, Teachers. Comfortable log dwellings and a school house are nearly completed. In consequence of attention to the erection of these, and of the necessary absence of the teacher, the former part of the year, and of sickness in the latter part, little has been done in the matter of instruction. Formerly Mr. Blanchard taught, and with a good degree of success, upon the *new system*. The school which is expected shortly to be opened in the new building will be taught in English. At the same time, instruction in Delaware, upon the new system will be imparted, so far as the Indians desire it.

The Post Office for all connected with the Delawares, is Westport, Jackson Co. Mo.

KAUZAUS,*

The country of this tribe lies on the Kauzau river, commencing 60 miles west of the state of Missouri, thence in a width of 30 miles, it extends west as far as the country can be inhabited.

About one third of the tribe reside in a village on the north bank of Kauzau river, within three miles of their eastern boundary; one third a few miles higher up, upon the south bank; and one third on the north bank, about 40 miles from their eastern boundary.

Their language, habits, and condition in life, are in effect, the same as those of the Osages. In matters of peace and war, the interest of the two tribes are blended; and they are virtually one people.

Like the Osages, the Kauzaus are ignorant, poor, and wretched in the extreme; and are as uncommonly servile and easily controlled by white men who mingle with them.

*Different persons have at various times, written the name of this tribe differently, as suited the fancy of each. We have chosen to adhere to the pronunciation of the natives themselves, which is Kau-zau.

All live in villages, where their huts are crowded closely, without order in their arrangement. Besides their houses of bark, and of flags, constructed like those of the Osages, they have a few of earth. These are circular and in form of a cone, the wall of which is about two feet in thickness, and is sustained by wooden pillars within. Like their other huts, they have no floor except the earth. The fire is in the centre, and the smoke escapes directly above. The door is low and narrow, so that in entering, a person must half crawl. The door, as in their other huts, is closed by a skin of some animal suspended therein.

At the lower village, the Gov't of the U. S. has fenced 20 acres of land and plowed 10 acres, and has erected for the principal Chief a good hewed log house.

Within the last year their smithery has been located on their own lands, near their lower village. The buildings formerly occupied by their smith, their former agency buildings, a house for the residence of one to aid them in agriculture, and a large stone building erected for the chief White Feather, are all within the country of the Delawares, 23 miles east of the Kauzau lands.

The wretched condition of the Kauzaus prefers strong claims upon the sympathies of a Christian public, and the prospect of success holds out great encouragement to benevolent efforts, for the amelioration of their condition.

Principal Chief is Nam-pa-war-rah, or White Feather. Other chiefs, are Ka-he-ga-wa-ta-ne-ga, Whin-ra-shu-ga, Ka-he-ge-wa-chi-chi, Min-gar-na-che, Ka-he-ga-shing-a.

Agent.—R. W. Cummins.

Interpreter.—Joseph James, a half Kauzau and half Frenchman. Compensation $300 per annum.

Blacksmith, Compensation, $480 per ann.

Assistant do. Comp. $240 per ann.

METHODIST MISSION.

Under the direction of the Miss. Soc. of the M. E. C.
Undertaken in 1835.

Missionaries.—Rev. Wm. Johnson, Mrs. Johnson.

KICKAPOOS.

The country of the Kickapoos lies north of the Delawares, extending up Missouri river to a point 30 miles direct;

thence westward, about 6 miles, and thence south 20 miles, to the Delaware line.—Including 768,000 acres.

They live on the south eastern extremity of their lands, near Cantonment Leavenworth.

In regard to civilization their condition is similar to that of the Peorias.

Principal Chiefs.—Pos-sa-che-haw, Kel-u-kuk, Mash-e-na. Kickapoo and Musk-o-ma.

Agent.—R. W. Cummins.

Blacksmith.—John P. Smith. Compensation, $480 per an.

Assistant do. —— ——, $240 per annum.

The U. S. have erected a School house and other buildings, attached thereto, worth $300.

U. S. School Teacher.—Rev. J. C. Beryman, of the Methodist Mission.

School.—Six scholars, instructed in English. Compensation, $480 per annum.

A church [house for worship] is being erected by the U. S. for the Kickapoos, the cost of which will be $700, Also, a saw and grist mill, nearly completed, worth $3000.

METHODIST MISSION.

Supported by the Missionary Society, of the Methodist. E. Church under the management of the Missouri Conference. Commenced in 1833.

Missionaries.—Rev. J. C. Berryman, Mrs. Berryman.

Mr. Berryman, receiving his support from the Methodist Missionary Society, applies the salary which he receives from government as teacher, to the support of the native scholars, and to other purposes of the mission. The Mission buildings, and the U. S. School house, are on the same ground.

The Post Office for all connected with the Kickapoos, excepting the Agent, is Fort Leavenworth, Western Territory.

KICKAPOO RELIGIOUS SOCIETY.

Kelukuk, alias the Kickapoo Prophet, one of the Kickapo. Chiefs, is a professed preacher, of an order which he himself originated some years ago. His adherents are about 400 in number; some of whom are small boys and girls.*

He professes to receive all that he teaches, immediately from the Great Spirit, by a supernatural agency. He teaches abstinence from the use of ardent spirits, the ob-

---

*About one half of them are Putawatomies, and the other half Kickapoos.

servation of the Sabbath, and some other good morals. He appears to have little knowledge of the doctrines of Christianity, only as his dogmas happen to agree with them.

Congregational worship is performed four days in the week, and lasts from one to three hours.

It consists of a kind of prayer expressed in broken sentences, often repeated, in a monotonous sing-song tone, equalling about two measures of a common psalm tune. All in unison, engage in this; and in order to preserve harmony in words, each holds in his or her hand, a small board about an inch and a half broad, and 8 or 10 inches long, upon which is engraved arbitrary characters, which they follow up with the finger, until the last character admonishes them that they have completed the prayer

These characters are five in number, the 1st represents the heart, the 2d, the heart and flesh, the 3d the life, the 4th their names, the 5th their kindred.

During the service, these characters are gone over several times, the first time the person supposes himself to be on earth; next, to be approaching the door of the house of God, in heaven, then at the door, &c.

Putting their finger to the lowest character, they say:

O, our Father, make our heart like thy heart, as good as thy heart, as strong as thy heart, &c. as good as thy house, as good as the door of thy house, as hard and as good as the ground about thy house, as strong as the staff thou walkest with, &c. &c.

O, our Father, make our heart and flesh like thine, as strong as thine, like thy house, door, staff, &c.

O, our Father, put our name with thy name, think of it as thou dost of thy house, door, staff, the ground about thy house, &c.

Make our kindred like thine, like thy house, door, staff, &c. &c. Make our life like thine, &c. &c.

From the above, may be inferred the mode and doctrines of their religious services; the exercises are, however, spun out to a length exceedingly tedious. Not the least allusion is made to sin against God, consequently no confession of, or repentance for sin is implied, nor atonement sought. In these things they seem to be more in darkness than other rude savages, all of whom in their *offerings* imply an acknowledgment of transgression against the Great Spirit and the necessity of repentance and atonement.

The step which they have taken from the state which is natural to Indians, has been retrograde into greater darkness. In matters of religion, Indians in their original condition, are the pupils of nature. A departure from this state, uninfluenced by the bible, must necessarily be backward. Whipping with a rod is one article of their creed, and is submitted to on account of transgression. But, as in their prayers, &c. no acknowledgement is made of sin against God, it appears that this suffering is submitted to merely on account of its salutary effects upon the present state of society among themselves.

The offender, whose crime may be known only to himself, applies to one of the four or five persons who are authorised to use the rod, and states that he has committed an offence for which he desires the whipper to inflict a given number of stripes upon his bare back. Having received the flagellation, which frequently brings the blood, the penitent immediately shakes hands with the executioner and others near, returning thanks for the favor conferred upon him, and declaring that he feels himself relieved from a heavy burthen.

Not long since, the prophet himself offended so notoriously; that he could not on account of the high station which he occupied, plead an exemption from the rigorous rule of whipping. But in order to lessen the mortification of publicly humbling himself, he called a council, at which it was concluded that there had been a general backsliding among them, and that a universal whipping would be proper. Accordingly a day was appointed, and every man, woman and child belonging to the society, received a due portion of stripes upon the bare back.

Polygamy is allowed. Kel-u-kuk, their leader, has two or more wives. The Prophet's popularity is on the wane as it ought to be. Eight of his party have recently forsaken him.

We have been astonished to hear it reported that the prophet was a *Christian*, and that he and his party were members of a Christian church! Had it not been for this report the foregoing article would not have been extended to its present length.

OTOES.

This tribe claims a portion of land in the fork between Missouri and Platte rivers. But their country is understood to extend southward from the Platte river down Missouri to Little Ne-ma-ha river, a distance of about 40 miles, thence their southern boundary extends westward up Little Nemaha to its source, and thence due west. Their western and northern boundaries are not particularly defined. Their southern boundary is about 35 miles north of the Kickapoo lands.

By treaty, such of their tribe as are related to the whites, have an interest in a tract adjoining the Missouri river, and extending from the little Nemaha to the Great Nemaha, a distance of about 20 miles, and ten miles wide. No Indians reside on this tract.

The condition of these people is similar to that of the Osages, and Kauzaus. They take the Buffaloe with less difficulty and danger than the former, and consequently suffer less with hunger.

The U. S. is erecting a School house for the Otoes, on a tract of land more suitable for the purposes of agriculture, than they have heretofore occupied, and on which they have consented to locate.

Principal Chief, Ietan.

Their Agency is on the South West bank of Missouri, 6 miles above its junction with the great Platte river.

Agent.—Maj. John Dougherty. Comp. $1500 per annum.
Blacksmith,—— Gilmore. Comp. $480 per annum.
Assistant do. Comp. $240 per annum.
Agriculturalist, —— Dougherty. Comp. $480 per ann.
U. S. School Teacher.—Rev. Moses Merrill. Comp. $480 per annum.

BAPTIST MISSION.

Under the management of the Bap. Gen. Mis. Con.

On the north bank of Platte river, 6 miles from its junction with Missouri river, and about 200 miles a little west of north from the mouth of Kauzau river. Commenced, Oct. 1833.

Missionaries.—Rev. Moses Merrill, Mrs. Merrill, Miss Cynthia Brown.

A small school has been sustained the greater part of the past year. The preparations which have been necessary for locating the mission permanently have greatly hindered other missionary labors. A favorable change, however, may be hoped for as soon as Mr. Merrill, the U. S. Smithery, and the Otoes become settled on the ground, selected for those purposes by the proper officers of government.

Post Office for all connected with this tribe is Fort Leavenworth, West. Ter.

OMAHAS.

The country of the Omahas adjoins the Platte river on the south, and the Missouri river on the N. East, their Northren and western boundaries are indefinite.

They are about settling on the bank of the Missouri, at a place recommended to them by the government, as being suited for agricultural purposes, about 60 miles north of the Otoes.

Their condition is in all respects similar to that of the Otoes, who are their friends and allies.

Principal Chief.—Big Elk.
Agent.—J. Dougherty.
Blacksmith.—Compensation $480.
Assistant do. $210.

BAPTIST MISSION.
Undertaken by the Bap. Gen. Mis. Con.

Within the last year a gentleman received the appointment of U. S. School Teacher for the Omahas, who was expected to be in connexion with the Baptist Board of Missions, according to labors which the Board had bestowed upon this subject. Ultimately this gentleman declined going to the Omaha country.

The Board then directed Rev. Chandler Curtis, who was temporarily at the Cherokee station, to repair to the Omahas, and his arrival among them is daily expected.

PAWNEES.

The country of the Pawnees is westward of the Otoes and Omahas. Their boundaries are not definite. Their villages are, chiefly, on the Great Platte, and its waters.

In their habits and condition they are farther removed from those of civilized man, than any tribe which we have noticed. Some of their huts are of earth, like those spoken of among the Kauzaus. In some instances they continue to cultivate the earth with the shoulder bone of the buffaloe. This being tied to a stick for a handle, serves the purposes of a spade or shovel. They obtain buffaloe with less difficulty than others, excepting the Otoes and Omahas, between whom and themselves there is an intimate connexion.

Agent.—John Dougherty.

BAPTIST MISSION.

The mission to the Otoes, which at first embraced the Omahas, was undertaken with reference to the Pawnees also; and this design is still maintained..

PRESBYTERIAN MISSION.

Under the direction of the Am. Bd. Com For. Miss.
Begun in 1834.
Missionaries.—Rev. John Dunbar, Mr. Allis. Not yet located.

For the purpose of acquiring the language of the Pawnees, of extending their acquaintance among them, and of securing their friendship, these two missionaries, separately, mingle with the Indians, and go with them on their hunting excursions. This course is as judicious as it is honorably self-denying.

Among the Pawnees is an inviting field for four missionary establishments.

PUNCAHS.

The Puncah is a small band, originally from the Pawnee tribe, on the Missouri, in the northern extremity of the country spoken of as the Indian territory. Their circumstances are similar to those of the Pawnees. They have no missionaries.

OTHER BAPTIST MISSIONARIES.

The author of this publication, and his wife, have been missionaries to the Indians ever since the year 1817. In August, 1828, they removed from among the tribes around Lake Michigan, to what is now termed the Indian territory. Their circumstances differ from those of other missionaries of the Baptist General Missionary Convention, inasmuch as their labors have not been located to a particular tribe, especially since they left the tribes of the north; but they have extended their labors to places and matters generally; and they have supported themselves without cost to the Missionary Convention. Their Post Office is Westport, Jackson Co. Mo.

MISSIONARIES IN GENERAL.

Excepting the missionaries noticed in the last article, and a few who have received appointments from government as school teachers, all others, of every denomination of Christians, are supported by the societies which patronize them severally; but they receive no more than a bare support. The amount allowed varies according to the expensiveness of living at each station, and is fixed by the missionary societies, so as barely to cover the necessary current expenditures of the several missionaries. None of them, therefore, receive any compensation which they can lay up as their own personal property. By this means, the voluntary surrender of the missionary to labors of benevolence for the benefit of the Indians, places him beyond the influence of temptation to acquire property. He does not receive even a promise of support for his family, should they out-live him; but, he trusts all to Providence.

Rev. Johnston Lykins exercises a general agency extending to the various tribes within the territory, according to instructions given him from time to time by the Baptist Bd. of Missions; and is duly authorized to fulfil this trust, by authority from the proper officer of government.

Rev. Thomas Johnson is Superintendent of all the missionary stations of the Mis. Soc. of the M. E. Ch. north of the Cherokees. His Post Office is Westport, Jackson Co. Mo.

Rev. Peter M. M'Gowan, under the direction of the same Society, is Superintendent of Methodist missions among the Cherokees and Creeks. P. O. Fort Gibson.

Rev. Joseph Kerr, is Superintendent of the Missions of the Western Foreign Missionary Society.

Missionary Societies are voluntary associations, composed of members of the several Christian churches in the United States which have embarked in the cause of missions.

The office of the American Board of Commissioners for Foreign Missions, is in Boston, Mass. Secretaries, Rev. Rufus Anderson, and Rev. David Green.

The office of the Board of Managers of the Baptist General Missionary Convention, is also in Boston, Mass. Corresponding Secretary, Rev. Lucius Bolles, D. D. Treasurer, Hon. Heman Lincoln.

The office of the Western Foreign Missionary Society, is in Pittsburgh, Pa.

The office of the Missionary Society of the Methodist Episcopal Church, is in New York. Corresponding Secretary, Rev. N. Bangs, D. D.

WANT OF MISSIONARIES.

We are sorry to be under the necessity of repeating the article under this head. We entreat the Christian community to reflect that another year's sufferings have been realized by destitute Indians; another year's loss of education has occurred with Indian youth; in which time many have passed beyond the reach of this necessary branch of improvement; and, alas, what multitudes have entered the darkness of death, without one ray of gospel light!! The *new system* of education affords uncommon facilities for doing good to these unfortunate people. Who, we ask, is willing to come to their relief?

More than 20 male missionaries, besides females, could, at this time, find inviting situations for usefulness, within the Indian Territory.

Preaching is not an essential qualification for missionaries. They should be men of good sense, ardent piety, persevering disposition, conciliating manners, contented with their own business without meddling with the business of others, industrious, frugal and economical, ready to enlist for life, and willing to labor through life without laying up a dollar for those of their families who may out-live them.

Provisions of the Government of the United States, for the education of the Indians within the Indian territory, and for their improvement in civilization generally.

Besides the annual appropriation of $10,000 for education purposes, a portion of which is applied within the Indian territory, and besides the schools which receive support from government already mentioned, the following provisions have been made, viz. for the

KAUZAUS.

By treaty of 1825, 36 sections of *good* land were to be selected and sold, and the proceeds applied to the education of Kauzau children *within* their country.

The number of acres was 23,040. The value of which, at the minimum price of government land, would be $28,800.

The cost of feeding, clothing, lodging, and instructing an Indian youth, if applied in conjunction with benevolent institutions, within the Indian country, may be kept within $50 per ann. At this rate, the proceeds of the Kauzau lands, had they been sold, as above calculated, would keep fifty children in school 11 years. Should the scholars be supported by their parents, the number which might be educated with the sum just stated, would be quadruple the above. A school house, books, and teacher, for 40 scholars, could be furnished for $500 per annum. At this rate, their education fund, to wit, $28,800, would keep 200 children in school 11 years.

These lands have been selected; but, unfortunately, the selection was not made by examination of the country, but upon the plats. The consequence is, that more than half the land is of little value.

The state of Missouri was allowed Seminary lands, in the same district of country. The claims of the Kauzaus were entitled to precedence. Missouri fixed the minimum price of her lands at two dollars per acre, and it was not until the greater part was sold that the price was reduced to $1 25 per acre.

Had the Kauzau lands been seltlled according to the provisions of the treaty, not an acre would have remained until this time unsold, and it could have been sold for two dollars per acre, which would have amounted to the sum of 46,080 dollars.

The difference between this sum and the calculation at $1 25 per acre is 17,280 dollars. This latter sum has been lost to this education fund. It would have kept 31 Kauzau children in school more than 11 years; and, if the youths had been supported by their parents, it would have kept 124 children in school the same length of time.

But the loss will more than double this calculation, as will be perceived by what follows:

The amount of Kauzau lands which had been sold prior to Oct. 1, 1835, was 8,457 $\frac{40}{100}$ acres. The quantity remaining unsold was 14,582 $\frac{20}{100}$ acres. A great portion of this unsold land, never will be sold for any thing. The loss, therefore, to the Kauzaus, will be very considerable.

The 8,457 $\frac{40}{100}$ acres mentioned above, have been sold for $1 25 per acre, amounting to $10,571. This sum is in the United States Treasury.

By the same treaty of 1825, provision was made for the application of 600 dollars per annum to aid them in agriculture.

The Buffaloe have retired so far to the west that these people cannot take them without great labor, and the danger of falling in with war parties of hostile tribes. They suffer extremely for want of food. The method which has been observed in the application of this annuity heretofore, has been unsuccessful. The tribe has derived no lasting benefit therefrom, except the fencing of 20 acres, and the plowing of 10 acres, of land.

600 dollars would pay for fencing, plowing, and properly preparing to receive seed, 75 acres of prairie land. Should this amount of land be prepared for them yearly, a few years would place them in comfortable circumstances. It is hoped that this will be done. Humanity pleads strongly for the Kauzaus, whose wretchedness is extreme.

OSAGES.

The treaty of 1825 provides "that the President of the U. S. shall employ such persons to aid the Osages in their agricultural pursuits as to him may seem expedient."

Under this provision the sum of $1200 a year has been expended by the government. This has been done without rendering any substantial benefit to the tribe beyond the fencing and plowing of 70 acres of land, mentioned on the preceding pages.

If the annuity of $1200 pr. an. were expended in fencing and plowing land, as has been suggested in relation to the Kauzaus, it would prepare for seed two fields of 75 acres each, or, 150 acres each year until they should need no more.

The same treaty of 1825, requires that 54 sections of land be laid off under the direction of the President of the U. States, and sold, and the proceeds applied to the support of schools for the education of the Osage children. The number of acres is 34,560. The value of which, if sold at the minimum price of the U. S. land, would be 43,200.

This sum, if applied according to our calculations for the Kauzaus, would support and instruct in school 100 children, eight years and a half. Should the children be supported by their parents, the above sum would afford instruction to 400 children, eight and a half years.

These lands have not been selected. It is hoped that, in view of the losses which have been sustained by the Kauzau education fund, the selection of the Osage education lands will not be long deferred.

DELAWARES.

The treaty with the Delawares of Sept. 1829, provides that 36 sections of the *best* land within the district which was at that time ceded to the U. S. be selected and sold, and the proceeds applied to the support of schools for the education of Delaware children.

These lands have not yet been selected. The quantity of acres is 23,040; the value of which at the minimum price of government land would be $28,800. According to our calculations for the Kauzaus, this sum would feed, clothe, and educate 50 youths 11 years, or, if supported by their parents, it would keep 200 children in school 11 years.

In the country in which the Delaware education lands are to be selected, the low grounds along the water courses are generally of the first quality, and the uplands are generally worthless, being exceedingly broken and rocky. Government will, no doubt, shortly order the location of these lands.

PUTAWATOMIES.

By the treaty of 1833, the Putawatomies are allowed the sum of 70,000 dollars for purposes of education. This sum, if applied according to the plan upon which we have based our calculations, would support in a boarding school 100 scholars 14 years. Or, if they should be supported by their parents, it would keep in school 400 scholars for the term of 14 years.

KICKAPOOS.

The treaty of Oct. 24, 1832, provides that the U. States shall pay $500 per annum, for ten successive years, for the support of a school, purchase of books, &c. for the benefit of the Kickapoo tribe, upon their own lands.

The school house and teacher which have been furnished them, have been in conformity with this stipulation.

The same treaty provides $4000 for labor and improvements on the Kickapoo lands. If the sum of $4000 should be applied in fencing and plowing prairie land, it would prepare for receiving seed, 12 fields of forty acres each. But it is probable, that, for the Kickapoos, it would be desirable to make some of their fields in wood lands, where the cost of preparing them would be greater than in prairie.

OTOES.

The treaty of 1830, secures to this tribe agricultural implements to the amount of $500 annually, until the year 1840. The treaty of Sept. 1833, continues this annuity of $500, ten years longer to be paid in the same articles.

The treaty of 1830 provides for a blacksmith for them ten years, and longer, if the President of the U. S. shall think it proper.

The treaty of 1833, stipulates that a flouring mill, to operate by horse power, shall be erected for the benefit of the tribe.

Also, the value of $1000, in live stock, will be given them, but, it will remain so far under the control of the proper officers of government, that the Otoes will not be allowed improvidently to waste it.

Two farmers are to reside in their country to assist them five years, and longer by the direction of the President of the United States. These two farmers could fence and plow 50 acres of land each year, and thus furnish them with 250 acres of land ready for seed, and enclosed in fields of convenient dimensions.

The treaty of July 1830, secures to sundry tribes mentioned therein $3000 annually for the term of ten years, for the education of their children. Of this sum the Otoes are entitled to $500 yearly.

In the treaty of 1833, an additional annuity of $500 is provided for education for the term of five years, or longer. The schools must be on the lands of the Otoes. While these education annuities continue they would support in a boarding school 20 Indian youths, or they would furnish instruction to 80 who were fed and clothed by their parents.

OMAHAS.

The treaty of July, 1830, provides that an annuity of $500 shall be paid to the Omahas, in agricultural implements, for, ten successive years, and longer, if the President of the United States shall think it proper.

Also, a Blacksmith and the necessary tools shall be furnished them the same length of time.

The sum of $500 for the term of ten years, is to be applied to the education of their children. This sum would keep in a boarding school, in the Omaha country, ten children, during the continuance of the allowance, or 40 youths, the same length of time, should they be supported by their parents.

PAWNEES.

The treaty of October, 1833, stipulates that the United States shall pay to the Pawnees annually for five years $2000 worth of agricultural implements, and this annuity is to be continued longer than five years, if the President deem it expedient.

Also, the value of $1000 in oxen, and other live stock is to be delivered to the tribe whenever the President of the U. S. shall believe that they are prepared to profit by them. This stock, after being taken into the tribe, is to be placed in charge of the proper authorities of the United States, to prevent the Indians from prematurely destroying it, thro' improvidence. This is an excellent arrangement. The live stock which was paid to the Osages and the Kauzaus was a disadvantage to them instead of a benefit. Their cultivated grounds were not enclosed with fences, and consequently they could not keep cattle and swine. In addition to this, their habitual improvidence was such that they had not patience to wait for future advantages from stock. The stock was immediately consumed for food, and only served to indulge them awhile in indolence.

Further, a sum not exceeding $2000 per annum for ten years, is to be expended in support of two smitheries, with two Blacksmiths in each, together with iron, steel, &c.

Four grist mills are to be erected for them, to operate by horse power.

Four farmers are to be provided for them, for the term of five years. The country of the Pawnees being more remote from white settlements than those of the Osages, and others, the cost of enclosing and plowing land would be increased. But if government should thus employ their farmers, 100 acres each year could conveniently be prepared for seed. This would give them five hundred acres of cultivated land enclosed with fences.

The sum of $1000 a year for ten years, is to be allowed for the establishment of schools. This sum will support in school 20 children during the ten years, or if they should be supported by their parents, 80 children could be kept in school the same length of time.

CHEROKEES.

It is stipulated in the treaty of the 6th May, 1828, that "the U. S. will pay $2000 annually to the Cherokees for ten years, to be expended under the direction of the President of the

U. S. in the education of their children *in their own country;* in letters and the mechanic arts. Also, $1,000 towards the purchase of a printing press and types."

CREEKS.

The treaty with the Creeks of March 24, 1832, stipulates that "$3000, to be expended as the President may direct, shall be allowed for the term of 20 years for teaching their children." This sum will support 60 scholars in a boarding school, or, give education in a common school to 240 scholars 20 years.

At a subsequent treaty held in Arkansas in 1833, another important provision was made for the education of Creek children.

CHOCTAWS.

The Treaty of Sept. 1830, provides for keeping 40 Choctaw youths, at school, under the direction of the President of the U. S. 20 years. Also, the sum of $2,500 is to be applied to the support of three teachers of schools, for the Choctaws 20 years.

There is also an unexpended balance of former annuities, amounting to about $25,000 which is to be applied to the support of schools at 12 different places, at each of which, a school house has been erected by the U. S. and paid for out of this fund.

MILITARY POSTS,

Within the Indian Territory.

FORT TOWSON.

In about N. Lat. 34 deg. and West Long. from Washington, 19 deg. It is within the Choctaw country, six miles north of Red river, and six miles west of the Kiamishi river, about 50 miles west of the eastern boundary of the Choctaws, 238 miles from Little Rock, Arkansas Territory, 280 miles from Natchitoches, La. and 120 miles from Fort Smith on the Arkansas river.

The erection of the Fort, at present occupied, was begun in the autumn of 1831. The situation is pleasant, the water is good, and the place is esteemed healthy. Four Companies of the 3d Infantry, compose the garrison.

OFFICERS.—Lieut. Col. J. H. Vose, *Commanding.*
Ass't Surgeons, Lucius O'Brien, M. C. Leavenworth,
Captains.—J. B. Clark, J. Dean, L. N. Morris, J. Garland,
1st Lieut's.—H. Bainbridge, E. B. Alexander, E. B. Babbitt, Com. Qr. Mr. W. Colcock.
2d Lieuts.—A. G. Baldwin, J. H. Taylor, S. B. Legate, W. O. Kello, Carey H. Fry, *Bvt.* J. O. Barnwell, *Bvt.* P. N. Barbour, George C. Gooding, Esq. *Suttler,* and *P. M.*

FORT GIBSON.

Fort Gibson is on the east bank of Neosho river, two miles north of Arkansas river, and two and a half miles below the junction of Arkansas and Verdigris rivers. It is within the country of the Cherokees, and about 43 miles west of their eastern boundary, about 55 miles on a direct course from Fort Smith, and about 140 miles north of Fort Towson.

It was established in 1823, by removal from Fort Smith.

Fort Gibson, or the mouth of Verdigris river may be considered the head of Steam Boat navigation.

The Garrison consists of nine companies of the 7th Infantry.

OFFICERS.—Bvt. Brig Gen. M. Arbuckle, Commanding the Posts on the south-western frontiers.
Lieut. Col. Wm. Whistler, commanding 7th Inftry.
Bvt. Lieut. Col. Burbank.
Bvt. Maj. George Birch. Act'g Maj.
Capt. Charles Thomas, Asst. Qr. Mas.
1st Lieut. D. S. Miles, Adj.
1st. Lieut. W. Seawell, Aid de Camp to Gen. Arbuckle.
2d Lieut. L. F. Carter, Asst. Com. Sub.
Saml. G. I. De Camp, M. D. Surgeon.
Asst. Surgeons, Henry Holt, Joseph H. Baily,
Bvt. Maj. Nath. Young.
Capt. E. S. Hawkins.
Capt. J. L. Dawson.
Capt. Francis Lee.
Capt. J. R. Stevenson.
Capt. J. A. Phillips.
Capt. N. Tellinghast.
1st Lieuts. G. I. Rains, S. W. Moore, V. V. Mather, J H. Holmes, S. Kinney, R. W. Ross, 2d. Lieuts. G. W. Cass, A. P. Whiting, R. S. Dix, R. C. Gatlin, A. F. Seaton, G. R. Paul, H. M. Havott, J. G. Read, A. Harris, F. Bretton. Bvt. A. Montgomery, Bvt.

Three companies of Dragoons are stationed at Fort Gibson.
Suttlers.—E. W. B. Nowland, Thos. E. Wilson.
OFFICERS.—Maj. R. B. Mason, Commanding.
Lemuel C. M. M'Phail, Asst. Surgeon.
Captains.—E. Trenon, D. Perkins, P. H. St. Cook.
1st. Lieuts.—James F. Izard, C. F. M. Noland, Jas. Allen.
2d Lieuts.—Wm. Eustis, L. B. Northrup, G. P. Kingsbury. J. M. Bowman.
Suttler.—Col. March.

FORT LEAVENWORTH.

Fort Leavenworth is on the S. W. Bank of Missouri river, 25 miles above the mouth of Kauzau river, and about 20 miles west of the state of Missouri. It was established in 1827.

The Post is at present, head quarters of the U. States Dragoons.

OFFICERS.

Col. H. Dodge, Commanding, Capt. David Hunter, Capt. Lemuel Ford, Capt. Matthew Duncan, Lieut. Lancaster P. Lupton, Lieut. Thos. Swords, Act'r Qr. Master, Lt. John Vandeveer, Lieut. E. Steen, Lieut. A. Territt, Act'g Com. Sub. Lieut. B. D. Moore, Lieut. G. B. Kingsbury, Lieut. A. Ury, Lieut. M'Comb.

Asst. Surgeons, Dr. B. F. Fellows, and Dr. Moore.
Post Office, Fort Leavenworth, West. Ter.

TRADING POSTS.

Among the Cherokees, Joel M. Bryan has a trading post.
Among the Creeks, A. P. Choteau and Seaborn Hill, have each a trading establishment.

The American Fur Company have a trading house near the Osage Agency, one among the Weas and their neighbors, one among the Shawanoes and their neighbors, one among the Kickapoos and Putawatomies, one among the the Kauzaus, and one on Missouri, above the mouth of the Platte river, in the vincinity of the Otoes, Omahas, Pawnees and others.

AFFINITY OF LANGUAGES.

Chickasaw and Choctaw are dialects of one language.
Putawatomies, Ottawas and Chippewas speak the same language.
The language spoken by the Osages, Quapaws and Kau-

zaus is the same. That of the Otoes and Ioways is the same, and between these and the Osage, Quapaw, Kauzau, Omaha and Winnebago languages, there is a near affinity.

Weas, Piankeshas, Peorias, Kaskaskias, and Miamies, severally, speak dialects of the same language.

Pawnees and Puncahs speak the same language.

WAR.

All the tribes in the territory, except the Pawnees, Otoes, Omahas and Puncahs, are liable to insult and injury from remote tribes, especially those towards the south west, and even the Pawnees and their allies have their enemies in the *far west*.

A portion of the Pawnees reside in the south, upon Red river. Until lately, warriors from the Pawnees of the south, and of the north, united with the Camanches of the remoter south west, and formed war parties, which annoyed traders to Santa Fee, and were particularly inimical to the Osages and Kauzaus, as well as troublesome to many hunting parties of the emigrant tribes.

In 1833 treaties of peace were concluded between the northern Pawnees and all the other tribes within the territory, and *all smoked the pipe of peace.*

In 1834, negociations of peace and friendship were held with the southern Pawnees. Thus far, all parties have been faithful to the pledges of friendship which have been mutually exchanged. Delawares, who, in 1833, retaliated with some severity upon the Pawnees, in 1834 and 1835, passed through their country, called at the encampments of Pawnees, and were received with warm expressions of friendship.

The last summer, Col. Dodge, with three companies, commanded by Captains L. Ford, and M. Duncan, and Lieut. L. P. Lupton, made an expedition of about 1600 miles. From Fort Leavenworth they ascended the Missouri, some distance above the Platte river; thence proceeded up the Platte river to the Rocky mountains; and along the mountains southward to Arkansas river, and down the Arkansas to the Santa Fee road, by which they returned to the post.

Upon this expedition, they fell in with warriors and others of the Otoes, the Omahas, the four bands of Pawnees, the Arickarees, the Arapahoes, the Chyennes, the Grosvontres of the prairies, the Blackfeet, and the Sioux.

No hostility was encountered on the expedition; but many councils were held with the different bands, which, it is hoped, will produce favorable results.

A brief expedition southward, was also made the past summer, by Capt. D. Hunter.

Also, Maj. Mason, of Fort Gibson, with part of his command, performed considerable service in the prairies west of that post. In the discharge of which duties some of the Infantry belonging to the post, were also engaged, all under command of Gen. Arbuckle.

Gen. Arbuckle, Gov. Stokes, and Col. F. W. Armstrong, were Commissioners on the part of the United States, to hold councils with the Pawnees of Red river, and others. They were escorted to the treaty grounds by the troops above mentioned. The first expedition to these Indians was made in 1834. The propriety of thus holding friendly negociations with those western roving tribes, who had little knowledge of our government, has already been developed in many well attested matters of fact.

GOVERNMENT.

Most of the tribes within the territory have expressed a desire to become united in one civil compact, and to be governed by laws similar to those of the United States.

Should the U. States provide for them a form of civil government, suited to their circumstances, a few among each of the emigrant tribes, and many among some of those tribes, would be found capable of filling responsible offices in the transaction of the affairs of their government.

The time has fully come for the adoption of this course. Objections to it, founded upon the uncultivated condition of the minds of the Indians, if they ever had any weight, have none now. Multitudes of Indians well understand the value of property, duly appreciate the individuality of right in property, and desire its security by equitable laws. Many of them desire to have a sufficient portion of land for a farm set off to them severally. They deprecate the agency system and its concomitant principles so far as they exist among them. They are ready to become a component part of the Commonwealth of the U. S. They desire no special privilege to be granted to them, nor special restriction to be imposed upon them, further than what would be necessary to their welfare, until the effects of the peculiar disabilities under which they have hitherto been placed, shall have so far disappeared both among themselves and us, as to allow them safely to take an equal place among existing states of the Union.

Objections to embodying them on our west through fear

that they may become formidable foes, are discovered to be unreasonable, because the Indians never did from choice fight us, and never will while their women and children are within our reach. In former wars they could carry their charge a little further into the depths of the forest, while the warriors returned to their work of mischief on our frontiers. Here it cannot so happen. An uninhabitable, open, and almost woodless plain, of at least four hundred miles extent, lies immediately beyond them. A prairie on which no Indian village ever did exist, and in which they could not remain.

The whole history of Indian warfare against the U. States, unequivocally testifies to the fact, that while we can keep them within sight and hearing of us, we can keep them at peace with us.

At the commencement of the last war a large delegation representing the whole of the Sauks, Foxes, and Ioways, came to St. Louis, and offered their services in the war in favour of the U. States.

Gen. Clark, the superintendent of Indian affairs, happened to be absent. The officer in charge of affairs did not feel himself authorised to negotiate with them upon this subject. They immediately set out to offer themselves to the British. On the return of the superintendent, he sent after them, but was able to overtake only a part of them. These stopped and consented to remain neutral. The main body of them, among whom was the since celebrated Black Hawk, joined the British in the war against us.

We can readily perceive how easily, by a proper management, those savages could have been prevented from imbruing their hands in the blood of our citizens. The same remarks will equally well apply to Putawatomies, Ottowas and others, so far as it was possible to keep them near to us. This I know to be true from a long personal acquaintance with them, and from frequent conversations with them upon these subjects.

Were it possible for a deterioration to take place among the Indians within the territory, in both mind, and manners, so far that they should abandon the hopes and prospects which at this time inspire pleasant anticipations unknown before to that wretched race, arising from their expected connexion with us; and should they, reckless of the foreseen conquence of certain destruction, become hostile to the U. S. still not a tomahawk would be lifted against us until they had abandoned the Territory, and fled to the wilderness of the north, towards the British settlements. There are many reasons, for

E

supposing that they would not go southward into the Mexican government, and if they should go west they could not stop until they had gone too far to be feared.

But, were it possible for us to conjecture that they might remain in the Territory after they had commenced hostilities, what should we have to fear from them? The whole number of Indians which we can hope to get into *this* Territory, *now* under consideration, would not exceed a fifth part of the present inhabitants of the state of Ohio. Now if one fifth part of the State of Ohio were to take up arms against the remainder of the United States, and remain where the latter could pour in their armies like an overwhelming flood, the result of such an unequal contest would do little injury to the stronger party.

But our subject is a plain common sense matter which can hardly require the aid of such reasoning as the foregoing. It is always expected that men will act in accordance with their supposed interests. It could not possibly be supposed a small portion of one of our states would be induced to sacrifice its interests so far as to dissolve its connexion with, and to commence an exterminating warfare upon all other parts of our country. The ties of interest that would bind the Indian Territory to the United States would be equally as strong as those which we have alluded to, and the infatuation which could induce disregard to them would be equally wild.

The objections to giving the Indians a territorial form of civil government which have been made upon constitutional principles are equally groundless. This is not the place to discuss constitutional questions. Yet, we may be allowed again, to appeal to common sense. The whole country inhabited by the Indians is, or has been, ours. It has or can become theirs only as we have made, or may make it so. We control both their persons and their property. In regard to the latter, we decide what they may sell, and what they may not, and who shall be the purchasers. These things being true, we can constitutionally direct their location, and direct their political affairs when they are located. We have always done so. We *are doing so now*, and, therefore, the matter cannot involve constitutional scruples. From its very nature it can only be a question of expediency and humanity.

We have always enacted laws for the regulation of Indian affairs, and have repealed them at pleasure. We have created agencies among them to attend to the execution of our laws and we have abolished them when we deemed it expedient to do so. If we should now believe that both their interest and ours require the entire abolition of the agency system, and the introduction of a mode of regulating their affairs similar to the mode of management of one of our Territories, the adoption of this better mode could not possibly be opposed by any constitutional obstacle. We might propose something objectionable in the *form*, because of its inexpediency, but the principle upon which we should act would be that upon which we had ever acted.

If we imagine that there ought to be conceded to the Indians some right on their part, to choose for themselves, and that it would be wrong in us to give them a form of civil government, and to take them under the wing of ours without their consent, then we are prepared to meet the question, by appealing to the good sense of the Indians. We say the time has come to *act* upon this matter. They are prepared to live under the laws of civilized nations. Twenty-two thousand, five hundred of the present inhabitants of the territory *have adopted written laws*, which in general, are based on republican principles, and are similar to those of their white neighbors. The Shawanoes have it in contemplation, shortly to do the same. They who are most civilized necessarily take the lead in these things, and their good sense and talents will be rewarded with an ascendancy among their less informed countrymen. The latter rejoice that some of their own brethren have become capable of managing their affairs, and expect to profit by their superior endowmenst.

INDIANS NOT WITHIN THE INDIAN TERRITORY.*

Tribes East of Mississippi.

Indians in N. England and New-York,	4715
Indians from New-York at Green Bay,	725
Wyandots in Ohio and Michigan,	623
Miamies,	1,200
Winnebagoes,	4,591
Chippewas,	6,793
Ottawas and Chippewas of Lake Michigan,	5,300
Chippeways, Ottawas and Putawatomics,	8,000
Putawatomies,	1,400
Menominees,	4,200
Creeks,	22,668
Cherokees,	10,000
Chickasaws,	5,429
Choctaws,	3,500
Seminoles,	2,420
Appalachicolas,	340

Tribes west of Mississippi river.

Sioux,	27,500	Black feet,	30,000
Iowas,	1,200	Camanches,	7,000
Sauks of Missouri,	500	Crows,	4,500
Sauks and Foxes,	6,400	Arrepahas, Kia-	
Assinaboines,	8,000	was, &c.	1,400
Crees,	3,000	Caddoes,	800
Gros ventres,	3,000	Snake and other	
Arrekaras,	3,000	tribes within	
Cheyennes,	2000	the Rocky Mts.	20,000
Minatarees,	1,500	Tribes west of the	
Mandans,	1,500	R. Mountains,	80,000

Throughout all the vast uncultivated regions north and south of the western territories of the United States, are Indians. The population becomes more sparse as we proceed northward, to a climate less accommodated to the comforts of uncivilized man, and becomes more dense, as we proceed southward to a more genial clime where subsistence is more easily obtained.

---

*This table refers to the territory belonging to the U. S. only. It is conjectural in regard to the remote tribes, and is probably very erroneous.

PLEA FOR THE ABORIGINES OF NORTH AMERICA.

Indifference to Indian improvement connected with the paucity of of their population.

We feel confident that there is a general indifference to the welfare of the aboriginal inhabitants of this continent, which is at variance with the rule of doing to others as we would that others should do unto us. It has never been otherwise, either in Europe or America, and whether it will be otherwise in future is not altogether certain. We write with a view of exhibiting, so far as our limits will allow, the true condition of these people, of promoting better feelings towards them than have heretofore existed, and of suggesting some easy methods of promoting their lasting prosperity.

One cause, it is presumed, of general indifference to the improvement of the Indians, is the paucity of Indian population. This matter seems to claim our first attention, inasmuch as the paralyzing effect which it has upon the mind will be likely to insinuate itself into all our reasoning. Whatever plea be urged in favour of the Indians, we are liable to be haunted with the reflection that their number is so small, that the subject of their reform can hardly be a matter of great importance.

We regret, that we are not able to obviate intirely this difficulty which hangs upon our subject, and to say that they are exceedingly numerous, yet we believe that, while the fewness of those for whom we plead may occasion some discouragement, it will, in view of the history of the past, prefer irresistable claims upon our justice and humanity. We shall be led to enquire under what circumstances they have been reduced from many millions to a *handful*, and the answer to this enquiry cannot fail to make a deep impression upon the feeling heart. We shall be compelled to date the origin of their diminution to the settlement of Europeans in their country, and the awful rapidity with which it has been carried on, will be found justly attributable to the devastating nature of the intercourse which the former have established with them.

But we seem to have labored under mistaken impressions in this matter. If our views may be inferred from what we have said and done for the improvement of the aborigines, their number is *not* so small as we have generally supposed. In the fact of underrating their number, we shall perceive a striking proof of indifference to their welfare. They for whose happiness

E 2

we feel solicitude have a place in our thoughts. Their numbers, their locations, and their circumstances are contemplated. It is not so with the Indians. They are scarcely remembered except as associated with some romantic flight of imagination.

Upon this subject we should naturally expect to find the most liberal views among those who had formed themselves into benevolent associations for the improvement of the condition of the natives. Some of these associations have existed many years, and yet their operations have been circumscribed to a few small tribes, amounting in the whole to a few thousands only, leaving the great mass of them almost unnoticed in regard to number, place and condition.

It is about two hundred years since evangelical efforts were commenced for the improvement of the condition of the Indians, and so feeble have these efforts been that from the best calculations which we have been able to make, not more than thirty three thousand are at this time, positively within their influence.

In this matter the apathy of the state resembles that of the church, the former has somewhat the advantage in a comparrison. Only about one third of the whole number within the territory of the United States have received attention.

Government may with propriety confine its Indian regulations to its own limits, but benevolent societies should not circumscribe their labours within the same sphere, much less should they sleep over the feeble efforts which they have put forth, and which extend to scarcely a tenth part of of those within the territory of the U. S. leaving unnoticed all others.

We are upon the borders of a vast wilderness, in comparrison to which, the settled portion of North America is small. Over the whole of this vast uncultivated region Indians are dispersed. We speak of this wilderness in the singular number, because it is but *one* vast uncultivated tract. The veracity of this statement is not impaired by imaginary lines which various civilized nations have drawn through it, merely for their own convenience in regard to their political intercourse.

When a mission is undertaken to the Sandwich Islands, we are reminded, and properly too, of the multitudes which inhabit them. When a mission to Burmah is undertaken, we are for our encouragement told of the millions within the empire. But missions to the inhabitants of this vast wilderness, on the borders of which we eat and sleep, have not been thus encouraged. Who ever heard of a missionary association originating a mission to the Indians as a people? No, the society undertakes a mission to the Osages, the Shawanoes, the Chippewas, or some other small portion of Indians. Its instructions to its missionary correspond with these small beginnings, and, too commonly, similar views and feelings are carried with him to the nut-shell sphere of his labours. By common consent it appears to have been made a small business. Nor is it the least exceptionable feature in this affair, that it is too generally supposed that moderate talents are sufficient for these moderate operations. Hereafter we shall do missionaries the justice to review this point. It is sufficient for our present purpose, to say that, whatever may be the talents or the devotion of the missionary to the Indians, he commonly fills a place in the estimation of others corresponding with the much or little importance which they attach to the field, and nature of his labors.

If it be said that benevolent associations, after furnishing this and that tribe with the means of improvement, design to extend their labors to others more remote; we answer by enquiring, why not pursue a similar course in relation to other heathen? In regard to other countries the society did not confine their imaginations to the sending of missionaries to a particular city or district, and impress the minds of their missionaries with views equally contracted, and then appeal to a benevolent public for aid in strains as feeble as the design which originated them was small. They resolved on a mission to the *country* embracing *all* its inhabitants. Their philanthropy was not affected by the jurisdiction of other nations, nor by that of the natives, the design was to be instrumental in converting *all* those heathen to Christianity. This design, than which none more noble ever actuated the mind of man towards his fellow man, was presented in bold relief to a Christian community, and, thank heaven, not unsuccessfully. In the choice of their missionary, corresponding views in him were essential to his being employed. The motto which hung over every proceeding was, "expect great things.—attempt great things."

Now turn and look towards missions to the aborigines of America. Alas! we sicken at the sight! If they deserve a motto at all, it might well be written over the small matters connected with them. Expect *little things*.—Attempt *little things*.

The blame which we design to imply in these remarks is not located upon any one denomination of Christians which has missions among the Indians. All are blameable. The nature of this plea for the aborigines will require us to notice this point hereafter, and we now advertise our reader that we do not hope to find among the different denominations of Christians one honorable exception.

WHOLE NUMBER OF INDIANS.

We have taken some pains to estimate the probable number of the aborigines within the North American wilderness. As our calculations cover extensive portions of country, unexplored by civilized man, and other vast portions little known even in the business of trapping, or of Indian trading, and much less as it respects the number of the native inhabitants, we can scarcely hope for even an approximation to precision.

In making our calculations we have pursued various methods, one of which has been, to take a given district within a medium latitude of the whole territory under consideration, of the number of Indians within which we had some knowledge, and where we supposed that the population over this given district, might compare with the average population of Indians generally, and, then suppose that as the extent of this district is to the whole Indian country, so is the population of this district to the whole number of Indians.

One of the districts assumed as data, we commence at the Sault de St. Marie, and imagine a line north of west through lake Superior, and another extending west of South by way of Green Bay, so that the extent assumed in the direction of the former line would equal about ten degrees of longitude, and the width of the district would be equal to three and a half degrees of latitude. Within this district we suppose there are 15,000 Indians; this compared with the whole extent of wilderness under consideration, gives 1,725,000. To which if we add Indians within the limits of, but not surrounded by, white inhabitants of the Mexican dominions, and others upon our extensive frontier northward, we may place the entire amount of Indians in North America at 1,800,000. This we believe will be esteemed a fair estimate by any one who will have patience to examine the subject.

Possibly our estimate is too low. The Indians live chiefly upon the spontaneous productions of nature. Consequently, in some countries, the means of subsistence can be more easily obtained than in others, and in those places population is expected to be proportionally dense. Hence in warmer climates the natives are more numerous than in colder, this, as a general rule is correct. Nevertheless it has led to some error, inasmuch as we have sometimes supposed the difference to be greater than what it really is. A. M'Kinzie, when travelling to the North-West between lat. 60 and 71 deg. noticed beaten paths, and other signs of human residence indicating an immense population.

For evidence that the population was great, let one who has passed along any river in the western country between the latitudes of 30 and 40 deg. N. and on which the Indian population is known to be as dense as in any other place in the interior of the country, compare the beaten paths which he has there seen with those described by M'Kinzie.

We should also bear in mind that these roads to the far north west, were made by human feet alone, horses or other animals not being used for servile purposes in those regions. The north is not so much less bountiful to the Indians than the south as we have generally supposed.

Our government has nothing to do with Indians who are beyond our Territorial limits. But as *Christians* our duties are not in like manner circumscribed. We should, therefore, be reminded, that within the settlements of Mexico, and immediately adjoining the vast wilderness under consideration, is a considerable Indian population, whose condition though somewhat improved in regard to food and raiment, is in other respects equally deplorable with those in the wilderness.

The best estimates at hand, make the entire population of Mexico, in 1808, 6,500,000, two fifths of which, or 2,600,000, are Indians, exclusive of those termed Mestizoes, descendants of whites and Indians, and Zambos, descendants of Negroes and Indians.

Adding Indians of the wilderness,	1,800,000
To those within the settlements of Mexico,	2,600,000
Gives us	4,400,000

which claim our kindness. Even four millions, four hundred thousand is a small number when compared with the millions of heathen in Asia, still we think that the number is such as to entitle the subject of Indian reform to much greater attention than it has heretofore received. Further, we believe that reflection upon this subject must result in conviction that they have claims upon us superior to any other people upon earth, however numerous they may be. We do not reason fairly when we suppose that the claims of one million are impaired because their number does not amount to five millions, or because ten millions elsewhere have claims upon us.

In contemplating labor for the improvement of the condition of heathen merely as an act of man towards his fellow man, it is predicated upon either justice or humanity, or rather upon both, for the obligation, which humanity imposes upon us, renders it morally unjust to withold from a needy fellow being, the assistance which we have it in our power to afford him. In addition to the claims of justice and humanity in common which all heathen have upon us, the natives of our forests have legal claims to an amount greater than we can ever liquidate. We are confident that this will appear in the sequel.

RELATIVE PROPORTION OF IMPROVED INDIANS.

We have above shown one million, eight hundred thousand, Indians in the wilderness adjoining us, which number for convenience, we may suppose to include the few remaining within the states. Of this number we suppose that ten thousand may be so far improved as to be classed, with some propriety, with civilized man, among these the portion that is pious considerably exceeds the average proportion of pious persons among the same number of citizens of the United States.

In addition to the above, there may be about 60,000, which have made advances toward civilization, some of them greater, and others less.

The whole number of those who have made some advances towards civilization, is to the number that have made none, as about two to forty-nine and a half. The whole number of the civilized is to the uncivilized as two, to three hundred and fifty eight, the whole number of those who are positively within the influence of missionary labours is, to the number of those who are not, as two to one hundred and nine.

CONDITION OF THE INDIANS.

Among such as have made no advances towards civilization there are shades of difference in regard to comfort. The more comfortable have obtained of the whites, some guns, axes, knives, blankets, and cotton and woollen cloths, &c. They use horses in hunting, and for carrying burthens, but never apply them to draft. Every man in addition to his gun, if he possess one, has his bow and arrows.

They have neither sheep, cattle nor swine, they do not manufacture any kind of cloth. In genial climates they cultivate from the fourth of an acre, to one acre of land to a family. They cultivate Indian corn, and some culinary vegetables, such as pumpkins, potatoes, &c. The field is cultivated alone with the hoe. Small spots of land the most easily prepared for seed are selected by them, and if enclosed at all, it is by brush or poles, either of which opposes a feeble resistance to an intrusive horse. A centinel usually guards the field from the time of planting in the spring, until the harvest in autumn. Many fields are without enclosure.

HOUSES.

Their houses are constructed of sticks about large enough for a summer house in a garden, on which is fastened either the bark of trees or rushes, or the skins of wild animals; without floors, the fire is placed on the earth in the centre.

DIVISION OF LABOR.

It is considered the business of the females to prepare the field, to cultivate it, and to harvest the crop, to erect the houses, procure fuel, prepare the food, take care of the horses, make the skins of animals into leather, and to make clothes of it. In removing from place to place, they are generally compelled to transport heavy burdens upon their backs. The budget is sustained by a strap of leather passing across the forehead.

The men do little else than hunt the wild animals, make bows and arrows, smoke the pipe, eat and sleep.

ROVING HABITS.

They remain in their villages from the time of planting corn in May and June, until September or October, when they leave their villages and spend the time in encampments in such places as are most favorable for procuring food for themselves and their horses.

Some of those in the prairies, when travelling, transport their tent poles by tying one end to a horse and allowing the other to drag on the ground.

DRESS.

The fashion of dress is much the same among all tribes, and usually appears to be the most convenient for them under their peculiar circumstances.

The males dress in leather mockasins for the feet, and leather leggings, a strip of cloth about the loins, and either a leather or cotton shirt.

The mockasins for the females are similar to those of the males, their leggings are shorter, and more frequently made of cloth, the cloth fastened around the waist with a belt, extends a little below the knee, a cotton shirt hangs loosely, a little below the belt, a blanket wrapped around the body serves for the outer garment by day, and for the bed at night.

Among tribes which are poorer, neither sex wears a garment to cover the body above the waist, excepting the blanket, or a Buffaloe's skin wrapped around as above, which is not used in warm weather. The young women usually wear a strip of cotton cloth about eight inches broad, passing obliquely across the breast, over one shoulder, and under the other arm. While they are at their villages in summer, all clothing except that about the waist, is frequently dispensed with.

TRIBES MORE WRETCHED.

Many of the tribes are more wretched than those of whom we have yet spoken. They generally reside near the Rocky Mountains, and between the mountains and the Pacific ocean, also east of the mountains upon the waters of M'Kinzies river, and those emptying into Hudson's Bay. In general their wretchedness increases as we go back from the sea.

In warm climates near California thousands of both sexes and of all ages are destitute of covering for any part of the body, among them a few may be observed, who, through a sense of decency, fasten a kind of fringe of grass, around the waist. Northward, and where the cold obliges them to wear clothes, many are as insensible to shame in the exposure to common observation, of every other part of the body as they are in regard to those of their hands and face. Hence may be inferred the extreme degradation of the minds of those people, and the shocking wretchedness of their condition in every respect. How deplorable the state of those people must be both physically and mentally, and as it regards both body and soul—time and eternity !!!

All, even the most grovelling and wretched manifest a fondess for ornament in dress. Trinkets are attached to the clothing, to the hair of the head, the nose, ears, neck, arms, hands and ancles, and paints are rubbed on the face and other parts of the body.

61

UNEXPLORED COUNTRY.

From the Columbia river, in about lat. 46 deg. southward about twelve degrees, and between the mountains and the Pacific, is much unexplored country. Also, from the sea-coast extending northwestward as far as Bhering's straights towards the interior, and Northward to Baffin's Bay, are vast portions of unexplored country. At particular points only has the traveller touched, and thence brought us intelligence of the condition of the inhabitants.

HORSES.

From the sources of Columbia, Missouri, Mississippi, and St. Lawrence rivers southward, all tribes own more or fewer horses. They were originally brought from the Spanish settlements in Mexico. Before we had become acquainted with those remote northwestern tribes, traffic in horses was carried on between them and the more southern tribes, which traffic is, to some extent continued. Farther north horses are not used.

AXES, AND OTHER MECHANIC TOOLS.

Most of the tribes have obtained of the whites a few useful implements of iron, such as knives, axes, &c. They who are too poor to own an iron axe, use an axe of stone, similar to many which have been found in the western states. It is a hard brown stone, worked somewhat into the shape of an axe, with a groove around the place where the eye should be, sunk deep enough to admit of fastening thereon a handle by means of strings. The upper end is somewhat flattened like the pole of an axe, and the other widened one way, and brought as nearly to an edge as practicable.

These axes may be employed in splitting wood, but not in cutting it. They are also of use as a mallet in fastening stakes in the earth in the construction of their dwellings, and in preparing snares in which to catch wild animals.

We found one of those stone axes on the St. Joseph river of Lake Michigan, which weighed about fifty pounds. It was of the common granite of that country. It was not shaped with skill equal to that employed upon smaller ones. The groove around the head, for the purpose of fastening the handle, was large in proportion to the size of the axe.

For what purpose it had been formed, is not easy to conjecture. It was not for use as an axe, because it was too large. Possibly they who manufactured this great axe were idolaters, who worshipped a huge image, whose bulk corresponded to the size of the axe, and into whose hands the axe was placed.

A piece of horn, or bone, sharpened at one end, is also used for the purpose of cleaving timber. With this horn chissel in one hand, and a mallet in the other, a native, in the preparation of his canoe, for which he selects a soft kind of wood, will make chips faster than could be imagined by one accustomed only to the use of iron, in such cases. The front teeth of the beaver, with which that animal cuts down trees more than 12 inches in diameter, are sometimes used as a chissel by the natives.

In the absence of an iron knife, copper has been so shaped as to supply its place. This was sometimes procured from the whites, and sometimes found by themselves in a pure state. With the poorer, a flint supplies the place of a knife. The flint is also used as a lancet in letting blood, scarrifying, &c.

Before their acquaintance with Europeans, southern tribes frequently used as a knife, a splinter of the reed, or cane, common to their country.

ARMS.

Their arrows are usually feathered at one end, and barbed at the other, with either iron, copper, flint, horn, or bone. A sharpened bone, fastened to a pole, forms a spear. A pointed horn, or bone, about a foot in length, a cudgel of wood, suitably shaped at the extremity, and a beam of an elk's horn, are also used for the purpose of dispatching an enemy, or an animal that has been caught in a snare.

MEANS OF OBTAINING SUBSISTENCE.

Few of the poorer tribes cultivate the soil. For subsistence they depend upon the spontaneous productions of nature. Fish, fowl, and quadrupeds, furnish the chief source of supplies.

One method of taking fish is, with hook and line, according to the practice with which we are familiar. The line is made of the inside soft bark of a tree. To this is tied a piece of horn or bone, suitably shaped, or else, two pieces so fastened together as to form a hook. In some places to the north west, nature has been so bountiful as to furnish a small hooked thorn, exceedingly sharp and hard, strong enough to catch a fish weighing half a pound.

Another, and more successful method of taking fish, is by a scoop net, formed, also, of the soft bark of trees, and let into the water in a manner similar to our own custom.

But the most successful method is by setting a net in the water. To places in rivers most favorable for fishing, the natives resort during the proper season, in order to procure a store for supplies during the season unfavorable for fishing; or, to prepare some for barter among neighboring tribes, whose fisheries are less productive.

Fish is dried by exposure to the sun, without salt, and is stored in houses prepared for the purpose.

In taking fowls, or quadrupeds, the bow and arrow are used when it can be done successfully. But fowls are caught with the greatest facility at the season when swans, geese, &c. having recently dropped their feathers, are either scarcely capable of flying at all, or, are often found exhausted by flying, especially in rainy weather, and so become a prey to the fleet Indian.

On the shores of lakes and rivers are particular places to which water fowls annually resort to build their nests, and to foster their young. To these the natives repair at the proper season to catch them as above described, and to catch the young ones before they are capable of flying.

On account of inattention, and a want of salt, a stock of fowl, flesh, or fish, recently taken, frequently becomes little better than a heap of carrion.

Elk, and deer, are sometimes taken in a snare, or noose, made of a small strong cord. Wild animals frequent particular places for the purpose of obtaining food or drink, and through dense foliage form paths. Along these, nooses are set in places favorable for entangling them.

Sometimes a pound is constructed of brush, poles, vines, and bark, sufficiently strong to defy the strength even of the buffaloe. The opening, in front, is wide, whence it gradually narrows to a point, or so nearly to a point as to present but one narrow way, which, unperceived, leads into an inextricable enclosure.

The buffaloe, deer, or elk, happening in the neighborhood, are induced to go towards the snare by the disclosure of a person in the opposite direction. The obstructions which had been formed for the purpose, confining the unsuspecting animals to the direction designed by their destroyers, they are unwarily taken by their pursuers.

Sometimes they are constructed on a hill which these animals have ascended and descended so frequently as to form a road. The natives, taking advantage of some turn on the hill side, fill up the beaten track so as to turn the animals towards a precipice. A company of animals are seen upon the high lands in the vicinity; the Indians are in readiness; the animals follow their usual beaten track, and perceive no obstruction until they have descended the first steep. At this moment the Indians close in upon their rear. The affrighted animals, in endeavoring to escape their pursuers, and, unable to go forward, turn into the way previously prepared for them. The pressure of the frighted animals in the rear, prevents those in front from returning, and crowds them down the precipice, so that they are either killed or crippled in falling.

Small animals, like the rackoon, are frequently caught in a trap, which, in the western states, is called a *dead-fall.*—This consists of a log of wood, or a rock, placed over another log of wood, or a path, or any place where the animal is most likely to pass, one end of which rests upon a trigger, which so intercepts the way that it is inevitably sprung by the animal in its passage, at which instant the log or rock falls on the victim and secures it.

Some small animals which burrough in the earth may be taken by inserting a spear into the den.

BOATS.

In the more northern parts, canoes are constructed of the bark of the Birch tree. They are larger or less, as circumstances require. They are very light, so that one, large enough to transport two or three persons, may be carried upon a man's shoulder. Upon lakes, and other large waters, some are large enough to carry many persons.

More southwardly, their canoes are made of a single tree, after the usual fashion of canoes on our rivers, and among the Indians near us. The labor of making a canoe sufficient to carry a dozen persons and their baggage, without the use of an iron tool, must be very great. First, the tree must be felled by means of fire at the root; or, if an accidental fire or the wind has favored them by prostrating a suitable tree, it must be sundered by fire. Next, it is to be brought to shape on the outside, and excavated within, by the application of fire; to hasten the process of which, as well as to give such a direction to the burning as to produce the proper form in the vessel, the coal is scraped off with some hard substance, as fast as it is charred.

The same tedious process must be resorted to in the construction of paddles, or oars for the canoe.*

In some instances, in the more southern parts, a vessel is formed by stretching the skin of the buffaloe, elk or deer over small pliant pieces of wood, similar to the manner of constructing a birch bark canoe in the north.

Frequently the buffaloe skin which serves for a robe for the body by day, and for its covering at night, is made to serve the purpose of a boat in crossing a river. Being spread upon the ground, the baggage is placed thereon, and if it be a mother in charge of an infant, the latter is also placed among the baggage. The edges of the skin are then brought together, so as to make the whole into a round bundle, like that of a washer woman. Being placed in the water, the person swims, and either pulls it by a cord held in the teeth, or pushes it forward.

The raft used for crossing deep waters, which consists of logs of wood, or reeds tied together, and which is well known to all who have travelled much in the wilderness, is usued occasionally by all tribes.

---

*Some very extravagant opinions have been formed relative to the inconvenience of the natives, for want of iron tools, as well as on many other accounts. The following, from Robinson's History of America, furnishes a specimen of those erroneous notions, though, in support of his opinion, the writer has quoted three authors.

He says " to fell a tree with no other instruments than hatchets of stone, was employment for a month. To form a canoe into shape, and to hollow it, consumed years, and it frequently began to rot before they were able to finish it. Their operations in agriculture were equally slow, and defective. In a country covered with wood of the hardest timber, the clearing of a small field destined for culture, required the united efforts of a tribe, and, was a work of much time and great toil. This was the business of the men."

The absurdities of the above, will be manifest by noticing that, 1st, stone axes were not used in felling trees, as we have heretofore remarked, 2d, a large tree may be either felled, or severed by fire in one or two days, 3d, a canoe sufficient to carry five men could be constructed by the use of fire, by that number of men, in a month, and if they had a suitable tree to work upon, and a convenient place for collecting wood for their fire, the canoe, with industry, could be made in half a month, 4th, the preparing of the field is invariably the business of the women, and not of the men, 5th, the removal of the trees was not necessary to the preparation of the field. For cultivation the natives select fertile spots, on which few trees or underwood grow. The trees are barked, and consequently die. The bark of a tree can be beaten off in a few minutes, with a stone or any hard substance sufficiently to prevent it from leafing. Twenty dead trees upon an acre of land would not materially injure the growth of the crop. Moreover dead timber is a great convenience to Indians on account of the facility with which they collect the fallen broken limbs for fuel, and the preference given to dry wood above that which is green. In the small Indian huts without chimnies, green wood cannot be used for fuel without occasioning intolerable smoke. On this account, and because it is, in other respects, more suitable for use in Indian houses, the tribes which use iron axes seldom burn green wood.

METHODS OF OBTAINING FIRE.

Since trading and trapping has become extensive in the Indian country, almost or quite all the tribes have obtained more or less iron from the whites, and steel and flint, with which to procure fire. Where they are not supplied with these, it is reported, that fire is produced by friction. A stick of dry wood is laid on the ground, to which one end of a hard dry stick is placed, while the upper end is pressed by the person's breast. This vertical stick, being either naturally in the form of a bow, or rendered so by pressure upon the upper end, is turned with the hand like a carpenter's wimble, and produces heat where it turns on the horizontal stick below.

M'Kenzie informs us that an uncommonly wretched tribe near the Great Bear Lake in about Lat. 66 deg. procured fire by "striking together a piece of pyrites and a flint stone over touchwood," (spunk) and that they were universally provided, each with a small bag containing those materials, the same as tribes near us are who carry flint, steel and spunk.

We have been informed by Indians, that anciently, when it was difficult to procure fire by the imperfect means which their ancestors possessed, it was usually preserved with great care, and was transported from place to place. A large piece of spunk or of some other decayed wood, was ignited and then enclosed in earth, and a wrapping of leaves, bark or skin, so placed around the spunk that the pressure would not become so great as to extinguish the fire and which excluded the air, excepting so much as was barely sufficient to preserve it. In this way a piece of spunk would last in transporting fire many days.

VESSELS TO HOLD WATER, &c.

One of their vessels used in carrying and in holding water is the stomach of a buffaloe, or the ponch of a less animal. As it would flatten down and leak its contents if it were set upon the ground, it is elevated upon three vertical sticks which are fastened to its brim.

Sometimes a wooden trough is used for a bucket: The bark of a tree taken in one entire piece, sufficiently large to allow of its being turned up at both ends, answers for a bucket. This is a common vessel with most of the tribes near us, especially with such as make sugar from the sugar tree, where it is used to receive the sweet water as it runs from the tree.

A better fashion of making a bucket of bark, is by bending it until it nearly assumes the form of vessels used by civilized men for similar purposes, the crevices of which are closed with gum from the pine tree.

Northwardly, buckets with some more labor are constructed of the filaments of the bark of trees, woven together like a basket, and rendered impervious to water by the pitch which exudes from the pine tree, or by some other glutinous substance.

A still better kind of water vessel is made of a hollow tree. The piece is brought to a proper length and thickness, when, with a knife, if one can be obtained, and if not, with a flint, a pointed piece of horn or bone, or the tooth of a beaver, a groove is formed within the hoop, and a bottom is inserted after the manner of constructing wooden vessels among us.

In a few instances, kettles among the natives have been discovered, large enough to contain two or three gallons, which had been chisselled out of solid rock, without an instrument of iron.

Some of the original inhabitants of that portion of the continent which is now settled by Europeans, manufactured earthen pots, pieces of which have frequently been dug out of the earth. At this time we have no knowledge of any tribe that manufactures earthen-ware.

COOKERY.

Roasting before the fire is a common and convenient method of cooking meat. Water is made to boil in a wooden or bark bucket, by inserting stones heated in the fire. This process of preparing food is tedious and troublesome, and although it may not render it less wholesome, must necessarily make it less palatable, than if it were prepared in the ordinary way in a vessel of metal.

When it is necessary to cook upon a large scale, meat is sometimes prepared by placing it in a heap, with leaves, or small brush or sticks between the pieces to keep them slightly asunder. The heap is covered with leaves, brush or grass, when a fire of wood is built over the whole, and continued until the meat is sufficiently stewed. It can easily be conceived that this process must necessarily impart to the food an unsavoury flavor.

Indians are often subjected to extreme hunger, and frequently die from actual starvation, as well as from cold. With many, wild berries, nuts, roots and esculent plants, are ut some seasons of the year, important articles of food. A kind of parsnip, found in morasses, said to be poisonous in its crude state, is rendered harmless and nutritive, by a peculiar process of roasting, or rather stewing, among heated rocks and earth, in a pit prepared for the purpose.

In the spring season of the year the bark of trees is peeled off, and the inner soft part is scraped from the harder, and in like manner the soft and juicy portion which adheres to the tree is procured. These scrapings are generally worked into a kind of soft dough, and then spread out to the sun to dry in the form of cakes. This is a substitute for bread.

With some of the tribes the manufacture of this bark bread is so considerable, that it becomes an article of traffic with others. An esculent root is by a similar process made into the form of bread.

The pacimmon fruit, well known in the western states, is also made into cakes, hardened by exposure to the sun. The ripe soft fruit is mashed in a vessel; after which the pulp is separated from the seed, and the rind, by pressing it through a strainer composed of small sticks fastened side by side.

These wretched people, of whom we speak, feed on animals which die of disease, and, frequently, after the flesh has become putrid. Their necessities are sometimes so great, that no kind of food that will contribute to the protraction of life, is rejected on account of its loathsomeness.

It has been reported that, from indifference, they were in the habit of eating *raw* flesh. This is not true. The pinchings of hunger are often extreme, and deprive them of patience to cook meat, when, as might be expected, they devour it raw and with the voracity of wolves. But when they have opportunity for preparing their food, they prefer it thoroughly cooked.

CANNIBALISM.

It has been frequently stated that cannibalism existed among some of the tribes. We believe that no tribe ever ate human flesh, even that of their enemies, merely as an article of food, except in such extreme cases of hunger as have sometimes driven others to this dreadful expedient for the prolongation of life, nor do we believe that any people, *ever* had a custom so horrid merely for the sake of food. When it does occur, it is either the result of insupportable hunger, as stated above, or the result of superstition. We cannot doubt that, from one or both of these causes, human flesh has been eaten by persons belonging to many of the Indian tribes. It is alone the flesh of the *enemy*, killed, or taken prisoner in battle, that is eaten. Most commonly the heart only is extracted and devoured. But sometimes persons who have been captives many months, are deliberately killed and prepared for eating, as they would kill and dress an ox. The whole of this horrid affair is accompanied with songs, dancing and hallooing, suitable, as they suppose, to the occasion. It is a ceremony engendered and fostered by superstition, and not an act performed for the gratification of the appetite.

The latest instance of the performance of this shocking ceremony, of which we have any knowledge, occurred in the Lake country since the year 1821*.

AMUSEMENT.

All Indians, however poor and wretched they may be manifest a fondness for music and dancing, and for playing at games of chance. For want of room, a description of these must be reserved for a succeeding number.

RELIGION.

No Indian tribe with which we are acquainted, from the most civilized to the most savage, is, at this time, known to be idolatrous. Their religious ceremonies are few, these, among all tribes, indicate a belief of those fundamental truths which teach man that he is accountable to his God. The author of our existence has interwoven these truths with the faculties of human understanding; knowledge of them is improved by scientific and religious culture. They are obscured by established and practical superstition. For an illustration of the former, we cite the people, wherever they be, who adhere to the doctrines and precepts of the Bible—the book which enjoins every virtue, both in regard to our relation to fellow-men, and to God, and forbids every vice. For an illustration of the latter, we have only to look to the people who, without the light of the Bible, have adopted a mythology loaded with unkind ceremonies, and sustained by ignorance and cruelty. Leave man without improvement, and without being made worse, and we have him in a state of *nature* ; and such is the condition of the unimproved Indian.

We are astonished that this subject as illustrated by the character of our Indians, has received so little attention from

---

* We wish not to state precisely either time or place.

the philosopher and the Christian. We read of man in primeval innocence, and we have a brief history of times immediately following his fall. But in both those periods, Jehovah communicated intelligence to man by methods which it has not been his pleasure to vouchsafe to the aborigines of America. As we follow man down towards the period of our own existence, his history becomes more fully written. It may, indeed, allow of the use of the term *savage* as distinguished from *civilized*, but it no where furnishes a case parrallel to that of the North American Indians. Other barbarous people kept flocks, subjected animals to servile purposes, or had made some improvement in the arts. The Indians, in their original state, had done neither. *

Their habits of life are such merely as have resulted from impressions which an unrestrained mind has received from surrounding natural circumstances, and are perfectly natural. Such also are their religious impressions. The latter being attributable to the structure of the human mind in its formation by the Creator, is virtually the same with all unrestrained human beings under whatever physical circumstances they may be placed, because the might, and the benignity of an overruling Providence, are taught by all creation, and the frailty and the imperfection of man are seen and felt wherever man exists. Whereas habits of life are according to the necessities of their situation. Hence, their religious opinions are even more uniform than their common habits of life.

It has been reported that about the time that Europeans first settled in America, several tribes were discovered which had no idea whatever of a Supreme Being, and no rites of religious worship. This we are confident was a mistake. They who reported were not prepared to comprehend the modes of thinking of men in a state of nature. Besides the prejudices under which they made their enquiries, their means of obtaining information were very imperfect.

The Indians were far from esteeming the whites as their real friends, even when the former appeared respectful in their demeanor. They, therefore, had many reasons for concealing their real views of religion. Man invariably attaches a sacredness to his religion, so far as he pretends to have any. It was natural for the Indians to suppose that the disclosure of their religious opinions and

---

*It is probable that the natives of New-Holland, who were unknown to the civilized world until about one hundred years after the discovery of America, more nearly resemble the native Americans in their circumstances, than any other people.

ceremonies to the whites, of whom they had formed a very unfavorable opinion, would be a profanity that would incur the displeasure of the Great Spirit. Even up to the present time, the religious ceremonies of the Delawares, Shawanoes, and many other tribes which have resided near the whites two hundred years, or more, are, in a great degree, kept secret from white people. It is often the case that tribes which are united in the most friendly intercourse, in all the ordinary transactions of life, are not allowed to participate in each others religious ceremonies.

Another, and almost invariable obstacle to the obtaining of correct information from the Indians upon important subjects of any kind, originates in the arrogance of the enquirer. The Indian is addressed as one who is exceedingly ignorant, and whose views of religion and of other important matters are ridiculous. Naturally possessing strong mental abilities, and being accustomed to judge of things from appearances, he readily discovers the vanity of the enquirer, and feels little inclination to indulge his curiosity at his own expense.

The remark may be worthy of a place here, that Indians, generally, are such competent judges of human nature, that when agents or commissioners of the United States enter into counsel with them, they readily perceive when a man is a novice in his business, and generally form an opinion of the talents of those with whom they are negotiating, about as correctly as civilized men would in the same length of time.

A few years since, it appeared in public prints that enquiries having been made of the Osages, it had been ascertained that they had no idea of a Supreme Being. In order to put our readers upon their guard when they read such accounts, we state here a few facts relative to the Osages, to show how erroneous the above account was.

Almost all adult Osages of both sexes, whether at their villages or on a journey, engage in service to the Great Spirit at break of day. They retire separately from the tent, and engage in a kind of prayer aloud, so that they are sometimes heard the distance of half a mile. Their words are uttered in a plaintive tone, and attended with apparent weeping. This howling, which to our ears seems hideous enough, lasts about ten minutes.

They frequently suspend human scalps over the graves of the dead. A bereaved husband or friend, in order to obtain a scalp for the above purpose, seeks the life of an enemy. Supposing that, having driven the enemy's spirit into the world of spirits, and suspended his scalp over the grave of the deceased, the spirit of the enemy becomes a slave to the spirit of the deceased friend. This service to departed friends is deemed so important, that it is perhaps the most fruitful source of Osage hostilities.

Fasts are common among the Osages, and women bedaub themselves with mud many months, as a badge of mourning for deceased husbands. Their name for the Supreme Being is Wohkonda. Yet while such ceremonies as the above were observed by the Osages, some honest men who mingled with them conjectured that they had no idea of the existence of a Supreme Being!

We can easily conceive that the natives, in their rude condition, are exceedingly superstitious. Our present limits will not allow us to dwell upon this subject.

METHODS OF RECKONING.

All tribes reckon time by *winters*, *moons*, and *nights*. Numbers are reckoned upon the decimal system, the same as among civilized men. We presume that they did not adopt this mode from a readiness to systematize, but that it was naturally suggested by the circumstance of having ten fingers upon the two hands. All the tribes, even those near us, and who have made some improvement in the habits of life, have great use for their fingers in reckoning.

With some of the tribes, of which the Ottawa is one while the decimal system is preserved, the numerical division actually commences with *five*. With, perhaps, an exception of the number nine, the radical names of numbers extend only to five. The next number is *one*, with an affix to denote that it is the first between five and ten. e. g. gotewoh is one, gotewohswe is six, neeshwoh is two, neeshwohswe is seven, &c. Over ten they proceed by ten and one two tens and one, and so on to ten tens, &c.

PHYSICIANS.

They have their physicians of both sexes, and the physician is always supposed to be a conjurer, who has recourse to charms and incantations.

HUNTING AND WAR.

It is probable that the Aborigines of America have not been so greatly misrepresented in any other traits of character as in those relating to their attachments to *hunting* and to *war*.

In contemplating the work of Indian reform, frequently

their attachment to the *life of a hunter*, and their *fondness for war*, are gravely brought to view as almost insurmountable obstacles to their improvement. This idea is illusory. Hunting is the business of the natives, in a hunting country, upon which they principally rely for subsistence. Fishing is the principal business in places where food can be more easily obtained by that business than by hunting. Agriculture is the principal business upon which a large majority of the citizens of the western states rely for a living. It would be no more absurd to suppose that the people of the western states could not be improved by schools, &c. on account of their fondness for farming, nor the people of N. England on account of their attachment to manufactures than to suppose that the Indians' attachment to hunting, fishing, digging wild roots, gathering berries, or making bread of the bark of trees, had rendered them unsusceptible of improvement.

The Indians, like all other people in the world, follow the employment which to them appears most convenient for procuring a livelihood, and their attachment to their modes of living are no stronger than the attachments of others are to their ordinary pursuits in life.

Should it be asked, if the Indians do not possess an unnatural fondness for hunting, why do not those upon our orders, more readily become agriculturalists and mechanics, when they have opportunities for witnessing the superior results of employments of this character? We must be allowed to answer, the fault is ours; and to exhibit this fact, and to plead for the correction of this error, are prominent features in the design of this plea for the aborogines.

The business of hunting allows them little opportunity for obtaining education. This is their misfortune, and not their crime. They have not a thirst for a knowledge of letters, because in their business they have no use for letters. All this is perfectly natural. We reject such pursuits and such studies as we deem unprofitable.

War among the Indians prevails precisely to the extent that it would with any other people if placed in similar circumstances, and no further. The existence of war in the general acceptation of the term, their modes of warfare, and the occurrence of battles and of acts of depredation, are such as naturally arise out of their circumstances in life in other respects. It is said that the Chippewas and Sioux have been at war with each other from time immemorial, without knowing how it originated, or understanding why it

G

should be continued. Hence it has been inferred that they were under the influence of an unnatural predilection for war. Not so. Civilized nations maintain peace with one another when commercial and other interests, teach them their mutual dependence upon one another. When questions of right are to be decided, the settled habits of their lives, and the plenitude of earthly comforts, afford leisure and opportunity for diplomatic negotiations. The various Indian tribes are not similarly united in bonds of common interest. A tribe may barter with a neighboring tribe, a few back loads of roots, for as much dried fish, but there exists between the various tribes nothing like national commerce. Each lives independently of the other. Our country is favoured with professional men from European nations, and those nations profit in a similar manner by sons of America. No such relationship exists between the different tribes of Indians.

When the rights contested by parties are nearly equal, they cannot be satisfactorily settled without negotiation, because each party is invariably partial to itself. This tribe recollects that last year, some of its members were murdered, or some of its property stolen, by a war party of that tribe. Without the disposition, even were it practicable, to compare past injuries, in order to ascertain which party is debtor to the other, the late injured party feels itself to be the loser and seeks redress in its own way, that is by retaliation; and it deserves particular notice, that this is the only mode by which redress for wrongs can be obtained by people who have not subjected themselves to subordination to general laws. This spirit of retaliation is necessarily reciprocal among tribes unfriendly to each other.

That man, depraved man, possesses a fiendish spirit, which leads to ignorance of, and disrespect for the rights of his fellow-man, and induces him to delight in depriving him of existence, is a truth written with blood, the record of which, is almost coeval with the world. But we deny, fearlessly deny that any evidence exists that this Satanic disposition is of ranker growth with the Indians than with others.

The horrors of war are diminished by the institutions of liberal governments. It can scarcely be said that the Indians have any settled institutions of any kind, or any national government. Their wars are therefore just such as any other nation of depraved men in similar circumstances would wage with their neighbors. Change those circumstances, and teach them to feel related to one another, not merely as foreign nations, but as so many tribes of one common family, or as so many states of one union, whose happiness could not be promoted, but by mutual dependance upon each other, and a mutual exchange of good offices, and all causes of war, would be as effectually excluded from among them, as they are from the states of our happy union.

No plausible reason has ever been assigned for the supposed inveterate predilection of the Indians for war, and we are confident that no good reason ever will be assigned. The idea is unphilosophical, not to say absurd. It cannot be attributed to the colour of their skin, for this could no more affect their minds than the colour of their hair. It cannot be attributed to kind or quantity of food, for they feed upon fowl, flesh, fish, corn, roots, berries, or bark, as necessity compels, and with scantiness or plenty, as success or disappointment attends their wretched pursuits in seeking supplies.

The opinion against which we plead is directly at variance with matters of fact. When we ascribe to a man among us a martial spirit, we mean that he is a warlike, fighting man, who feels less reluctance to combatting than some others, and, consequently, is courageous. The Indians in their native condition evince an uncommon want of courage, both in their wars with one another, and with the whites. The hard fought battles which have ocurred on our frontiers have been fought with Indians who had acquired courage by their intercourse with the whites.

The facts that a few dozens of Europeans on their first settlement in America, stopped when and where they pleased, and made permanent settlements, in defiance of the ten thousand Indians who desired their expulsion, and who frequently attempted it, is evidence incontrovertible, of the validity of our argument.

But we need not go back to history to obtain proof of the point for which we contend. We have, at this time, Indians near us, who are almost, though not entirely in their native condition in regard to war. These are not a warlike, courageous people, but precisely the reverse. The Osages and Pawnees will fight in a prairie half a day and not kill half a dozen men. One of these battles occurred on the Arkansas river, within the last five years, where in half a day's fighting only three lives were lost, because each party was unwilling to risk tiself within killing distance.

More recently sixty-three Pawnees and Camanches surrounded nine white men upon Arkansas, when they were seven miles from their associates at camp, and in an open prairie. If, at any time, an Indian deemed himself too near or safety, he invariably gave back at the presentation of a whiteman's gun. In going the seven miles to their camp, the white men necessarily had to pass over ground, which afforded the enemy great advantages. Notwithstanding which, and the disparity of their numbers, and the similarity of their arms, every white man reached camp unhurt.

Still later, three Shawanoes were proceeding westward upon the Santa Fee road with a view of overtaking a company of white men, when they were attacked by about 30 Pawnees and Camanches. The Shawanoes were surrounded and compelled to sculk as well as they could until night came on, when, *unhurt*, they escaped with two scalps which they had taken from their enemies in the skirmish.

We state these occurrences as samples of many which might be adduced to prove that the aborigines in their native condition, are not courageous, and to exhibit a specimen of difference between Indians with their original feelings, and those who have acquired courage by their intercourse with the whites.

Horrid massacres are sometimes made by one party of Indians upon another, but generally their wars are perpetuated without energy. An instance similar to many that exist, is found in relation to the Kauzaus and Pawnees. The former reside on the Kauzau river, and number only about fifteen hundred souls. The latter number about ten thousand, and until very recently their settlements commenced on the same river, not one hundred miles from the former. The parties have been hostile to each other longer than either can recollect. There is no mountain or other natural barrier between them to prevent the stronger from making a descent upon the weaker, and exterminating it. But this has not been done. Though by small predatory war parties, they have yearly taken from each other a few horses, and a few scalps. We admit that battles have been fought which were of such magnitude as to entitle the parties to the name of armies. But these have been exceedingly rare.

Both in a general battle, and in a skirmish of a few individuals, the victorious are usually merciless and cruel in the extreme, to the vanquished who fall within the reach of their rage. This is to be expected from a people whose minds and manners have not, in the remotest degree, felt the influences of Christianity.

The cruelty of the Indians in war is frequently, though not always, extended to their white enemies, who are so unfortunate as to fall into their hands. They have apparently taken delight in dashing out the brains of the infant in the presence of its captive mother, and have studied to render the agonies of the victims of their hate, both long and severe. But their unbounded ferocity towards a vanquished foe, is not a mark of courage, but of cowardice. It is not an evidence of an uncommon propensity to war, but, of an uncommon aversion thereto.

Our remarks in this place are of a general nature. Instances of noble courage have sometimes occurred among the Indians, and also honorable instances of humanity towards prisoners. Whatever may be the sufferings of white female prisoners among them, they generally escape insults, which too often to the disgrace of human nature, are suffered by unprotected females whom the fortune of war places at the will of the soldiery of other nations. Here the conduct of the savages forms a striking contrast to that of civilized nations : a contrast too honorable to the wild man of America not to be remembered to the end of time.

The list of arguments which might be drawn from sound philosophy and plain matters of fact, seems to us to be almost endless in favor of the point for which we here contend, that the aborigines do not possess an uncommon propensity to war.

Human beings cannot always sleep; they must talk; they must act. Indians have no scientific topics of conversation to indulge in; no commercial intercourse to manage; no machinery to contrive to make the simple wise; no national or corporation laws to enact, and no spirit of enterprize to foster. The sphere within which they move, is limited by their present necessities, except as they are induced to transcend it by barely so much fondness for pre-eminence, so much love of power, and so much diabolical hate, as are interwoven with the human mind. The white man among them hears them talk about hunting, to the exclusion of conversation on topics relating to the business of life among civilized people; and fancies that they have an uncommon propensity to hunting, because they spend their time chiefly in that employment, and indulge in conversation respecting it, when, in fact, it happens so, merely because the poor creatures have no better employment, and because they, like other people, indulge in conversation upon the chief business of their lives.

When, in addition to the love of gain, the Indian feels, in a degree, the love of preeminence and honor, both of which are natural to man, he contemplates hostilities against his neighbors, and feats of war, past or to come, necessarily be-

G2

come subjects of conversation. Hence, white men have inferred their predilection for war, forgetting that with them, these innate passions of the mind, to wit, a thirst for honor and power, and a sordid love of gain, could expand in no other way. In these latter remarks we shall not be understood as excluding from the causes of their wars, a malignant heart common to all men.

ERROR OF SUPPOSING THAT INDIANS POSSESS PECULIAR PROPENSITIES.

In making out our plea for the aborigines, we feel confident that our object will be attained with least difficulty, by a candid admission of facts, evil as well as good, in relation to them. Viewing them in their true condition, it may be difficult to repress a dropping tear over fallen, depraved, wretched, unimproved, human nature. While we sympathize with their sufferings, pity their ignorance, and wonder at their superstition, we are shocked by their crimes, and shudder for their fate. Still, we are confident, that one of their greatest misfortunes has been, that they have been misrepresented by white men who have mingled with them, or who have written respecting them from the information of others. This man studiously conceals their vices, and would persuade the world that they are a virtuous people, while that seems to imagine them to be, naturally, too vicious to be capable of performing virtuous acts. One labors to prove that they are uncommonly wise, while another argues that their minds are too obtuse to be susceptible of improvement. All, however, seem to agree in supposing that they possess a structure of mind and disposition, in some respects, *peculiar* to themselves, and among these peculiarities, is their supposed predilection for hunting and war, which is ascribed to them by common consent. All this is visionary and erroneous. The external circumstances of the Indians are such as are peculiar to themselves; but their minds and dispositions have nothing peculiar belonging to them.

Could this erroneous impression upon the minds of white men be effaced, the larger portion of the difficulties attending our Indian relations would be obviated. If we could feel, that, excepting their habits of life, the Indians are precisely like other people, neither worse nor better, with neither less nor more natural understanding, with propensities precisely similar to the propensities of other nations, we should allow them equal claims upon our sympathies with others, would regulate our conduct towards them by the same rules, would respect their rights with the same scrupulosity, and for their improvement we should employ the same means that we apply to the improvement of others. Instead of lengthy metaphysical disquisitions about man in his rude state, and how he advances step by step towards civilization, when, by the by, man had never, since his creation, been known to exist in the rude state presupposed, until our acquaintance with the aborigines of America; and instead of prescriptions of remedies for the relief of the Indians, as peculiar in their operations, as the phrenzied imaginations of men have conceived the Indian character to be, we should turn to our own firesides, and remember that our sons and daughters would all sink into savageism, were it not for the means with which a kind Providence has furnised us to prevent it; means, the influence of which has not been brought to bear upon the Indians. We should reflect that Indian children come into the world with precisely such propensities as our own possess; and, under similar circumstances, might be expected to act a similar part. To all which, it would be suitable to add, the reflection that the preventives of ruin, and the facilities to improvement with which we are blessed, have been communicated to us through the kindness and instrumentality of others, and that it would be proper for us to become instruments of relief even to the neglected Indian.

We err in supposing that the civilized portion of the human family has advanced, step by step, from the point most remote from civilization to its present condition, and hence, ascribe some natural defect to the Indians because they have not improved. The rude state in which we date our origin never existed, except in our bewildered imaginations. Adam and Cain tilled the ground, Abel was a herdsman, Noah and his family entered upon the business of agriculture, and the necessary mechanic arts, as soon as they left the ark.

If men, by events unknown to us, were cast upon a continent like ours, deprived of the helps to improvement which were granted to Adam and Noah, where necessity did not dictate a different course in their conduct, a period, longer or shorter, would elapse, before they would rise from their wretched condition. The aborigines of America are these people;—the only people, we repeat it, that, previously to our acquaintance with them, had ever been known to exist upon earth, in a state of nature. The period in which they have remained unimproved has been long, but we have no evidence that it would have been shorter with any other people, had they been placed in similar circumstances.

If cast upon our continent without the use of iron, to aid in agriculture, and in mechanic arts, and without seed from their mother country for their fields, their necessities would impel them to seek food from the spontaneous productions of nature. The world before them was wide, and they long continued this method of obtaining a living.

CIVIL GOVERNMENT, AND IMPROVEMENT IN THE ARTS OF LIFE.

On the discovery of America by Europeans, the natives were scattered over it in a state of anarchy; but not in that condition which follows the destruction of government by sedition. We have just grounds to believe that civil government, properly speaking, had never existed among them. It may be presumed, that, as they multiplied, they spread abroad over the country, without organization into civil government, and as the game diminished in the vicinity of an occupied place by the increase of those who consumed it, bands divided and subdivided, and pitched their tents where the necessaries of life could be more easily obtained. This has been the course of their conduct since our acquaintance with them.

To naked Indians, the attractions of the warmer climates would naturally be greater than those of the colder, hence population became more dense in the former than in the latter. In proportion to the increase of population, was the difficulty of obtaining subsistence upon the uncultivated productions of nature. In those places, circumstances would naturally suggest the idea of cultivating the soil, and there the earlier efforts towards civilization were made, as in Mexico, &c.

Some tribes in California, and in other parts of those warm countries were exceedingly wretched. But speaking in general terms, the cultivation of the soil, and efforts of mechanism diminished as we proceeded northward.

Precisely in proportion to the improvement which they had made in agriculture and the mechanic arts, were the municipal regulations of the tribes severally. Hunters did not need laws, and they acknowledged none. Such as acquired some property by industry, felt the necessity of civil government in proportion to the rights which they had to secure. The principles of individuality of right in property, and of civil government, naturally cherish each other, out of the former springs a spirit of enterprise and improvement, the latter binds society together for purposes of mutual safety, encouragement, and assistance.

In regard to manual labor, the Mexicans had made greater improvement than others, and among them existed the nearest resemblance to civilized government. Civil government and improvement in the arts, are necessarily coetaneous. The one cannot exist without the other. Deprive a community of municipal laws, and society is destroyed. A decline of the arts and sciences, and a consequent increase of wretchedness necessarily ensues. Deprive our happy United States of its Constitution, thence proceed to demolish the constitution of the several states, and all the minutia of civil government within each, and how wretched would our condition be! Notwithstanding the extensive knowledge of the arts of life which we now possess, we should daily become less comfortable, and with the Bible in our hands we should become less virtuous, until we sunk down to the wretchedness of the Indians in their unimproved state.

The more ambitious might become chieftans of such parties as they could rally, but without some judicial regulations for the administration of justice within their several spheres the standing of each would become merely nominal, like that of an Indian Chief, who has little of that which is real in his office, and even that little, he would not possess, were it not for the shadow of civil compact that exists among them. Civil government under some name is the adhesive principle which unites man to his fellow man, for mutual benefits, and without it he cannot improve the arts and sciences.

Were we deprived of civil government we should have no common interests to defend against an invading foe. If Individual interests were threatened, and common sense should, from similarity of circumstances bring us together to oppose the invasion of the rights of all, we could make no effectual resistance without organization. Unprotected from the invasion of others, and unassisted by one another, we should continue to degenerate until we had reached the lowest point in human wretchedness. Nothing could prevent it but the re-establishment of civil government; and this would prevent it as certainly as that the rising of the sun illuminates our dwellings.

This is the condition of the aborogines of America, excepting so far as the shadow of civil government does exist among them. Why then should we attribute to them some peculiar propensity to degeneracy, when we perceive, that if we were deprived of civil government, as nearly as they are, and were thrown into a state of anarchy similar to theirs, our condition would become equally deplorable?

The Indians, even in their unimproved state, have a semblance of civil government and a contracted round of religious ceremonies. But they have no greater portion of either than human beings must necessarily possess. Man being a social and a religious being, does necessarily feel, to some extent, the influence of principles relating to society in this world, and society in the next. We have above stated the incontrovertible fact, that the difference in the condition of various Indian tribes has been in due proportion to the extent to which each had become subordinate to the bonds of society, subordinate to civil government.

THE CAUSE OF INDIAN DEGENERACY.

We have now arrived at the true source of Indian degeneracy, to wit, the absence of civil government, or its laxity where it does exist. Nothing can be more obvious than that people cannot improve in the arts and sciences without being united in civil government, by which they become united for mutual comfort, and for the mutual defence of their comforts. The Indians, first, by causes which existed solely among themselves, and secondly, by the nature of the policy of European intercourse, so far as it has been extended among them, have been detained in circumstances in which, it has been impossible, in the nature of things, for them to be any thing better than what we now find them to be. For their wretchedness, before we were acquainted with them, we are not blameable. But for the augmentation of their miseries by our mistaken and destructive policy, we cannot be innocent.

The division of Indians into distinct bands, each headed by a chief, has been fostered by their habits of procuring subsistence from the spontaneous productions of nature. The absence of civil government left every one, in some measure, to act for himself, and necessarily cherished their roving habits, at the same time that their unsettled condition as naturally fostered their indifference to civil government. These two circumstances continually influenced each other, and on the discovery of America by Europeans, had been but slightly altered in a few places, in which a degree of civil government, and improvement in the arts were existent. The principle of chieftancy necessarily belongs to the rudeness of Indian condition, and so long as the former exists, it will foster the latter. A spirit of insubordination, the achievment of some act of magnitude in savage life, or even age, may create a man a chief. Hence chiefs multiply in proportion to the outspreading of Indian population. With their narrow conceptions of the future, it is not surprising that they who are ambitious to become chiefs should limit their ambition to the little sphere of their several chieftancies. Without the abolition of this Indian custom, which, we repeat it, necessarily belongs to uncivilized, and not to civilized man, we can no more hope for the elevation of Indians to the blessings of a civilized state, than we could hope to heal a wound while a splintered bone rankled within.

This Indian custom, found at the very root of their rudeness, has been invariably fostered by the nature of European intercourse. We appoint an agent or agents to each tribe, and thus perpetuate the distinctive character of the tribes severally. We recognize the chiefs as such, and hence cherish the practices attendant upon the existence of chieftancies.

The Indian agency system is but a *part* of that of which we are speaking, and chimes well with it. It is an awkward anomaly in civil government, producing unnecessary cost and vexation to us, and promotive of the rapid decline of the Indians. Let us not be misunderstood. We are not blaming *men*, we are blaming measures. And this we do fearlessly, believing that we shall be sustained by the deliberate judgment of all Indian Agents who have had an opportunity to witness the effects of the system upon the aborigines.

The system of Indian agencies and Indian chieftaincies, is, throughout, at variance with the fundamental principles of civilization, and, therefore, should be abolished.

When the Spaniards discovered this country, they took possession of it in the name of their Sovereign. They never once thought that it might possibly belong to the people who inhabited it. Other Europeans, at divers times, touched at different places northward, as far as the continent has been explored, and took possession of places in the names of their respective Sovereigns, equally unconscious, it would seem, that the millions who, in those times, inhabited this country, could have claims to it. The boundaries of the claims of Europeans, sometimes became a matter of inquiry among them, but there was none with regard to the claims of the Indians. They were supposed to have no rights. Hence the charters of European Sovereigns to their subjects covered the whole continent. In this respect all imitated the example of the Spaniards. The settlements of New England, and of Virginia, were begun upon the same principles.—

Neither was made under the impression that the country belonged to its aboriginal inhabitants, and, with the design, that, if the rightful owners should not consent to the settlement of foreigners in it, they would return to Europe. Settlements were made under the impression that the Indians had no right to forbid it, and with the determination to remain, whatever might be the views of the Indians concerning it. When the latter attempted to arrest the settlement of the whites by force, and were defeated, they were not treated as a conquered nation which had been contending for their country and their rights. They were treated as rebels against government; some were put to death, and others were sold for slaves. This usage was not confined to the Spanish dominions; it extended northward, and prevailed in New England.

The practice of putting prisoners to death, or selling them for slaves, as being rebels against government, because they had taken up arms in defence of their country and their rights, was not continued after our colonies became united. This honorable change of conduct towards the wretched natives, was a true token of the superior excellence of the government of the United States over others. While it indicated the kind influence of our institutions, it became ominous of the entire correction of the evil policy which had been entailed upon us. But this evil policy has not yet been corrected; hence we are not quite innocent.

We have marked out states and territories through the Indian country, regardless of any claims which they might have. At the treaty of Ghent, the Commissioners on the part of the U. S. and those of Great Britain, agreed that a given line of latitude should divide the possessions of the two governments. The whole length of the line across to the Pacific ocean, run through Indian country. The same things occurred in fixing the boundaries between the U. States and Mexico.

Treaties have been held with various tribes, ostensiby for the purpose of extinguishing their titles to the soil they inhabited; but the nature of those titles was never defined.— In those treaties, the whites invariably gave the terms. Not one was ever made when the parties met under equal circumstances, and under such circumstances as would legalize a contract according to the laws of civilized nations. In proof of this we state the following facts, which we select from among many others, all of which speak the same unequivocal language. England has possessions in the north

Russia in the north west, Mexico in the south, and the U. States in the centre. The claims of each are acknowledged by others. But neither founds its claim upon the circumstance of having extinguished the Indian title to its territory. The United States do not professedly claim a foot of land by virtue of conveyance from the Indians. Its claims are based upon other considerations.

The extinguishment of Indian title, so called, by treaty, has been merely a measure to get them off the land with the least difficulty either to us or to them. By treaties we took the land, and gave them something for their consent to leave it. This was all that was implied by treaty, for, the country we intended to have, whether the Indians treated or not. This policy did not originate with the U. States. Its origin was anterior to the existence of our government, and we are persuaded that no government has treated the Indians with so little unkindness as ours. We speak of wrongs not for the purpose of inflicting a wound but for the purpose of healing one which our country, under the influence of its humane institutions, has long felt.

We know of no one state in the Union more deeply implicated than another. One policy has, from the first, pervaded the whole. The boundaries of each state are agreed upon by all the states. The right of the government to describe the boundaries of a state, when, to more than half of it, the Indian title has not been extinguished, has been doubted, by no state, and the claims of *none* are predicated upon a legal conveyance from the Indians.

The Indians, therefore, in all places within the territory claimed by us, have only been tenants at the will of our government. It was impossible, therefore, for them to feel, extensively, a spirit of improvement. So far as circumstances allowed, individuals of uncommon energy, under all their discouragements, have improved. They have become agriculturalists, mechanics, merchants, school teachers, physicians, preachers, &c. But these cases must necessarily, in a degree, be isolated, because of their detached, unconnected condition as a people.

This incoherence of condition has been fostered by the policy of their white neighbors. We have recognised each tribe as being independent of all others, and as such, have appointed an agent to attend them. The chiefs of each have been encouraged to remain contented with the little authority of their several chieftaincies, without conceiving a nobler design for general union and general effort. The control which, through our agents, we exercise over them in the management of their affairs, necessarily cherishes their ideas of remaining in separate bands, as they were in their original state, and prevents them from perceiving the want of civil government. Each feels itself wholly dependent upon us, without the hope of profiting by that dependence. It is permitted to manage its *small* internal affairs, provided it be done consistently with the general rules which we have established in relation to them. This little authority left to them, beguiles them into a kind of contentment with their degraded condition.

They have had no permanent resting place which they could call their *own*, and over which they had supreme control. The tribes could not become united in one civil community, such as is essential to improvement, and, in a word, they could not become any thing better than they have been, for our policy confined them to the very condition in which they have remained.

We have already seen that without civil government, no people could possibly thrive. Our intercourse regulations deprived them of the possibility of enjoying the blessings of civil government. They have not been allowed a participation in the affairs of our government, and they could not form a government of their own, because our policy kept them assunder. Each tribe was but a sojourner in its place, under the management of a people to whose interests it had no claims.

We cannot blame the aborigines for not having generally adopted habits of civilized life, when we perceive that the disabilities under which Europeans have placed them, are such as would quickly reduce to a similar state of wretchedness, even the people of the United States.

Separated from each other as tribes, and yet the several members of each not being taught the individuality of right in property, except in a small degree; in the absence of civil government, and without the prospect of better condition, they are generally listless and indolent. The efforts of Christians and other philanthropists to instruct them in science and religion, have not been rewarded with success equal to their expectations. This circumstance is not surprising, when we consider what is necessary to our own improvement, and perceive that this has been denied them.

Even the Bible, should we disregard its requirements in relation to subjection to civil government, would not save us from ruin as a people. How then can we hope for a salutary application of its other doctrines to a people not in possession of this privilege, which is of vital importance to ourselves?

It is the absence of this civil order, of national character, of individuality of right in property, and the consequent want of incentives to industry and interprise, that so frequently baffles efforts for their improvement. While they are kept destitute of these necessary things, it is as unreasonable to attempt their substantial improvement even with the Bible in our hands, as it would be to row a boat with oars upon one side only, or, to run a carriage with a wheel missing. But, let it be borne in mind that we depart from the doctrines of the bible, as well as from the dictates of common sense, when we seek the improvement of the Indians without civil government and its concomitant blessings.

If we would benefit those people substantially, save them from extermination, and elevate them to an equality with others, this is the place at which we should begin. This first, and indispensible step, we are sorry to say has not, even yet, been taken!!

About twelve years efforts have been making to secure to such of the aborigines as are among and near us, a permanent residence, in a body, in a country where the influence of our prejudices and of our local interests would be least felt by them, to give them a form of civil government, and to constitute them citizens of the United States. But so many have been the obstacles to the adoption of this kind and salutary measure, that it is still rather in embryo, than in existence.

Among the causes which have occasioned delay, are, 1st, the apathy which almost universally prevails, both in the church, and in the state, to the improvement of the condition of the Indians, 2d, the inveteracy of the irrational and vexatious policy in the management of Indian affairs, entailed upon us by our European ancestors; and 3d, the absurd notion that peculiarities are attached to Indian character which render their improvement almost impracticable.

May we hope that brighter days are dawning upon this unhappy race of men, or must they die?

Give the Indians, who could be reached by the measure, a common home. Let individuals hold land in severalty, while the surplus lands remain the common property of each district within which it lies. Give them a form of civil government, and so far as practicable, let it be administered by themselves, make them citizens of the United States, so that we and they shall have mutual interest, and mutual regard for those interests, and they will then be brought within the reach of the means of instruction, both in the arts and sciences, which are essential to the comfort of man in life, and in the doctrines of Christianity, which are essential to the salvation of the soul.

They would then possess no more facilities to improvement than what we know to be *essential* to our own prosperity. Thus situated we might as confidently affirm that they would become improved, as we can now affirm that we *are* improved.

Here, then we have the remnants of these people, with nothing mystical about them. With no unnatural predilection for war nor propensity to hunting, nor unnatural attachment to other customs opposed to their improvement, possessing minds not inferior to any other people. They would rejoice in the improvement of their condition, and they are ready to receive the blessings at our hands, which we here propose to give them, and which are solely under our control. Many of them are anxious to arise and repair the desolations of former generations.

With the increased weight of a thousand considerations which crowded upon our mind in this place, the question again recurs, must they perish? shall we withhold from them life on earth and life in heaven, when they stand ready to receive both, imploring the boon at our hands, by their ten thousand woes!

We have but barely entered upon this subject, and with a view of reaching the point in argument at which we have arrived, before we had filled the space allowed for this article, in this number of the Register, we have not been able to do justice to many points at which we have glanced, and have been obliged to omit much that lay in our way. The subject will be continued, should providence allow us to issue another number of the Register.

———⊶※⊷———

The statement was omitted in the proper place, that the publisher of the Register is himself *alone* accountable for its contents.

His Post Office is Westport, Jackson county, Missouri.

THE   No. 3.

ANNUAL REGISTER

OF

INDIAN AFFAIRS

WITHIN

THE INDIAN (OR WESTERN) TERRITORY.

PUBLISHED BY ISAAC M'COY.

SHAWANOE BAPTIST MISSION HOUSE, INDIAN TERRITORY,

MAY, 1837.

———●※●———

SHAWANOE BAPTIST MISSION, IND. TER.

J. G. PRATT, PRINTER.

1837.

Ben Perryman, Chief of the Creeks,
Painted by George Catlin (1796-1872)
Courtesy of Gilcrease Museum
Tulsa, Oklahoma

ADVERTISEMENT.

It was the design of the publisher to issue this number of the Register on the first of January of the present year, but a necessary absence from home for several months, occasioned a delay until this time. This delay is the less regretted on account of some reasons which we have discovered, for supposing that the first of January is *not* the best time for the work to be issued. It is designed to be a document to which reference may be safely made, by all interested in such Indian matters as it attempts to exhibit. It is desirable therefore, that each number should be ready for delivery at, or before the opening of each session of Congress. On this account, no time could be less suitable than that at which the preceding numbers have been issued. It is expected, that hereafter it will appear during the recess of Congress, and not much prior to the meeting of that body.

Our materials for this number, were chiefly collected prior to January last. Hence, some valuable information respecting the affairs of the present year, must be unavoidably postponed to 1838. Such matters, however, of the present year, as we have been able to obtain correct accounts of, will be noticed.

Readers who may discover any inaccuracies in statistics, are respectfully requested to inform us, that the error may be corrected in the succeeding number.

The work is issued gratuitously; and, it being designed to promote the welfare of a noble, but suffering race of men, thousands of whom still linger in sight of our fulness of comfort; readers are earnestly requested to diffuse as widely as practicable, such useful information as they suppose it contains.

Our subject is one of general interest, and in treating of it we shall be uninfluenced by either political or sectarian partialities. We have, however, already learned, that while we hope to escape the censure of *parties* in politics, and *sects* in religion, we shall subject ourselves to the blame of *individuals*. But we are determined neither to color a matter for the sake of pleasing, nor to conceal it for fear of offending.

It is much to be lamented, that most persons who have either spoken or written about the aborigines of America, seem to have been too much influenced by the phantasies which accompany romance. We advertise the reader, that we write about a people whose circumstances in life are, indeed peculiar to themselves, but whose minds are like those of all other people. They can be made either better or worse, by the same causes which operate to produce these effects upon others.

Jotham Meeker
*Courtesy of The Kansas State Historical Society
Topeka, Kansas*

ANNUAL REGISTER.

The policy of locating the nearer Indian tribes within the country west of the states of Missouri and Arkansas; and of organizing a civil government for their benefit, appears to be now pretty well settled in the minds of our citizens.— The necessity of the measure becomes daily more apparent, and its ultimate success more certain. The local situation of the country, its freedom from political embarrassments which have attended other places; and its physical resources, all highly commend it for such a purpose.

This scheme is an untried experiment in the work of Indian reform; and consequently a departure from the long existing policy of European intercourse with the Indian tribes. In the transition from the former to the latter policy, it was not to be expected that a popular government, like ours, could proceed systematically. Different opinions, various feelings, and clashing interests, were to be met.— Hence some measures whose character gave them claims to priority, have been preceded by others.

The boundaries of the Indian Territory have not yet been established by law, notwithstanding this step seemed to be demanded by the nature of the case, early in the enterprize. We are happy to find, however, that this matter now appears to be distinctly under the consideration of government; and no doubt is entertained that the boundaries of the Territory, will, ere long be fixed.

By the common consent of the public, and by bills reported to both Houses of Congress at the last session, by the appropriate Committees on Indian Affairs, we feel authorized to believe that those boundaries when established, will not vary materially from the following:

Beginning where the line of the 23d deg. of longitude crosses Puncah river, and running down said river to the Missouri river; thence down the Missouri river to the state of Missouri; thence along the western boundary of the states of Missouri and Arkansas to Red River; thence up Red River to the 23rd degree of long.; and thence north to the beginning.

These bounds would make it a little more than equal to a

tract 600 miles long, and 200 miles wide. It should be borne in mind however, that much on the west, the whole distance of 600 miles north and south, is at present uninhabitable on account of the scarcity of wood; though the soil is generally good, and in process of time, will become timbered. In view of this defect, it is generally supposed that the country as above described, though fully adequate in extent, would not be too large for the purposes contemplated. It could not be diminished on either the north, east, or south side, without the inevitable exclusion of some tribes, and great damage to the whole; but if curtailed on the west, by a line from a point on Red River, only 200 miles west of the state of Arkansas, running northwardly to the beginning, it would not be the less valuable to the owners. As the country is described above, it embraces much uninhabitable prairie land, and this uninhabitable prairie continues west four or five hundred miles to the Rocky Mountains.

Between the settlements within the Indian Territory and the Rocky Mountains, no Indians ever resided, and none will ever reside until these plains become timbered. Within the Territory are much coal and salt water, and some lead and iron ore.

REMARKS.

The Osages and all south of them, are in charge of Capt. William Armstrong, acting superintendent and agent for the Choctaws. All north of the Osages, are under the superintendency of Gen. William Clark, who resides in St Louis, about three hundred miles east of the Indian Territory.

A Sub-agent is not an officer subordinate to an Agent; the duties and responsibilities of the two are the same. The only difference is, that the compensation of an Agent is $1500 per annum, and the compensation of a Sub-agent is $750 per annum.

Annual reports are made by the Agents and Sub-agents; which, through the superintendents, come before the commissioner of Indian Affairs, the Hon. C. A. Harris, in Washington city.

These reports exhibit the amount of aid afforded the Indians in agricultural implements; live stock; the erection of dwelling houses and mills; and in the fencing and ploughing of fields; the names and salaries of interpreters; of farmers, blacksmiths, wheelwrights, and school teachers employed by the Government; the condition of schools, supported and managed exclusively by the Government, together with the location and condition of the schools immediately in charge of the missionaries. In a word, these reports are intended to exhibit in statistical form, all matters within the several agencies which require the consideration of the Commissioner of Indian Affairs.

When missionary buildings are erected by a missionary society, one object of which, is an English school for Indian youth, the missionary acting as agent for the society, reports the fact, with the costs of the buildings to the U. S. Indian Agent, or Sub-agent for the tribe. The latter examines them in person, and reports their character and what he believes to be their value. Upon these reports, and at the request of the society, the Government, if in possession of the means, pays to the society two thirds of the value of the buildings.

The Agent or Sub-agent examines the schools annually before he makes his report. All missionary establishments are formed under the authority of Government, and receive more or less pecuniary assistance from it. The means of assistance are either provided by treaty stipulations, or by the appropriation annually of a civilization fund of $10,000.

INDIGENOUS TRIBES.

Osage, about	5,510	Pawnee, about	10,000
Kauzau, "	1,606	Puncah, "	800
Omaha, "	1,400	Quapaw, "	600
Otoe and Missouria,	1,600		
		In all	21,516

EMIGRANT TRIBES.

*Choctaw, about	15,300	Shawanoe of Kauzau riv.	823
†Cherokee, "	6,072	Delaware,	921
‡Creek, "	19,253	Kickapoo,	625
Senecas & Shawanoes of Neosho,	462	Putawatomie,	444
Wea,	206	Emigrant,	44,484
Piankasha,	157	Indigenous,	21,516
Peoria & Kaskaskias,	142		
Ottawa,	79	In all	66,000

*Including 200 white men married in the nation, and exclusive of 600 negro slaves.
†This number had reached the Creek country prior to 1837, and it includes about 500 slaves.
‡Including about 800 slaves.

CHOCTAWS.

The southern boundary of the Choctaw country is Red river, south of which is the province of Texas. On the east they adjoin the state of Arkansas; are bounded north by Arkansas and Canadian rivers, and on the west by the almost woodless prairie regions. The extent of their country from north to south is about 150 miles; and from east to west, the habitable portion is about 200 miles.

Their country is supplied with numerous springs of salt water, at two of which the natives are preparing to manufacture salt.

Their settlements are divided, politically, into three districts, viz:—1st. Mushulatubbee district on the north. 2d. Poshemataha district on the south west, adjoining Red river. 3d. Red River district on the south east, adjoining the state of Arkansas.

About three or four thousand of the tribe have not yet settled in their new country; some of whom are in the country which they formerly inhabited; others are dispersed in the adjoining states, and some in the province of Texas. The latter are in a wretched condition. Besides a moderate augmentation of numbers by emigration, they *increase*, but not rapidly, by births.

None of the settled emigrants reside in villages. They have suffered much by sickness. More than 2000 have died since emigration commenced. This mortality, however, is not attributable to the unhealthiness of the country generally, but to such causes as have usually produced similar distresses in the formation of new settlements in wilderness countries.

Notwithstanding their afflictions, and the discouraging losses of property, incident to early settlers, a growing spirit of improvement is widely prevalent. Their houses and fields indicate a good degree of industry. They own a considerable number of horses, cattle, sheep and hogs; wagons, and ploughs. All live by their industry at their homes.

If any engage in hunting, it is for pleasure and not for a livelihood. About six hundred bales of cotton have been raised from their own fields for foreign market the past year.

They have received from Government 88 looms, 220 spinning wheels, and 220 pairs of cards; and are yet to receive 312 looms, 780 spinning wheels, and 780 pairs of cards. Making in all 1000 spinning wheels, 1000 pairs of cards, and 400 looms. These added to what they possessed previously, will make the amount of those articles very considerable. In Red River district are two sets of mills, one of which is a flouring mill, the other a flouring and saw mill; both owned by natives.

They have eight native merchants, who brought into the country the past year about $80,000 worth of goods. Some are mechanics. But a large majority are agriculturalists. Within the tribe are about 600 negro slaves.

For their government they have adopted a written constitution upon republican principles, with slight exceptions. It provides for a general Council, or Legislative body, to consist of the three principal Chiefs, and thirty counsellors chosen annually by the people; that is, ten in each district. The Legislative Council meets once a year. It is supplied with a speaker and clerk. Two of their Chiefs have the vetoe prerogative, but when an act is passed by two thirds of the Legislative Council, it becomes a law. Eighteen *Light Horse* men, enforce the laws of the nation.

They have enacted some wholesome laws relative to the crimes of murder, theft, lost property, fences, widows and orphans, witchcraft, &c. Legal counsel and trial by jury are allowed to all. Severe laws have been enacted against the introduction of ardent spirits; and these laws are enforced with becoming zeal, so that the evil of intemperance, which is so awfully destructive to Indians generally, is now little known in the Choctaw country.

The English mode of dress, has been adopted to a considerable extent, especially among the females, and is daily becoming more common. Many of the Choctaws may properly be classed with civilized men, while a large portion of the residue are little inferior to them in point of improvement.

There are favorable openings for religious teachers in some parts of their country, which have heretofore been very destitute.

Each district has its principal chief. These chiefs are elected by the people for the term of four years.

It is expected that the Chickasaws will settle within the limits of the Choctaw country. In 1828, a delegation of the former visited, and were pleased with it. The Choctaws refuse to sell any of their land, but offer to receive them as their own people, assigning as a reason, that as they "were once one people," it was proper for them again to unite.— They proposed to allow their friends a district of their own. Each district to have its own chiefs and head men, and all to be equally represented in the General Council, and united under one government, to be denominated Choctaw.

It appeared that if this consolidation should be effected, the Chickasaws would become indebted to the Choctaws some two or three thousand dollars, because the former had received from the U. States, the full amount for which they had sold their lands east of Mississippi. Whereas the Choctaws had taken this country, a portion of which they were now giving to the Chickasaws, as a part of the price for which they had sold their lands east of the Mississippi.

These propositions have recently been made to a delegation of Chickasaws who visited the Choctaws on this business; and it is believed, they will be agreed to by both parties.

PRINCIPAL CHIEFS.

Mushulatubbee district,		Joseph Kincaid,
Poshemataha	do.	Nitahachi,
Red River	do.	Thomas Leflore.

AGENCY, &c.

Their agency is south of, and near to Arkansas river, and fourteen miles west of the eastern Choctaw boundary.

Agent and acting Supt. William Armstrong. Compensation $1500, per annum. (Post office at the Agency.)

Clerk, Geo. W. Clark. Compensation		$1000	per an.
Daniel McCurtain Interpreter,	"	300	" "
Jefferson Wallace, blacksmith, }	Red River	600	" "
Big John (native) asst. do. }	district.	240	" "
Christian Spring, blacksmith, }	Poshemata-	600	" "
Harris Frayiuse (native) asst. }	ha district.	240	" "
Lewis Harman, blacksmith, }	Mushula-	600	" "
Tho. McCustain (native) asst. }	tubbee dis.	240	" "

SCHOOLS SUPPORTED BY THE U. STATES, AGREEABLY TO TREATY STIPULATIONS.

1st—Teacher pr. treaty Oct. 20, 1830, resigned.			
2d—Ramsay D. Potts,—compensation		$833,33,	per an.
3d—H. G. Rind,	"	833,33	" "
4th—Joseph Smedley,	1825 "	500,00	" "
5th—Alanson Allen,	"	500,00	" "
6th—Eber Tucker,	"	500,00	" "
7th—Moses Perry,	"	500,00	" "
8th—J. B. Benton,	"	500,00	" "
9th—H. K. Copeland	"	500,00	" "

The number of scholars taught at the above schools is 210.

Two other schools are not supplied with teachers,—making three vacancies.

67 Choctaw youths are at the Choctaw Academy in Kentucky.

PRESBYTERIAN MISSION,
Under the direction of the A. B. C. F. M.

1st. BETHABARA STATION.—On Mountain fork of Little River, Poshemataha district. Commenced in 1832.

Missionaries.—Rev. Loring S. Williams, Mrs. Williams.

A school of 20 scholars taught by John Quincy Adams, a native Choctaw. Instruction is imparted in both English and Choctaw. The scholars are supported by their parents. The teacher is supported by a Youths' Missionary society in Philadelphia.

An English school of 30 scholars, taught half the year by a female, Miss L. M. Williams. Scholars supported by their parents.

Two Sabbath schools, embracing about 60 scholars.

Mr. Copeland, U. States school teacher.

Church.—Organized Aug. 19, 1832.

Native Church members, 115 ⎫
White   do.   5 ⎬ In all 123.
Black   do.   3 ⎭

Since the organization of the Church 30 have died, apparently in the faith of the gospel, and 19 have been dismissed to form another Church.

2d. WHEELOCK STATION.—On Little river, Poshemataha district. Begun in 1832.

Missionaries.—Rev. Alfred Wright, Mrs. Wright.

School.—the scholars supported by their parents. Also, a Sabbath school.

Church.—Organized December 9, 1832.

Native Church members, 62, ⎫ In all 67.
White   do.   5, ⎭

A considerable number of Church members have died, who exhibited evidence of genuine piety.

3d. CLEAR CREEK STATION.—Near Red River, Poshemataha district. Commenced in 1833.

Missionaries.—Rev. Ebenezer Hotchkin, Mrs. Hotchkin, Miss Ann Burnham.

School.—Taught by Mr. Hotchkin, 13 scholars.

Post Office for all the above stations is Eagletown, Choctaw nation, (west.)

4th. BETHEL STATION.—Six miles west of Wheelock St.

Missionaries.—Mr. Samuel Moulton, Mrs. Moulton. Begun in 1834.

School.—12 scholars, some instructed in Choctaw, and some in English. Supported by their parents. Also a Sabbath school.

5th. LUKFOATA STATION.—Ten miles west of Bethabara Station. Commenced in 1834.

Missionaries.—Rev. Joel Woods, Mrs. Woods.

School.—25 scholars.

Church.—Bok Tuklo Church, organized May 18, 1834.

Native members, 18,⎫ 19.
Black do. 1,⎭

Six members of this Church have died in the faith.

School.—Taught by Allen Kerney, a native, 27 scholars. Two Sabbath schools.

6th. PINE RIDGE STATION.—Two miles west of Fort Towson, Poshemataha district.

Missionaries.—Rev. Cyrus Kingsbury, Mrs. Kingsbury, Miss Burnham. Commenced in 1835.

School.—Taught by Miss Burnham, 15 scholars.

7th STATION.—*Missionaries*—Rev. Mr. Byington, Mrs. Byington, and Miss Merrill.

School.—Taught by Miss Merrill, 27 scholars.

Post Office for the three latter stations is Fort Towson, Western Territory.

Another school is on Red River, taught by Jesse Cole, a native, 15 scholars.

Books in the Choctaw language, written upon the common principles of English orthography, and printed upon our English types, have been well received among them; and many of these books are used in schools. In all cases tuition is without cost to the natives, and in most cases, books also.

METHODIST MISSION.

On Little river, 11 miles eastwardly from Fort Towson. Originated in 1831.

Missionaries.—Rev. Moses Perry, U. S. school teacher.

They have several Sunday schools, and several hundred Church members, among whom are four or five native exhorters.

Post Office, Fort Towson, Western Territory.

BAPTIST MISSIONS.

Connected with the Baptist General Missionary Convention.

1st STATION.—Canadian river, 30 miles west of the Choctaw Agency, Mushulatubbee district, commenced in June, 1833.

Missionary—Rev. Joseph Smedley, (Mrs. Smedley has died.) Mr. S. is under appointment and pay of the U. S. as school teacher, in conformity with treaty stipulations.

Post Office, Choctaw Agency, Western Territory.

2D STATION.—About twelve miles westward of Fort Towson, and six miles north of Red River, in Red River district.

Missionaries—Mr. Ramsay D. Potts, Mrs. Potts. Mr. P. is also under appointment and pay of the United States as teacher. according to treaty provisions.

Post Office, Fort Towson, W. T.

3D STATION.—Rev. Eber Tucker, U. States school teacher.

4TH STATION.—Dr. Alanson Allen, " " "

An elementary school book, in the Choctaw language, upon the *New System* of writing Indian, (see an explanation of it under head of Shawanoe Mission,) was compiled and printed at the Shawanoe Baptist Mission House in 1835, and forwarded to the Choctaw country for use.

CHEROKEES.

The Cherokee country is bounded as follows: beginning on the north bank of Arkansas river, where the western line of the state of Arkansas crosses the river; thence north 7 deg. 35 min. W. along the line of the state of Arkansas 77 miles, to the S. W. corner of the state of Missouri; thence north along the line of Missouri, 8 miles, 64. 50 ch. to Seneca river; thence along the southern boundary of the Senecas, to Neosho river; thence up said river to the Osage lands; thence west with the southern boundary of Osage lands, 288¼ miles; thence south to the Creek lands; and east along the northern line of the Creeks, to a point about 43 miles west of the state of Arkansas, and 25 miles north of Arkansas river; thence south to Verdigris river; thence down Verdigris to Arkansas river; thence down Arkansas river, to the mouth of Neosho river; thence S. 53 deg., W. one mile; thence S. 18 deg. 18 min., W. 33 miles, 28. 80 ch.; thence south 4 miles, to the junction of the North Fork and Canadian rivers; thence down the latter to Arkansas river; and thence down Arkansas to the beginning.

They also own a tract, described by beginning at the southeast corner of the Osage lands, and running north with the Osage line 50 miles; thence east 25 miles, to the western

B

line of Missouri; thence south on said line 50 miles; thence west 25 miles to the beginning.

The Cherokees have asked the Govt. of the U. States for a *patent* for their land. With the view of giving them a patent, orders have been issued for completing the survey of their country. The matter will, ere long, be properly reported to the Government and the patent issued.

This is a measure that has been wisely and generously prompted by the Govt. of the U. States. Similar encouragement has been given to divers other tribes to ask for *patents*, and it is hoped that they will be induced to avail themselves of the offer. It is a measure which would contribute greatly towards destroying the influence of mischievous insinuations of white men, that Indians will not be secured in their possessions. It would tend to quiet suspicions among the Indians, and consequently, would be promotive of many advantages.

They own numerous salt springs, three of which are worked by Cherokees. The amount of salt manufactured is probably about 100 bushels per day.

They also own two lead mines. Their salt works and their lead mines are in the eastern portion of their country; and all the settlements yet formed are within this eastern portion, which embraces about two and a half millions of acres.

Politically, this eastern portion of their country is divided into four districts, viz:—Lee's Creek dist., Flint dist., Illinois dist. and Neosho dist.

It may properly be said that the Cherokees have adopted the habits of civilized man. There is no village in their country; they are, generally, agriculturalists; a few are mechanics, salt manufacturers, merchants, &c.

They probably own 3,000 horses, 11,000 horned cattle, 15,500 hogs, 600 sheep, 110 wagons, a plough and often several ploughs to each farm, several hundred spinning wheels, and 100 looms.

They cultivate all kinds of culinary vegetables common to the western country; raise corn in abundance, and have commenced the growing of wheat. Their fields are enclosed with rail fences. They have, generally, good log dwellings, (for a new country,) many of which have stone chimneys to them, with plank floors, all erected by themselves. Their houses are furnished with plain tables, chairs and bedsteads; and with table and kitchen furniture, nearly, or quite, equal to the dwellings of white people in new countries.

Charles Rogers and David Milton each own a grist mill;

A. Brown owns a grist and saw mill; Dr. John Thornton owns a saw mill, and is erecting a grist mill; cost of both when completed will be $2000; John Drew owns a saw mill.

Their form of civil government resembles that of one of our states. Their Legislature consists of upper and lower houses, each of which has a President and Secretary; meets annually in autumn, and may be convened at other times by order of the principal Chiefs.

Each district has two judges, and also two light-horse men, (sheriffs) who are prompt in the discharge of the duties of their trust.

PRINCIPAL CHIEFS.

1st. Major John Jolly—2d. Joseph Vann—3d. James Rogers. Their Post Office is Fort Gibson.

NATIVE MERCHANTS.

David Webber, capital $14000—Lewis Rogers, capital $5000—Lura, Price and Paine, capital $5000.

Dr. John Thornton is a native Physician, who received a medical education in the United States.

AGENCY, &C.

M. Stokes late Sub-agent, now Agent, resides at Fort Gibson. Compensation $1500.

Jack Spear, (native) interpreter. Com.	$300
Jacob Gentry, blacksmith, with an asst. " for both,	840
John Richmond do. " " " " "	840
Harvey Wyatt, do. " " " " "	840
Henry Freshour, do. " " " " "	840
James A. Hart, wheelwright "	600
Thos. N. Findlay, wagon maker. "	600

PRESBYTERIAN MISSIONS.
Under the patronage of the Am. Bd. Com. For. Mis.

1st. DWIGHT STATION.—20 miles west of the state of Arkansas, and 12 miles north of Arkansas river. Commenced in 1829. Has 30 buildings, consisting of dwellings, school house, dining hall, store, barn, carpenter's and blacksmith's shops, &c.

Missionaries.—Rev. Cephas Washburn, Mrs. Washburn, James Orr, Mrs. Orr, Asa Hitchcock, Mrs. Hitchcock, Jacob Hitchcock, Mrs. Hitchcock, Aaron Gray, Miss Stetson, Miss Esther Smith, Mr. Adjuton and Miss Bradshaw. The two latter became connected with the station the preceding year. Post Office at Dwight.

Schools.—The male school consists of 30 scholars, boarded at the cost of the mission.

One half of the scholars are instructed in the Cherokee language, and the other half in English.

The female school embraces 32 scholars; 30 of whom are boarded by the mission, and two by their parents.

The Cherokee Mission Church was organized at Old Dwight, in Arkansas territory.

Native Church members, 43,
Black   "   "   3, } In all 62.
White   "   "   16,

2d. FAIRFIELD STATION.—On Salisaw Creek, 15 miles N. West of Dwight. Originated in 1829.

Missionaries.—Mrs. Palmer went to the state of Ohio for the improvement of her health, where she died. Present missionaries, Rev. Marcus Palmer, M. D., Mrs. Palmer late Miss Jerusha Johnson, Dr. Evans.

School.—50 scholars, taught by Dr. Evans, some in English and some in Cherokee.

Church.—Native Church members, 41,
Black   "   "   4, } In all 50.
White   "   "   5,

Post Office at Dwight.

FORKS OF ILLINOIS STATION. Begun in 1830.

Missionaries.—Rev. Samuel A. Worcester, Mrs. Worcester, John F. Wheeler, printer. For the want of suitable buildings at this place, the printing press has been in operation the past year; in buildings at the late Union missionary station.

Have been printed in Cherokee, upon Guess' System, one small book, Cherokee Almanac, Scripture tracts, and 2d edition of Hymns.

Printed in Choctaw, according to Pickerings' orthography, sundry religious tracts, viz: The book of Jonah, Catherine Brown, The Worth of a Dollar, Neglected Garden, and others; one spelling book.

Printed in Muscogee, according to Pick. orthog. two small books.

Not far from this station, Mr. Samuel Newton, missionary, has a school of 20 scholars, taught gratuitously, but supported by their parents.

Instruction in the Cherokee language, as given at the above mentioned stations, is upon the syllabic system, invented by Mr. Guess, a native Cherokee.

Post Office, Fort Gibson.

METHODIST MISSION.*

Under the patronage of the Arkansas Conference.

Originated in 1831.—Missionaries, Mr. Butolf, Rev. John W. Hunton. Two schools have been taught the past year. Church members, in all 245. Native preacher, Young Wolf. Native exhorters, William M'Intosh, (who is also interpreter,) Samuel Wolf, Titus Grapevine.

The schools are instructed in English, and taught gratuitously. The scholars are supported by their parents.

BAPTIST MISSION.

Under the patronage of the Baptist General Mis. Convention.

Near the eastern boundary of the Cherokee country.— Commenced Nov. 10, 1832.

Missionaries.—Rev. S. Aldrich who was located at this station has died. On his decease the mission was left in charge of Rev. Chandler Curtis, who was temporarily at the station, and who has since left, and has entered upon a mission to the Omahas. The station is at present unoccupied.

The Church was established in the Cherokee nation within the state of Georgia, and emigrated to Arkansas in 1832.

Native Church members, 7
Black   "   "   6 } In all 21.
White   "   "   8

CREEKS,—(Properly MUS-CO-GEES†).

The country of the Muscogees joins Canadian river and the lands of the Choctaws on the south, and the Cherokee lands on the east and north. Their eastern limit is about 62 miles from N. to S.; thence their country extends westward as far as the quantity of wood will admit of habitation.

They own salt springs west of their settlements, not yet worked. The celebrated salt rock, on the Red fork of Arkansas, where from time immemorial, the natives have collected salt, will likely prove to be near the line from east to west, between the Creeks and Cherokees.

---

* We have not received accounts of the condition of the Methodist missions on Arkansas and Red River, as we had expected, and we are therefore compelled to present a more meagre account respecting them than is desirable. This difficulty has been increased in consequence of the frequent changes which take place in relation to the sphere of labor of their ministers severally. It is common for one man to labor only one year in a place.

† Accent the second syllable, and sound g hard.

The settlements which they have formed are on Arkansas, Verdigris, North Fork, and Canadian rivers, on the eastern portion of their lands. None reside in villages. Their fields are invariably enclosed with rail fences. They cultivate corn extensively, so that within their settlements, there have been fifty or sixty thousand bushels more than they needed for home consumptiom. They cultivate the variety of culinary vegetables common among the whites, and raise wheat and highland rice in small quantities.

They spin, weave, sew, knit, and follow other pursuits of industry common in the west.

Their dwellings are composed of logs, erected by themselves, and resembling those of their frontier white neighbors; and many of them are furnished with plain, decent furniture, such as farmers generally own.

They have one grist mill erected at the expense of the owner.

They own horses, cattle, sheep, hogs, ploughs, wagons, cotton spinning wheels, and looms.

The Muscogees are governed by *written laws*, in spirit resembling laws of the United States. These laws are enacted by a general council of the nation, which convenes as often as circumstances require.

Their Sheriffs, who execute the decisions of the Council, and of the Judges, are termed *Light Horse men*, and are exceedingly prompt in the discharge of their duties.

The Creeks have been remarkable for respectful and dignified attention bestowed upon matters submitted to their consideration by officers of the government of the U. States, and by those who are emplyed in labors of benevolence among them. There are favorable openings for benevolent efforts for aiding them in their promising career of improvement; in the western settlements, on the north of Arkansas river, and in the southern settlements upon Canadian river.

Principal Chiefs.—Rolly M'Intosh, Upolhlohola, Neamahtla, Neameeko;* Fushatchemeko, commanding general of the militia; Chilly M'Intosh, and Jacob Derrisaw, judges.

There are chiefs and head men in every settlement, who severally manage their local affairs, these form the general council of the nation which enacts laws, &c.

---

*A perfect account of chieftaincies cannot be given at this time, because some questions respecting them, which have arisen by means of the late emigration are not yet decided.

Late Sub-agent, Francis Audrain.	Com.	$750	per an.
Present Agent, Col. Sanford,	"	1500	" "
Mr. Johnson, blacksmith,	"	480	" "
A striker,	"	240	" "
Joseph Blair, wagon maker,	"	600	" "

BAPTIST MISSIONS.
Under the management of the Bap. Gen. Mis. Con.

1st STATION.—North of Arkansas river, and four miles west of Verdigris river: Missionary labors were commenced in Oct. 1829, by John Davis, a native Muscogee. The station was regularly organized in Oct. 1832.

Missionaries.—Rev. D. B. Rollin, Mrs. Rollin, were missionaries at this station until October last, when they left and located at the Shawanoe mission house. The Rev. Mr. Kellam and wife, of N. York, have recently been appointed missionaries to this station.

Church.—Muscogee Baptist Church was constituted Sept. 9, 1832.

Native Church members, 22
Black   "   "   57 } In all 82.
White   "   "   3

One native female member has died.

2d STATION.—On Canadian river, about twenty miles from the first.

Missionaries—Rev. John Davis, Mrs. Davis, both natives. Mr. Davis began to labor separately in February, 1834.

The school book, and gospel by John, in Muscogee, written upon the New System, introduced among the Muscogees in 1835, by Mr. Davis, have been read by a considerable number. A pious young Creek has been employed to teach upon the New System.

So far as the principles of the New System have been developed by application, increasing expectations have been raised respecting its utility.

The Post Office for all within the Creek country is Fort Gibson, Arkansas.

PRESBYTERIAN MISSION.
Under the direction of the Am. Bd. Com. For. Mis.
Not in operation.

METHODIST MISSION.
Under the patronage of the Arkansas Conference.
Not in operation.

SENECAS, &c.

These consist of three bands, viz:
Senecas, 200
Senecas and Shawanoes, 211 } 461.
Mohawks, 50

The lands of the Senecas proper, adjoin those of the Cherokees on the south, and, adjoining the state of Missouri 13 miles and 30 chains, extend west to Neosho river.

The lands of the mixed band of Senecas and Shawanoes, extend north, between the state of Missouri and Neosho river, so far as to include 60,000 acres.

Seneca Chiefs.—Geo. Curley Eye, 1st Civil Chief.
Comstick, 2d " "
Capt. Good Hunter, 1st War Chief,
Seneca Steel, 2d " "
Small Cloud Spicer,
Thos. Brant, } Head men.
Tall Chief,

Seneca and Shawanoe Chiefs.—Civil John, 1st Civil Chief, Pe-wy-ha, 2d do. Skillowa, 3d do.

Onondaqua Isaac, and Capt. Read, Head men.

Mohawk Chiefs.—Isaac White, Principal Chief,—George Heron, 2d Chief.

They are within the Cherokee Agency.

James Pool, U. S. blacksmith, with an asst.
Compensation for both, $840
Robert Lowther, blacksmith, with an asst.
Compensation for both, 840
A. Halcomb, miller.

As a people, they are in some measure civilized. Most of them can speak English. All cultivate land for support, and grow potatoes and other garden vegetables; and corn sufficient to support them and their live stock. Their fields are enclosed with rail fences. None reside in villages. They own about 800 horses, 1200 cattle, 13 yoke of oxen, 200 hogs, 5 wagons, and 67 ploughs.

They have one tailor, and one cooper; and many, of them can use edged tools.

Their dwellings are neat hewed log cabins, erected by themselves. Within them are bedsteads, chairs, and tables, of their own manufacturing.

They own one grist and saw mill, erected at the cost of the U. States. One of their number, Mr. John Brown, is a merchant.

They are generally favorably disposed towards civilized

habits, and evince a desire to improve their condition, except in the matter of education. They have no school, and desire none.

About 36 persons can read in the Mohawk language, the book of Common Prayer, and the gospel by St. Mark, translated into Mohawk by Captain Joseph Brant in 1787, which contains 505 octavo pages. Also, they read the gospel by St. Luke, translated by II. A. Hill, and printed in 1827, by the American Bible Society.

Among them is a Church of 50 members, denominating themselves Episcopalians. Captain Bowless, who lead in their public religious exercises, is dead. In their service they read portions of the book of Common Prayer, sing, &c. They have no house of public worship.

Their condition calls for the early attention of missionary societies.

OSAGES, (Properly WOS-SOSH-E.*)

The country of the Osages lies north of the western portion of the Cherokee lands, commencing 25 miles west of the state of Missouri; and thence in a width of 50 miles, extends west as far as the country can be inhabited.

About one half of the tribe reside on the eastern portion of their lands. The residue are in the Cherokee country. The latter form three villages, the two larger of which are on Verdigris river, and the smaller on Neosho river. The small band upon Neosho have made some advances towards civilized life. They have fenced small quantities of land with rail fences. A few have erected very ordinary log cabins, and keep a small number of cattle and hogs, and occasionly have used the plough.

The residue of the tribe have made no improvement.† Their fields are small, say one acre or less to a family, and enclosed by the insertion of stakes in the earth, to which a line, or two lines of small poles are fastened horizontally with the bark of trees.

Their huts are constructed by inserting small poles in the ground, the smaller ends of which are bent over the room and united, so as to produce the form of a cone, some eight

---

*O as in not, accent the second syllable.
†The most barbarous tribes keep horses and dogs, and cultivate a small quantity of corn and other vegetables. So that these things are not an indication of improvement.

or nine feet high. On the outside is fastened, either broad pieces of bark, which forms a kind of weather-boarding, or a mat of flags or of bulrushes, sewed together with threads of bark. The fire is placed in the centre, the smoke of which escapes through an aperture in the top. Many of these houses are oblong, and contain two or three fire places, and a great number of families. All the Osages live in villages, in which their houses are crowded close together without order.

Some of their shelters are covered with buffalo or elk skins; and these, as well as those covered with flags, are portable.

Their villages are merely *summer* residences. In winter they change encampments, as the prospects of grazing for their horses suggests.

Within their houses, are neither tables, chairs, nor bedsteads, unless we fancy an exception in a platform raised about two feet high, upon stakes set in the earth. This platform extends along the side of the hut, and may serve for a seat, a table, or a bedstead. This, however, is generally dispensed with.

The leggings and the mockasins for the feet, are seldom worn, except in cold weather, or when travelling in the grass. —Excepting these and the temporary garments fastened about the waist and extending downward, neither the males, nor the married females have any covering for the body, except a buffalo skin, or a blanket, thrown loosely around them. This robe is their garment by day, and their bed at night.

The younger females usually wear a plain strip of cloth, eight or nine inches broad, resting upon one shoulder, and passing over the breast, and under the oposite arm.

The Osages are not fierce and warlike, as has been generally represented; on the contrary, they are uncommonly servile and manageable.

Whilst the condition of depraved man, unimproved, is pitiable in the extreme, there is something noble to be admired in these pupils of nature.

Game near them is exceedingly scarce. They go upwards of one hundred miles before they find buffalo, and then they are frequently either frighted, or whipped back empty by their enemies. They suffer much for want of food and raiment, and they *are wretched in the extreme.*

Favorable openings for benevolent efforts for the improvement of their condition, present themselves in at least four places.

Cleremont is principal Chief. Subordinate Chiefs are Mo-ne-push-ee, Tow-un-ma-kee, Sho-ba-shing-a, Nung-e-wash-e, O-wau-sau-be, Ne-she-mo-ne, Mau-shau-ke-tau.

Their Agency house is among the villages of the north eastern part of their lands.

Sub-agent, P. S. Choteau, salary $750 per an. The interpreter receives $300 per an.

They have a blacksmith with a salary of $480 per an. and a striker with a salary of $240.

The missions to this tribe have been discontinued, and it is now destitute and apparently friendless.

QUAPAWS.

The band of Quapaws was originally connected with the Osages. Some years they resided within the territory of Arkansas. Their lands lie immediately north of the Senecas and Shawanoes; and extend north between the state of Missouri on the east, and Neosho river on the west, so far as to include 96000 acres.

Their country is south east of, and near to the country of the Osages.

Their habits are somewhat more improved, and their circumstances more comfortable than those of their kindred, the Osages.

They are in charge of the Cherokee Agent, Mr. Stokes. S. B. Bright, agriculturalist, appointed by virtue of treaty stipulations.

They are destitute of religious and literary teachers, and ought to be supplied without delay.

PUTAWATOMIES.

By treaty of Chicago, in 1833, the Putawatomies agreed to remove westward, and accepted of an extensive country on the N. E. side of Missouri river, above the state of Missouri; with this they were not satisfied after seeing it. The consequence has been, that about 400 of them who had emigrated with the Kickapoos, and about 1700 later emigrants have remained in an unsettled, and most of them in a wretched condition.

In February 11, 1837, a treaty was held with the Putawatomies of Indiana; by which Government agreed to convey to them by patent, a country adequate to their wants, on the Osage river, within the Indian Territory. These lands have since been selected by order of the Commissioner of Indian Affairs, and also a site for their Sub-agency. They lie south of the Peorias and Ottawas; commencing about 20 miles west of the state of Missouri, and extending west for quantity.

Adjoining the Putawatomies on the east, south, and to some extent on the north, is still unappropriated country, sufficient, it is supposed, for the settlement of the Ottawas of Michigan, the Miamies, the Wyandauts, and the New York Indians.

The Putawatomies now in this country, are expected soon to become located in their permanent home, to which all subsequent emigrants of the tribe will directly go.

Principal Chief of the former emigrants, Qua-qua-taw.

Subordinate Chiefs, Wau-pu-nim, or, white dog, Mich-e-ke-kau-ba, or bad boy, and Nosha-kum.

Sub-agent, A. L. Davis; compensation $750 per an.

BAPTIST MISSION.

Under the patronage of the Baptist General Mis. Convention.

CAREY MISSIONARY STATION, in Michigan territory, was among the Putawatomies. The treaty of Sept. 20, 1828, includes an article favorable to the removal of the establishment to the west of Mississippi. In accordance with which, matters are held in readiness to resume the operations of the institution as soon as the Putawatomies shall become settled.

Since the suspension of labors at Carey, some of the missionaries who belonged to that station, have been employed for the benefit of other tribes. In the mean time, those matters have been in charge of Mr. Robert Simerwell, and Mrs. Simerwell, missionaries; who are at present, at the Shawanoe mission house, awaiting the location of the Putawatomies. On resuming labors at their permanent station, they will be reinforced. Mr. Simerwell has written three small books, upon the New System, which have been printed in Putawatomie. He visits such of the tribe as have reached this country, and teaches upon the New System.

Post Office for Mr. Davis and Mr. Simerwell, Westport, Jackson county, Missouri.

WEAS AND PIANKESHAS.

These are bands of Miamies. Their country is north of the Putawatomies, adjoins the state of Missouri on the east, the Shawanoes on the north, and Peorias and Kaskaskias on the west. It embraces 160,000 acres.

These people cultivate little over an acre of land to a family. Some of their fields are fenced with rails, and some are enclosed with poles only, like those of the Osages. Some of their dwellings are of logs, and others are of bark. They own a few cattle and hogs. Upon the whole it may be said that the condition of this tribe is slowly improving.

Principal Chief, Swan.
Sub-agent, A. L. Davis.
Blacksmith, William Carlisle. Comp. $480 per an. who also labors for the Peorias and Kaskaskias.
Assistant do. "   "   "   " $240 "   "

Presbyterian Mission.—Under the management of the Western For. Mis. So. commenced April, 1834.

Missionaries.—Mr. Henry Bradley, Mrs. Bradley, Miss Nancy Henderson, Mrs. Bradley, Mr. Duncan.

Church.—Constituted in 1836.

Native Church members, 7 } In all 12.
White   "   " 5 }

School.—Attended in the Indian village, but not regularly. Instructed gratuitously in English. Scholars supported by their parents.

Post Office for all connected with this tribe, is Westport, Jackson county, Missouri.

PEORIAS AND KASKASKIAS.

These are also bands of Miamies. Their land lies immediately west of the Weas, adjoins the Shawanoes on the north, and the Ottawas on the west. They own 96,000 acres.

The fields which they have made themselves are small, though they are generally enclosed with rail fences. The number of their cattle and swine is greater than those of their neighbors, the Weas. Some of their dwellings are composed of logs, and others are of bark. The condition of these people is improving.

Chiefs.—White Skin, Peoria Jim, Paschal, and Gemasah.
Sub-agent, A. L. Davis.

C

METHODIST MISSION.
Under the management of the Mis. Society of the M. E. Church.

Commenced in 1832.
Missionaries.—Rev. N. M. Talbot, Mrs. Talbot.
School.—14 scholars, instructed in English, and supported by their parents, excepting one meal a day furnished at the mission house.
Church.—Native Church members, 42*⎫ In all 46.
White   "   "   4 ⎭

The Post Office of all connected with these bands, is Westport, Jackson co. Mo.

OTTAWAS.

This band owns 36,000 acres of land, immediately west of the Peorias and Kaskaskias, and south of the Shawanoes. They have recently settled upon their lands; have made rail fences, and in other respects, commenced in a manner that indicates a disposition to improve their condition. Their condition, as it regards civilization, is similar to that of the Peorias.

Treaties have recently been held with the main body of the Ottawa tribe in Michigan territory, according to which, it is understood that they are to leave that country in the course of five years; and to become settled within the Indian Territory.

Chiefs.—Ok-wun-ox-e and She-kauk.
Sub-agent, A. L. Davis.

BAPTIST MISSION.

Missionaries.—Jotham Meeker, Mrs. Meeker.
While Mr. M. resided at Shawanoe mission in charge of the printing concern, he occasionly visited the Ottawas.— He has recently located permanently among them.

The Post Office for all connected with this band, is Westport, Jackson co. Mo.

---

*In the reports of native members of the Methodist Church, at the different missionary stations, the accounts are not limited to such as are hopefully pious, but they embrace all who are united with the Church, for the purposes of religious instruction and improvement. The numbers who are supposed to be pious, we have not the means of knowing.

SHAWANOES.*

IMMEDIATELY on the north of the Weas and Piankashas, the Peorias and Kaskaskias, and the Ottawas, lies the country of the Shawanoes; extending along the line of the state of Missouri north, 28 miles to Missouri river, at its junction with Kauzau river; thence up Kauzau river to a point 60 miles on a direct course, to the lands of the Kauzau Indians; thence south on the Kauzau line six miles; thence west, with a width of about 19 miles, to a north and south line 120 miles west of the state of Missouri. Their tract embraces 1,600,000 acres.

The Shawanoes reside in the north eastern corner of their country, near the line of Missouri, and near the Kauzau river.

Generally, their dwellings are neat hewed log cabins, erected with their own hands; and within them is a small amount of furniture. Their fields are enclosed with rail fences, and are sufficiently large to yield them corn and culinary vegetables plentifully. They keep cattle and swine, work oxen, and use horses for draught; and own some ploughs, wagons and carts.

In conformity with treaty stipulations, Government has erected for them a saw and grist mill; the cost of which, has been about $8000.

Principal Chief, John Perry. Other Chiefs, Black Feather, Sa-mau-kau, Little Fox, Letho, and Black Hoof.

Agent, Richard W. Cummins; entitled Agent for the northern Indian Agency. Compensation $1500 per annum. Agency house near the line of the state of Missouri, seven miles south of the Missouri river.

1st. Blacksmith,	Comp. $480 per an.
Asst. do.	" 240 " "
2d. Blacksmith, William Donelson,	" 480 " "
Asst. do.	" 240 " "

METHODIST MISSION.

Under the patronage of the Mis. Soc. of the M. E. Church.
Originated in 1830.

Missionaries.—Rev. Thomas Johnson, Mrs. Johnson, Rev. N. T. Shaler, Rev. D. G. Gregory, Mr. Holland.

School.—35 scholars. Instructed in English gratuitously. 19 are supported by the mission, and live in the mission family. The residue receive one meal a day at the mission

---

*Pronounced by themselves, Sau-wau-no; pronounced by other Indians, Shau-wau-no.

house, and otherwise are supported by their parents. Six of them are learning the cabinet making business; and two are learning the business of shoe making.

The missionaries have instructed some of the Shawanoes to read in their native language; and some of these have become teachers of others. Instruction in Indian is systematically placed under the immediate notice of native class leaders of the Church.

A small book in the Shawanoe language, on religious subjects, embracing some hymns, has been published by the missionaries, and introduced among the people of their charge with good effect.

Church.—Native Church members, 80 } 86.
  White   "   "   6 }

Among these native Church members are some who take an active part in the performance of public religious exercises, pray in their families, &c..

BAPTIST MISSION.

Under the direction of the Baptist General Mis. Convention.

Missionaries.—Rev. Johnston Lykins, Mrs. Lykins, Rev. D. B. Rollin, Mrs. Rollin, Mr. J. G. Pratt, Mrs. Pratt. Robert Simerwell and Mrs. Simerwell, are temporarily here.

Native Church members, 9, viz: 3 Shawanoes, one Osage, and 5 Delawares; and 11 white persons; in all 20.

Two native members have died, who gave evidence of genuine piety.

At the Shawanoe station is a printing press, under the management of John G. Pratt.

Since the establishment of the printing press, there have been printed in the Delaware language, three small books; in Shawanoe, three, of a larger size for the Baptists, and one for the Methodists; in Putawatomie, three; in Otoe, three, all small; selections from which have been re-printed for the benefit of the Presbyterian missionaries among the Ioways; in Choctaw, one; in Muscogee, one elementary school book, and the gospel by John; and in Wea, one school book for the Presbyterians. Also, a considerable number of hymns have been printed in various Indian languages. Besides which, there is issued from the press, a small monthly periodical, edited by Mr. Lykins, entitled "*Shauwaunowe Kesauthwau,*"—Shawanoe Sun.

In this periodical, such of the Shawanoes as have learned to read in their own language take a deep interest. Some of them have furnished matter for the work from their own pens.

All of the above prints are upon the *New System* of writing Indian, with a slight exception which occured in the Wea. book. In this system the common types are used, but not for the purpose of *spelling*. That is to say, the learner is not required to repeat the names of two, three, or more letters, from the combination of which he derives the sound of a syllable, and, when he has obtained the requisite syllables, to unite them, and form a word. Vowel sounds are denoted by letters which never vary their several uses. Each of the other letters indicate the position of the organs of speech, preceding or following vowels, with the exception of two or three, as, for instance, S, denotes merely the *hissing*, in which consists the real value of that letter in the word *see*, e. g. this character T, directs the reader to place the end of the tongue to the upper part of the mouth with a slight pressure from within, the voice opens on O, and he necessarily pronounces TO; transpose the characters, and adhere to the same principles, and he necessarily pronounces OT. In like manner all other characters are used, none of which vary their uses.

Hence, when the learner has acquired a knowledge of the use of each character, or in other words, when he has learned the alphabet, he is at once capable of reading.

Indian habits render them averse to study. The labor of becoming familiar with certain sounds, as is necessary in the process of spelling, is, in general, exceedingly irksome, and vastly more so when learning to read English. Upon the New System one may begin to read in a few days, or in a few weeks at farthest, and understanding what he reads, he finds amusement in the exercise.

Upon the New System, what we term *bad spelling* cannot happen. A word is necessarily written precisely as it is pronounced; because each letter is the invariable sign either of a certain vowel sound, or of a certain position of the organs of speech.

The imperious demands of other duties have allowed little time to the few missionaries to attend to teaching the natives to read upon the new plan. Nevertheless, between one and two hundred of the Shawanoes, Delawares, and Putawatomies, have become capable of reading, and some of them can write; a large portion of them are adults, who never would have learned to read English, and some of them old men, who use spectacles. Never since the education of the aborigines was first attempted, have so many learned to read with so little labor and cost, as in the cases under consideration, and this is the more remarkable for this reason, that they are chiefly adults.

Such is the simplicity of the system, that as soon as one begins to read, he is capable of teaching others; and many of the Shawanoes and Delawares, have thus learned to read from their associates, without the knowledge of the missionaries.

The invention of this system is a favorable indication of Providence, which promises much benefit to the Indians.—Could an ample supply of missionaries be brought to the work, all the tribes in the vast wilderness inhabited by them, might shortly be taught to read religious tracts, &c. A revolution among them might speedily be effected, the benefit of which to our country, as such, would be great, and the advantages to them *infinite*.

The English school taught at the mission has been suspended for the present, for want of a teacher.

One male and one female Indian youth, live in the mission family, the former of whom is an apprentice to the printing business.

The Post Office for all connected with the Shawanoes, is Westport, Jackson co. Mo.

DELAWARES, (Properly LIN-NOP-PE.)

The lands of the Delawares lie north of the Shawanoes, and in the forks of the Kauzau and Missouri rivers, extending up the former to the Kauzau lands; thence north 24 miles to the N. E. corner of the Kauzau survey. It extends up the Missouri river to Cantonment Leavenworth, a distance of about 23 miles on a direct course; thence with a line westward to a point 10 miles north of the N. E. corner of the Kauzau lands; and then in a slip only 10 miles wide, it extends west along the northern boundary of the Kauzaus, to the distance of 208 miles from the state of Missouri.

The Delawares reside on the eastern portion of their country, not far from the junction of the Missouri and Kauzau rivers. They generally occupy good hewed log cabins, and have some furniture within them. They enclose their fields with rail fences; keep cattle and hogs, apply horses to draught, and use oxen and ploughs. They cultivate corn and garden vegetables sufficient for their use, and have commenced the culture of wheat.

In compliance with treaty stipulations, the United States

have erected for the Delawares a grist and saw mill, worth about $2950; have fenced and ploughed 105 acres of land, and have erected a school house and buildings attached thereto, worth $278, 50; and have furnished them cattle, worth $2000.

The school house erected by the U. States for a public school is unoccupied.

Principal Chiefs.—Capt. Nah-ko-mund, Capt. Catch-him. and Non non-da-gon.

Agent.—R. W. Cummins.

Blacksmith.—Mr. Newton. Compensation, $480 per an.
Asst. "   "   240 " "

—— Allen, miller, to attend the mills and keep them in repair. Compensation, $500 per an.

METHODIST MISSION.
Directed by the Mis. Soc. M. E. C.

Begun in 1831.

Missionaries.—Rev. E. T. Peery, Mrs. Peery, Rev. W. C. Ellefrit.

School.—16 scholars.

Native Church members, 71 ⎫ 73.
White   "   "   2 ⎭

BAPTIST MISSION.
Under the management of the Bap. Gen. Mis. Con.

Commenced in 1832. This Mission is under the superintendence of Rev. Mr. Lykins, missionary among the Shawanoes. Other missionaries at the Shawanoe station also visit this. The converts here are members of the Church which meet at the Shawanoe mission house.

School.—Ira D. Blanchard and Mrs. Blanchard, teachers. Early in 1837, an English school at the mission house was opened under encouraging prospects, which was subsequently suspended. It will be resumed soon. Forty-five, mostly adults, have been taught to read their own language upon the New System.

The Post Office for all connected with the Delawares is Westport, Jackson county Mo.

KAUZAUS.*

The country of this tribe lies on the Kauzau river, commencing 60 miles west of the state of Missouri; thence in a width of 30 miles, it extends west as far as the country can be inhabited.

About one third of the tribe reside in a village, on the north bank of Kauzau river, within three miles of their eastern boundary; one third a few miles higher up, upon the south bank; and one third on the north bank, about 40 miles from their eastern boundary.

Their language, habits, and condition in life, are in effect, the same as those of the Osages. In matters of peace and war, the interest of the two tribes are blended; and they are virtually one people.

Like the Osages, the Kauzaus are ignorant, poor, and wretched in the extreme; and are as uncommonly servile and easily controlled by white men who mingle with them.

All live in villages, where their huts are crowded closely, without order in their arrangement. Besides their houses of bark, and of flags, constructed like those of the Osages, they have a few of earth. These are circular and in form of a cone, the wall of which is about two feet in thickness, and is sustained by wooden pillars within. Like their other huts, they have no floor except the earth. The fire is in the centre, and the smoke escapes directly above. The door is low and narrow, so that in entering, a person must half crawl. The door, as in their other huts, is closed by a skin of some animal suspended therein.

At the lower village, the Govt. of the U. S. has erected for the principal Chief a good hewed log house; and within the last year, fenced and ploughed three fields for them; one containing 130 acres, one 140, and one of six acres; in all 276 acres. Also, ploughed 10 acres previously fenced.— They have now 297 acres of land which have been fenced and ploughed by the Government. These fields were by the Iindians, pretty well cultivated in corn the last year, so that they have been better supplied with food than usually. This seems to have inspired them with new hopes. They have promised to do still more the present year, and have expressed an inclination to breed cattle and hogs.

In relation to this matter, Government has adopted the true policy. That which uncivilized Indians are most in

---

*Different persons have at various times, written the name of this tribe differently, as suited the fancy of each. We have chosen to adhere to the pronunciation of the natives themselves, which is Kau-zau.

want of is a *field* made ready to receive seed, which they may cultivate with their own hands. Different habits, want of skill in making fence and ploughing, and want of implements of agriculture, present discouragements rather too great for the first efforts for improvement. When the earth is mellowed for seed, and the crop secured by a fence, the amount of labor required will be so amply, and so speedily rewarded, that they will readily cultivate grain, and garden vegetables sufficient for their use. Relieved from the sufferings of hunger, their attention to other labors, and to instruction in letters and religion will become practicable.

The former policy of employing agriculturalists for the Indians, merely to set them an example, to give them advice and verbal instructions in agriculture, and to repair their implements, has proved entirely unsuccessful. To employ farmers to raise grain, &c. for the consumption of the Indians, would be equally unsuccessful. It would merely indulge idleness, and the prevailing apathy from which we desire to arouse them.

The buildings formerly occupied by their smith, their former agency buildings, a house for the residence of one to aid them in agriculture, and a large stone building erected for the Chief White Feather, are all within the country of the Delawares, 23 miles east of the Kauzau lands.

The wretched condition of the Kauzaus prefers strong claims upon the sympathies of a Christian public, and the prospect of success holds out great encouragement to benevolent efforts, for the amelioration of their condition.

Principal Chief.—Nam-pa-war-rah, or White Feather.—Other Chiefs, are Ka-he-ga-wa-ta-ne-ga, Whin-ra-shu-ga, Ka-he-ge-wa-chi-chi, Min-gar-na-che; Ka-he-ga-shing-a.

Agent.—R. W. Cummins.

Interpreter.—Joseph James, a half Kauzau and half Frenchman. Compensation, $300 per annum.

Blacksmith.—Compensatin, $480 per an.
Asst. "   "   250 " "

METHODIST MISSION.
Under the direction of the Mis. Soc. of the M. E. C.
Undertaken in 1835.
Missionaries.—Rev. William Johnson, Mrs. Johnson, Post Office, Westport, Jackson county Mo.

KICKAPOOS.

THE country of the Kickapoos lies north of the Delawares, extending up Missouri river to a point 30 miles direct; thence westward, about 45 miles; and thence south 20 miles, to the Delaware line. Including 768,000 acres.

They live on the south eastern extremity of their lands, near Cantonment Leavenworth.

In regard to civilization, their condition is similar to that of the Peorias.

Principal Chiefs.—Pos-sa-che-haw, Ken-u-kuk, Mash-e-na, Kickapoo and Musk-o-ma.

Agent.—R. W. Cummins.

Blacksmith.—John P. Smith. Compensation, $480 per an.
Asst. "   "   240 " "

The U. S. have erected a school house and other buildings, attached thereto, worth $300.

School.—13 scholars, instructed in English. U. S. school teacher, Rev. J. C. Berryman of the Methodist mission.—Compensation, $480 per an.

A Church [house for worship] has been erected by the U. S. for the Kickapoos, the cost of which was $700. Also, a saw and grist mill, have been completed, worth $3000.

METHODIST MISSION.

Supported by the Missionary Society of the Methodist E. Church, under the management of the Missouri Conference. Commenced in 1833.

Missionaries.—Rev. J. C. Berryman, Mrs. Berryman.

Mr. B. receiving his support from the Methodist Missionary Society, applies the salary which he receives from Government as teacher, to the support of the native scholars, and to other purposes of the mission. The mission buildings, and the U. S. school house, are on the same ground.

The Post Office for all connected with the Kickapoos, excepting the Agent, is Fort Leavenworth, Western Territory.

KICKAPOO RELIGIOUS SOCIETY.

Kenekuk, commonly called the Kickapoo Prophet, is a Chief, who is a porfessed preacher, of an order of religion which he himself originated some years ago. His adherents are about 400 in number, about one half of whom are Putawatomies, and some of whom are small boys and girls.

He professes to receive all that he teaches, immediately from the Great Spirit by a supernatural agency. He teaches abstinence from the use of ardent spirits, the observation of the Sabbath, and some other good morals. He appears to have little knowledge of the doctrines of Christianity, only as his dogmas happen to agree with them. By some, however, it is thought that he and his party are improving in Christian knowledge and morals. We should be happy to possess evidence of this fact, but we do not, and are compelled to doubt it.

Congregational worship is performed at regular seasons, and lasts from one to three hours.

It may be amusing, as a matter of curiosity, to see a specimen of the effusion of a savage mind in framing a system of religious worship.

The religious opinions of Indians who have received no impressions from other people, are remarkably uniform; excluding the absurdity of idol worship, and embracing the fundamental truths of the existence and overruling providence of God, man's accountability to him, the immortality of the soul, future rewards and punishments, a consciousness of guilt for offences against God, &c. their external ceremonies embrace sacrifices for the purpose of propitiating the Deity; and festivals accompanied with music, dancing, speeches, &c. for the indulgence of their religious impressions. The formula of the Prophet, has evidently not been framed from ideas purely *Indian*. It seems to resemble more the ceremonies of the Roman Catholics, than the forms of any other Christian denomination.

Besides the speeches of the Prophet, their religious exercises consist of a kind of prayer expressed in broken sentences, often repeated, in a monotonous sing-song tone, equaling about two measures of a common psalm tune. All in unison, engage in this; and in order to preserve harmony in words, each holds in his or her hand, a small board about an inch and a half broad, and eight or ten inches long, upon which is engraved arbitrary characters, which they follow up with the finger, until the last character admonishes them that they have completed the prayer.

These characters are five in number, the 1st represents the heart, the 2d, the heart and flesh, the 3d the life, the 4th their names, the 5th their kindred.

During the service, these characters are gone over several times, the first time the person supposes himself to be on earth; next, to be approaching the door of the house of God, in heaven, then *at* the door, &c.

Putting their finger to the lowest character, they say:
O our Father, think of our heart as thou dost of thy door, &c.

O our Father, bless our heart and its clothing, [meaning the flesh] make it like thine, as strong as thine, &c. like thy house, the door of thy house—the ground about thy house, thy staff, &c.

O our Father, put our name with thine, think of it as thou dost of thy house, door, ground about thy house, staff, &c.

O our Father, make our kindred like thine, thy house, door, ground about thy house, staff, &c.

The repetitions are exceedingly frequent, almost the same words of a short sentence being repeated many times, and all aparently unmeaning.

Certain men are appointed to use the rod on occasions of worship, for the purpose of maintaining order. The rod, also, is applied by these men as a kind of church discipline in cases of transgression.

The offender, whose crime may be known only to himself, applies to one of the four or five persons who are authorised to use the rod, and states that he has committed an offence for which he desires the whipper to inflict a given number of stripes upon his bare back. Having received the flagellation, which frequently brings the blood, the penitent immediately shakes hands with the executioner and others near, returning thanks for the favor conferred upon him, and declaring that he feels himself relieved from a heavy burthen.

The Prophet has two or three wives.

OTOES.

This tribe claims a portion of land in the fork between Missouri and Platte rivers. But their country is understood to extend southward from the Platte river, down Missouri to Little Ne-ma-ha river, a distance of about 40 miles; thence their southern boundary extends westward up Little Ne-ma-ha to its source; and thence due west. Their western and northern boundaries are not particularly defined. Their southern boundary is about 35 miles north of the Kickapoo lands.

By treaty, such of their tribe as are related to the whites, have an interest in a tract adjoining the Missouri river, and extending from the Little Ne-ma-ha to the Great Ne-ma-ha, a distance of about twenty miles, and ten miles wide. No Indians reside on this tract.

The condition of these people is similar to that of the Osages, and Kauzaus. They take the buffalo with less difficulty and danger than the former, and consequently suffer less with hunger.

The Otoes have been induced by the Govt. of the U. S. to locate on the north bank of the Great Platte river, about six or eight miles west of Missouri river. About one half of the tribe spent the last summer at this place; and erected houses of earth according to the description given of similar houses among the Kauzaus, though many of them are much larger. Some of these earthen houses are fifty feet in diameter.

The Government has erected for them a school house, at this place, and has fenced and ploughed for them 130 acres of land.

Agent.—Maj. John Dougherty. Comp. $1500 per an.
Martin Dorion, interpreter.
Blacksmith.—Samuel Gilmore. " 480 " "
Asst. " " 210 " "
Agriculturalists.—Joseph L. Dougherty, 600 " "
James Case. " 600 " "
U. S. *School Teacher.*—Rev. Moses Merrill. Comp. $480 per an.

BAPTIST MISSION.

Under the management of the Baptist General Mis. Convention.

On the north bank of Platte river, six miles from its junction with Missouri river, and about 200 miles a little west of north from the mouth of Kauzau river. Commenced, October, 1833.

Missionaries.—Rev. Moses Merrill, Mrs. Merrill.

A small school has been sustained a part of the past year.

Post Office for all connected with this tribe, is Fort Leavenworth, West. Ter.

OMAHAS.

The country of the Omahas adjoins the Platte river on the south, and the Missouri river on the N. E. their northern and western boundaries are indefinite.

They have made a village on the south west bank of Missouri, at a place chosen for them by the Government, about 120 miles above the Otoe village. There they have built houses of earth, similar to those of the Otoes.

D

Their condition is in all respects, similar to that of the Otoes, who are their friends and allies.

Principal Chief.—Big Elk.
Agent.—J Dougherty.
Blacksmith.—Comp. $480 } Located on the new site for
Asst. "   "   240 } Omaha settlement.
U. S. School Teacher, Chandler Curtis.

BAPTIST MISSION.
Undertaken by the Bap. Gen. Mis. Con.

Rev. Chandler Curtis, who had transiently been at the Cherokee mission, and Mrs. Curtis, late Miss Colburn of the Creek mission, left the Shawanoe mission house early in November last, with the view of establishing a mission at the Omaha village. The Board of Missions has made a liberal appropriation for the erection of mission buildings; and Mr. Curtis has received the appointment from Govt. of school teacher, according to treaty stipulations.

Post Office for all connected with this tribe, Fort Leavenworth, West. Ter.

PAWNEES.

The country of the Pawnees is westward of the Otoes and Omahas. Their boundaries are not definite. Their villages are chiefly on the Great Platte, and its waters.

In their habits and condition, they are farther removed from those of civilized man, than any tribe which we have noticed. Some of their huts are of earth, like those spoken of among the Kauzaus. In some instances, they continue to cultivate the earth with the shoulder bone of the buffalo. This being tied to a stick for a handle, serves the purposes of a spade or shovel. They obtain buffalo with less difficulty than others, excepting the Otoes and Omahas.

Agent.—John Dougherty.
Blacksmith.—Charles C. Rentz. Comp. $480 per annum.
Hitherto the Pawnee smith has been located at the Otoe Agency.

BAPTIST MISSION.

The mission to the Otoes, which at first embraced the Omahas, was undertaken with reference to the Pawnees also; and this design is still maintained.

PRESBYTERIAN MISSION.
Under the direction of the Am. Bd. Com. For. Mis.
Begun in 1834.
Missionaries.—Mr. Allis, Mrs. Allis, Rev. John Dunbar, Dr. Benedict Saturlee. Not yet located.

For the purpose of acquiring the language of the Pawnees, of extending their acquaintance among them, and of securing their friendship, these missionaries, separately, mingle with the Indians, and go with them on their hunting excursions. This course is as judicious as it is honorably self-denying.

Among the Pawnees is an inviting field for four missionary establishments.

Post Office for all connected with the Pawnees, is Fort Leavenworth Indian Ter.

PUNCAHS.

The Puncah is a small band, originally from the Omaha tribe, on the Missouri, in the northern extremity of the country spoken of as the Indian Territory. Their circumstances are similar to those of the Pawnees. They have no missionaries.

OTHER BAPTIST MISSIONARIES.

The author of this publication, and his wife, have been missionaries to the Indians ever since the year 1817. In August, 1828, they removed from among the tribes around Lake Michigan, to what is now termed the Indian Territory. Their circumstances differ from those of other missionaries, inasmuch as their labors have not been located to a particular tribe, especially since they left the tribes of the north; but they have extended their labors to places and matters generally; and they support themselves without cost to the Missionary Convention. Their Post Office is Westport, Jackson co. Mo.

MISSIONARIES IN GENERAL.

Excepting the missionaries noticed in the last article, and a few who have received appointments from Government as school teachers, all others, of every denomination of Christians, are supported by the societies which patronize them severally; but they receive no more than a bare support.

The amount allowed varies according to the expensiveness of living at each station, and is fixed by the missionary societies, so as barely to cover the necessary current expenditures of the several missionaries. None of them, therefore, receive any compensation which they can lay up as their own personal property. By this means, the voluntary surrender of the missionary to labors of benevolence for the benefit of the Indians, places him beyond the influence of temptation to acquire property. He does not receive even a promise of support for his family, should they out-live him; but, he trusts all to Providence.

In the action of Government, missionaries are recognized as being in its service, and, like Agents, Sub-agents, and others authorised to reside in the Indian country, enjoy its protection. Should a missionary be convicted of a violation of the laws regulating intercourse with the Indian tribes, Government would expel him; but this circumstance would not be an obstacle to prevent the occupying of the station by an approved missionary.

By a regulation in the Dept. of Indian Affairs, misssionaries are required to report to the U. S. Agent within whose Agency they are, their establishments, and their operations, so far as schools are concerned; stating the cost of their buildings, their location, the names of the teachers, the number of scholars, their success &c.

Rev. Johnston Lykins exercises a general agency, extending to the various tribes within the territory, according to instructions given him from time to time, by the Baptist Bd. of Missions; and is duly authorised to fulfil this trust, by authority from the proper officer of Government.

Rev. Thomas Johnson is Superintendent of all the missionary stations of the Mis. Soc. of the M. E. Ch. north of the Cherokees.

Rev. Peter M. M'Gowan, under the direction of the same Society, is Superintendent of Methodist missions among the Cherokees and Creeks. Post Office, Fort Gibson.

Rev. Joseph Kerr, late Superintendent of the missions of the Western Foreign Missionary Society, has discontinued his labors.

Missionary Societies are voluntary associations, composed of members of the several Christian Churches in the United States, which have embarked in the cause of missions.

The office of the American Board of Commissioners for Foreign Missions, is in Boston, Mass. Secretaries, Rev. Rufus Anderson, and Rev. David Green.

The office of the Board of Managers of the Baptist General Missionary Convention, is also in Boston, Mass. Corresponding Secretary, Rev. Lucius Bolles, D. D. . Treasurer, Hon. Heman Lincoln.

The office of the Western Foreign Missionary Society, is in Pittsburgh, Pa. Cor. Sec. Walter Lowrie, Esq.

The office of the Missionary Society of the Methodist Episcopal Church, is in New York. Corresponding Secretary, Rev. N. Bangs, D. D.

WANT OF MISSIONARIES.

In a little over two years, the whole increase of missionaries, of the three denominations of Presbyterians, Methodists, and Baptists, has been *two* males and *eleven* females.

In the same length of time, the increase of Indian population has been *nineteen thousand seven hundred and thirty-eight.* The increase of the Indians has been about 43 pr. ct. and the increase of male missionaries has been less than one pr. ct. This is a startling fact, which we desire our readers to notice particularly.

We have been pleading for more benevolent, devoted, energetic men, to teach the Indians the practices of virtue and the path to heaven. But so unsuccessful have we been, that in a period of less than three years, the wants of the Indians have augmented more than forty times as fast as the number of the men we have prayed for, and who were necessary to supply those wants. Why are we so far behind in the work of Indian reform? We never had half as many men as the nature of the work required; and yet, if we would make the amount of benevolent effort for a given number of Indians only what it was three years since, we must at once bring into the field 43 more missionaries.

This fact must be a severe rebuke to a benevolent people, such as are now addressed. Have we not been guilty of a neglect of duty? and what extenuation of our guilt can we plead, either before God or man? Were we in darkness, we should not be blameable for not holding to others the lamp of life. Were we struggling with the embarrassments of wars, with persecutions, or any common calamity which necessarily demanded increasing attention to ourselves, neglect of others, might receive some paliation. This is not our situation. Never was a people so highly favored in all these respects as we. Neither have we been kept from works of benevolence by increasing obstacles to render success more doubtful. So far from it, we have the most unquestionable assurance that a time so favorable for rendering substantial benefit to the Indians, never before presented itself to the benevolent.

Provisions of the Government of the United States, for the education of the Indians within the Indian Territory, and for their improvement in civilization generally.

BESIDES the annual appropriation of $10,000 for education purposes, a portion of which is applied within the Indian territory, and besides the schools which receive support from Government already mentioned, the following provisions have been made, viz: for the

KAUZAUS.

By treaty of 1825, 36 sections of *good* land were to be selected and sold, and the proceeds applied to the education of Kauzau children *within* their country.

The number of acres was 23,040. The value of which, at the minimum price of Government land, would be $28,800.

The cost of feeding, clothing, lodging, and instructing an Indian youth, if applied in conjunction with benevolent institutions, within the Indian country, may be kept within $50 per an. At this rate, the proceeds of the Kauzau lands, had they been sold, as above calculated, would keep fifty children in school eleven years. Should the scholars be supported by their parents, the number which might be educated with the sum just stated, would be quadruple the above. A school house, books, and teacher, for 40 scholars, could be furnished for $500 per annum. At this rate, their education fund, to wit, $28,800, would keep 200 children in school eleven years.

These lands have been selected; but unfortunately, the selection was not made by examination of the country, but upon the plats. The consequence is, that more than half the land is of little value.

The state of Missouri was allowed seminary lands, in the same district of country. The claims of the Kauzaus were entitled to precedence. Missouri fixed the minimum price of her lands at two dollars per acre, and it was not until the greater part was sold, that the price was reduced to $1 25 per acre.

Had the Kauzau lands been selected according to the provisions of the treaty, not an acre would have remained until this time unsold, and it could have been sold for two dollars per acre, which would have amounted to the sum of $16,080.

The difference between this sum and the calculation at $1 25 per acre is $17,280. This latter sum has been lost to this education fund. It would have kept 31 Kauzau children in school more than 11 years; and, if the youths had been supported by their parents, it would have kept 124 children in school the same length of time.

But the loss will more than double this calculation, as will be perceived by what follows:

The amount of Kauzau lands which had been sold prior to Oct. 1, 1835, was $8,457\frac{80}{100}$ acres. The quantity remaining unsold was $14,582\frac{20}{100}$ acres. A great portion of this unsold land, never will be sold for any thing. the loss, therefore, to the Kauzaus will be very considerable.

The $8,457\frac{80}{100}$ acres mentioned above, have been sold for $1 25 per acre, amounting to $10,571. This sum is in the U. States Treasury.

By the same treaty of 1825, provision was made for the application of $600 per annum, to aid them in agriculture.

OSAGES.

The treaty of 1825 provides "that the President of the U. S. shall employ such persons to aid the Osages in their agricultural pursuits as to him may seem expedient."

Under this provision, the sum of $1200 a year has been expended by the Government. This has been done without rendering any substantial benefit to the tribe, beyond the fencing and ploughing of 70 acres of land, mentioned on the preceding pages.

If the annuity of $1200 per an. were expended in fencing and ploughing land, as was done the last year for the Kauzaus, it would prepare for seed two fields of 75 acres each, or 150 acres each year, until they should need no more.

The same treaty of 1825, requires that 54 sections of land be laid off under the direction of the President of the U. States, and sold, and the proceeds applied to the support of schools for the education of the Osage children. The number of acres is 34,560. The value of which, if sold at the minimum price of the U. S. land, would be $43,200.

This sum, if applied according to our calculations for the Kauzaus, would support and instruct in school 100 children eight years and a half. Should the children be supported by their parents, the above sum would afford instruction to 400 children eight and a half years.

These lands have not been selected. It is hoped, that in view of the losses which have been sustained by the Kauzau education fund, the selection of the Osage education lands will not be long deferred.

DELAWARES.

The treaty with the Delawares of Sept. 1829, provides that 36 sections of the *best* land within the district which was at that time ceded to the U. S. be selected and sold, and the proceeds applied to the support of schools for the education of Delaware children.

These lands have not yet been selected. The quantity of acres, is 23,040; the vlaue of which, at the minimum price of Government land, would be $28,800. According to our calculations for the Kauzaus, this sum would feed, clothe, and educate 59 youths 11 years, or if supported by their parents, it would keep 200 children in school 11 years.

In the country in which the Delaware education lands are to be selected, the low grounds along the water courses are generally of the first quality, and the uplands are generally worthless, being exceedingly broken and rocky.

Measures have very properly been adopted for selecting and selling these lands without delay.

PUTAWATOMIES.

By the treaty of 1833, the Putawatomies are allowed the sum of $70,000, "for purposes of education, and the encouragement of the domestic arts." They desire that, for the present, only the interest of this sum be expended. The Interest of $70,000, at five per cent. per anunm would be $3500, a year. This would keep at a mission school in the Indian couutry, 70 Indian youths; or if the children should be fed and clothed by their parents, it would afford instruction to 280, kept perpetually in school.

Also, in the same treaty, is provided the sum of "$150,000 to be applied to the erection of mills, farm houses, Indian houses, and blacksmiths' shops: to agricultural improvements, to the purchase of agricultural implements, and [live] stock; and for the support of such physicians, millers, farmers, blacksmiths, and other mechanics, as the President of the U. S. shall think proper to appoint."

KICKAPOOS.

The treaty of Oct. 24, 1832, provides that the U. States shall pay $500 per annum, for ten successive years, for the support of a school, purchase of books, &c. for the benefit of the Kickapoo tribe, upon their own lands.

The school house and teacher which have been furnished them, have been in conformity with this stipulation.

The same treaty, provides 4000 dollars for labor and improvements on the Kickapoo lands. If the sum of 4000 dollars should be applied in fencing and ploughing prairie land, it would prepare for receiving seed, 12 fields of 40 acres each. But it is probable, that for the Kickapoos, it would be desirable to make some fields in wood lands, where the cost of preparing them would be greater than in prairie.

OTOES.

The treaty of 1830, secures to this tribe agricultural implements, to the amount of 500 dollars annually, until the year 1840. The treaty of Sept. 1833, continues this annuity of 500 dollars, ten years longer, to be paid in the same articles.

The treaty of 1830, provides for a blacksmith, and an assistant blacksmith, for the term of ten years, and longer, if the President of the U. S. shall think proper. The smiths have been employed and are at work for them.

The treaty of 1833, stipulates that a flouring mill, to operate by horse power, shall be erected for the benefit of the tribe.

Also, the value of 1000 dollars, in live stock, will be given them; but it will remain so far under the control of the proper officers of Government, that the Otoes will not be allowed improvidently to waste it.

Two farmers are to reside in their country to assist them five years, and longer by the direction of the President of the United States. These two farmers could fence and plough 50 acres of land each year, and thus furnish them with 250 acres of land ready for seed, and enclosed in fields of convenient dimensions.

The two farmers have been employed, and have already fenced and ploughed 130 acres of prairie land for them.

The treaty of July, 1830, secures to sundry tribes mentioned therein, 3000 dollars annually for the term of ten years, for the education of their children. Of this sum, the Otoes are entitled to 500 dollars yearly.

In the treaty of 1833, an additional annuity of 500 dollars is provided for education, for the term of five years, or longer. While these education annuities continue, they would support in a boarding school 20 Indian youths, or they would furnish instruction to 80 who were fed and clothed by their parents.

OMAHAS.

The treaty of July, 1830, provides that an annuity of 500 dollars shall be paid to the Omahas, in agricultural implements, for ten successive years, and longer, if the President of the United States shall think proper.

Also, a blacksmith and the necessary tools, shall be furnished them the same length of time. The blacksmith is at work at their new village.

A treaty has been held with this tribe, by which, their claims to a tract of country which has lately been attached to the state of Missouri have been extinguished. This treaty provides for fencing and ploughing 100 acres of land.

The sum of five hundred dollars for the term of ten years, is to be applied to the education of their children. This sum would keep in a boarding school, in the Omaha country, ten children, during the continuance of the allowance, or 40 youths the same length of time, should they be supported by their parents.

PAWNEES.

The treaty of October, 1833, stipulates that the United States shall pay to the Pawnees annually for five years $2000 worth of agricultural implements, and this annuity is to be continued longer than five years, if the President deem it expedient.

Also, the value of $1000 in oxen, and other live stock is to be delivered to the tribe whenever the President of the U. S. shall believe that they are prepared to profit by them. This stock, after being taken into the tribe, is to be placed in charge of the proper authorities of the United States, to prevent the Indians from prematurely destroying it, through improvidence. This is an excellent arrangement. The live stock which was paid to the Osages and the Kauzaus, was a disadvantage to them instead of a benefit. Their cultivated grounds were not enclosed with fences, and consequently they could not keep cattle and swine. In addition to this, their habitual improvidence was such that they had not patience to wait for future advantages from stock. The stock was immediately consumed for food, and only served to indulge them awhile in indolence.

Further, a sum not exceeding $2000 per annum for ten years, is to be expended in support of two smitheries, with two blacksmiths in each, together with iron, steel, &c.

Four grist mills are to be erected for them, to operate by horse power.

Four farmers are to be provided for them, for the term of five years. The country of the Pawnees being more remote from white settlements than that of the Osages, and others, the cost of enclosing and ploughing land would be increased. But if Government should thus employ their farmers, 100 acres each year could conveniently be prepared for seed. this would give them five hundred acres of cultivated land enclosed with fences.

The sum of $1000 a year for ten years, is to be allowed for the establishment of schools. This sum will support in school 20 children during the ten years; or if they should be supported by their parents, 80 children could be kept in school the same length of time.

CHEROKEES.

It is stipulated in the treaty of the 6th May, 1823, that "the U. S. will pay $2000 annually to the Cherokees for ten years, to be expended under the direction of the President of the U. S. in the education of their children *in their own country,* in letters and the mechanic arts. Also, $1000 towards the purchase of a printing press and types."

By the treaty of December 29, 1835, the sum of $150,000 is provided for the support of common schools, and such a literary institution of a higher order, as may be established in the Indian country. The above sum is to be added to an education fund of 50,000 dollars, which previously existed, making the sum of 200,000 dollars, which is to remain a permanent school fund, the interest of which shall be consumed. The application of this money will be directed by the Cherokee nation, under the supervision of the President of the U. States.

CREEKS.

The treaty with the Creeks of March 24, 1832, stipulates that "3000 dollars, to be expended as the President may direct, shall be allowed for the term of 20 years for teaching their children."

At a treaty on Arkansas, Feb. 14, 1833, it was stipulated that 1000 dollars annually, during the pleasure of the President and Congress, should be applied, under the direction of the former, to the purposes of education.

These two annuities, amounting to 4000 dollars, would support 80 scholars in a boarding school, or would instruct constantly 320 scholars who should be supported by their parents.

CHOCTAWS.

The treaty of Sept. 1830, provides for keeping 40 Choctaw youths at school, under the direction of the President of the U. S. 20 years. Also, the sum of 2,500 dollars is to be applied to the support of three teachers of schools, for the Choctaws 20 years.

There is also an unexpended ballance of former annuities, amounting to about 25,000 dollars, which is to be applied to the support of schools at twelve different places, at each of which, a school house has been erected by the U. S. and paid for out of this fund.

MILITARY POSTS,

Within the Indian Territory.

FORT TOWSON.

In about north lat. 24 deg. and west long. from Washingington, 19 deg. It is within the Choctaw country, six miles north of Red River, and six miles west of the Kiamishi river, about 50 miles west of the eastern boundary of the Choctaws; 238 miles from Little Rock, Arkansas state; 280 miles from Natchitoches, La. and 120 miles from Fort Smith on the Arkansas river.

The erection of the Fort, at present occupied, was begun in the autumn of 1831. The situation is pleasant, the water is good, and the place is esteemed healthy.

FORT GIBSON.

Fort Gibson is on the east bank of Neosho river, two miles north of Arkansas river, and two and a half miles below the junction of Arkansas and Verdigris rivers. It is within the country of the Cherokees, and about 43 miles west of their eastern boundary; about 55 miles on a direct course from Fort Smith, and about 140 miles north of Fort Towson.

It was established in 1823, by removal from Fort Smith.

Fort Gibson, or the mouth of Verdigris river, may be considered the head of steam boat navigation.

FORT LEAVENWORTH.

Fort Leavenworth is on the S. W. bank of Missouri river, 25 miles above the mouth of Kauzau river, and about 20 miles west of the state of Missouri. It was established in 1827.

The post is at present, head quarters of the U. States Dragoons.

FORT COFFEE.

Fort Coffee is on the south bank of Arkansas, above Fort Smith, about 12 miles west of the state of Arkansas. It was established in 1825.

FORT SMITH is unoccupied.

TRADING POSTS.

Among the Cherokees, Joel M. Bryan has a trading post.

Among the Creeks, A. P. Choteau and Seaborn Hill, have each a trading establishment, with a branch on Canadian river.

The American Fur Company have a trading house near the Osage Agency; one among the Weas and their neighbors; one among the Shawanoes and their neighbors; one among the Kickapoos and Putawatomies; one among the Kauzaus, and one on Missouri, above the mouth of the Platte river, in the vicinity of the Otoes, Omahas, Pawnees, and others.

AFFINITY OF LANGUAGES.

Chickasaw and Choctaw are dialects of one language.

Putawatomies, Ottawas and Chippewas speak the same language.

The language spoken by the Osages, Quapaws and Kauzaus is the same. That of the Otoes and Iowas is the same;

E

and between these and the Osage, Quapaw, Kauzau, Omaha, Puncah, and Winnebago languages, there is a near affinity.

Weas, Piankashas, Peorias, Kaskaskias, and Miamies, severally, speak dialects of the same language.

There is a near resemblance between the Pawnee and Arickara languages.

WAR.

All the tribes in the territory, except the Pawnees, Otoes, Omahas and Puncahs, are liable to insult and injury from remote tribes, especially those towards the south west, and even the Pawnees and their allies have their enemies in the *far west.*

A portion of the Pawnees reside in the south, upon Red River. Until lately, warriors from the Pawnees of the south, and of the north, united with the Camanches of the remoter south west, and formed war parties, which annoyed traders to Santa Fe, and were particularly inimical to the Osages and Kauzaus, as well as troublesome to many hunting parties of the emigrant tribes.

In 1833, treaties of peace were concluded between the northern Pawnees and all the other tribes within the Territory, and *all smoked the pipe of peace.*

In 1834, negotiations of peace and friendship were held with the southern Pawnees. For twelve or eighteen months, those treaties were strictly observed by all parties, and there is up to this time *professed* friendship existing among all the tribes, excepting the Omahas and Pawnees. But we are sorry to say, that in two or three instances, the peace has been disturbed by others.

In 1835, a hunting party of Delawares, some four or five hundred miles from their settlements, towards Santa Fe, killed twelve Pawnees. The Delawares say that they detected the Pawnees in the act of stealing their horses from camp about break of day, and fired on them and killed one. The Pawnees fled, and were pursued. They sought either concealment or shelter in a sink hole in the earth. There they were surrounded and all murdered excepting one. The Delawares having wreaked their vengeance, were called off by their leader, who said "they had killed enough," and allowed one Pawnee to escape.

The Delawares, by one or two of their party, sent home to their tribe the scalps of eleven of the murdered, as trophies of a noble deed. But they were much disappointed on finding that their scalps produced regret and grief instead of savage rejoicings. The partiality of the Delaware chiefs for their own party, induced a desire to exculpate it as far as practicable. Nevertheless, they showed evident signs of dissatisfaction with what had happened.

There is some reason to hope that the Pawnees will not retaliate.

The Kauzaus have also murdered one or more Pawnees in violation of the late treaties of peace and amity. We have not obtained the particulars of these outrages, though we have seen the bones of one of the murdered.

Sometime in the summer of 1836, the Pawnees, from causes which we have not heard stated, murdered an Omaha woman. The Omahas resolved to avenge the murder, and fitted out a war party, which had a skirmish about the first of April, 1837, in which four or five Pawnees were killed. A Pawnee female was subsequently killed. War parties have since gone out. Hostile feelings exist, and preparations for offence and defence have been made.

Among these rude people, quarrels are much like those of children—begun and ended with facility. The U. S. Agent for those tribes will no doubt, speedily put a stop to hostilities.

The former Creek emigrants were of what is termed the M'Intosh party. In 1828, a delegation of Creeks from the east of Mississippi, was sent to examine the country designed by the Government for the settlement of the Creek nation west of Mississippi. The delegation was kindly received by the emigrants; and, lest their kindred remaining on the east of the Mississippi should feel some aversion to emigration, under an apprehension that they might meet with some angry feelings among the M'Intosh party, on account of the murder of old General M'Intosh in the former wars, they held a council and prepared a written communication to their countrymen in the east, in which they affectionately invited them into their new country, under assurances that former grudges were buried.

Since the commencement of the recent rapid emigrations, which have been hurried on by the late hostilities in the Creek country east of the Mississippi, some fears have been justly apprehended that old quarrels might be resuscitated through imprudencies to which human nature is incident.— But in view of the kind feelings of the early emigrants in 1828, as stated above, of the good sense which belongs to the chiefs of that party, and the sound judgment of the chiefs of the later emigrants, we believe that all hostility and political variance may be prevented by a prudent management on the part of the Govt. of the U. States.

The principal cause of difficulties now, will be the question which party shall have the ascendency. But all such party feuds, may be quieted by the organization of the Indian Territory. That organization, it is true, will not alter the internal regulations of any tribe without its consent. But both parties of the Creeks will perceive that in joining the proposed confederacy, and enlarging their code of laws, all their chiefs and head men may be honorably provided for with office, without the inconvenience of putting down any one. This tranquilizing measure, would amalgamate the parties in one.

We are confident that serious difficulties will not really arise out of the circumstance of General M'Intosh's death in a former war; and we hope that Government will early afford them an opportunity of an amicable, and honorable settlement of all questions relative to the right of chieftaincies; and of entering upon a career of improvement among men of the highest attainments; of which the Creeks are physically and mentally capable.

Special attention from our Government is due to the Creeks, and it is hoped that it will not be withheld. Some of them have recently left the land of war. They are related to the Seminoles, where war has scarcely terminated. That any of them should have had the temerity to take up arms against the U. States, is deeply to be regretted, and the fact is in itself unjustifiable. Nevertheless, there are extenuating circumstances in the affair, which ought not to be overlooked. Some, at least, of the causes which led to the late Creek hostilities, may be traced to unprincipled white men, whose misdeeds could not be prevented by our Government. Many of the Indians, both Creeks and Seminoles, knew that they had been grossly imposed on. Driven to desparation, they sought either redress or revenge. They sought a redress of grievances in an improper way; involving Government in war, for crimes of individuals, which it could not prevent.

We may still shake the rod over them, and by that means save our scalps, and prevent them from scalping one another, but such a course would not gratify the feelings of forbearance and sympathy which have been elicited by considerations suggested above.

GOVERNMENT.

Most of the tribes within the Territory have expressed a

desire to become united in one civil compact, and to be governed by laws similar to those of the United States.

Should the U. States, as it is contemplated, provide for them a form of civil government, suited to their circumstances, a few among each of the emigrant tribes, and many among some of them, would be found capable of filling responsible offices in the transaction of the affairs of their government.

The time is fully come for the adoption of this course.—Objections to it, founded upon the uncultivated condition of the minds of the Indians, if they ever had any weight, have none now. Multitudes of Indians well understand the value of property, duly appreciate the individuality of right in property, and desire its security by equitable laws. Many of them desire to have a sufficient portion of land for a farm set off to them severally. They deprecate the agency system, and its concomitant principles, so far as they exist among them. They are ready to become a component part of the Commonwealth of the U. S. They desire no special privilege to be granted to them, nor special restriction to be imposed upon them, further than what would be necessary to their welfare, until the effects of the peculiar disabilities under which they have hitherto been placed, shall have so far disappeared, both among themselves and us, as to allow them safely to take an equal place among existing states of the Union.

The organization of civil government among the tribes of the Territory becomes more necessary, as the Indian population increases. It has increased about 18000 the last year, and the increase will probably be much greater the succeeding year.

It is known to every body that peace among Indian tribes must ever be precarious upon the principles of savage life. In order to tranquilize turbulent spirits, and to paralyze mischievous efforts, the tribes must be united under the influence of law; so that wrongs may be redressed without resorting to the savage custom of retaliation. They must not be left as so many distinct communities, or petty sovereignties, each independent of all others. In such a state of things, physical strength will be the ruling principle, and the tomahawk must decide controversy. Their interests as a people must become united, so that harmony of feeling may prevail.

Suppose that the state of Missouri were disorganized, and the inhabitants divided into nineteen bands, united under as many chiefs, with their subordinates, no one any more under the restraint of law than the individuals of the several Indian tribes, and the whole unconnected with the states adjoining them: would it be strange if, in such a state of anarchy, we should become troublesome neighbors to one another and to those around us? We could hope for nothing better among the Indians; because human nature is the same among them that it is among us.

If, however, they become united among themselves, like the several counties of a state, and if the confederacy become a component part of the United States, and territories, all cause of quarreling among themselves, or of giving trouble to us, would be as effectually excluded, as it is from the state of Missouri at present.

That they are prepared to become thus organized under a territorial form of government, there can be no doubt. The Choctaws, Cherokees, Creeks, Senecas, Weas and Piankashas, Peorias and Kaskaskias, Ottawas, Shawanoes, Delawares, Putawatomies, and Kickapoos, embracing a population of about 44484, may be said to subsist by domestic industry. When the savage state has so far disappeared that people obtain subsistence at their homes by agriculture, they are undoubtedly prepared to submit to laws. But should the matter be delayed, upon the supposition of unfitness, so far from becoming better prepared, precisely the reverse must be the fact. *Nothing* can be gained in Indian improvement by delay in this matter, and *every thing* may be lost.

Now the tribes are concentrating their settlements in the Territory, each brings into it, its imperfections as well as its better traits of character. In their present incoherent condition, we may easily conceive of conflicting views, and interests, which would be reconciled by the introduction of the means which coalesce discordant materials on our side of the line, and by no other.

Objections to giving the Indians a territorial form of goverment, made on constitutional grounds, are evidently untenable. According to the invariable action of our General Government, of the state governments, and of every other government that has had any thing to do with the Indians, they have only been tenants at will, as it regarded place of residence, while in other respects they were required to submit to just such intercourse regulations as were prescribed for them. We have enacted laws for the regulation of Indian Affairs, and have repealed them at pleasure. We have decided what property they might sell and what they might not, and with whom they should deal. In a word, we have in all respects controlled them and their affairs, as far as we chose. We have appointed our Agents to reside among them, to enforce the intercourse regulations which we had created. If, therefore, we should now introduce among them, regulations resembling those by which one of our territories is governed, though more simple, it would be in strict conformity with the principle of managing Indian affairs, adopted by all civilized powers. We might propose something objectionable in its *form*, because of its inexpediency, but the principle would be that upon which we have always acted. The constitutionality of the act could no more be called in question than the constitutionality of all our acts regulating trade and intercourse with the Indians, ever since the existence of our government. Even were we to introduce a code of laws, and compel them to submit to them, it would be no departure from former principles.— We say again, that we have already introduced precisely such regulations as *we* chose, and have required their submission to them. If what we have done has been no violation of the constitution of the U. States, then, what we propose to do cannot possibly be a violation of that instrument.

But, it is not proposed to use coercion in this matter. It is proposed merely to afford them an opportunity of accepting and adopting a form of civil government. The overture is to be made, and if any tribe choose not to accept it, the tribe will remain in the same relation to the Government and to other tribes as it did before.

If, after exercising the power of controlling Indian affairs ever since we have been acquainted with them, scruples should in this matter, and at this late day, arise relative to the moral right of doing so, and it be contended that the Indians had a right to choose for themselves, it will be more a matter of surprise than of regret.—Yes, it is desirable that the matter be left to their choice; and let Government make the overture, and we will warrant its acceptance.

We repeat it, the time has fully come to *act* upon this matter. The tribes within the Territory, are prepared to live under the laws of civilized nations. More than forty thousand of the present inhabitants of the Territory, (if we include the late emigrant Creeks,) *have adopted written laws;* which in general are based upon republican principles, and are similar to those of their white neighbors; others have it in contemplation to do the same. Almost all of the less civilized tribes have expressed a desire to form the confederacy and adopt laws, as is proposed, viz: The Pawnees, Omahas, Otoes, Kickapoos, Kauzaus, Putawatomies, Delawares, Shawanoes, Weas and Piankashas, Peorias and Kaskaskias, Ottawas, and Osages.

They who are farthest advanced in civilization, will necessarily take the lead in the affairs of a civil and general government. Their talents and acquirements will be rewarded with an ascendency among their less informed countrymen. The latter also understand this, and rejoice that some of their own *red skinned* people have become capable of managing their affairs, and hope to profit by their superior endowments.

It is understood that the Cherokee, Choctaw, and Creek tribes, will severally desire to establish a territorial government seperately for themselves, and as such, become united to the Governmeut of the U. States. That they should be thus inclined at the first blush of the subject, is not surprising. It indicates a degree of national pride, which augurs well for the success of the experiment proposed. But, upon due reflection, the same reasons which induce the several counties of one of our states to prefer a union in order to constitute a body politic of convenient magnitude, rather than for each to form a state of itself, will induce those tribes to prefer a union.

WHOLE NUMBER OF INDIANS.

Tribes East of Mississippi.

Indians in N. England and New York,	4,176
Indians from New York at Green Bay,	725
Wyandots in Ohio and Michigan,	575
Miamies,	1,100
Winnebagoes,	4,500
Chippewas,	6,793
Ottawas and Chippewas of Lake Michigan,	5,300
Chippewas, Ottawas and Putawatomies,	8,000
Putawatomies,	1,400
Menominees,	4,200
Creeks,	4,000
Cherokees,	16,000
Chickasaws,	5,400
Choctaws,	3,500
Seminoles,	2,600
Appalachicolas,	400
	68,669

Tribes West of Mississippi river.

Sioux,	27,500	Black feet,	30,000
Iowas,	1,200	Camanches,	7,000
Sauks of Missouri,	500	Crows,	4,500
Sauks and Foxes,	6,400	Arrepahas, Kia-	
Assinaboines,	8,000	was. &c.	1,400
Crees,	3,000	Caddoes,	2,000
Grosventres,	3,000	Snake and other	
Arickaras,	3,000	tribes within	
Cheyennes,	2,000	the Rocky Mts.	20,000
Minatarees,	1,500	Tribes west of the	
Mandans,	1,500	R. Mountains,	80,000
Indians in Mexico,			3,600,000
Near the northern boundary of the government of the U. S. and within the territories claimed by other governments,			1,520,431
Tribes within the Indian Territory,			66,000
In all,			5,400,000

The population becomes more sparse as we proceed northward, to a clime less accommodated to the comforts of uncivilized man, and becomes more dense as we proceed southward to a more genial clime, where subsistence is more easily obtained.

This table is conjectural in regard to the remote tribes, and is probably very erroneous.

PLEA FOR THE ABORIGINES OF NORTH AMERICA.
(*Continued from No. 2.*)

In extending our plea for the Indians, we must necessarily touch upon some points previously noticed, because our remarks have been too brief to do justice to them; and because their importance in relation to the work of Indian reform is such, that they should be constantly held up to view.

In all our designs and doings for the benefit of the aborigines of our country, we should keep in mind that, with the slight exception of a few within the States, they are inhabitants of *one vast country*. They are not separated from each other and thrown into divers divisions by intervening settlements of other people. The portion of North America.

which has been settled by the European race, is yet small compared with that inhabited by the originals.

We have taken some pains to estimate the probable number of the Indians. The data of our calculations were given in the preceding number of this work. We supposed that in the settlements of Mexico were 3,600,000, and that within what might more properly be termed the *wilderness* portion of the country, were 1,800,000. Making in the whole 5,400,000.

Since making the foregoing statements, we have become satisfied that our estimate of Mexican Indians were too low by at least one million. We therefore feel pretty confident that we are still below the true amount, in stating at this time the number of Mexican Indians at 3,600,000, which added to 1,800,000 in the more uncultivated parts of the country, and within the United States, make 5,400,000.

This estimate does not include about 2,500,000 mixed offspring of whites and Indians, and about 1,000,000 of descendents of Indians and negroes.

We have no doubt that as the affairs af Mexico become better known to us, developements respecting the original inhabitants will acquire additional interest, both in relation to numerical strength, and to their former and present condition.

When the Spaniards first entered Mexico, their extravagance was unparalleled in magnifying the numbers of the inhabitants, as well as their civil institutions and general improvements in the arts of life. Hundreds were magnified to thousands; and in a country of poor, naked, miserable, barbarians, headed by what are now termed *Indian Chiefs*, they found Empires, and Kingdoms, Emperors, Kings, Lords, &c. It is less astonishing that their exaggerations should have gained credence in the dark days of superstition in which those florid accounts were made, than that any should believe them at this time. We are surprised to find modern writers referring to the ancient Mexicans, as a people far advanced in civilization. Hereafter, we design to prove by the showing of the Spaniards' story itself, and by a comparison of the Mexicans with other aboriginals of the continent, that, notwithstanding the former had made some advances *towards* civilization, they were far from it. They were still in the savage state, a poor miserable people; and, like all savage tribes, defenceless for want of the organization of civil institutions among themselves, and for the want of courage in war.

The extravagance of the Spanish accounts alluded to, are

to be accounted for in a vain desire to magnify their own achievements in conquering empires and dethroning kings, with a handful of soldiers.

Eclesiastics, too, for similar reasons, gave florid accounts of what they had done for the conversion to the Christian religion, of those kings and kingdoms. To have told the world that those among whom they had achieved such religious wonders, were a poor, artless people, in their native condition—a condition beneath that of any other nation that had been known to inhabit the world—that they possessed nothing more of religion than necessarily attached itself to rational beings; and that, although they had received the sign of the cross, and had submitted to other Catholic mumeries, neither their minds, morals, nor comforts, had been improved thereby, would not have comported with their vanity.

While we thus caution our readers against the exaggerated accounts, alluded to above, we would have it understood, nevertheless, that the original inhabitants of Mexico undoubtedly numbered many millions. The mildness of the climate, the luxuriance of the soil, and the facility with which food may be obtained in warm countries, from exuberant plants of spontaneous growth, or cultivated vegetables, all tended to the increase of the population.

In no part of North America, has the havoc of European arms been so great as in Mexico. Hundreds of thousands were destroyed in the course of a few years. While surrounding tribes remained inimical to the Spanish settlements, the inhabitants of Mexico proper, became a conquered people; and subject to such regulations as the Spaniards chose to adopt. Those regulations were less hurtful to the Indians than the intercourse regulations of the Anglo-Americans. Without entering into a comparison of those intercourse regulations, it is sufficient for our purpose, in this place, to state the fact, that within the territories of the U. States, and of Great Britain, the tribes, in times of peace, have rapidly melted away, while in Mexico it has been otherwise. As yet, we are not sufficiently acquainted with the subject, to be able to state precisely the extent to which the regulations of the one country, have been more hurtful than those of the other, but that there is a vast difference in favor of those of the Spanish Americans, is proved by the fact that there they continue to live by millions, whilst with us, their decline has been much more rapid.

In our enterprises of benevolence for the relief of the Indians, we have commonly left out of consideration such as were in Mexico. But why should we exclude them? Their condition, it is true, in regard to food and raiment, is no doubt a great deal more comfortable than that of Indians wholly uncivilized; but it is, perhaps, not superior to that of the more civilized Choctaws, Cherokees, and Creeks; and, in regard to mental cultivation, they are no doubt greatly behind those tribes. We risk little in saying, that the nineteen tribes of Indians, within what we term the Indian Territory, can more easily be united, and rendered subordinate to wholesome laws, than the Indians of Mexico. Further, so far as the matter of religion goes, (and it should go farther in inducing benevolent action, than every other consideration,) the Mexican Indians are certainly in a condition more deplorable. than the Pawnees, Camanches, or any others of the uncultivated tribes of our acquaintance.

If, then, in the mere matters of eating and wearing, joined to a very imperfect knowledge of agriculture and the mechanic arts, they are only equal to some of our more comfortable neighboring tribes, while in every other respect they are not superior to the most ignorant and depraved, no good reason can be conceived for not including them within the sphere of benevolent effort for that unhappy race of men.

In these views, we anticipate a cordial acquiescence by American citizens in general. In our incipient* labors, therefore, in the work of Indian improvement, we contemplate 5,400,000 souls as the recipients of our munificence.

We have supposed that one cause of the general indifference to Indian improvement, of which we have heretofore complained, is an impression that there are but few to derive benefit from any thing that may be done for them. But, certainly five and a half millions of souls in one country, and that country adjoining our own, constitute a body of people sufficiently large to prefer strong claims upon our efforts, and to promise in their improvement a large reward of gratification in the success of our labors for their relief.

It is remarkable, that in any thing which has been done in relation to the Indians, either politically or religiously, they have not been contemplated as a *whole*—as a nation, or body of people, but our thoughts and acts have extended to one tribe at a time. The tribe is composed of but a small number of souls, and the interest which we feel in contriving, is equally small; and the energy with which we act upon

---

* We say *incipient labors*, because to the work of Indian reform has recently been applied impetus unknown before, and which we trust will be augmented, until, becoming commensurate to the design, it will ultimately terminate in success.

those contrivances correspondingly feeble. We are aware that this habit of which we complain, corresponds with the ideas and habits of the Indians; but this fact, so far from furnishing an apology for our error, makes it appear the more glaring. Why should the institutions which civilized nations have formed in relation to a savage people, and which were designed to draw them off from the rudeness of savageism, be in principle so far assimilated to the spirit of their rude customs as to cherish their continuance?

It is, doubtless, greatly to the disadvantage of the work of Indian reform, that it is cut up into pieces.—This is intended for the benefit of this tribe, and that for another tribe, without reference to the relation which should be sustained between the tribes. The work is undertaken in reference to tribes severally; and not as a work begun for the benefit of the five and a half millions of Indians, introduced among the tribes near us as a part of the main body.

We therefore remind our readers, that the organization of an Indian Territory, is a work begun for the benefit of the five and a half millions of inhabitants in this vast country. A portion of this country, of suitable extent for one Territory only, is at present under consideration, in our political and religious action upon the subject.

This Territory becoming organized, and the experiment promising to become successful, other suitable places will be selected for like purposes. Instead of leaving the aboriginals scattered over this vast Territory, under the influence of their savage customs, and giving place to us only by the diminution of their numbers by death,* it is proposed to collocate them in divers places, under circumstances which will allow them to live, and to cultivate the arts and sciences as other civilized people. By this process, they will make room for the wide spreading of white population; not by becoming exterminated, but by the improvement of their condition.

Upon the subject of the organization of the Indian Territory, we are happy to be able to present some interesting documents, from a source which adds greatly to their worth.

---

*This is lamentably true. We commonly speak of having crowded the Indians farther and farther back into the wilderness, but it would be more correct to say that we have crowded them out of the world. Where are the millions which lined the Atlantic coasts, and inhabited the countries now marked out into states? Have we driven them west? They are not here! The aborigines here are far less numerous than they were in those days when the millions existed where our settlements now are. No; they are gone! Here are remnants of some of those tribes, but too few in number to make the population equal to what it was here formerly.

F

To these our readers are referred with great satisfaction. They will discover, that in the progress of this question, for the last ten or twelve years, Government has, though slowly, yet constantly been approaching the true ground in this affair; and here, it will be perceived by the references, which we now make, that it is fairly reached. Public documents from the Congress of the U. States, fairly respond to the calls that have been made by the Executive. These documents state the true cause of Indian decline and misery; point out the sure and the only remedy; and take hold of the subject with the design of carrying out practically the principles which they avow.

"*In Senate of the United States, March* 15, 1836. *Read and ordered to be printed.*—Mr. Tipton *made the following Report, with Senate bill No.* 159:

"*The Committee on Indian Affairs, to whom was referred the bill supplementary to an act entitled "An act to provide for an exchange of lands with the Indians residing in any of the States or Territories, and for their removal west of the river Mississippi," approved the twenty-eighth of May, eighteen hundred and thirty, present the following report:*

"That, in treaties and in all other laws regulating trade and intercourse with the Indian tribes, is expressed, either directly or by implication, the desire of the Government of the United States to perpetuate the existence of the aboriginal inhabitants of our country, and to elevate them to the rank of civilized man. To this expression of kind feelings has been added positive efforts for the improvement of their condition.

"These efforts have not been rewarded with success proportioned to the benevolence which prompted them. Causes, the influence of which has operated to produce this failure, are too numeros to be noticed in this report. The committee will limit their remarks to such only as appear to claim attention in reference to the accompanying bill; some of which at least, have not, in their opinion, heretofore received sufficient attention. It has generally been supposed that, in four particulars, the aboriginal race were under the influence of peculiarities of constitution, namely: 1st, An irresistible thirst for ardent spirits. 2d, An unnatural predilection for war. 3d, An inordinate fondness for the hunter state; and, 4th, An unconquerable aversion to the improvement of condition. Failures of efforts for the improvement of the condition of the Indians have generally been attributed to some or to all of these causes.

"In reference to the 1st, to wit, an irresistible thirst for ardent spirits, the committee would remark, it could hardly be said to be a peculiar propensity of the savage state, because it did not exist in that state until their acquaintance with the whites. They suppose that the indulgence of the Indians in the use of intoxicating liquors must have its origin, and must find its support, in other causes than in a peculiarity of constitution. The Indian is known to relish food common to man, he slakes his thirst at the same fountain and with equal gratification with the white man, and sound philosophy seems to deny that he possesses any peculiarity of appetite.

"The inordinate indulgence in the use of ardent spirits of the nations near us, is justly attributable to their degradation as a people. No odium is attached to drunkenness to forbid it; and placed where the prospect of attaining to some enviable station in life, or of accomplishing some desirable purpose, cannot operate to promote a love of life, they indulge their present appetites, regardless of future consequences. In this matter there can be but little difference between men whose prospects have been blighted by a reverse of fortune, and those whose fortunes never furnished prospects. Both are exposed to strong temptations to intoxication.

"In relation to the 2d, namely, an uncommon passion for war, the committee would remark, that they feel unable to reconcile a strong predilection for war to the want of courage which has ever been evinced by Indian tribes in their original condition. A few whites have been able at any time to form settlements amidst thousands of opposing Indians. If the generation of nations that have grown up on our own borders have been courageous, it strengthens the argument that the principle of courage has been fostered by their proximity to the whites, and that it does not, in a high degree, prevail in the savage state.

"The history of Indian warfare among themselves, and of the formation of acquaintance between white men and the various tribes, corroborate these statements.

"3d. That they naturally possess a peculiar attachment to the hunter state, seems also to lack proof. A partiality for a particular branch of business is formed by external circumstances, and cannot be innate. The child of a blacksmith becomes fond of that branch of business from the circumstance of seeing his father at the forge, and of being taught to hope for a living therefrom; but it would be absurd to suppose that the son was born with a predilection for smithing in consequence of his father being a smith. Hunting is a *business* in savage life, and war too, is as properly a business of life as working at the forge, and the principles which may be applied to the latter case, are equally applicable to the two former. None can suppose that parents entail upon posterity a fondness for particular branches of business in life, and yet this is presupposed in the assumption that the Indians possess an inborn fondness either for hunting or for war. White men who have resided among them from early life are no less fond of hunting than the natives, and they are generally more resolute in war.

"4th. The causes of their indifference generally to the improvement of their condition, will find a full explanation in a brief notice of the things which are *essential* to our improvement, should we discover that they were not within the reach of those necessary things.

"Indians possess such vague notions of the first principles of social life, that the property of the husband and of the wife are kept separate, as belonging to them separately; the combined interests of the parties mutually stimulating to united efforts for the acquisition of the comforts of life, as exists among civilized nations, is not known here. Hence follows want of discipline towards their youth, who generally grow to maturity without parental restraint, and prepared only for savage life; the evil increases as the principles of polygamy prevail.

"Among a people who have not adopted the radical principles of social compact, we cannot expect to find established order in regard to any thing. Every one does what is right in his own eyes; hence the reward of industry is not secured. The more indolent and improvident spunge upon the more industrious and economical, to the suppression of a spirit of enterprise..

"They are not subordinate to law; hence the custom of retaliation prevails. They are subject to no government except the slight restraint which chiefs may exercise. The man inherits the chieftaincy or he acquires it by feats of savage life, or from his age, combined with his fortune, in having numerous relations and acquaintances to feel from some cause a degree of dependence upon him; but the control of the chief can be rejected at pleasure by any one, or by any set of persons, who may choose to secede and form a separate band; or if they become dissatisfied with the conduct of the chief, he may be summarily dispatched, and another may take his place.

"No international laws exist between the various tribes; each is independent of others, and each band is independent of other bands of the same tribe, except as fortuitous wants may render it otherwise. This independence extends down to individuals, destroying in its course the social relations essential to improvement, not sparing even those between husband and wife, parents and children.

"These things belong to savage life, and, like a torrent to which no effectual barrier is opposed, carry on in savageism all the remote tribes. Whether it can become generally otherwise, with those on our own borders, remains yet to be tested. But as we are entering upon an experiment in Indian reform, it should be particularly noticed, that hitherto our intercourse regulations have been such as to render it impracticable for them to change their condition in regard to the above defects. We have recognized each tribe as independent of all others, and have acknowledged the chiefs of each. No prospect of any other condition in these respects has been placed before them. They are taught to remain contented with their own several little spheres.— Should uncommon intellect prompt some to aspire to a less degraded condition, the attainment of the end is impracticable; they cannot become united, for many of the tribes are kept asunder by intervening white population, and where this is not the case, our policy restricts each tribe to its isolated condition. Even here, within the small sphere of each tribe, the mind has not latitude for enlargement by the exercise of sovereignty; they are mere dependents upon others, and upon others of separate interests. They exercise barely so much volition in the management of their affairs as others choose to permit.

"While this state of degradation has deprived them of incentives to improvement, their decline would have been less rapid could they have lived wholly alone. But this could not be; there was of necessity an intercourse between them and their white neighbors: in this intercourse, as might have been expected in their case, they were more exposed to the temptations of vice than to the influence of the restraints of virtue. Thus situated, they have in no instance flourished as a people; and thus situated, it might be asked, what people upon earth would flourish? Apply the case to ourselves; abolish all international laws with neighboring nations, the constitution of the United States, and all law within every State, until no civil organization of society remained, not even so much as that which would acknowledge that an individual could have a separate right to land; until even husband and wife were not bound together for mutual and social interests; and until the laws of parental restraint ceased to operate, and every one, both in youth and in manhood, was left to do what seemed right in his own eyes; and our destruction would be rapid; a few generations would reduce us to wretchedness as deplorable as that of the Indians.

"Our policy in relation to Indian affairs is of European origin; had our intercourse regulations originated in that knowledge of human nature and that regard for human rights which characterize the United States at this day, they would doubtless have been different from what they are.

"It was early perceived that the insular condition of the tribes severally had a tendency to keep them destitute of law, and that without law it was in the nature of things impossible for them to improve in the arts and sciences. Hence, as early as the treaty of September, 1778, encouragement was held out to the Delawares to unite with the other tribes, and for the confederacy to 'form a State, whereof the Delaware nation should be the head, and have a representation in Congress;' but difficulties attended the execution of the design of forming the tribes into a civil community, which were not easily either foreseen or obviated—among these, the selection of a suitable place was not the least. Had they been located in the interior of the United States, the history of the past plainly foretold their decline in future. At any point on the sea coast or on the shores of the lakes, they would have been equally insecure.

"It appears that increasing interest was taken in this subject as we follow its history down toward the present time. Mr. Monroe, in 1825, recommended the cllection of the tribes for the purpose under consideration. But even then the difficulty of finding a suitable place for them had not vanished. He proposed locating some of them in the west, whither many of them have already gone, and another portion of them in the Ouisconsin Territory, between Lake Michigan and the Mississippi river.

"As we improved our knowledge of the character of the country west of the territory of Arkansas and the state of Missouri, and southwest of Missouri river, the difficulties which hung upon the matter of selecting an eligible place disappeared. It was ascertained that here was an immense body of fertile soil, elevated and healthy in appearance, beyond almost any new country that had been settled on the western waters—well adapted to culture and grazing, and lying within the latitudes within which the tribes generally resided. This country is west of all white settlements. In length, it lies north and south, in breadth, the portion which is sufficiently wooded to make it convenient for the residence of man, is about two hundred miles. Beyond this, extending north and south farther than the district under consideration, is an open and almost woodless plain, four or five hundred miles in width, in which, on account of the scarcity of wood, no human being ever had a permanent residence. No vestige of Indian villages is found within this vast prairie. It is uninhabitable. With this uninhabitable region immediately on the west of the Indian Territory, they cannot be surrounded by white population. They are on an *outside* of us, and in a place which will ever remain an *outside*.

"Further: as we approach this country, the water courses meet us coming from west to east, and thus directing commerce not into, or through the Indian country, but from it eastwardly. This region, too, is under the control of the Government of the United States; not being subject to the claims of any State, out of which embarrassing questions of jurisdiction might arise. The localities of the place are such, also, as to diminish temptation to the discontented to stir up hostilities towards the United States: no other place, within the jurisdiction of the United States, furnishes equal security from the malign influence of foreign emissaries.— They are far from our northern boundaries. They cannot be approached from the west, on account of their great distance from the ocean, the intervening mountains, and especially on account of so much prairie immediately adjoining them. They are accessible to foreigners only on the south, through the province of Texas; and here they adjoin a country of so much prairie, that a barrier to foreign intercourse is interposed, almost equal to that on the west.

"Indians never make war upon our frontiers without having looked out a place of retreat for their women and children. In the event of war, they could not retreat westward, because no hiding place could be found within this vast prairie.

"In addition to the resources of the country before mentioned, nature has been liberal in her supplies of lead and iron ore, of salt water, and coal. The time has been when the game sought by the hunter was near and abundant; but, in a country of so much prairie, and so little wood, the game, for want of hiding places from their pursuers, and in which to foster their young, soon becomes scarce. Every year the buffalo retire further from the settlements towards the Rocky Mountains, and smaller animals become more scarce. This circumstance, it is believed, will promote the improvement of the Indians. Even at this time, few, comparatively, belonging to the emigrant tribes, rely upon the chase as the chief source of supplies.

"Here it is proposed to locate the tribes within and near our settlements. Within the country described by the bill, are, at this time, seven indigenous tribes, numbering, in the whole, about twenty-two thousand; and portions of twelve emigrant tribes, numbering about twenty-seven thousand; in all, forty-nine thousand. The bill merely proposes to make such provisions for them as will enable them to lay hold of such means of improvement as we well understand are necessary to sustain our own elevated condition, and without which man cannot be in the possession of the blessings of civilization.

"It is believed to be essential that the Indian should be taught the rights of persons, and all the relations of domestic life, the various titles forming the law of personal property, the division of property and labor, that each is heir to the fruit of his own labor, and that he shall be protected in its enjoyment. These, it is believed, are the foundations of society, and form the first step to human happiness.

"It is proposed to unite the tribes as one people, and to allow them to meet annually by delegates to enact laws for the government of the whole, without infringing the rights of the tribes severally to manage their own internal affairs. In general, the nature of those laws is left to themselves, under the impression that this course would be most gratifying and encouraging to them, and would most readily inspire them with the disposition so necessary to improvement, of thinking and acting for themselves, and because they could better judge to what extent the establishment of law would at present be acceptable to them; but lest through inexperience they should enact laws that would be injurious in their operations, the whole is made subject to the approval of the President of the United States.

"As without law, it is impossible for man to improve in the arts of living, and in science and virtue, which elevate his moral condition, so under the administration of wholesome laws suited to the condition of the tribes, the various auxiliaries to improvement will be brought into successful operation.

"Education will be sought when the state of society has become such as to render education useful in the business of life. This is not the case in the savage state. The security of property by law will tend to eradicate the custom of community of right in property, so well calculated to stifle a spirit of enterprise; a man will become the owner of a piece of land in his individual capacity; its value will be enhanced by improvement; and this property will descend to the benfit of his children: hence will be originated something of *settled design* and of *fixed purpose* with regard to the future—things which do not belong to savage life, the absence of which cherishes improvidence, recklessness, and apathy.

"The bill provides for only two offices to be filled by citizens of the United States, viz: a superintendent of Indian affairs and a clerk. Their improvement will be better promoted by allowing offices of profit or honor to be filled by themselves, so far as they can find among them men possessing the requisite qualifications.

"As a measure calculated in no ordinary degree to promote the general design of the bill, it provides that an agent for the confederacy, to be selected under such regulations as the President of the United States shall believe will consist with harmony of feeling among the several tribes, shall remain at the seat of Government of the United States during each session of Congress. The sphere of his duties will embrace the interests of all within the confederacy. He must be an Indian, and his pay will be equal to that of a member of Congress.

"In addition to political disabilities under whic hour intercourse regulations have placed them, the blighting influence of which has already been noticed, the Indians are exposed to a repulsive prejudice, universal among the whites, which draws a line of distinction between the two in all the social relations of life, greatly to the disadvantage of the Indians. This prejudice originated in Indian degradation, and can be corrected only by Indian improvement. The sensible among them feel it; and many a well educated native has abandoned civilization among the whites, because he was thrown into the back ground in society, and has returned to savage life, where he could enjoy equality of condition.

"It is believed that the provisions of the bill are calculated to place the Indians beyond the influence of this discouraging prejudice. No whites will reside among them, except such as are specially permitted to do so for their benefit by the Government of the United States. They will live to themselves, and each will feel that he is eligible to the highest distinctions of the society by which he is surrounded; that his talents and virtue may be suitably rewarded; in a word, the whole community will perceive that the highest felicities of civilization are attainable, and, unless they be men of passions unlike all others, these causes will produce effects similar to the effects of the same causes when operating upon others. The better informed will find the reward of merit in their promotion, while the less informed will find protection in the same source. Of the nineteen tribes or parts of tribes now within the Territory, three of them, embracing a population of about 23,000 souls, are governed severally by written laws: some of the smaller and less informed tribes have also manifested a disposition to adopt written laws, and some of them have expressed a desire to have a portion of land, sufficient for a farm, laid off for their uses severally. Sixteen of the tribes have expressed a desire to become united, for the purposes contemplated in the bill. Delegates from two others have expressed themselves in favor of the measure, and before subscribing their consent, asked time only to refer the subject to their several tribes for their decision, according to their custom of transacting such business. From the other tribe, which completes the number of the nineteen, though no official communication has been received on the subject, such information has been obtained as leaves no doubt that it would most heartily enter into the confederacy.

"In view of these and of kindred considerations, it appears that, so far as relates to the condition of the Indians, they are prepared for the adoption of the measure proposed by the bill. In reference to ourselves, if reasons for the adoption of the measures proposed, drawn from considerations of economy, could have any influence, the subject furnishes them. We have been reconciled to the expensiveness of our Indian relations, from the supposition that the money thus expended benefitted that unfortunate people. This has been a delusion. Situated as the Indians have been, a fair conclusion drawn from facts is, that annuities, and other expenses to Government in the management of Indian affairs, have, taken as a whole, proved to be the reverse of what was designed. The committee would not intimate a desire to withhold any moneyed consideration due them. But they believe that the change of condition proposed would occasion an application of those moneys to their positive benefit, in the promotion of their improvement; but motives for action in this matter are drawn from higher considerations than those of dollars and cents.

"It is not believed that the hunting savage acquired right to all the regions which he roved, to the exclusion of the cultivator of the soil, merely because the former happened to be first on the ground. The claims of the hunter state would be exorbitant, to the restriction of civilization within limits too narrow. Our necessities compelled us to take the country which we inhabit, and to circumscribe the aboriginal tribes about us to smaller spheres than they originally claimed. While we plead justification in taking the country because we could not live without it, justice requires that ample remuneration should be made to the aboriginal occupants. That the claims of the Indians arising out of these circumstances have been fully liquidated, none will contend. Their claims have acquired strength by our reiterated declarations of friendship and desire to do them good. The prosecution of our former policy can never satisfy those claims, because it renders them no substantial benefit. We have continued our own mode of procedure in relation to them, and we control it in all its ramifications. They submit to all we do without presuming to think that any better way could be devised.

"We, then, as the stronger, acting towards and for this weak and dependent people, should leave untried no feasible plan of affording them substantial relief.

"In this way, alone, can we satisfy the claims which our relation to them has originated.

"If we should give them the facilities to improvement which are essential to our own preservation in a state of civilization, we should do what has not yet been done for them; if, then, they should perish, we should be clear; we had performed our duty. If the experiment should be successful, and the Indians should become elevated to the comforts of civilization, it would add a page to our history that would be read with satisfaction to the end of time."

From a report made to the House of Representatives in Congress, May 20, 1834, by Hon. Horace Everett, from the Committe of Indian Afairs, we make the following extracts. Premising that the bill to which it refers has, under some modifications, been kept before Congress every session since its introduction:

"Whatever difference of opinion may heretofore have existed, the policy of the Government, in regard to the future condition of these tribes of Indians, may now be regarded as definitely settled. To induce them to remove west of the Mississippi, to a territory set apart to their use and government forever; to secure to them their final home; to elevate their intellectual, moral, and civil condition, and to fit them for the enjoyment of the blessings of a free government, is that policy. And a further hope is now encouraged, that whenever their advance in civilization should warrant the measure, and they desire it, that they may be admitted as a State to become a member of the Union.

"To carry that object into effect is the object of this bill.

"The Western Territory will be bounded on the east by Arkansas and Missouri.......To the whole of it the original Indian title has been extinguished, and the tribes now within it derive their title from the United States. It is believed to be more than sufficient for them, and for those who have agreed to emigrate to it. The soil and climate are all that can be desired, to reward industry, and to prolong life.

"This territory is to be dedicated to the use of the Indian tribes forever by a guaranty the most sacred known. among civilized communities—*the faith of the nation*. The committee are aware that this guaranty, *the faith of the nation*, has not been illustrated by the history of the past, in a manner satisfactory to the Indian tribes. They are not surprised that they should now ask, 'What new security can you give us to the lands in the west, that you did not, in times past, give us to our lands in the east?'

"It is admitted that we have given to them guaranties which we have not fulfilled, pledges which we have not redeemed; not because we desired not to fulfil them, but because it was believed by the Government that we had no right, originally, to give them, and therefore had no power to redeem them. The Indians, however, will do us the justice to say, that we never held ourselves absolved from the obligation of indemnifying them, and of acknowledging that these very cessions of land at the west are a portion of the indemnity. Our inability to perform our treaty guaranties arose from the conflicts between the rights of the States and of the United States. Nor is it surprising that questions, arising out of such conflicts, which have bewildered wiser heads, should not be readily comprehended or appreciated by the unlettered Indian.

"The case is now free from all the embarrassments of conflicting rights. The guaranty now stands as an obligation which the Government will at all future time have power to perform; we can look around it, there is no doubt, no obscurity about it; even to the Indian eye it is clear and as well defined as the edge of the circle of the sun. The United States extinguished the Indian title to the Western Territory; that territory then became their absolute property. By the constitution Congress has an unqualified power to dispose of the territory belonging to the United States; and now Congress proposes, by charters, to grant and apportion this territory among the Indian tribes. The United States and the Indians are the sole parties."

The bills before Congress to which the two aforementioned reports refer, are virtually the same. For the purpose of rendering it less liable to objection, and to secure its final passage, that before the Senate goes less into detail than that before the House. The substance of these bills is the following:

1st. The boundaries of the Territory are fixed, and the lands secured to the tribes severally owning, by patents from the Government of the United States, with such restrictions only as are necessary to prevent white men from purchasing them.

2d. A General Council of delegates fairly chosen by the several tribes is to be convened once a year, or oftener, by order of the Superintendent. which Council shall enact laws for the benefit of the confederacy generally. These laws will not take effect until approved by the President of the United States.

3d. A delegate, who must be a native, chosen by the confederacy, shall remain at the city of Washington during each session of Congress, to attend to the affairs of the Territory, whose pay and emoluments shall be equal to those of a member of Congress. For the sake of harmony, the mode of choosing this delegate, in the first instance, as well as the mode of choosing the first delegates to the Legislative Council, will be prescribed by the President of the U. S.

4th. All offices within the Territory, excepting those of Superintendent and Secretary, will be filled by Indians, if such as are competent can be obtained.

Fully to our purpose is the following from the last message of President Jackson to Congress: "I again invite your attention to the importance of providing a well digested and comprehensive system for the protection, supervision and improvement of the various tribes now planted in the Indian country. The suggestions submitted by the Commissioner of Indian Affairs, [Hon. C. A. Harris] and enforced by the Secretary on this subject, are entitled to your profound consideration. The best hopes of humanity in regard to the aboriginal race, the welfare of our rapidly extending settlements, and the honor of the U. States, are all deeply involved in the relations existing between this Government and the emigrating tribes."

G

To the list of sensible documents to which we have the happiness of refering on this occasion, is the report of the acting Secretary of War, the Hon. C. F. Butler, of Dec. 3d, 1836, from which we extract the following:

"We may now be said to have consummated the policy of emigration, and to have entered on an era full of interest to both parties. It involves the best hopes of humanity in respect to the Indian tribes; and though, to the U. States, its issues cannot be equally momentous, they yet deeply concern our prosperity and honor. It therefore behooves us, at this juncture, seriously to examine the relations which exist between the U. States and the inhabitants of the Indian country, to look into the duties which devolve on us, and to mature a system of measures for their just and constant execution.

"In almost every treaty providing for the emigration of an Indian tribe, the impossibility of preserving it from extinction, if left within the limits of the States or organized territories of the U. States, and thus exposed to the advances of white population, is expressly recognized. The advantages which the tribe will derive from its establishment in a territory to be exclusively occupied by red men, under the solemn guaranties and the paternal care of the United States, are uniformly insisted on. In the treaty with the Choctaws, of the 27th September, 1830, the wish of the tribe to be allowed the privilege of a delegate in the House of Representatives of the U. States, is expressly mentioned; and though not alluded to by the Commissioners of the U. States, yet they insert it in the treaty, 'that Congress may consider of, and decide the application.' In the late treaty with the Cherokees east of the Mississippi, it is expressly stipulated 'that they shall be entitled to a delegate in the House of Representatives whenever Congress shall make provision for the same.' It is not to be doubted that the hopes thus held out to those tribes had an important influence in determining them to consent to emigrate to their new homes in the west.

"Although some of the Indians have made considerable advances in civilization, they all need the guardianship of the U. States. To leave them to the barbarism of their own institutions, with the inadequate assistance of an Agent, and the slight control of the General Superintendent, would be imprudent as it regards ourselves, and unjust towards them. Under such a system hostilities will frequently break out between the different tribes, and sometimes between them and the inhabitants of our frontiers, attended in both cases by the usual consequences of savage warfare. To fulfil, in their true spirit, the engagements into which we have entered, we must institute a comprehensive system of guardianship adapted to the circumstances and wants of the people, and calculated to lead them, gradually and safely, to the exercise of self government.

"The daily presence of a native delegate on the floor of the House of Representatives of the United States, presenting, as occasion may require, to that dignified assembly, the interests of his people, would more than any other single act, attest to the world, and to the Indian tribes the sincerity of our endeavors for their preservation and happiness. In the successful issues of those endeavors we shall find a more precious and durable accession to the glory of our country, than any triumph we can achieve in arts or in arms."

The Commissioner of Indian Affairs, the Hon. C. A. Harris, in his annual report of Dec. 1, 1836, and in his special report of Jan. 9, 1837, exhibits with uncommon force the propriety of organizing the Indian Territory. In the documents to which we allude there is little abstract reasoning, but the necessity of the measure is prominently set forth by a plain exhibition of facts, stated in a business-like manner. Here is no danger of mistake—facts speak for themselves, and confirm the justness of the sentiments implied in the following sentence: "The large augmentation of their numbers, and the consequent changes in their condition and circumstances, appear to me, to give new importance to the establishment of a government for the Indian tribes west of the Mississippi."

From the time That the aborigines of America were first discovered by Europeans, the flights of fancy common to romance seem to have beset all who wrote about them. Indians were supposed to possess some traits of character peculiar to themselves—predilections for war and hunting, and for being savages, which belonged to no other race of beings.—Do what you would for his improvement, an Indian would be an *Indian* still. It will be perceived that the foregoing documents have not been framed under the influence of such delusions. They speak the language of common sense, and suppose the Indians to possess minds and dispositions similar to those of other nations, and may be influenced by the same causes which operate upon others. They presuppose that the causes of Indian ruin are such as would ruin others, and that when the means which are essential to the improvement of others are applied to them the result will be the same.

We are sick of the stale stories of Indian peculiarities, told for more than three hundred years, and all who desire the prosperity of the misrepresented Indians, have reason to rejoice that men who are among the *first* in our nation both in merit and office, are, by a plain, common sense and benevolent course, about to correct those old whims about *hunting*, and *war*, and *aversion to improvement*.

We are persuaded that our plea for the Indians cannot be rendered more forcible than by furnishing such specimens of good sense coupled with benevolence.

An opinion, which we are confident, is unphilosophical and absurd, has long prevailed extensively, that this aboriginal race of men must ultimately become extinct. Some of the bad consequences of this error, are, all our efforts to produce a different result are weakened; only partial, and not complete success is hoped for, and therefore labors for their improvement are not entered upon with energy. We quiet our consciences for past neglect of effort, by supposing that had we performed an active part for their relief, the result would ultimately have been the same; and, still worse, this hopelessness which is indulged in regard to the destiny of these people, has rendered us less observing and economical in the management of their affairs.

In years past, Indian matters have been more out of sight than any other business belonging to our Government. Liberal appropriations have been made for benefiting the Indians in various ways. This was the expression of kind feelings for an unfortunate people, and nothing more than the mere expression of good will was supposed to be practicable. Therefore the application of those appropriations were not made with due care. Often they did not reach the case of the Indians at all, and frequently when they did, it was by a misuse which produced more evil than good. White men who fattened on the spoils quieted their consciences by supposing it was fair game for every one, and he was most to be admired who was most successful. Great good to the Indians was not hoped for, and was therefore left out of the question.

But why suppose that the aboriginal race must necessarily become extinct? We have seen that under all the privations of savage life they increased in numbers. They cannot, therefore, be naturally subject to any physical, or to any moral degenerating defect to destroy them. It is only when they come in contact with white men that their decline begins. Among white men, therefore, and not among the Indians are we to look for the cause of their diminution of numbers. But our institutions do not contain these life-destroying principles, for we have a happy demonstration of their better tendency. In subsequent history which shall tell this story of intercourse between the white and red man, a *darker* shade will be seen than any that could be produced by savage customs, or be inferred from civil institutions.—This destruction of numbers will be attributed to a dereliction of duty on our part, resulting from a want of desire to preserve them. To what else can it be attributed? The causes are with us, and not with them, and as these causes do not belong to our institutions, they must necessarily be attributed to our delinquency.

The notion that Indians begin their existence with prepossessions in favor of savage customs, and averse to civil institutions is too absurd to be met by argument. Their predilections, therefore, like those of other people, must all be formed by extraneous circumstances. By surrounding circumstances a white man may be made a savage, as has been demonstrated in numberless instances; and by surrounding circumstances a red man may be made subordinate to civil institutions. While all men are susceptible of improvement, all naturally possess a tendency to degenerate. The state of man which we term *civilized*, is produced by the operation of outward means; for want of these man remains in his natural condition. The original condition of the Indians is this state of nature. We cannot hope for the improvement of the condition of the Indians, until they enjoy the means *essential* to the improvement of others. *These means, hitherto they have not enjoyed.* In the application of these means we may as confidently hope for the civilization of the Indians, as we hope that under their influence the next generation among us will be borne up above savageism. As, therefore, we hope for the improvement of the condition of the Indians, we abandon the notion that they must necessarily become extinct.

The design of Government to embody the Indians under the influence of law, will secure to them all that is requisite in the case, and, unless they are a race of men unlike all others, they will flourish under the influence of the means which render others prosperous. We are, therefore, no longer allowed to despair of the prosperity of this people, but to expect it confidently.

From the best data that can be obtained it appears, that

the Choctaws, Cherokees, and Creeks, are increasing in numbers. In the course of two years, there is shown an increase of 121 among the Delawares, 73 among the Shawanoes, 50 among the Kickapoos, 4 among the Ottawas, and 2 among the Peorias and Kaskaskias. The Quapaws, and the Senecas and Shawanoes of Neosho, are stationary. The Weas and Piankashas have decreased 43. The Osages, Kauzaus, Pawnees, Otoes, Omahas, and Puncahs, are all supposed to be decreasing; and, in proportion to their numbers, the diminution among the Putawatomies is more rapid than that of any other tribe.

Proposed Tour of Observation.

It is much to be regretted that so little is known respecting the Indians remote from the settlements of the whites. The information which we possess, is little more than what has been merely incidentally given us by persons who travelled on the business of trapping or trading. We believe that no one has ever explored any portion of the remoter parts of the vast region inhabited by Indians, whose chief purpose was to ascertain their local situation, numbers or condition.

From Mexico, as well as elsewhere, we have little more than doubtful statements, and conjectural estimates. A more thorough knowledge of these matters, in Mexico and the wilder regions, is daily becoming more desirable; and many considerations remotely affecting the affairs of the Government of the U. States, and intimately connected with the cause of benevolence, call louder and louder for an effort to obtain it.

In this age of benevolent enterprize, we are happy to have an opportunity of recommending that a tour of inquiry and observation be undertaken for the purposes under consideration. Our experience would greatly diminish difficulties which were once formidable in travelling in a wilderness, and in mingling with Indian tribes little acquainted with white people. The local situation of the tribes severally could be ascertained, and a probable estimate of their numbers be made. Their habits of life and their modes of thinking, their traditions and religious ceremonies could, to some extent, be dicovered, and some idea could be formed of the prospects of doing them good, of the most eligible mode of doing it, and of the most promising place.

That portion of the tour which would extend to Mexico, would, no doubt, develope the most interesting and useful facts. Truth, even at this remote period, could be made to supply, in many instances, the place of old Spanish fables and fictions. From some imperfect accounts we have obtained respecting the aboriginal inhabitants of that country, we are persuaded that the benevolent would discover a field for action whose extent, and "whitening for harvest" would excite astonishment, inducing wonder that a field so inviting, and so near, had remained so long undiscovered, and unoccupied.

Much scientific knowledge could be obtained on such a tour. We should be enabled to contemplate Indian affairs as a *whole*, and contrive the grand scheme of benevolence so that it should fully meet the case.

Reasons in favor of our proposition rapidly accumulate upon reflection on the subject. Our limits here allow us barely to solicit for it a serious consideration, believeing that few, if any, will differ from us in opinion, and hoping that the measure proposed will not be long delayed.

Brief view of the Past and the Present.

On our discovery of America we found a people in a state of nature, who had undergone no change by moral culture or social discipline. It was a condition deplorable on account of hardships, cruelty, and crime. Yet, under all its privations, they increased in numbers. This must be admitted, unless we suppose that they had been cast upon this continent in greater numbers than when we discovered them. There is no evidence that they had ever been more civilized than they were at that time. Ancient fortifications, tumuli, and all indications of prior existence, prove that they had been savage, and not civilized men.

We found them in vast numbers, but their millions opposed a feeble resistance to their invaders. In the south, they were massacred by tens of thousands, in their disconcerted and ineffectual efforts to keep possession of their country. Sometimes one nation was employed to murder another, to gratify Spanish avarice and ambition. Thousands were enslaved, and the inhabitants of entire countries were divided among their invaders as property. Ship loads were decoyed from other countries by professions of friendship, to supply the places of others who had preceded them, and had perished under the weight of their oppression. Their mortality when slaves on the plantations or in the mines, was fearfully great.

North of the Spanish territories, their sufferings from the hands of their conquerors were much less severe though similar in character. They were subjected to slavery as well as to the havoc of wars, and of European diseases. Every where their country was taken possession of, regardless of the desire of its inhabitants. No *legal* bargains were made in the purchase of lands, because the nominal purchaser had resolved on taking possession of them, and, being the stronger, held the rod over the weaker and dictated the terms to it, which the latter dare not refuse. Justice sometimes spake, and pleaded that the conquered had some right to the soil which none beside themselves had ever possessed, but was answered that the Indians were *savages*, under the influence of a strange passion for *war* and *hunting*, and a *queer aversion to improvement*, and therefore, it was not improper for better people to dispossess them. When humanity spoke, and entreated for forbearance from oppressions which occasioned such a fearful waste of life. Fancy, without stopping to notice the real fact, pleaded the reverse of truth, that they were diminishing by wars and pestilence, prior to the arrival of the whites. When conscience pleaded that strange, uncouth, and cruel as might be the savages, being human beings, they claimed, at least, our sympathies, and ought to be made acquainted with religious and civil institutions, it was answered, the savage is untameable—whatever may be done to civilize and Christianize him, the Indian will be an Indian still; and when reason would be heard, she was silenced by the summary answer, the Indians are destined to become extinct.

Thus has the flood of calamity beaten upon this wretched race until many tribes have indeed been driven out of existence, while others are reduced to a few. Happily for those that remain, they do not live in the days when ignorance and superstition, scarcely less frightful than pagan night, predominates over their conquerors.

It is not easy for a people to divest themselves of sentiments, however absurd, or of habits, however unjust in their effects, which have been entailed upon them by the generations which preceded them. Such is the case with the people of the United States in reference to this injured and neglected people. We have imbibed the sentiments and feelings of our ancestors, and have clung to their policy. But the influence of our religious and civil institutions has broken the spell. We are awaking from our reveries, and begin to see the subject in its proper character.

We feel astonished that any had ever dreamed that the laws of nature had changed, and had produced a race of men morally unlike all others, or had rendered inoperative, in relation to these, the means which improve all others.— In the light of common sense we look upon the past, and contemplate the future. We regret the past errors, under which millions have gone beyond the reach of redress for their grievances, and as we cannot now do justice to the former generations, we become the more firmly resolved to assist the present. The hurry of our onward reach in science and in wealth, need not be interrupted by a pause for metaphysical inquiry—what shall be done; the case is plain. Here are rational beings, who, like others, eat and sleep, and think and act, according to the laws of human nature. Therefore, we have only to apply the means which produce our prosperity, and they will bring this people up to our level.

In the American Revolution we recognize the dawn of civil and religious liberty, which are to fill the world with light, and truth, and justice. We account ourselves happy in being the people to usher in this Halcyon era; and it is under the healthful action of our free institutions, that the vapors are removed which have mystified the subject of Indian Affairs. Yes, the sound judgment, and scrupulous sense of justice of our Government, specimens of which we have given in the extracts from public documents, &c. which we have quoted, utter a voice to the lingering remnants of tribes whose numbers once were great, saying, "Your warfare is accomplished. The wilderness and the solitary place shall be glad, and the desert shall rejoice." While philanthropy, the true index of our greatness, extends her voice from Maine to Louisiana, "Come and let us strengthen the tribes that remain and are ready to perish, and say to them fear not, for, on account of your sufferings, blessings shall be doubly heaped upon you."

ERRATA.

Page 58 6th line from the top, for 3,600,000 read 2,600,000.
" " 9th " " " " for 5,400,000 read 4,400,000.
" " 11th " " " " for *were* read *was*.
" 59 22d " " " " for *exuberant* read *esculent*.

Clermont, Chief of the Osages
Painted by George Catlin (1796-1872)
Courtesy of Gilcrease Museum
Tulsa, Oklahoma

Gratuitous.   THE   No. 4.

ANNUAL REGISTER

OF

INDIAN AFFAIRS

WITHIN

THE INDIAN TERRITORY.

PUBLISHED BY ISAAC M'COY.

SHAWANOE BAPTIST MISSION HOUSE, INDIAN TERRITORY, 1838.

WASHINGTON:
PRINTED BY PETER FORCE.
....
1838.

CONTENTS.

	Page.
Advertisement,	3
Historic facts, and plans for Indian improvement,	7
Internal government of the respective tribes,	14
Locations, &c.	15
Seat of Government,	18
Surveys,	ibid.
Land Titles,	20
General description of the country,	22
Small Pox	ibid.
Hostilities,	23
Provisions for the indigent,	28
Villages,	ibid.
Ardent Spirits,	ibid.
Mails,	31
New System of Writing,	ibid.
Management of Indian Affairs,	34
Numbers,	36
Choctaws,	ibid.
Chickasaws,	40
Cherokees,	45
Creeks,	49
Seminoles,	52
Senecas, &c.	53
Osages,	54
Quapaws,	57
Putawatomies,	58
Weas and Piankashas,	59
Peorias and Kaskaskias,	60
Ottawas,	ibid.
Shawanoes,	61
Delawares,	64
Kauzaus,	65

	Page.
Kickapoos,	67
Sauks,	68
Ioways,	ibid.
Otoes,	69
Omahas,	70
Pawnees,	71
Puncahs,	72
Other Baptist Missionaries,	ibid.
Missionaries in General,	73
Want of Missionaries,	74
Temperance Societies,	ibid.
Provisions of the Government of the U. S. for the education of the Indians, and for their improvement in civilization,	75
Kauzaus,	ibid.
Osages,	76
Delawares,	77
Putawatomies,	ibid.
Kickapoos,	ibid.
Otoes,	78
Omahas,	79
Pawnees,	ibid.
Cherokees,	80
Creeks,	ibid.
Choctaws,	81
Sauks,	ibid.
Ioways,	ibid.
Chickasaws,	82
Military Posts,	ibid.
Trading Posts,	84
Affinity of Languages,	ibid.
Names of Tribes,	ibid.
Whole number of Indians,	85
Plea for the Aborigines,	86

ADVERTISEMENT.

The publishing of the present number has been delayed longer than is desirable.

It is exceedingly difficult to obtain the information necessary to make the Register what it purports to be. No aid of importance can be obtained from public prints. The publisher is compelled to collect his materials chiefly within the Territory, which is yet a comparative wilderness, under disadvantages and uncertainties similar to those which attend a botanist in collecting his plants, or a mineralogist his minerals.

Here we have no mails, excepting in two or three cases, in which the route from the East barely enters the Territory a few miles. A correspondence with New-York or Boston, which are more than 1,000 miles distant from us, is less tedious, and far more certain, than with either the northern or the southern parts of the Indian Territory. With a few worthy exceptions, we have also found it impossible to engage correspondents, who would promptly furnish such statements of facts as came within the sphere of their knowledge. Our repeated appeals to individuals for information, are sometimes wholly unavailing, and often answered with partial, or at most *general* statements.

In the autumn of the last year, by a tour which was extended to the southern extremity of the Territory, and by similar opportunities in relation to the northern portion, we hoped we had engaged correspondents, who would place within our reach such statistics as would make the work of compiling future numbers comparatively light. In this we have been disappointed.

We have also had on hand other duties in relation to Indian matters, the calls of which have been imperious. On this account we thought for a while that the present number could not be issued. Its failure would have been a circumstance which we should have had many reasons for regretting, especially at this eventful juncture in Indian affairs. To prevent such a failure, we have been obliged to make extra exertions, in order to accomplish within a limited time this, in addition to the labor which seemed of itself fully equal to our strength. We also found it not convenient to get the work printed in the office from which preceding numbers had issued. But with all the disadvantages under which we compile and publish the present number, we hope its imperfections will not be such as to mislead the reader. We shall endeavour, as heretofore, to make it, to the extent our limits will allow, a book which may safely be referred to by all interested in Indian Affairs. Matters doubtful or indefinite will be stated as such.

The work is issued gratuitously; yet we shall be gratified if those who receive it within the Indian country, would return the compliment by furnishing corrections of any mistakes which they may detect, and information of changes in affairs, which will be necessary in compiling the next number. The sphere of our distribution is the United States and its Territories, consequently we are unable to send many into any one neighborhood; we have therefore to request those into whose hands it shall come, and whose sentiments shall justify it, to give such attention to the work, and such direction in its circulation, as will be best calculated to promote its utility.

As heretofore, we are resolved not to be biased by prejudices. We write on a subject alike interesting to all parties, whether political or religious. Our object is to promote the welfare of a suffering, but noble race of men; and to impart such information respecting them as will shed light upon the path of duty, which their white neighbors should pursue in relation to them.

Our remarks are confined chiefly, though not exclusively, to what we denominate the Indian Territory.

Our Indian relations are assuming a more rational character. The irregularities and absurdities of the past are daily developing, and we are happy in believing that generally throughout our country, both in the Church and in the State, as a knowledge of what is right increases, there gradually increases also a disposition to act accordingly.

Dr. Johnston Lykins
*Courtesy of the Kansas State Historical Society
Topeka, Kansas*

Non-on-da-gon, Chief of the Delawares
Painted by George Catlin
Courtesy of Gilcrease Museum
Tulsa, Oklahoma

ANNUAL REGISTER.

HISTORIC FACTS, AND PLANS FOR INDIAN IMPROVEMENT.

The removing of the tribes from the East to the West of the Mississippi, was begun by our Government, in accordance with the former policy of removal, merely for the sake of making room for white settlements. But about the same time, the benign influence of our institutions became such, that nobler ends were sought. The permanent good of the Indians was contemplated, as well as our own convenience. Prosperous and happy ourselves, beyond what any other nation had ever been, and daily becoming more so, and improving in a knowledge of the rights of others, the condition of the aborigines attracted attention, and elicited sympathies in a degree somewhat proportioned to the favorable circumstances in which we found ourselves. We perceived the original inhabitants of our favored land sinking while we were rising—and their decline appearing to be accelerated in proportion to our growing prosperity. The cause could not be attributed to any innate self-destroying passion or propensity in the Indian, because philosophy and even common sense teach that all human beings are radically the same, mentally as well as physically. Speaking of man generally, there exists no greater dissimilarity of intellect than of physical appearance. We know, that as certainly as that men possess hands which can be employed in the arts, they possess minds susceptible of science. Nature has, in no instance, left her productions disproportionate. Or more properly, the God of Nature manifests consistency in all his works.

When, therefore, an enlightened community felt disposed to inquire into the causes of Indian decline, it was clearly perceived to be a baleful policy, introduced by the first discoverers of our continent, adopted by all who succeeded them, and *entailed* upon our Government by that which preceded it. European acquaintance with the natives begun, and was carried on upon the principle that the latter did not own the country in which they were found. Hence their country was parcelled out among their conquerors, and they themselves made subject to such restraints and disabilities as their conquerors respectively chose. These restrictions have invariably been fraught with mischief to the Indians. They circumscribed the sphere of intellect and enterprise within the narrow limits of their tribe. Our laws of intercourse allowed them to retain so much of their ancient forms as were injurious, and deprived them of what had rendered savage life tolerable, without allowing them a participation in the facilities for improvement which belong to civilized life. To suppose that Indians could improve when excluded from a participation in the institutions of other tribes, and of other nations, and when the utmost that they could hope for was a state of dependance upon the will of those who had thus consigned them to degradation and impotence, would be as absurd as to suppose that because an acorn was imbedded in a soil sufficiently warm and moist to cause it to germinate, it would produce a lofty oak when circumscribed to narrow limits within an impenetrable wall. Unconnected with one another, and with all other nations of the earth, having no interest in the things by which they were surrounded, and destitute of prospects to elicit a spirit of enterprise, the tribes naturally degenerated; and we easily perceive now that such was the natural result of the circumstances in which European policy had placed them.

Discovering the cause of the malady, we inquired for the remedy. From an early stage in our acquaintance up to the present, they had, to a limited extent, been furnished with moral and literary instructers. But, viewing them as a people, our best efforts had proved to be mere palliatives, which had not arrested the progress of disease.

To make it *possible* for them to improve, they must be so situated that they can feel the influence of the social relations of life, including that branch which we denominate *law*. The lines of distinction between them and us are too strongly marked, to make it either profitable to them, or pleasant to us, for them to amalgamate as citizens with ours. They must dwell alone, united among themselves, for mutual encouragement and assistance, and in such a relation to us as will not make them liable to injury, by our superiority of information and power, but where they will be fostered by our Government's care and our people's benevolence. Such a location could not be found east of the Mississippi River, for there each tribe was so hemmed in by white population, that others could not unite with it. Moreover, State claims, the origin of which was prior to the existence of our Government, and which our Government could not control, extended over all the country between the Atlantic and the Mississippi.

Therefore, the first place westward, at which a limit to our settlements could be fixed, was on the west side of the Mississippi River. Here, also, white settlements had been formed previously to our purchasing the country of the French Government. In our bargain, by which the country became ours, these settlers had to be provided for. Hence the States of Missouri and Arkansas were originated. The western limits of these States might have been drawn nearer to the Mississippi River than they were, which would have allowed of the commencement of Indian settlements farther east than has been the case. But Indian settlements could not begin until they had passed the western boundaries of those two States. First, there was no place of sufficient extent unincumbered by white settlements; and, secondly, the General Government could not annul claims which it had frequently acknowledged, and which were of more ancient date than its own existence.

The anxieties which these anomalous circumstances were calculated to produce in the benevolent mind, which sought an opportunity to do justice to the Indians, were happily removed, by discovering that, west of the States alluded to above, was a country adequate in extent, and ample in its resources, for the purposes required, and unincumbered by *State claims*. This country belonged exclusively to the Government of the United States, excepting the claims of the indigenous tribes of Indians, which could, without difficulty, be so adjusted as not to injure them, nor to embarrass the designs of Government in relation to emigrants.

As we proceed westward from the Mississippi the prairie lands become more extensive, and the timbered lands less, until wood almost wholly disappears, in one vast plain of four or five hundred miles in width from east to west, and of a much greater extent north and south. As the Territory of Arkansas was first described, by actual survey, it was discovered that it extended farther west than either the convenience of its inhabitants required, or the interests of the Indians would justify. Therefore the western boundary of Arkansas was brought back east forty miles, making the territory narrower from the Mississippi west by forty miles, and leaving this slip, forty miles in width, for the settlement of Indians. The survey of the lines between the whites and the Indians was completed in 1831.

The influence of custom is often greater than we are aware. The policy which had given tone to all our regulations of intercourse with the Indian tribes, had been matured by centuries,

2

and every step by which the whites extended their territory, had been, in some degree, connected with the Indians, so that our policy had become as familiar as it was old. To embody the tribes, and place them in a country of their own, under the influence of *law*, and in a territorial connexion with our States, was too great an innovation upon long established customs, to be done without opposition. Prejudice magnified difficulties and misrepresented facts; imagination wrought frightful anticipations; while the unholier principles of avarice, presented a still more determined opposition.

It was easily foreseen, that the effect of the plan proposed, would be the abolition of Indian agencies, and all the costly appendages of office and operation belonging to the agency system, and, notwithstanding the change would necessarily be so slow, that the present incumbents could hardly fear interruption during the period for which, under existing regulations, they could reasonably hope to enjoy their offices, still it was natural to dislike the plan, which would put the original sytem on the wane. Some, too, not feeling a sufficient interest in Indian matters to make themselves acquainted with the subject, professed not to believe that the new system would work any better effect than the old. Missionary Societies and their Missionaries had their stations located in divers places, and felt an unwillingness that they should be broken up by the removal of the natives. The more northern tribes had annuities coming to them, which were large, compared with their numbers. Many found it convenient for the tribes, respectively, to remain in their original places, because these annuities would then be paid them, near to the former, who found in the circumstance an easy and lucrative speculation.

The Indians, who, let it be distinctly noticed, have always been under the control of the whites, who could persuade them to do any thing, either right or wrong, were, in many instances, made to object to locating in the new country in prospect of the new state of things. Frightful stories were told them, to alarm their fears.—The wild Indians of the West would scalp them; the resources of the country were inadequate to a comfortable subsistence; the Southern tribes were told that the new country was too cold; and the Northern tribes that it was too hot; and all were told that the Government was insincere in its promises, that there they would find a secure abode. The past was referred to, and the inference drawn, that the future would be equally precarious; and, from first to last, the aid of the tenderest sympathies of the human heart were invoked, by reiterating, ten thousand times—" Here are the graves of your fathers." Nevertheless, the deformities of the former policy have been constantly unfolding, and the proposed system steadily gaining favor, both with the white and red people.

In reducing the theory to practice, the concurrence of both the President and the Congress of the United States was necessary. The former found it easy to decide in favor of the measure, but the latter, consisting of many members, brought together from various portions of the United States, have found it less convenient to harmonize their views. Difference of opinion, however, has not occasioned such formidable obstacles to a favorable decision, as the fact that most members have felt a deeper interest in the success of other matters, and therefore the Indian measure under consideration has been thrown aside, and not acted upon. In the press of business, many members seem to content themselves by supposing that, for the present, it will be sufficient for them to follow the footsteps of their predecessors, make the usual appropriations, &c., and leave things to run in their ordinary channels.

Mr. Munroe appeared in favor of the measure. Mr. Adams, it was understood, was also in favor of it; and General Jackson and Mr. Van Buren have both strongly recommended it to the favorable consideration of Congress.

The subject, in a tangible form, has been before Congress several of the sessions last past. At the last session, the bill providing for carrying the plan into full operation passed the Senate by a majority of thirty-nine to six. The bill was sent to the House for its concurrence. The House had a bill of its own before it, similar in its provisions to the Senate's bill. Both bills were reported to the House by the Committee of Indian Affairs, having passed to that stage, when they could properly be called up for the final consideration and action of the House. In this place, unfortunately for the subject, the bills were left behind, by the press of other matters. From the large majority in favor of the bill in the Senate, it is fair to infer that, had a decisive vote been taken in the House, it would have become a law.

In 1837, under instructions from the Department of Indian Affairs, the subject was distinctly submitted to the consideration of the Delawares, Shawanoes, Kickapoos, Putawatomies, Sauks, Ioways, Kauzaus, Weas, Piankashas, Peorias and Kaskaskias, and Ottawas, and each of these tribes expressed a desire that Government should carry into operation the plan proposed. — Each tribe made a written communication to the Government on the subject, of which the following is a sample.

"SHAWANOE COUNCIL HOUSE,
"*Indian Territory, July* 12, 1837.
"Hon. C. A. HARRIS,
"*Commissioner of Indian Affairs.*

"SIR: We, the undersigned chiefs and head-men of the Shawanoes, met in council, have heard read to us, by Isaac McCoy, a paper which you had sent him, and which has been under consideration in Congress, for the benefit of the Indian tribes within this Western country, to which, through the same person, we now return our answer, which we request you to lay before Congress.

"The substance of the paper to which we allude, we understand to be as follows, viz :—

1st. "The country between the Puncah and Red Rivers, and southwest of Missouri River, and west of the States of Missouri and Arkansas, to the distance of two or three hundred miles, is to be set apart exclusively for the use of Indians, excepting the amount necessary for military posts, roads, and public highways, and for the residence of such persons as may be allowed to reside in the Indian country, by the laws regulating intercourse with the Indian tribes, and that the lands granted to the tribes severally shall be secured to them by patents from the Government of the United States, under such restrictions as shall secure the lands from becoming the property of an adjoining State or Territory, or of either individuals or companies of white persons.

2d. "That the Superintendent of the Indian District shall call into general council, once a year, or oftener, a prescribed number of chiefs or principal men, appointed by their respective tribes, according to directions given them. That, in this council, the tribes, by their representatives, shall unite, for purposes of peace and friendship, and shall make such regulations for the benefit of the confederacy as may, from time to time, appear necessary, the said regulations to be submitted to the consideration of the President of the United States, and not to take effect until approved by him. That all tribes within the district be at liberty to join the confederacy, and that none be required to do it without its consent, and that each tribe may make its own internal regulations, consistently with those of a general nature.

3d. "That the confederation shall send an Indian, as its delegate, to Washington City, to remain there during each session of Congress, to attend to such matters as the interests of the confederation, or of the tribes and individuals severally require, whose pay and emoluments shall be equal to those of a member of Congress.

"With the foregoing propositions we are well pleased, and we do earnestly request the President and Congress of the United States to carry them into effect as soon as practicable."

Signed by thirteen chiefs and principal men, in behalf of the whole.

In 1838, the author of this work and Capt. W. Armstrong were instructed to submit the bill, which passed the Senate at the last session of Congress, to the Choctaws, Cherokees, and Creeks, for their consideration. The matter was brought before the general council of the Choctaws in a formal manner. The prominent points, concerning which their views were solicited, were distinctly stated. The council declined giving a direct answer. They replied, in general terms, disapproving of the bill, without assigning any reason, except that they would esteem its adoption "the first step towards their removal farther towards the setting sun." They assigned no reason for this conjecture, of which the design of the bill was precisely the reverse.

The subject was not, in a formal manner, brought before the Cherokees and Creeks. It was ascertained, however, that the people generally, among the Choctaws, Cherokees, and Creeks, had been induced to believe that the bill was a kind of treaty, in which the United States designed, in some covert manner, to defraud them of their present homes. It is evident that they are entirely mistaken in regard to the purport of the bill, and their misapprehension has, no doubt, been produced by mischievous and avaricious men, who profit by the degradation of the Indians.

It is not known that any of the tribes object to any provision of the bill. Their objections, in relation to the subject, are invariably made against points not embraced in it. It is evident, indeed, that the bill provides for precisely such a state of things as they desire, though they have been persuaded to fear that some other meaning may be attached to it.

To the extent of the confederation proposed, it is probable the Choctaws feel averse, desiring that their own nation should constitute a Government; but to the principles proposed in the bill under consideration, they are evidently not opposed, because they have already adopted the very essence of them, in relation to the government of their own tribes, as the reader will perceive in the article headed *Choctaws*.

In September last, the Cherokees held a special council, to which all the emigrant tribes were invited, the most prominent object of which appeared to be, the establishment of regulations of intercourse among the tribes, similar in design to the provisions of the bill. That international laws. among the tribes, for the preservation of peace, are necessary to their prosperity, is understood by every tribe, down to those least informed. That such regulations cannot be longer deferred by our Government, which is bound to preserve peace among the tribes, without danger of serious difficulties among them, and between them and the citizens of the United States, is evident to us. This will appear more clear to the reader, in the article under the head of *Hostilities.*

INTERNAL GOVERNMENT OF THE RESPECTIVE TRIBES.

On the internal government of the respective tribes, our remarks in this place will be of a general nature, reserving a more particular account for the statements which appear under the name of each tribe.

The Choctaws, Chickasaws, Cherokees, Creeks, and Seminoles, embracing a population of 66,600, are governed by written laws, enacted by themselves. All the other tribes are without law, excepting the customs which pertain to savage life.

The Delawares have recently held a general council among themselves, and resolved that laws were necessary, and that they would commence, by enacting such as were most obviously indispensable. They resolved that the matter which most distinctly called for immediate legislation, was the evil of intemperance. They immediately prepared a written communication to two citizens of the United States, in whom they had confidence, giving information of the above resolutions, and soliciting assistance in the framing of laws, and advice in relation to executing them.

All customs pertaining to savage life, which bear any resemblance to laws, are predicated upon the principle of retaliation. There is no regulation or law for the punishment of any crime. The thief is not liable to punishment by his tribe. The injured can obtain no redress only by stealing in return, or otherwise taking, without consent, a sufficiency, if he can find it, of the property of the first offender, to countervail the damage. The murderer escapes with impunity, unless a friend of the murdered undertake to avenge the deed, by taking the life of the offender. These matters, though of serious moment, are left to the caprice of circumstances and of passion. No tribunal investigates the nature of the offence, or adjudges the award. If, in the estimation of a friend of the murderer, the avenger takes life improperly, he takes the life of the latter in return.

LOCATIONS, &c.

Each tribe has received an assignment of land fully adequate in extent and resources, making allowance for increase of population for several generations to come.

Some of the first locations, being made by treaty stipulations, at a great distance from the Indian country, and when neither of the parties was acquainted with the ground, have been found to be not as judicious as they might have been made, with a better knowledge of the country. About two years since, a more rational course was adopted by Government than had been followed in the more incipient stages of the subject. The plan contemplated the removal of all the tribes from the east of the Mississippi, even those within the State of New-York, and their location within the Indian Territory. A view was taken of the population of each tribe to be removed, and then inquiry was made, whether the lands which yet remained unappropriated within the Indian Territory would be sufficient for their settlement. The result of the examination was favorable. Notwithstanding too much land had been assigned to some of the earlier emigrants, it was found that, by a careful division, there was yet enough remaining for the accommodation of those which had not arrived.

Since the spring of 1837, lands have been selected for the Putawatomies; for a band of Ottawas, of Ohio, denominated the Ottawas of Roche de Boueff and Wolf Rapids; for a band denominated the Chippewas, of Swan Creek and Black River; for a band called the Chippewas of Saginaw; and for the Ottawas of Michigan. In parcelling out these lands, the country was thoroughly examined, and suitable portions left for the Miamies of Indiana, and the Indians of New York.

A considerable portion of the Ottawas of Roche de Boueff and Wolf Rapids removed to their land in 1837, and took possession of it. In the same year a delegation from the Chippewas of Swan Creek and Black River, and a delegation from the Chippewas of Saginaw, were shown their respective tracts. In the same year, also, a delegation, representing different bands within the State of New-York, was shown the country set apart for them. It was understood that each of these delegations was willing to accept the country which had been assigned to it.—Some delay, however, in relation to emigration, has been occasioned by points unsettled in the negotiations, by which they were to relinquish their former residences.

Within the present year, (1838,) a delegation of Ottawas and Chippewas, representing these nations as recognised in the treaty of 1836, have been shown a country which they have accepted.

It is expected that the Wyandots, of Ohio, will be located near the Ottawas and Shawanoes. For the Winnebagoes, the Menominees, and the Sauks and Foxes of the Mississippi, there is suitable country north of the Delawares, Sauks, and Ioways, and south of the great Platte River. With the Winnebagoes, who are at present within the Wisconsin Territory, east of the Mississippi River, a treaty has been made, which was ratified by the Senate of the United States in June last, by which they are to find a temporary residence west of, and pretty near to, the Mississippi River, within the Ioway Territory, in which treaty also provision is made for an examination, by them, of the country within the Indian Territory.

The main body of the Sauks and Foxes are at present within the Ioway Territory. But their settlement within the Indian territory, at no distant day, is confidently expected; and this circumstance, we have no doubt, will be kept in view in making assignments of land to other tribes.

By treaty with the Chickasaws, they were to procure a home for themselves. This they have done within the Choctaw country. A more particular account of which will be given under the head of *Choctaws*.

The Seminoles are locating within the Creek country, and will receive attention under the head of *Creeks*.

By treaty of Prairie Du Chien, of 1830, a tract between the Great and Little Nemaha Rivers, extending up each, from its junction with the Missouri, ten miles on a direct course, was set apart for half-breed Omahas, Ioways, Otoes, and Sioux of the Yancton and Santie bands. The quantity within this tract has been ascertained, by actual survey, to be 143,647 acres. In 1837, the Superintedent of Surveys was directed to cause the exterior boundaries of the tract to be surveyed. This has been done. He was also required to ascertain the number, the names, &c., of the claimants, and to inquire into the expediency of subdividing the tract; and should this appear proper, he was to proceed to make such a division as would be equitable among the claimants. He reported that it appeared *inexpedient* to subdivide the tract. It appeared that none of the half-breeds, or their relations, ever had resided on this tract, and that they probably never would. The reasons why the land had been set apart for this purpose at the treaty did not appear very distinct, but it was probably done as a matter of favor, the extent of which could not have been great in the anticipation of any of the parties concerned. It was, therefore, recommended that, instead of a division, and a parcelling out of the land to the owners severally, their titles should be extinguished by the Government. This would be the most advantageous to the owners. The expense to Government would be small. The claimants could not, in justice, expect much, and the extinguishment of these claims would add value to the lands left for the Sauks and Foxes, the Menominees, and the Winnebagoes. The above recommendation, it is expected, will be carried into effect.

From Red River, which is the Southern boundary of the Territory, North, the half-breed tract noticed above, is the first land the title to which it seems necessary that the Government should extinguish, in order to enable it to carry out the plan of Indian location. This, and a country between it and the Great Platte River, on the North, Government should acquire the control of, for the purpose of future locations. It is not really necessary that Government should make any other purchases.

The boundaries of the Pawnees, Otoes, Omahas, and Puncahs, on the North of the Great Platte, have not been definitely agreed upon. The time is not distant when a negotiation between these tribes, under the supervision of the Government, will be found expedient, for the purpose of fixing definitely their respective boundaries.

The Osages and the Kauzaus are virtually the same people. It has long been deemed desirable that they should be placed near each other, upon the lands of the latter. It is known that the Kayzaus desire to sell a portion of the lands now held by them. It is also believed that a similar desire will be found to exist among the Osages, in relation to their lands, and instances of dissatisfaction between them and their red neighbors on the South, and their white neighbors on the East, within twelve months past, have been such as to render the location under consideration more desirable, not only to all Indians concerned, but to the whites also.

3

SEAT OF GOVERNMENT.

In 1832, when Secretary Eaton retired from office, he was about to instruct the Superintendent of Surveys, then in his employ, to set apart a portion of the unappropriated lands, in a central part of the contemplated Territory, for the Seat of Government of the Territory, should it become organized. It was thought advisable that a few miles square should be reserved from cession to any tribe, in which reservation all the tribes should have a common interest, on which should be erected all public buildings, and should be settled all persons whose offices made it necessary for them to reside at or near them. It was proposed to lay off the district in town lots and farm lots, the latter to contain say from 40 to 80 or 100 acres. That a member of any tribe would be at liberty to select and occupy one of these lots. Nothing further was done in relation to this matter, until 1837, when orders were issued from the Department of Indian Affairs to the Superintendent of Surveys, to select and report a place suitable for the above objects. The selection was accordingly made of a valuable tract, of about seven miles square on the Osage River. It is nearly equi-distant from the Northern and Southern extremities of the Territory, and a little over sixteen miles West of the State of Missouri.

SURVEYS.

Only the exterior boundaries of lands have, as yet, been surveyed. Within the years 1836, '7, and '8, the following Surveys have been made, viz: The Northern boundaries of the Osage and of the Kauzau lands, amounting to 330 miles. The lands of the Senecas, Senecas and Shawanoes, and Quapaws, all completed. The Cherokee surveys have been completed, by running 622 miles. The half-breed lands, and the lands of the Sauks, Ioways, Putawatomies, and the Ottawas of Roche de Boueff and Wolf Rapids, have been surveyed. The Delaware surveys have been completed, and the surveys of the district for the Seat of Government have been completed.

Rivers form the Southern and Northern boundaries of the lands of the Choctaws. To complete the survey of the exterior boundaries of their country, it would be necessary to follow Red River from the Western boundary of the State of Arkansas, up Westward to the Mexican boundary, thence run North to the Canadian River, and thence follow the Canadian River down to its junction with Arkansas.

To complete the survey of the boundaries of the Creek lands, after surveying the lands of the Choctaws, it would be necessary to draw their Western boundary about sixty miles in length.

The Osage and the Kauzau surveys would be completed by drawing their Western boundaries, the former fifty miles, and the latter thirty.

The surveys of the Weas and Piankashas, Peorias and Kaskaskias, Shawanoes and Kickapoos, are complete.

In 1837, the Putawatomies petitioned the Government to lay off a small portion of their country in farm lots, which they proposed to assign to such individuals as desired to hold land in severalty. The amount needed at that time was small. It can easily be imagined that many strong reasons could be urged in favor of the measure. Perhaps none will doubt its being one of vital importance in the work of Indian improvement. Individuality of right in property, and especially in landed property, appears obviously to be a fundamental principle, without which civilization must progress slowly and never be complete.

In this case the Putawatomies plead that they had been induced by the agents of the Government to expect such a subdivision of land as they prayed for, and that their present circumstances required it, in order that a fair distribution of the better portions might be made among them. Without doubting that the measure would be advantageous to the Indians, the committee of Congress, to which the subject was referred, on account of a question unconnected with the salutary effect the adoption of the measure would have upon the interests of the petitioners, reported against it. The Putawatomies continue to urge it, and it is hoped that its adoption will not be long postponed.

In recommending this measure to the consideration of Congress, the Secretary of War exhibited another evidence of the fostering care of Government in favor of this late "scattered and peeled people." The individual owner was to be invested with a title that would make it secure to him and his heirs. To prevent the weak from being oppressed by the strong, the title was to be inalienable in favor of an Indian for a given number of years, and forever in relation to white men. In the mean time the interest of the individual in the portion of country which remained a common property to his tribe, would not be affected beyond the small amount of his farm lot. Some of the Ottawas and Shawanoes are imbibing the same consistent views relative to exclusive ownership in land which they may improve, under a hope that after them their heirs may enjoy its benefits. This measure, when once introduced, will be rapidly adopted throughout the Territory.

LAND TITLES.

It is creditable to the age in which we live, that a vexatious question concerning the title of the aborigines to the lands they occupy, which has remained unsettled during the centuries of our acquaintance with them, and which has been a prolific source of mutual inconvenience, should now be settled, and be established upon principles of humanity and justice.

The tenure by which the Indians held lands has always been of doubtful character. As original occupants, the country seemed to be *bona fide* theirs; but as a people unimproved, or at most less civilized than Europeans, the latter claimed the right to dispossess them. All Europeans who formed settlements in America, the most humane not excepted, did it under the pretext of *right*. When a negotiation for territory took place with the Indian, and he was in a greater or less degree rewarded for the relinquishment of his claim, it was a measure resorted to merely because it offered less violence to reason and humanity, and was less inconvenient than direct coercion. But the European invariably controlled the terms, and was resolved not to leave the country, whether the Indian agreed that he should remain in it or not. If the latter refused to accept the consideration offered him for his land, he *must nevertheless leave it.*

The condition of the Indians being an anomaly in the history of man, their relation to their conquerors has remained so too. Treaties were held with them, the forms of which seemed to imply the presence of two parties capable of acting, but this in *matter of fact* was not so. The wording of treaties appeared to be full and explicit, and to imply all that the Indian could desire. Nevertheless the force of Indian treaties has been frequently declared to be doubtful. Since the formation of the Government of the United States, it could not be otherwise on the east of the Mississippi river, and we have often regretted that this fact received so little attention in the agitation of Indian matters.

Previous to the formation of our Government, two of the Colonies claimed the country westward to the Mississippi river. In the cession of these lands to the General Government, the latter became bound to lay off the country into States or Territories. Upon these lands were numerous Indian tribes. By the arrangement, negotiations for land were, after this, to be held between the United States and the Indians, and all assurances given the latter that they were the real owners of the residue of lands which they had not ceded, were illusive, because an obligation previously created compelled the General Government to lay it off into States, and to grant within them the usual privileges of citizenship. The General Government did not possess the right to make any tribe the substantial owner of the land it occupied.

Many of the tribes within the Indian Territory are entitled to patents for their land by treaty, and by an act of Congress of May 28, 1830, all the tribes are entitled to patents. Within about two years past most of the tribes have been distinctly informed that the Government would issue patents to each as soon as its surveys were completed. No obstacle exists to the making of such conveyances by the General Government, for *here are no State claims.*

The tenure by which the tribes will hereafter hold land, will be materially different from what the nature of things allowed on the east of the Mississippi.

By both the Indians and the whites, it has always been conceded that Indian chiefs and principal men possessed the right to sell the lands of the tribe. Now, when a patent is issued to a tribe, each and every member of that tribe, whether old or young, male or female, in or out of power, will become a real and common owner of the soil, and the right of the owner, without consent, cannot be extinguished by another. The ordinary process of Commissioners on the part of the United States, negotiating with chiefs and principal men for a cession of land by the latter to the former, cannot take place in relation to a tribe which holds its lands by a patent from the United States Government.

Patents, in the first place, will issue from the proper office of the United States Government to the tribes severally, for their respective tracts of country. Should individual members of tribes obtain a right in fee simple to farm lots, or other portions, the patents, will issue from an office belonging to, and solely under the control of, the tribe to which such persons respectively belong.

To the Cherokee nation a patent has been given. This is an event full of interest to all who desire the prosperity of the Indians. The latter will more properly appreciate it, as the principles which it involves shall develope themselves; and by all it will ever be remembered as the harbinger of freedom and prosperity to a people long degraded.

The surveys of the lands of several other tribes having been completed, it is expected that patents will shortly be issued to them.

GENERAL DESCRIPTION OF THE COUNTRY.

The country contemplated as the Indian Territory, is comprised within the following boundaries: Puncah and Missouri rivers on the North and Northeast, the States of Missouri and Arkansas on the East, the Red River, which is the northern boundary of Texas, on the South, and the western limit of habitable country, say two hundred miles west of the States of Missouri and Arkansas, on the West. It is about six hundred miles long from north to south, and two hundred broad from east to west.

It lies within latitudes which have taken the Southern tribes somewhat north of their original places east of the Mississippi, and the Northern tribes a less distance south of their former homes.

The soil is generally very fertile. By far the greater part of it is destitute of wood. The plains are covered with a heavy coat of grass. It contains iron and lead ore, and much coal and salt water. To the eye of the observer no country west of the Alleghanies appears more favorably situated for health. Emigrants to the southern portions have suffered much from sickness, but the cause must be sought in other circumstances than the character of the country.

Both in extent and resources the country is fully adequate to the wants of the inhabitants, with reasonable calculations, for many years to come.

On account of the vast prairie on their west, which extends four or five hundred miles, white settlements could not surround them, even were there no other obstacles.

Game, convenient to the settlements, has become scarce. All of the emigrant tribes rely almost wholly on agriculture for subsistence.

SMALL POX.

In 1837, the small pox appeared on a steam-boat that was ascending the Missouri River, and was communicated to several tribes in the upper country, some of which have been nearly all destroyed, and at the latest dates from that country it still prevailed. It is conjectured by traders in that country, that previous to the 1st January, 1838, 15,000 had perished by this dreadful disease.

The Pawnees, and some others within the upper parts of the Indian Territory, caught the disease, but its ravages among them were not extensive. The disease had been very destructive among them in the year 1831. Hence none but children born since that period were liable to it.

In the summer of 1838, the small pox appeared among the Southern tribes, to wit: the Choctaws, Chickasaws, Cherokees, Creeks, and Seminoles; and it continues there to go on with its work of wo and death. There is also great reason to fear that it will spread among the remoter tribes to the Southwest, extending to the Pacific Ocean.

Something has been done by the Government, and by humane individuals, to arrest its frightful march by vaccination, but these efforts have been too partial to be effectual. Hitherto attempts to vaccinate under instructions from Government, have been carried on in too much haste. Often the virus is not good, and from this, or from some other cause, the operation is ineffectual. Those persons afterward contract the small pox, and the circumstance gives rise to the belief that vaccination is useless, or worse than useless.

It has been recommended to the Government to adopt a systematic course of vaccination among the tribes as soon as possible. To insure success, a physician should be required to limit his labors to a district, or to a band, until it had, in his opinion, been secured against the contagion of small pox. He should examine the vaccinated to ascertain if the operation had been effectual, and should repeat it where it had not. As soon as he had completed his work in one district, or upon one band of Indians, let him proceed to another. He should be required to keep a register of the names of the heads of families, and of the number and location of each family, and to make frequent reports to the proper officers of Government; and he should be bound by oath faithfully to discharge the duties of this solemn trust.

In 1837, the small pox was brought by sea to the tribes about the Columbia River upon the Northwest coast. For a while it was pretty destructive, but its progress was arrested by vaccination by the British fur company.

HOSTILITIES.

In 1833, the Government convened councils of a general nature, of delegates from various tribes, and induced them to exchange mutual promises to be at peace with one another.—

This measure, though it touched the subject but slightly, nevertheless, produced a good effect. All parties, for some time abstained from depredation and murder. These councils not being repeated, the parties felt less restraint, and ultimately returned to their former unkind treatment of one another; and thefts and murders have become more frequent with each succeeding year.

The Osages are accused of destroying hogs, and cattle belonging to the neighboring tribes to a considerable amount. Horse stealing is frequent in divers places, carried on by the worthless of different tribes. By some the work is almost reduced to system. They will steal horses in the southern parts of the Territory, or in Texas, and convey north, and there steal others, and take back on their return.

But besides the renegadoes, whose crimes are disapproved by their well principled countrymen, there are others engaged in these, and in worse practices, for which they are honored by their respective tribes, according to Indian custom. The Kauzaus have brought into their villages at least thirty stolen horses within the last summer and autumn. The Osages have stolen, perhaps a greater number, among which are some valuable horses belonging to the citizens of the United States. In August last, a large drove of horses was stolen from one of the Osage villages.

In April, 1838, a few Pawnees made a friendly visit to the Sauks and Ioways in Missouri. As they were returning to their homes, a party of Kauzaus fell in with them and attacked them, and killed one.

In August last the Kauzaus and Osages sent out a war party, consisting of about eighty warriors. They surprised a party of Pawnees, and took eleven scalps. Four of their men were killed and two wounded. A few of the united party separated from the main body. These also had a battle, and took five scalps, making seventeen killed by those tribes, of whom we have obtained certain information. Reports of other murders committed by other tribes, have been in circulation. On the 1st September last, a war party of about twenty Kauzaus were out, the result of which we have not heard.

In the months of June, July and August, the Rev. M. Merrill, missionary to the Otoes, accompanied that tribe on their buffalo hunt, which lasted more than two months.* They saw three war parties of Pawnees; the first was a party of thirty, who had been to the Cheyennes to steal horses. They had, first, a skirmish with the Cheyennes, and had been defeated,

* This party consisted of 800 souls—men, women and children. They killed 1500 buffaloes.

with the loss of one killed and one badly wounded. They next fell in with a party of Osages, and were again defeated with the loss of two men killed.

The second was a party of ten, which had started to the Osage villages to steal horses. One of their party was bitten by a snake, which induced them to return without accomplishing any thing.

The third party said they were going to the Cheyennes to steal horses, but it was believed that they designed committing depredations upon the Osages.

Near the western boundary of the Cherokee country a bloody battle was fought the last summer, (1838) between the Kiawas and Camanches on the one side, and the Cheyennes on the other.

A detachment of dragoons, in command of Lieut. Northup, was on an expedition in that country, and arrived at the ground two days after the battle. The Kiawas and Camanches were encamped, and had heard of the approach of the detachment. As the Cheyennes advanced to attack their enemies, they were met by the latter about a mile from the encampment. The latter were slowly beaten back into their encampment, though disputing desperately every inch of ground. The whole scene was in an open prairie. The women dug holes in the earth, in which to hide themselves and children. The Cheyennes continued to make dreadful havoc of their wretched enemies, and would have soon reduced the whole to a heap of corpses, when a messenger from camp mounted a horse, and set off to meet the detachment of dragoons, to solicit assistance. As he was leaving, a Cheyenne, who understood the language of the Camanches, was informed by one of the latter, that the messenger had gone to hasten the white men and Osages, whom they every moment expected to come to their assistance. The Cheyennes instantly retired, leaving fourteen dead on the ground, besides the dead that had been carried off during the action. Fifty-eight of the Kiawas and Camanches were killed. More than one hundred horses lay dead on the ground, chiefly within the encampment.

From time immemorial, many of the Osages have been in the habit of spending the winter in the country east of their present villages, from fifty to one hundred and fifty miles. This country is now within the State of Missouri, and covered by a very sparse white population. The latter found the Osages troublesome, and in the autumn of 1837 drove them back to their own side of the line, and in several instances, in which the Osages seemed obstinately inclined to remain, they were severely whipped. The Osages, exceedingly distressed for food, being almost

4

in a state of actual starvation, for some time continued, at the risk of life and limb, to cross the line by stealth, with women and children, for the purpose of hunting the game for food. The whites having reason to fear that habit and hunger might have such influence upon these wretched people, that a greater force than they could embody would become necessary for their expulsion, adopted measures to increase their strength, and in the month of October an army of five hundred militia came to their assistance. They scoured the country along the line, a distance of upwards of one hundred miles, and found about one hundred of these miserable beings, men, women and children, and conveyed them across the line into the Indian country. Notwithstanding these admonitions, the more severe of which had been so deeply impressed upon the back as to be seen and felt for many weeks, hunger within, and staring in the countenances of others, including mothers, wives and children, urged them to continue secretly to cross the line. Their sign was frequently discovered by the white inhabitants, who believed that their stocks of cattle and swine suffered by these incursions.

In March, 1838, it was discovered that two hogs had been killed by a party of Osages. Nineteen of the citizens armed themselves with rifles, and went in pursuit, with a view of flogging the depredators. The latter were overtaken near the line between the whites and Indians. The Osages were in camp; the number of the men about twenty, besides the women and children. The whites asked for the persons who had committed the depredation. Some altercation followed, and in the mean time an Osage was seen loading his gun, with which he said he designed to kill one of the party with whom he was quarrelling. While he was in the act of loading, he was shot dead by two of the party. Others fired on both sides. The Osages fled into the woods, having two men killed and one wounded. Two of the whites were wounded, one of whom died a few days afterwards.

Two or three companies of dragoons from Fort Leavenworth hastened into the neighborhood of the Osages, but there appearing no disposition to hostilities, every thing soon became tranquil.

It is hoped that the adoption of measures for the suppression of these disorders will not be long delayed by the Government. The Indians should be required to restore, or pay for all stolen property, whether taken from a red or white man; and murderers should be promptly punished.

Some eight or ten years ago, the Camanches and other roving bands of the Southwest, annoyed traders from the State of

Missouri who passed through the Indian Territory to Santa Fe. But those Indians have now formed a friendly acquaintance with the Choctaws, Chickasaws and Creeks, and have become friendly to both white and red.

Indians within the Territory carry on a trade with those remoter tribes, which is increasing in briskness. The former take out goods, and exchange for mules, peltries and furs.

The settlements of the Indians extend up the Missouri River from the Territory. The first are bands of Sioux. On Red River, which is the southern boundary, a few bands are located: namely, the Wàkò, Taùweâsh and Withchetau, on both banks of the river, about two hundred miles west of the State of Arkansas, in all about six hundred souls. Two other small bands, viz. Tawarèka and Kăjï, numbering about six hundred souls, reside at no great distance from the above, in a southwest direction. It is among, and by way of these small bands, that the traffic spoken of above is carried on.

More than once it has been conjectured by some, that designs of hostility against the white settlements were fomenting among some of the tribes. That some individuals who have emigrated from the east to the west of the Mississippi, under circumstances exceedingly grating to them, have felt the influence of unkind feelings towards the United States, none can doubt; but we confidently believe that no measure of hostility has ever been conceived against the white settlements by any tribe within the Territory since emigration commenced. For upwards of ten years, our business has been chiefly with the tribes within the Territory. Under very favorable opportunities we have carefully noticed passing events, in relation to this matter, and we feel assured that we are not mistaken.

In 1837, a call was made on some of the emigrant tribes, for a regiment of volunteers to join the United States army, in Florida, against the hostile Seminoles. About eighty Delawares, and about the same number of Shawanoes, responded to the call, joined the army in Florida, and performed a service of six months. It was evidently not congenial to their feelings to join in this war, but a desire to give evidence of respect for, and fidelity to the Government of the United States, and the desire to realize the liberal wages offered, prevailed.

About five hundred Choctaws also mustered for the same service, but ascertaining that their pay would not be equal to what they had expected, they declined the service.

PROVISIONS FOR THE INDIGENT.

At the session of Congress of 1837–8, an appropriation of $150,000 was made "for affording temporary subsistence to such Indians, west of the Mississippi as, by reason of their recent emigration, &c., were unable to subsist themselves."

Great praise is due to the liberality of the spirit which prompted this measure, but its propriety may well be doubted. Special cases occur, one of which the reader will observe under the head *Osages*, which make it proper for Government to offer relief in the means of subsistence. But usually such relief comes too late, and as frequently it fosters idleness and improvidence. Much of the live stock, and property of various kinds, which have been furnished the Indians in fulfilment of treaty stipulations, has been worse than wasted, because given to them when they were unprepared to apply it usefully.

VILLAGES.

All the indigenous tribes live in villages, in which their houses are crowded closely, without regard to order, excepting a few which missionaries have prevailed upon to enter upon a more hopeful course of agriculture.

Not one village, properly so called, exists among the emigrant tribes, though some settlements, among those most improved, seem to be approximating a village appearance.

In the unimproved state, all bands, whether large or small, keep close together—not only their dwellings are thus situated, but when travelling on hunting excursions with old and young, male and female, a village is formed at every encampment, and demolished on their departure from it. In the earlier stages of improvement, they scatter and make separate settlements, on account of the greater convenience in agricultural pursuits. As in the march of improvement, mechanics and merchants multiply, they necessarily begin to congregate, and mutual convenience leads ultimately to the formation of regular towns.

ARDENT SPIRITS.

Drunkenness is the greatest of all the evils which *immediately* assail the Indians, yet this is what physicians would term a symptomatic malady, and not really the disease. The appetites of Indians are like those of other human beings, and they are no more inclined to intoxicating drinks, on account of appetite, than others. In almost every instance, Indians hesitate to drink ardent spirits, when it is first offered them. Some tribes have been known to reject its use for several years. Few of the Osages had become drunkards up to the year 1828, though they had long been exposed to the temptation. But with them there is less moral restraint than in more improved society. Want of self-respect, and recklessness in regard to life and comfort, throw wide open the door to excessive indulgence. With unimproved Indians, drunkenness is neither considered a sin nor a shame in either sex; and without either prospect or hope of better condition for themselves or their posterity, present sensual gratification predominates. To this there is no counterbalancing influence. Hence unimproved natives are given to intoxication, and the evil becoming common, it clings to society in its improving stages.

No effectual remedy for this evil can be found, except in the elevation of the Indian character; and that it can be removed in this way is as certain as that the whites are less addicted to this vice than the Indians. The desideratum is the means of promoting moral principles among people indulging excessively in this degrading vice. We are confident that the object is attainable. Heretofore we have been too indifferent to this subject. It is true Congress has enacted some good laws for the suppression of the evil, but these laws are not executed with fidelity. It is not known—it is not even believed that temperance in any degree has been promoted among the Indians, in consequence of our laws forbidding the furnishing of Indians with ardent spirits. It is conveyed into the Choctaw, Cherokee, and Creek countries, by wagon loads. It has been estimated by some persons of intelligence, whose opportunities of knowing were most favorable, that in the year 1837, not less than $40,000 worth of whiskey was sold by white men to Cherokees and Creeks alone.

Now, if Government agents were brought under an accountability, which would induce them to be vigilant, they could, and they would search for intoxicating liquors, and would destroy all that could be found in the Indian country. The Indians do not drink in secret; their Bacchanalian revels are constantly resounding in the ears of every body. The depôts of whiskey are known to all through the surrounding country. Nothing, therefore, is wanting, but to require the agents, upon the penalty of losing their offices for neglect of duty, to take measures by which they would at all times be informed, without delay, when, and by whom, whiskey had been introduced, and to repair to the place immediately, and destroy it. If they should meet with resistance in the discharge of their duty, let them call on one of the garrisons for military aid. If liquor should be smuggled into the country and concealed, let the offenders, whether white or red, be imprisoned at one of the garrisons, and liberated only on the assurance of better behavior in future.

That this course would succeed, we have had satisfactory evidence in a few praiseworthy experiments which have come within our knowledge. It would occasion additional labor to the agents, but this could not give rise to objection, because the Government is ready to make ample compensation for their services. The task would be less difficult than some would suppose, because agents would be sustained, in most instances, by a very large majority of the Indians themselves, and in every instance, by the more respectable and influential portion of the tribe. The character and influence of the agents would become greatly elevated by such a course. Commonly, the *talks* of agents to the Indians on the evils of intemperance, are esteemed by them idle and insincere. But if agents would meet the subject decidedly in practice, the Indians would esteem it manly and dignified. We have known a few honorable instances of the destruction of ardent spirits by the agents, and the result has been in confirmation of the opinions here expressed.

Along the line between the whites and Indians, whiskey shops will always be found. The rules which we propose would not prevent the intemperate from crossing the line and visiting these houses, but, if they were prevented from carrying it across the line and introducing it into their settlements, the sales which could be made at these whiskey houses, would be too poor to allow of their existence.

The remoter tribes, towards the Rocky Mountains, are furnished with vast quantities of ardent spirits. Besides places of less note, there is one high up on the Missouri River, which carries on the traffic upon a large scale; and there is another, of no less magnitude, high up on the Arkansas River. To these regular posts it is commonly conveyed in the form of alcohol, in order to diminish its weight in transportation, and it is diluted for use afterwards. To the post on the Missouri it is conveyed by steamboats, and to that on the Arkansas, and to other places, it is most commonly taken in wagons, or packed upon mules. Thousands of gallons of alcohol are yearly conveyed through the Indian Territory near where we now write. Seven or eight wagons loaded went through in one company the last summer. These transportations are not made by Indians, but by white people, and, therefore, could the more easily be prevented.

Vast quantities of whiskey are now manufactured in the Spanish country near Santa Fe, and conveyed into the territory of the United States, along the mountains, on mules.

We forbear attempting to describe the evils of intoxication among the Indian tribes, because they are inconceivably great, and we might as well attempt a description of the awful devastations of the most profuse vomitings of Vesuvius.

MAILS.

At Fort Leavenworth the mail barely crosses the Missouri River, which is the line of the Indian Territory.

From the State of Arkansas, a mail route to Fort Gibson passes through the Cherokee country, in which are two or three post-offices. Another mail route lies between Forts Gibson and Towson, passing offices at Fort Coffee and the Choctaw Agency; and from Fort Towson a route leads eastwardly into the State of Arkansas, passing an office at Eagletown, in the Choctaw country.

It would be a great convenience to white men authorized to reside in the Indian country, and to many of the Indians, if a direct mail route could be established, commencing at the southern extremity of the Territory and extending north as far as the Great Platte River. Improvement in mail facilities would tend greatly to the improvement of the Indians. These advantages to them would be much increased, if they could be allowed to receive by mail, prints free of postage. There are a good many readers among them, and the number is increasing. Though the postage on a newspaper or magazine is small, yet in the incipient stages of improvement, many of them are unwilling to incur the expense.

NEW SYSTEM OF WRITING.

To each Indian language, and to each dialect of language, belong peculiar sounds, which cannot be obtained by the use of the English alphabet. To designate syllables which could not be spelt, or sounds which could not be obtained by the ordinary use of letters, writers who would write intelligibly, have been compelled to introduce arbitrary characters, each according to his fancy. It can easily be perceived that serious inconveniences attend this course of things.

Mr. Guess, a Cherokee, had discovered that the language of his tribe could be written with about eighty syllabic characters. Guess' plan was tried in relation to some other languages, and found to be inapplicable, because characters would be multiplied beyond the bounds of convenience.

To remedy the evils which attended the ordinary methods of writing Indian, and to avoid the complexity attending the universal application of Guess' system, the idea suggested itself to Mr. Jotham Meeker, then a missionary at the Sault de St. Marie, of using characters to designate, not syllables, but certain positions of the organs of speech. By the addition of this third principle, to so much of the two former as were apparently necessary, he discovered that much would be gained.

Subsequently, Mr. Meeker became located at the Shawanoe Mission-House, where, by himself and fellow missionaries, the scheme which was first thought of merely for the purpose of supplying defects in other modes of writing, was carried out, and reduced to a distinct system, and successfully applied.

In the new system, spelling is entirely excluded, and the tedious process is avoided of familiarizing the memory with certain names of characters, [letters] and then recollecting that after combining these names, an arbitrary sound [syllable] must be uttered. This sound, unmeaning in itself, must be borne in mind, until by a similar process, a second, third, or fourth be obtained; and then these arbitrary sounds must be combined to make a *word*. With an unlettered Indian, whose thoughts have never been disciplined upon any matter, the study of orthography is exceedingly irksome, especially in a language which he does not understand. Nothing can be further from his habits, than to strain his thoughts to acquire a knowledge of something like the art of *causing a paper to talk*, when he is unprepared to appreciate the result.

On the new system, every sound is indicated by a character, [letter] which in Indian languages, are usually about eight or ten, the greater part of which, but not all, are what, in other systems are denominated vowel sounds. The other characters [letters] merely indicate the position of the organs of speech, preceding or following these sounds, by which the beginning or ending of sounds is modified. This modification, as we easily perceive, except in simple vowel sounds, is necessary to the articulation of a syllable. No character has a name, because the characters are not combined for the process of spelling.

Not more than twenty-three characters have yet been found necessary in writing any Indian language. A knowledge of the use of these can be acquired by the learner in as short a time as he can learn the names of the letters of the English alphabet. As soon as he has learned the use of the characters, he is capable of reading; because, by placing the organs of speech, as indicated by the characters severally as they occur, and uttering a sound, as is in like manner denoted by a character, he necessarily expresses a word. Speech consists alone of this simple process. It is the excellence of the new system, that it is the natural painting of speech on paper, by characters which never vary their uses, unincumbered by every thing complex in the art of reading.

The common English types are used, to save the expense of founding others; and, chiefly, because one who knows the use of those letters can learn to read with them on the new system, with the greater facility.

A person capable of reading any language, written upon the principles of orthography, can, in the course of an *hour*, learn to read a book in any Indian language, so as to be well understood by one acquainted with that language: therefore, writings on the new system, can be used by all who are capable of reading any book. An Indian who never knew the use of a letter, can learn to read his own language in the course of a few days; that is, he can learn to read in the same time that it would require him to learn the names of from sixteen to twenty-three letters of the English alphabet.—Many instances have occurred, in which adult Indians, ignorant of letters, have learned to read their own language upon this system, by merely occasionally falling in company with some of their people who had learned to read, and receiving a little instruction from them.

In the development of the new system, is recognised the dawn of brightening days for the obscure aborigines; and animating prospects rapidly widening, commensurate with their country and their condition. By it, some of the more formidable obstacles to Indian reform, are, in a great measure, obviated. With the aid of an interpreter, one may write in a language which he does not understand. He may write a portion of scripture, a religious tract, or other useful writing; and can teach the natives to read and to *write* it also. The facility with which a knowledge of reading is acquired, would enable a teacher; who could mingle with a tribe, even in their rudest condition, to introduce the art of reading, and circulate his tracts.

Could there be found a competent number of devoted Christians, as zealous for the salvation of the Indians, as traders are in acquiring their peltries and furs, bidding defiance to hunger and fatigue—to the perpetual snows of the Rocky Mountains, or the frosts of the higher latitudes, and penetrating to the remotest hordes of these miserable mortals; the arts of reading and writing could be rapidly introduced among every tribe in the vast wilderness which they inhabit. Even the most rude could, in a few days, as they would occasionally rest from pursuing the game, or from the fatigue of digging roots for subsistence, learn to read useful books. What astonishing facilities would be afforded to such, as in future would do these people good, by the previous introduction of the arts of reading and writing! The new system is applicable to any language, but more advantageously to some than to others. It is hoped that it will be generally adopted by teachers, who find it necessary to impart instruction in the Indian languages. We also solicit for it the serious consideration of missionary teachers, in other countries, destitute of a written language.

Education in Indian languages cannot supersede the necessity of education in English, so far as the latter is practicable; but by means of the new system, tens of thousands of Indians might be taught to read, whose condition would never allow them to learn to read, or to understand the English language. The application of the new system would result in a speedy enlargement of mind, a love of order, and a relish for education and improvement generally.

MANAGEMENT OF INDIAN AFFAIRS.

The immediate management of all Indian Affairs, excepting war measures, is by the Commissioner of Indian Affairs, subject to the Secretary of War. The present Commissioner is T. Hartley Crawford, Esq., who has recently succeeded C. A. Harris, Esq., resigned.

Governors of Territories are ex-officio Superintendents of Indian Affairs. H. R. Schoolcraft, Esq., Agent for Chippewas and others, is also a Superintendent, but without additional emoluments. Capt. William Armstrong, Agent for Choctaws, is Acting Superintendent for the tribes south of the northern boundary of the Osages, without additional emoluments. By special act of Congress, a Superintendency has long existed in St. Louis, Missouri, which includes all the tribes within the Indian Territory north of the Osages, and other tribes north as far as the Superintendency of the Governor of Ioway. The late incumbent, Gen. William Clark, has deceased.

The nature of the duties and responsibilities of Agents and Sub-agents is the same. The one is not an officer subordinate to the other, as seems implied in the title. The compensation of an Agent is $1,500 per annum, and the compensation of a Sub-agent $750 per annum.

Instructions are given by the Commissioner of Indian Affairs to the Superintendents, and by the latter to Agents and Sub-agents, who respectively report back through the same channel.

These reports exhibit the amount of aid afforded the Indians in agricultural implements, live stock, the erection of dwelling houses and mills, and in the fencing and ploughing of fields, the names and salaries of interpreters, of farmers, blacksmiths, wheelwrights, and school teachers, employed by the Government; the condition of schools, supported and managed exclusively by the Government, together with the location and condition of the schools immediately in charge of the missionaries. In a word, these reports are intended to exhibit, in statistical form, all matters within the several Agencies which require the consideration of the Commissioner of Indian Affairs.

When missionary buildings are erected by a Missionary Society, one object of which is, an English school for Indian youth, the missionary, acting as agent for the society, reports the fact, with the costs of the buildings, to the U. S. Indian Agent or Sub-agent for the tribe. The latter examines them in person, and reports their character, and what he believes to be their value. Upon these reports, and at the request of the society, the Government, if in possession of the means, pays to the society two-thirds of the value of the buildings.

The Agent or Sub-agent examines the schools annually, before he makes his report. All missionary establishments are formed under the authority of Government, and receive more or less pecuniary assistance from it. The means of assistance are either provided by treaty stipulations, or by the appropriation annually of a civilization fund of $10,000.

INDIGENOUS TRIBES.

Osage, about	- 5,510	Pawnee, about	-	10,000
Kauzau, "	- 1,750	Puncah, "	-	800
Omaha, "	- 1,400	Quapaw, "	-	600
Otoe and Missouria,	1,600			
		In all	-	21,660

EMIGRANT TRIBES.

(1) Choctaw, about	15,000	Ottawas,	- -	240
Chickasaws, "	5,500	Shawanoes,	- -	823
(2) Cherokees, "	22,000	Delawares,	- -	921
(3) Creeks, "	22,500	Kickapoos,	- -	400
(4) Seminoles, "	1,600	Sauks,	- -	600
Senecas & Shawanoes,	461	Ioways,	- -	1,000
Putawatomies, about	1,650			
Weas, - -	206	Emigrant,	- -	73,200
Piankashas, - -	157	Indigenous,	- -	21,660
Peorias & Kaskaskias,	142			
		In all	(5)	94,860

CHOCTAWS.

The Southern boundary of the Choctaw country is Red River, South of which is Texas. They adjoin the State of Arkansas on the East; are bounded North by Arkansas and Canadian Rivers, and on the West by a line dividing the Territory of the United States from that of Mexico. The extent of their country is about 150 miles, from North to South, and, from East to West, the habitable portion is about 200 miles. Want of wood renders the western part uninhabitable at present.

Their country is supplied with numerous springs of salt water, at two of which the Choctaws are manufacturing salt.

No villages have yet been properly formed in their country, though the settlements of Eagletown, Doaksville, and Pheasant Bluff, are places which begin to assume a village appearance. They have suffered much by sickness, the causes of which are

(1) Including 200 white men married in the nation, and exclusive of 600 negro slaves.
(2) This table was prepared when the latter emigrants were on the road to the West. It pre-supposes that nearly all had arrived. It includes negro slaves, which may amount to 1,200.
(3) Including about 900 negro slaves.
(4) Including 393 negro slaves.
(5) With some of the later emigrants there have been diminutions, by deaths, which we are unable to state, and which, if known, would reduce the sum as stated above.

probably such as usually occasion sickness to settlers in new countries. The appearance of the country is very favorable to health. They are improving in civilization and comfort. Their houses and fields indicate a good degree of industry. Many have large farms. They own much live stock, such as horses, cattle, sheep, and swine; are pretty well supplied with farming utensils. They own about 600 negro slaves.

They own three flouring mills, two cotton gins, eighty-eight looms, and two hundred and twenty spinning-wheels. They have thirteen native merchants, besides white men engaged in the same business. Their national council house is nearly equidistant between the northern and southern boundaries of their country, and about forty miles west of the State of Arkansas. It is an excellent log building, with a council hall and two committee rooms.

About three or four thousand Choctaws have not yet settled in their country, some of whom are in the country they formerly inhabited, east of the Mississsippi. A small band live in Texas, about eighty miles south of Red River, opposite Fort Towson. At the time of general emigration of the tribe, a band of about three hundred and fifty settled still farther south in Texas, between the rivers Brasos and Trinity. Besides these, there are others in divers places in Texas, who emigrated thither at various times, twenty, thirty, or forty years ago.

In respect to civilization, there is great difference among them. Some have fully adopted the habits of civilized man, many are in comfortable circumstances in life, and some may be said to be wealthy. From these more favorable circumstances all grades of condition exist, down to the Indian who has advanced but little in civilization.

The best evidence of the improving condition of the Choctaws, is seen in an entire change in their Government, which they have effected, from the barbarous to the civilized. We cannot now assemble chiefs and head-men among them, and transact business with them relating to their people, as is the custom among uncivilized tribes. The system of chieftaincies has been abolished.

The tribe denominates itself "The Choctaw Nation." It has adopted a written Constitution of Government, similar to the Constitution of the United States. Their Declaration of Rights secures to all equal privileges, liberty of conscience, excluding all religious tests; it secures trial by jury, and, in a word, it provides for all that is felt to be necessary in the incipient stages of political existence. The Constitution may be amended by the National Council.

Their country is divided into four judicial districts. Three of these districts annually elect, by popular vote, each nine members of the National Council, and the fourth elects, by the same mode, thirteen members, in all forty. These are allowed three dollars a day, while engaged in legislating. Within each district an officer, denominated a Chief, is elected for the term of four years. The National Council meets, annually, on the first Monday in October. It consists of forty members, the necessary clerks, a light-horseman, [Sergeant-at-arms,] and door-keeper. It is also attended by the chiefs, who have an honorary seat provided for them by the side of the Speaker, but they have no voice in debate in Council. Their signatures are necessary to the passage of a law. They may veto an act, but it may become a law, by the concurrence of two-thirds of the Council notwithstanding. The Council is styled "The General Council of the Choctaw Nation." It adopts by-laws for its government while in session. It elects a Speaker and other requisite officers, appoints appropriate committees to adjust matters for legislation. All writings are in English, but are read off in the Choctaw language. All discussions are carried on in the Choctaw language. Each member, when about to speak, rises, and respectfully addresses the Speaker, using the Choctaw word for *Speaker*, adding the syllable *ma*, which nearly corresponds with the English Mr., or Sir. The question is put in the form customary in legislative bodies, and the vote is given by rising.— The preliminary of a law is, "Be it enacted by the General Council of the Choctaw Nation." In future the Constitution and laws will be printed in both the Choctaw and English language. By the Constitution, the Government is composed of four departments, viz:—Legislative, Executive, Judicial, and Military. Three judges are elected by the people in each district, who hold inferior and superior courts within their respective districts. Ten light-horsemen in each district perform the duties of sheriffs, and the sum of $200 per annum is allowed to each district for their compensation. An act has recently been passed for the organization of the militia.

Individual Indians have frequently become civilized, and subject to the laws of white men, but the Choctaws furnish the first instance among the aboriginal tribes of America, of self-government, divested of the barbarous customs which belong to the savage state. It is truly gratifying that the laws of a commonwealth have been established within the Indian Territory, so soon after the plan of organizing an Indian Government had been undertaken by the Government of the United States. It evinces the capacity of the natives to think and act for themselves, and it may be looked upon as a sure presage of the success ultimately of the design of the Government to place all the tribes in the enjoyment of such blessings.

The following brief narrative of the manner in which our business was attended to by the last General Council, to which we presented for consideration the bill for the organization of the Indian Territory, does not fully comport with the design of the Register, nevertheless, as it relates to a period which will be marked as a new era in the history of the Indians, and as the reader cannot feel perfectly satisfied with general remarks, because, if we would understand the true condition of a people we must have before us an unvarnished story of their affairs, in common life, we will insert it.

On our arrival we informed a member of the Council that we had been commissioned to transact business with the Choctaws, and inquired in what manner it could be brought before them. He said a written notice must be sent to the Speaker; and politely offered to serve us in presenting any papers that we desired. A communication was accordingly conveyed to the Speaker, who, in due form, submitted it to the consideration of the Council. It was decided by vote that we should, at a given time, be introduced into the Council. A seat was prepared, an interpreter appointed, and a committee of two sent to inform us, and to conduct us to our seat. Having received our communication, the subject was for the present dismissed by the Council, to be considered in its proper place in the order of business.

There was in the vicinity only one house of public entertainment. For want of room in the tavern, and for the sake of economy, a majority of the members, and of others in attendance, boarded themselves in camp. This session lasted much longer than had been anticipated. The consequence was some inconvenience for want of supplies, and great anxiety to adjourn, which, with many, was increased on account of their business requiring their presence at their homes. Notwithstanding this state of anxiety, on a Saturday night they unanimously voted not to sit on the Sabbath, and by a unanimous vote, invited a Minister of the Gospel to preach in the Hall, and appointed an interpreter, and a committee to notify him. All this was done without a hint from a white man to prompt it. A congregation never behaved with more propriety under the preaching of a chaplain in Congress-Hall than did this in the National Hall of the Choctaws.

Our business was referred to a committee, which reported. The Council, in the discussion of the subject, and in making out its response, sat with closed doors. Their communication was sent to us by a messenger.

We then informed one of the members that we should be happy to take leave of the Council in a formal and friendly manner. They passed a resolution, by which they sent a member and invited us within the bar, and heard from us a brief farewell address, at the conclusion of which the Speaker and all the members rose from their seats, and remained standing until we had retired.

They sit in Council with heads uncovered, excepting some in Indian costume, who wear turbans. There were many animated speeches. We could not understand a single sentence, but were charmed with the gracefulness with which the speakers disengaged themselves from their seats, and delivered their speeches. Intonation of voice was sweet, and gesticulation appropriate; both of them free from those extremes of *high* and *low*, of *storm* and *calm*, which too often injure speeches in legislative bodies. Some of those who were prominent in debate were full-blooded Indians, in the Indian costume.

Many of the counsellors, no doubt, will soon figure as statesmen. We forbear in this place to mention names, because we should be compelled either to do injustice to some, or to fill up too much space. On one occasion a very animated debate arose, in which two ardent young men responded to each other, in two or three pretty long speeches, in which they used *written notes*.

CHICKASAWS.

By mutual agreement, the Chickasaw tribe has become merged in the Choctaws. In the treaty with the United States, by which the former ceded their country east of the Mississippi, they agreed to provide for themselves a home. This they have done within the Choctaw country, for a consideration, to be paid to the latter, of $530,000. They are allowed the privilege of settling in a body; and for that purpose an extensive tract of land, embracing much valuable soil, has been assigned on the western portion of the Choctaw country, to constitute a district, denominated the Chickasaw District. Nevertheless they are at liberty to settle elsewhere in the Choctaw country, and Choctaws are at liberty to settle within the Chickasaw District.

Few of them have yet located permanently. Large companies are yet residing in tents. This unsettled condition is attended with deterioration in every thing that belongs to civilization, comfort, and morals.

Their habits in regard to civilization are similar to those of the Choctaws. Though now a component part of the Choctaw nation, the annuities, and other moneys, which are the proceeds of the sale of their lands east of the Mississippi, are exclusively theirs. The amount of these dues and investments are such as to make the tribe uncommonly rich. It proves a great evil to them that Government is under the necessity, upon their demands, of paying them large sums of money, in their unsettled condition. It tends greatly to intemperance and idleness, and their kindred evils. It is hoped that Government will withhold from these and all other tribes, moneys, and all other things due them by treaties, so far as those engagements will allow, until the recipients are in a condition to apply those considerations to their benefit. Otherwise, while whiskey sellers, and others of vulturine principles will be benefited, the Indians will be injured by such unseasonable payments.

PRINCIPAL CHIEFS.

Mushulatubbee District,		Col. John M'Kinney,
Pushmetahau	do.	Pierre Juzan,
Opukshenube	do.	Oakchiah, (acting,)
Chickasaw	do.	George Colbert.

AGENCY, &c.

The Choctaw Agency is south of, and near to Arkansas River, and fourteen miles west of the Eastern Choctaw boundary.

Mushulatubbee District.

Capt. William Armstrong, Agent and acting Superintendent. Compensation, - - - - $1500 per an.
   Thomas Irwin, Clerk to Supt., compensation, 1000 "
   William Riddle, (native) Interpreter, " 300 "
   ——— Harris, blacksmith, } natives, " 600 "
   Saml. McCurtain, striker, } " 240 "

U. S. School Teachers.

1st.—William Wilson, (Presb.) " 833 "
2d.—Rev. Joseph Smedley (Bap.) " 500 "
3d.—Alanson Allen, M. D. (Bap.) " 500 "
4th.—Thompson McKinney, (native) " 500 "

Scholars in all 60. Post Office at the Agency.

PUSHMETAHAU DISTRICT.

Christian Spring, U. S. blacksmith. Comp.	$600	per an.
Big John, (native) striker "	240	" "
1st—Rev. R. D. Potts, (Baptist) U. S. school teacher	800	" "
2d—Rev. Ebenezer Hotchkin (Prest.) U. S. school teacher	500	" "
3d—Rev. Chas. G. Hatch (Bap.) U. S. school teacher	500	" "

Scholars in all 45. Post Office at Fort Towson.

OPUKSHENUBBE DISTRICT.

George Nelson, U. S. blacksmith, Comp.	$600	per an.
Isaac Nelson, striker	240	" "
1st—Rev. H. G. Rind, (Methodist) U. S. school teacher	833	" "
2d—Rev. Moses Perry, (Meth.) U. S. school teacher	500	" "
3d—John T. Lewis, U. S. school teacher	500	" "
4th—John Watson, " "	500	" "
5th—Peter Autin, (Presb.) U. S. school teacher	500	" "

Scholars in all 75.

In all twelve schools, supported by the United States, according to treaty stipulations,—average number of scholars to each, 15—in all 180. Instructed chiefly in English; a few scholars instructed in Choctaw—all supported by their parents.

About 60 male Choctaw youths are kept in the Choctaw academy in the State of Kentucky.

PRESBYTERIAN MISSION,

Under the direction of the A. B. C. F. M.

BETHABARA STATION has been discontinued. Rev. L. S. Williams and lady, missionaries, and Mr. Copeland, United States school teacher, have resigned; and two daily schools and two Sunday schools have been discontinued.

The church is in charge of Rev. Mr. Byington, missionary, with Mrs. Byington, and Mr. Abner D. Jones, teacher, and Mrs. Jones. Miss Merrill has retired from missionary labors.

Native Church members, 99 ⎫
White do. 7 ⎬ In all 110.
Colored do. 4 ⎭

School.—15 scholars are taught in both English and Choctaw, and supported by their parents.

Post Office, Eagletown.

In this neighborhood is a Native Missionary Society, which, in 1837, contributed for missionary purposes among themselves, about $100.

WHEELOCK STATION.

WHEELOCK STATION, on Little River, commenced in 1832.

Missionaries.—Rev. Alfred Wright, Mrs. Wright; Mr. Jared Olmstead, teacher.

School.—On the list of scholars 30. Regular in attendance 10. Supported by their parents. Also a Sabbath school.

Connected with this mission is a school on Red River, taught by a native.

Church.—Organized December 9, 1832.

Native Church members 64 }
White   do.   2 } In all 67.
Colored   do.   1 }

The native members of this Church in 1837, contributed for missionary purposes $25.

Post Office, Fort Towson.

CLEAR CREEK STATION.—Has been discontinued by the removal of the Missionaries to another place.

BETHEL STATION.—Begun in 1834.

Missionaries.—Mr. Peter Autin, Mrs. Autin, Mrs. Nancy E. Barnes.

School.—This is the United States school, previously noticed, taught in English, by Mr. Autin, and the children supported by their parents. Also a Sabbath school.

Post Office, Eagletown.

LUKFOATA STATION.—Now called Greenfield Station. Commenced in 1834.

Missionaries.—Rev. Joel Woods, Mrs. Woods; Miss Clough, teacher.

School.—35 scholars on the list. Taught in English and Choctaw. Supported by their parents. The school lately taught by Allen Kerney, a native, has been discontinued. Two Sabbath schools.

Church.—Organized May 18th, 1834.

Native Church members 18 } In all 19.
Colored   do.   1 }

The native Church members have contributed considerably towards the support of the Gospel.

Post Office, Eagletown.

PINE RIDGE STATION.—Commenced in 1835.
Missionaries.—Rev. Cyrus Kingsbury, Mrs. Kingsbury, Miss Burnham, teacher.
School.—20 scholars taught in Choctaw and English.—Supported by their parents.
Church.—Native members 1, White 22, Colored 2—in all 25. The greater portion of these belong to the United States troops, at Fort Towson.
Post Office, Fort Towson.

KIAMISHI STATION.—Commenced in 1837.
Missionaries.—Rev. Ebenezer Hotchkin, Mrs. Hotchkin.
School.—It is the United States school taught by Mr. Hotchkin, previously noticed.

Books in the Choctaw language, written upon the common principles of orthography, and printed upon our English types, with a few additional characters to denote peculiar sounds, have been well received, and many of these books are used in schools.

In all cases tuition is without cost to the natives, and in most instances, books also.

METHODIST MISSION.*

1st STATION.—Missionary, Rev. J. W. P. McKenzie, Mrs. McKenzie.
Schools.—A small school irregularly attended. Female school of 14 scholars, all supported by their parents.
Natives in society amount to several hundreds.

2d STATION.—Missionary, Rev. Moses Perry, teacher of U. States school, previously noticed.

3d STATION.—Rev. H. G. Rhind, teacher of United States school, as previously stated.

4th STATION.—Missionary, Rev. Mr. Allen, Mrs. Allen. They have a school.

Rev. Mr. Seaman, itinerant preacher. Post Office, Fort Towson.

BAPTIST MISSIONS.

1st STATION.—Commenced in June, 1833, on Canadian River.

---

* Methodist Missionaries unite with them in *society* natives who evince a willingness to receive religious instructions, though they be not really pious. We have never obtained a particular statement of the probable number of those who give evidence of genuine piety. Some of them are pious. These remarks apply to all Methodist stations.

Missionary.—Rev. Joseph Smedley, teacher of U. States school, previously noticed.

Post Office, Choctaw Agency.

2d STATION.—Missionaries, Rev. Ramsay D. Potts, Mrs. Potts, Miss Taylor. Mr. Potts is teacher of the United States school, as stated before. Miss Taylor teaches a flourishing school. Scholars of both schools taught in English, and supported by their parents.

Church.—Constituted in 1837.

Post Office, Fort Towson.

3d STATION.—Discontinued. Missionary, Rev. E. Tucker, United States school teacher, resigned.

4th STATION.—Dr. Alanson Allen teaches the United States school, as before mentioned.

Post Office, Choctaw Agency.

5th STATION.—Rev Charles G. Hatch, United States school teacher, as noticed before. Mr. Hatch commenced in 1837.

Post Office, Fort Towson.

An elementary book in the Choctaw language, upon the *New System* of writing Indian, [see an explanation of it under its appropriate head] was compiled and printed at the Shawanoe Baptist Mission House, in 1835, but has not been brought into use among the Choctaws.

CHEROKEES.

The Cherokee country is bounded as follows: beginning on the north bank of Arkansas River, where the western line of the State of Arkansas crosses the river: thence north 7° 35′ W. along the line of the State of Arkansas 77 miles to the S. W. corner of the State of Missouri; thence north along the line of Missouri, 8 miles, 64.50 ch. to Seneca River; thence west along the southern boundary of the Senecas, to Neosho River; thence up said river to the Osage lands; thence west with the southern boundary of Osage lands, 288½ miles; thence south to the Creek lands; and east along the northern line of the Creeks, to a point about 43 miles west of the State of Arkansas, and 25 miles north of Arkansas River; thence south to Verdigris River; thence down Verdigris to Arkansas River; thence down Arkansas River, to the mouth of Neosho River; thence S. 53 deg., W. one mile; thence S. 18 deg. 18 min., W. 33 miles, 28.80 ch.; thence south 4 miles, to the junction of the North Fork and Canadian

Rivers; thence down the latter to Arkansas River; and thence down Arkansas to the beginning.

They also own a tract, described by beginning at the southeast corner of the Osage lands, and running north with the Osage line 50 miles; thence east 25 miles, to the western line of Missouri; thence south on said line 50 miles; thence west 25 miles to the beginning.

They own numerous salt springs, three of which are worked by Cherokees. The amount of salt manufactured is probably about 100 bushels per day.

They also own two lead mines. Their salt works and their lead mines are in the eastern portion of their country; and all the settlements yet formed are within this eastern portion, which embraces about two and a half millions of acres.

Like the Choctaw, the Cherokee nation embraces all conceivable conditions between refinement, intelligence and wealth, and the opposite extremes but little removed from the original state. The earlier emigrants are, perhaps, in more comfortable condition than the same proportion of any other tribe within the Territory. But with the large accession of late emigrants, there has necessarily been an augmentation of uncomfortableness.

Some of them own immense herds of cattle. We counted upwards of 200 at one time within sight, grazing on the prairies, belonging to one man; and it was thought he owned about one hundred more. It was thought by some intelligent white men in their country, that within five years past they had sold between six and seven thousand head of cattle.

They probably own 3,000 horses, 15,500 hogs, 600 sheep, 110 wagons, a plough, and often several ploughs to each farm, several hundred spinning-wheels, and 100 looms.

They cultivate all kinds of culinary vegetables common to the Western country; raise corn in abundance, and have commenced the growing of wheat. Their fields are enclosed with rail fences. They have, generally, good log dwellings, (for a new country,) many of which have stone chimneys to them, with plank floors, all erected by themselves. Their houses are furnished with plain tables, chairs, and bedsteads; and with table and kitchen furniture, nearly, or quite, equal to the dwellings of white people in new countries.

They have seven native merchants, one regular physician, and, *unfortunately*, several steam doctors. Several of them have, at divers times, become partners in large contracts for furnishing the United States' Army and emigrant Indians. The traveller finds among them houses of public entertainment, with neat and comfortable accommodations.

The Cherokee Government, though highly creditable to them, is not fully systematic and judicious like that of the Choctaws. This may be accounted for by the unsettled condition of the affairs of the Cherokees for some years past. The laws extant in the Territory are such as have been adopted by the earlier emigrants, since their settlement in this country, and are not a transfer of the code to which the larger portion of the tribe were subordinate on the east of the Mississippi.

Their settlements are divided into four districts, each of which elects, for the term of two years, two members of the National Council—the title of which is, "The General Council of the Cherokee Nation." By law it meets annually on the first Monday in October. They have three chiefs, which, till lately, have been chosen by the General Council. Hereafter they are to be elected by the people. The approval of the chiefs is necessary to the passage of a law; but an act upon which they have fixed their veto, may become a law by the vote of two-thirds of the Council. The Council consists of two branches. The lower is denominated the *Committee*, and the upper the *Council*. The concurrence of both is necessary to the passage of a law. The chiefs may call a Council at pleasure, and in several other respects they retain, in some degree, the authority common to Indian chiefs. Two judges belong to each district, which hold courts when necessary. Two officers, denominated Light-horsemen, in each district, perform the duties of sheriffs. A company of six or seven, denominated Light-horsemen, the leader of whom is styled Captain, constitute a national corps of Regulators, to prevent infractions of the law, and to bring to justice offenders.

One band of 200 or 300 Cherokees, have resided about ten years in Texas, about 80 miles south of Red River, opposite Fort Towson. It is said they are in comfortable circumstances.

Principal Chiefs.—Major John Jolly, John Brown, John Luna. Post Office, Fort Gibson.

AGENCY, &c.

Gov. M. Stokes, Agent, resides at Fort Gibson, compensation, - - - - $1500 per ann.
Jack Spear, (native,) interpreter, Comp. 500 "
Jacob Gentry, blacksmith, with an ass't, " 840 "
John Richmond, do. " " " 840 "
Harvey Wyatt, do. " " " 840 "
Henry Freshour, do. " " " 840 "
James A. Hart, wheelwright, " 600 "
Thomas N. Findlay, wagonmaker, " 600 "

PRESBYTERIAN MISSIONS,
Under the patronage of the Am. Bd. Com. For. Miss.

1st. DWIGHT STATION.—Twenty miles east of the State of Arkansas. Commenced in 1829. Has 30 buildings, consisting of school-house, dining-hall, store, barn, mill, carpenter's and blacksmith's shops, &c.

Missionaries.—Rev. Cephas Washburn, Mrs. Washburn, James Orr, Mrs. Orr, Asa Hitchcock, Mrs. Hitchcock, Jacob Hitchcock, Mrs. Hitchcock, Miss Stetson, Miss Esther Smith, Miss Bradshaw. Mr. Aaron Gray, late of this station, has died. Mr. Adjuton has resigned on account of ill health.

Post Office, Kidron, Cherokee Nation, Ark.

Schools.—The male school contains 31 scholars, boarded at the cost of the mission, and 6 boarded at their homes—in all 37. All of whom are instructed in English, and some of them also instructed in Cherokee.

Of a female school, 39 board at the mission, and 7 at their homes—in all 46. Twelve pupils of the schools, who are orphans, are clothed by the mission. The residue of the scholars are clothed by their parents. Also a Sabbath school and Bible class.

About three hours a day are devoted to labor by the males in agriculture, and by the females in the domestic branches. Applications for admission into the schools are much more than can be granted. For want of the means of support the missionaries have been compelled to refuse admittance to sixty in the course of two months.

Cherokee Mission Church.—Organized at Old Dwight, in the State of Arkansas. Present number of

Native Members, 46 }
Colored,   "   1 } In all 61.
White,   "   14 }

Post Office, Kidron, Ind. Ter.

2d. FAIRFIELD STATION.—Originated in 1829.
Missionaries.—Rev. Marcus Palmer, Mrs. Palmer.
School.—Fifty scholars, some instructed in English, and some in Cherokee. A Sabbath school and a Bible class.

Church.—Native Church Members, 41 }
Colored,   "   "   4 } In all 50.
White,   "   "   5 }

Post Office, Kidron.

3d. FORKS OF ILLINOIS, now called PARK HILL STATION.—Begun in 1830.
Missionaries.—Rev. Samuel A. Worcester, Mrs. Worcester.

John F. Wheeler, printer. Here is a printing press in successful operation, on portions of the sacred scriptures, elementary school books, tracts, almanacs, &c., chiefly for the use of the Cherokees and Choctaws.

Connected with Park Hill, are missionaries Samuel Newton, teacher and catechist, Mrs. Newton, Miss Sarah Ann Palmer.

School.—Twenty scholars, supported by their parents. Also a Sabbath school and Bible class.

Post Office, Park Hill.

Instruction as imparted in Cherokee, at all of the aforementioned stations, is on the syllabic system invented by Mr. Guess, a native Cherokee.

4th STATION.—Rev. John Huss, Mrs. Huss—both natives.

METHODIST MISSIONS.

FORKS OF ILLINOIS STATION.—*Missionaries*, Rev. Mr Burtolph, Mrs. Burtolph, Rev. Mr. Essex.

School.—About 15 scholars.

Post Office, Park Hill, Ind. Ter.

SALISON STATION.—*Missionary*, Rev. Mr. Graham.

School.—About 15 scholars, supported by their parents.

Young Wolf, Boston, John Fields, and John Duncan, are native licensed preachers.

Among the late emigrant Cherokees are some hundreds of professors of religion, belonging to Baptists, Presbyterians, and Methodists, who cannot be reported by us at the present time.

CREEKS.

The country of the Creeks, or Muscogees, joins Canadian River and the lands of the Choctaws on the south, and the Cherokee lands on the east and north. Their eastern limit is about 62 miles from north to south—thence their country extends westward to the Mexican boundary, though wood becomes so scarce westward that settlements cannot extend so far. Their settlements at present extend westward from their eastern boundary about 100 miles.

Their country is fertile, and exhibits a healthy appearance, though the inhabitants, thus far, have suffered much by sickness. The causes must be such as commonly afflict the earlier settlements in new countries.

Of the latter Creek emigrants which reached Arkansas in

the winter and spring of 1837, about 200 died on the road, and after their arrival, and before the 1st of October, about 3500 of them had died, chiefly of bilious fevers. In the same year, 1837, about 300 of the earlier emigrants died. This statement is made upon the authority of an officer of Government, of respectability, the nature of whose business afforded him an opportunity of knowing the condition of these people.

The latter emigrants generally believe that their country is unhealthy. A good deal of dissatisfaction exists among them in relation to their location. Many of them would prefer to be beyond the jurisdiction of the United States Government, and not a few emigrated from the east with the design of going into Texas. The hope of removing beyond their present locations has, with many, been a very serious hindrance to improvement. It is reported, upon authority that scarcely leaves room for doubt, that more than $20,000 had been entrusted to an agent, who was a member of their tribe, to purchase land in Texas. The agent died in Texas, and the condition of the trust, if it was made, is not known to us.

They own salt springs west of their settlements. None reside in villages, though two or three places begin to assume the appearance of hamlets. They cultivate corn, and all the vegetables common to the climate and country. They spin, weave, sew, and follow other pursuits of industry. Their fields and dwellings resemble those of white people in new settlements. Many of them have large stocks of cattle. The contractors for furnishing supplies to emigrant Indians, have purchased of the earlier emigrants vast quantities of corn. Among others, the annexed amounts of purchases have been made from the following persons, prior to the crop of 1837—

Of Lewis Perryman,	$3650 worth of corn.
" Mr. Hardrich,	4500 " "
" Daniel Grayson,	1500 " "
" Richard Grayson,	1500 " "
" George Grayson,	1500 " "
" Mrs. J. McIntosh, (wid.)	1400 " "
In all	$14,050 worth of corn.

Before the crop of 1837 had been harvested, contracts were made for upwards of $25,000 worth of corn. Vast quantities still remained unsold. Even the latter emigrants, who arrived in their country the winter and spring previous to the cropping season of 1837, though they had to prepare new fields, in the months of September and October, of the same year, sold to the contractors $10,000 worth of corn. They have two native merchants.

The condition of the Creeks, in regard to civil Government, is less like that of civilized man, than is that of the Cherokees. The first emigrants, denominated the M'Intosh party, brought with them written laws from their mother country, by which, with such modifications as appeared necessary, they have ever since been governed. The latter emigrants, the principal chief of whom is Little Doctor, supported by Hopoelhyoholo, have adopted written laws since their arrival. The seat of council of the former party is on Arkansas, and that of the latter on Canadian River, about fifty miles apart. Chieftaincies are hereditary, as is common among Indian tribes, and, with some exceptions, embrace the privileges usually belonging to Indian chiefs. Each of the parties holds general councils, composed of principal and subordinate chiefs, and of those who are merely denominated Counsellors. Different bands exist, which, on the east of the Mississippi, composed districts. Each of these bands may hold a council or court, and try, and punish offenders; they decide and execute. A General Council may be called at any time. Laws are made only by the General Council, and, latterly, almost all offences are tried, and punishments inflicted, by it; some of its number being detailed for executioners.

Notwithstanding the Creeks, as a people, are in the rear of the Choctaws and Cherokees in regard to civilization, there is much intelligence, refinement, and wealth among them.

Principal Chiefs.—Rolly M'Intosh, Little Doctor, Hopoelhyoholo, Tuckebachemeko, Kauchehtustunege, Ufalabache.

Fushachemeko, Commanding General, Chilly M'Intosh and Jacob Derrisaw, Judges.

Col. James Logan, U. S. Agent—Agency eight miles from Fort Gibson—compensation, $1,500 per annum.

James Johnson, U. S. blacksmith, with a striker, (native,) compensation, $660 per annum.

Alvin Tubbs, U. S. blacksmith, with a striker, compensation, $660 per annum.

Two other smiths and strikers, at the same, compensation, $1,320 per annum.

P. G. Pollock, teacher of U. S. school, compensation, $750 per annum.

Rev. Mr. Kellam, (Baptist,) do.

BAPTIST MISSIONS.

1st STATION.—On Arkansas, commenced in October, 1829,

by John Davis, a native Muscogee. Regularly organized in October, 1832.

Missionaries.—Rev. Mr. Kellam, Mrs. Kellam, Rev. Mr. Mason, Mrs. Mason. Mr. Kellam is teacher of U. S. school above mentioned.

Church.—Constituted September 9, 1832.

Native Church members, 19 ⎫
Colored   "   "   50 ⎬ In all 73.
White   "   "   4 ⎭

2d STATION.—On Canadian River, commenced February, 1834.

Missionary.—Rev. John Davis, (native.) Mrs. Davis, (native,) has died.

Books written upon the New System have been introduced among the Creeks to a limited extent, by Mr. Davis, with success, so far as the experiment has been made.

Post Office for all within the Creek country is Fort Gibson.

SEMINOLES.

In the spring of 1836, about four hundred Seminoles emigrated from the east, and settled on the North fork of Canadian River. In October, 1837, they were reduced by sickness nearly one half.

During these awful times of mortality among the Creeks and Seminoles, the dead were frequently deposited in hollow standing or fallen trees, and the opening closed by billets of wood. A hollow standing tree frequently has an opening near the root; through this opening the corpse was inserted, and extended up the hollow of the trunk of the tree, so that it was left standing on the feet. Many abandoned their houses, after having deposited some of their dead in a temporary enclosure of boards above the ground. Guns and other articles of property were often buried with the corpse, according to Indian custom.

Subsequent to the arrival of the four hundred of whom we have spoken, and prior to October, 1838, one thousand six hundred and thirty-three had reached their new homes. Total number of emigrants, two thousand and thirty-three. Of these perhaps not more than one thousand six hundred remain alive.

The Seminoles, as a band, have become merged in the Creek nation. Politically, they are no longer a distinct people, either in regard to location or Government.

SENECAS, &c.

These consist of three bands, viz:—
- Senecas, - - - - 200 ⎫
- Senecas and Shawanoes, - - 211 ⎬ 461
- Mohawks, - - - - 50 ⎭

The lands of the Senecas proper, adjoin those of the Cherokees on the South, and, adjoining the State of Missouri thirteen miles and thirty chains; extend West to Neosho River.

The lands of the mixed band of Senecas and Shawanoes, extend North, between the State of Missouri and Neosho River, so far as to include 60,000 acres.

Seneca Chiefs.—Comstick, 1st Civil Chief, George Curley Eye, 2d Civil Chief. Captain Good Hunter, 1st War Chief. Seneca Steel, late 2d War Chief, is dead.

Small Cloud Spicer, Head-man. Thomas Brant and Tall Chief, late Head-men, are dead.

Seneca and Shawanoe Chiefs.—Civil John, 1st Civil Chief, Pe-wy-ha, 2d Civil Chief, Skillowa, 3d Civil Chief.

Onondaqua Isaac and Capt. Read, late Head-men, are dead.

Mohawk Chiefs.—Isaac White, late Principal Chief, is dead. George Heron, Chief.

R. A. Calloway, Esq., Sub-agent, compensation, $750 per annum.

One Interpreter, compensation, $300 per annum.

Two blacksmiths and strikers, compensation for each, $840 per annum.

One miller, compensation, $600 per annum.

As a people, they are, in some measure, civilized. Most of them can speak English. All cultivate land for support, and grow potatoes and other garden vegetables, and corn sufficient to support them and their live stock. Their fields are enclosed with rail fences. None reside in villages. They own about eight hundred horses, one thousand two hundred cattle, thirteen yoke of oxen, two hundred hogs, five wagons, and sixty-seven ploughs.

Their dwellings are neat hewed log cabins, erected by themselves. Within them are bedsteads, chairs, and tables, of their own manufacturing.

They own one grist and saw mill, erected at the cost of the United States.

They are generally favorably disposed towards civilization, and evince a desire to improve their condition, except in the matter of education; and latterly a few, especially of the Mohawks, have appeared favorable to schools.

METHODIST MISSION.

The Rev. Mr. Smyth and Mrs. Smyth, missionaries, lately commenced a mission, embracing a school among these people, but the aversion of some of the Indians to the operations, induced Mr. Smyth to remove across the line into the State of Missouri.

OSAGES.

The country of the Osages lies north of the western portion of the Cherokee lands, commencing twenty-five miles west of the State of Missouri, and thence, in a width of fifty miles, extends west as far as the country can be inhabited.

About one-half of the tribe reside on the eastern portion of their lands. The residue are in the Cherokee country, in two villages, on Verdigris River.

The tribe has made scarcely any improvement. Their fields are small, say one acre or less to a family, and enclosed by the insertion of stakes in the earth, to which a line, or two lines, of small poles are fastened horizontally with the bark of trees.

Their huts are constructed by inserting small poles in the ground, the smaller ends of which are bent over the room and united, so as to produce the form of a cone, some eight or nine feet high. On the outside are fastened, either broad pieces of bark, which form a kind of weather-boarding, or mats of flags or bulrushes, sewed together with threads of bark. The fire is placed in the centre, the smoke of which escapes through an aperture in the top. Many of these houses are oblong, and contain two or three fire-places, and a greater number of families. All the Osages live in villages, in which their houses are crowded close together, without order.

Some of their shelters are covered with buffalo or elk skins; and these, as well as those covered with flags, are portable.

Their villages are merely *summer* residences. In winter they change encampments, as the prospects of grazing for their horses suggests.

Within their houses are neither tables, chairs, nor bedsteads, unless we fancy an exception in a platform raised about two feet high, upon stakes set in the earth. This platform extends along the side of the hut, and may serve for a seat, a table, or a bedstead. This, however, is generally dispensed with.

The leggings and mockasins for the feet are seldom worn, except in cold weather, or when travelling in the grass. Excepting these, and the temporary garments fastened about the waist, and extending downward, neither the males nor the married females have any covering for the body, except a buffalo skin, or a blanket thrown loosely around them. This robe is their garment by day, and their bed at night.

The younger females usually wear a plain strip of cloth, eight or nine inches broad, resting upon one shoulder, and passing over the breast, and under the opposite arm.

The Osages are not fierce and warlike, as has been generally represented; on the contrary, they are uncommonly servile and manageable.

Whilst the condition of depraved man, unimproved, is pitiable in the extreme, there is something noble to be admired in these pupils of nature.

Game near them is exceedingly scarce. They go upwards of one hundred miles before they find buffalo, and then they are frequently either frighted, or whipped back empty, by their enemies. They suffer much for want of food and raiment, and they *are wretched in the extreme.*

Favorable openings for benevolent efforts for the improvement of their condition, present themselves in several places.

For some time the miseries of the Osages had been augmenting from various causes, until in the latter part of the year 1837, they became insupportable, and difficulties followed, of which the reader has been informed under the head of *Hostilities*. During nearly two years, with the exception of a few weeks, they had not enjoyed the advice or assistance in any manner of an Agent. They were without blacksmith or agriculturalist, with both of which they had once been supplied; and they were destitute of a known friend, either among the red or white people; while they were incapable themselves of devising means for their own relief, or of foreseeing an end of their accumulating woes.

In November, 1837, an account of the deplorable condition of the Osages was communicated to the Department of Indian Affairs, with a prayer that immediate relief be afforded them. The matter received prompt attention by the Commissioner of Indian Affairs, under the direction of the Secretary of War; and when the subject came before Congress, attention to it was equally prompt. A law was passed by which the Department was authorized to offer to such of the Osages as were suffering for want of food, which doubtless included nearly all, the value of their next year's annuity in provisions; and authorizing the fencing and ploughing of land for cultivation, in 1838.

Early efforts were made by the Department of Indian Affairs to carry these humane designs into execution. A Sub-agent was appointed, and directed to repair immediately to the Osages. A special agent was employed to procure men, teams, and utensils, to fence and plough prairie land, and it was hoped that 500 acres of land would soon be inclosed and prepared to receive seed. This latter was a wise measure, calculated to do substantial good, by encouraging industry, by which these poor people could be delivered from the necessity of depredating upon their neighbors.

Thus far the success of these undertakings has not quite equalled the desires which prompted them.

The Osages have so long been in the habit of anticipating their annuities a year before they become due from the Government, that few, if any, suppose they have any right to annuities for any other purposes than that of paying their debts. Therefore, hungry as they were, with wives and children, aged and infirm, they were induced to say that they would not accept of bread and meat instead of money. This choice was, no doubt, prompted by their creditors.

Teams and farming utensils were purchased, sufficient to carry on rapidly, the improvements in farming, but the preliminaries necessarily consumed so much time, that little has been done the past summer. The materials for preparing the fields are still on hand, and it is hoped will be successfully used next year.

In 1833 a field of about seventy acres was made for them by the Government, the fence around which has been destroyed. About two-thirds of this field was ploughed under the late arrangements. About fifteen acres of new prairie land ploughed, and a few acres in a field formerly cultivated by a missionary. No rails for fences, have been made.

The encouragement, though small, given them last spring, so far inspired hope and prompted industry, that the Osages raised more corn than usual, on their own unfenced little patches.

Their late Sub-agent, Doctor E. James, has resigned, and they have been placed in charge of R. A. Caloway, Sub-agent for Quapaws, Senecas, &c. They have no blacksmith, and no person residing with them in the employment of Government, except the interpreter, who is one of their own people.

BAPTIST MISSION

It has been resolved by the Baptist Board of Missions to establish a mission among these suffering people. In 1827 a young Delaware who had obtained some English education, and who could speak Osage, was hired to aid in compiling a small book in the Osage language, upon the *New System* of writing. He was conducted to the vicinity of the Osage country, with the design of introducing him as a teacher among them, when the difficulties which occurred between them and the neighboring white citizens, as stated in a preceding page, made it necessary to suspend operations, which will be renewed, and it is hoped, followed up with an energy corresponding with the evils which are sought to be remedied. For the promotion of this mission, liberal donations have been made by three ladies in the State of Delaware, long known in the spheres of benevolence.

Chiefs.—Cleremont, Monepushe. Towunmakee, Shobshinga, Nungewashe, Owausaube, Maushauketau, Kiahegetungee, and Black Dog.

QUAPAWS.

The band of Quapaws was originally connected with the Osages. Some years they resided within the Territory of Arkansas. Their lands lie immediately north of the Senecas and Shawanoes; and extend north between the State of Missouri on the east, and Neosho river on the west, so far as to include 96,000 acres.

Their country is south east of, and near to the country of the Osages.

Their habits are somewhat more improved, and their circumstances more comfortable than those of their kindred, the Osages.

About three-fourths of them have erected small log dwellings, with chimnies.* The dwellings of others are of bark. They have rail fences, and all their improvements have been made by themselves. They subsist by industry at home. They probably own 100 head of cattle, and 200 head of hogs. They have two natives who are coopers, one a repairer of guns, and one an assistant blacksmith. Unfortunately for them they settled on the lands of the Senecas and Shawanoes, from which they must soon remove, when they will settle upon their own lands.

* A house of bark, flags, brush, or skins, indicates the original condition of Indians. A dwelling constructed of wood, in the rudest manner, is an improvement. And a chimney to a dwelling is evidence of still further improvement.

A small band of forty or fifty Quapaws live in Texas, about forty miles south of the Choctaw country. About thirty souls have recently emigrated from Texas, and, by permission, have settled among the Choctaws.

Chiefs.—Kaketoh, 1st; Kiahega Teday, 2d; Tishetau Waukonta, 3d.

R. A. Caloway, Esq., Sub-agent,	Comp.	$750	per an.
Pere Peet, (half-breed) Interpreter,	"	300	"
S. B. Bright, agriculturalist,	"	600	"
George Nutting, blacksmith, with a native striker,	"	840	"

They are destitute of religious and literary teachers, and ought to be supplied without delay.

PUTAWATOMIES.

It has happened unfortunately, that in emigrating to the West, the Putawatomie tribe has become divided. About from 1,000 to 1500 have located on the north east side of the Missouri River, about 240 miles from the country designed for the permanent residence of the tribe. They are not within the limits of what is called the Indian Territory. In the autumn of the present year Commissioners were appointed to negotiate with that band for their removal, and their union with the main body of the tribe.

Nothing more was effected by this negotiation than an agreement on the part of those Putawatomies to examine the country assigned them more thoroughly than they had yet done.

About four or five hundred of the tribe have stopped near the Sauks, on the Mississippi, and manifest some inclination to remain there.

The country assigned the Putawatomies lies on the sources of the Osage and Neosho Rivers. It commences sixteen miles and four chains west of the State of Missouri, and in a width of twenty-four miles, extends west two hundred miles.

Having lately arrived in the country, they are in an unsettled condition.

Chiefs.—Topinepee, Principal. Waupenim, Miche Kekaubee, Noshakum, Quaquata, Naswaugee, Magaukwok.

Major A. L. Davis, U. S. Sub-agent, comp. $750 per an.
John Jones, temporary Interpreter. " 300 "

BAPTIST MISSION.

This Mission is a continuation of the Carey Mission in Michigan, the origin of which was in November 1817. Commencement of the present station 1837.

Missionaries.—Mr. Robert Simerwell, Mrs. Simerwell.

Mr. Simerwell has written three small books, upon the new system, which have been printed in Putawatomie. He teaches in the Putawatomie language, by visiting the settlements. Has also a Sunday school at his house.

METHODIST MISSION.

Commenced in 1838.
Missionaries.—Rev. E. T. Peery, Mrs. Peery.

CATHOLIC MISSION.

Rev. Mr. Petit, and Rev. Mr. ———, Catholics, are in the Putawatomie country, as Missionaries, but have not yet made locations.

Post Office for all among the Putawatomies, is Westport, Jackson County, Missouri.

WEAS AND PIANKASHAS.

These are bands of Miamies. Their country is north of the Putawatomies, adjoins the State of Missouri on the east, the Shawanoes on the north, and Peorias and Kaskaskias on the west. It embraces 160,000 acres.

These people own a few cattle and swine. About one half of their dwellings are constructed of logs, and the other half of bark, in true Indian style. Their fences are made of rails. They cultivate corn and culinary vegetables sufficient for a comfortable supply.

The Piankasha band is less improved than the Wea. The latter have made their fences themselves; for the former, a field of about fifty acres has been made by the United States.

Chiefs.—Swan, Gotokapooh, Bull, Charley.

Major A. L. Davis, Sub-agent.

The term for which they were entitled to a blacksmith has expired, and they now have none.

PRESBYTERIAN MISSION.

Commenced April, 1834, under the management of the Western Foreign Missionary Society, which, in 1837, relinquished it. It continues to be occupied by—

Missionaries.—Mr. Henry Bradley, Mrs. Bradley. All the other Missionaries have left.

Church.—Constituted in 1836.
Native Church members, - 7
White, " " - 2 } In all 9.

Post Office, Westport, Jackson County, Missouri.

PEORIAS AND KASKASKIAS.

These are also bands of the Miamies. Their land lies immediately west of the Weas, adjoins the Shawanoes on the north, and the Ottawas on the west. They own 96,000 acres.

The fields which they have made themselves are small, though they are generally enclosed with rail fences. The number of their cattle and swine is greater than those of their neighbors, the Weas. Their dwellings are composed of logs. The condition of these people is improving.

Chiefs.—White Skin, Peoria Jim, Paschal, and Gemasah.
Sub-agent, A. L. Davis.

METHODIST MISSION.

Commenced in 1832.

Missionaries.—Rev. N. M. Talbot, Mrs. Talbot, Mr. Reuben Aldrige.

School.—Fifteen scholars taught in English, and supported by their parents. In Society, forty natives and three whites. In all forty-three.

Many of these people understand the Shawanoe language, and use, in religious exercises, the hymn-book in that language, prepared and printed at the Shawanoe Baptist Mission House.

OTTAWAS.

The first band of Ottawa emigrants received a tract of land, containing 36,000 acres. A band which arrived subsequently, received 40,000 acres, adjoining the first.

Their lands lie immediately west of the Peorias and Kaskaskias, and south of the Shawanoes.

They all live in good log cabins. Have fields enclosed with rail fences, and raise a comfortable supply of corn and garden vegetables, and now have wheat growing. Own cattle and swine. They have purchased a cheap grist mill, worth about $250.

About 5,000 Ottawas remain in Michigan, and are expected, ere long, to join their countrymen in the Indian Territory. No tribe will be placed west of the Ottawas, so that their country may be extended westward as far as circumstances may require.

Chiefs.—Okwunoxe, Kompchau, Wosseoneguet, Waseun, Nekitchewa, Waweeshqua.

Major A. L. Davis, Sub-agent.

BAPTIST MISSION.

Commenced June, 1837.

Missionaries.—Rev. Jotham Meeker, Mrs. Meeker.

School.—Ten scholars in regular attendance, instructed in English, and supported by their parents. Instruction in the Ottawa language has, to some extent, been imparted by visits to the houses of the Indians. A small book in the Ottawa language, upon the *New System*, has been compiled and printed.

Post Office, Westport, Jackson County, Missouri.

SHAWANOES.

Immediately on the north of the Weas and Piankashas, the Peorias and Kaskaskias, and the Ottawas, lies the country of the Shawanoes; extending along the line of the State of Missouri, north twenty-eight miles, to Missouri River, at its junction with Kauzau River; thence up Kauza River to a point, sixty miles on a direct course, to the lands of the Kauzau Indians; thence south on the Kauzau line six miles; thence west, with a width of about nineteen miles, to a north and south line, one hundred and twenty miles west of the State of Missouri.— Their tract embraces 1,600,000 acres.

The Shawanoes reside in the northeastern corner of their country, near the line of Missouri, and near the Kauzau River.

Generally, their dwellings are neat hewed log cabins, erected with their own hands, and within them is a small amount of furniture. Their fields are enclosed with rail fences, and are sufficiently large to yield them corn and culinary vegetables plentifully. They keep cattle and swine, work oxen, and use horses for draught, and own some ploughs, wagons, and carts.

In conformity with treaty stipulations, Government has erected for them a saw and grist mill, the cost of which has been abut $8,000.

The Shawanoes, like many other emigrant tribes, are much scattered. Besides the two bands on Neosho, already mentioned, a band lives on the Trinity River, in Texas, and others in divers places.

Principal Chief, John Perry. Other Chiefs, Black Feather, Sa-mau-kau, Little Fox, Letho, and Black Hoof.

Agent, Richard W. Cummins, entitled Agent for the Northern Indian Agency. Compensation, $1,500 per annum. Agency house near the line of the State of Missouri, seven miles south of the Missouri River.

1st Blacksmith, R. Dunlap, compensation, $480 per annum.
Asst. do. " 240 "
2d Blacksmith, William Donelson, 480 "
Asst. do. " 240 "

METHODIST MISSION.

Under the patronage of the Mis. Soc. of the M. E. Church.

Originated in 1830.

Missionaries.—Rev. Thomas Johnson, Mrs. Johnson, Mr. Lorenzo Waugh.

School.—Thirty-two scholars, instructed in English. Eleven of them, viz: eight girls and three boys, live in the mission family, and are supported by the mission. The residue of the scholars are furnished one meal a day at the mission house, and are otherwise supported by their parents. Some of the girls have learned to weave; all sew, knit, &c. Three male youths have left the institution, who had learned the cabinet-making business, and become capable of making pretty good furniture. The institution has furnished them with tools, to enable them to set up work-shops for themselves. Other boys are making pleasing improvement in a knowledge of some of the more useful mechanic arts taught at the Mission House.

Natives in Society, - - 80 } In all 86.*
White, " - - 6 }

Religious exercises are sometimes performed in English, interpreted into Shawanoe; and sometimes in Shawanoe. In the

* This statement is made from the report of 1837; none later having been received by the Editor.

latter, Shawanoe hymns, published by the missionaries, are used. A small book in Shawanoe, on religious subjects, is in use.

BAPTIST MISSION.

Under the direction of the Baptist General Mis. Convention.

Missionaries.—Rev. Johnston Lykins, Mrs. Lykins, Rev. D. B. Rollin, Mrs. Rollin, Mr. J. G. Pratt, and Mrs. Pratt.

Native Church members, nine, viz: three Shawanoes, one Ottawa, and five Delawares; and eleven white persons. In all twenty.

At the Shawanoe station is a printing press, under the management of John G. Pratt.

Since the establishment of the printing press, there have been printed, in the Delaware language, three small books; in Shawanoe, three, of a larger size, and part of the gospel by Matthew, for the Baptists, and one for the Methodists; in Putawatomie, four; in Otoe, three, all small. Selections from which have been re-printed for the benefit of the Presbyterian missionaries among the Ioways; in Choctaw, one; in Muscogee, one elementary school book, and the gospel by John; in Osage, one; in Ottawa, one; in Kauzau, one. This last was for the Methodists. And in Wea, one school book for the Presbyterians. A revised harmony of the gospels is now in press, the greater portion of which has been printed for the Baptists.— Also, three numbers of the Annual Register of Indian Affairs, and one number of Periodical Account of Baptist Missions. One of the above, in Shawanoe, has been re-printed, the first edition having been exhausted. Also, a considerable number of hymns have been printed in various Indian languages. Besides which, there is issued from the press, a small monthly periodical, edited by Mr. Lykins, entitled "*Shauwaunowe Kesauthwau,*"—Shawanoe Sun.

In this periodical, such of the Shawanoes as have learned to read in their own language take a deep interest. Some of them have furnished matter for the work from their own pens. On account of ill health, but more particularly on account of the absence of the editor, on business, the publication of the paper was suspended some months. A circumstance much to be regretted. The editor has returned, and its publication has been resumed.

All the above prints are upon the New System of writing Indian, with a slight exception, which occurred in the Wea book.

64

FRIENDS' (QUAKER) MISSION.

Commenced June, 1837. This is a continuation of a mission commenced many years since in the State of Ohio.

Missionaries.—Moses Pearson, Mrs. Pearson.

School.—Seventeen scholars, instructed in English, fed and clothed by the mission. Attendance not regular.

Post Office for all connected with the Shawanoes, is Westport, Jackson County, Missouri.

DELAWARES.

The lands of the Delawares lie north of the Shawanoes, and in the forks of the Kauzau and Missouri Rivers, extending up the former to the Kauzau lands; thence north 24 miles to the N. E. corner of the Kauzau survey. It extends up the Missouri River to Cantonement Leavenworth, a distance of about 23 miles on a direct course; thence with a line westward to a point 10 miles north of the N. E. corner of the Kauzau lands; and then in a slip only 10 miles wide, it extends west along the northern boundary of the Kauzaus, to the distance of 208 miles from the State of Missouri.

The Delawares reside on the eastern portion of their country, not far from the junction of the Missouri and Kauzau Rivers. They generally occupy good hewed log cabins, and have some furniture within them. They enclose their fields with rail fences; keep cattle and hogs, apply horses to draught, and use oxen and ploughs. They cultivate corn and garden vegetables sufficient for their use, and have commenced the culture of wheat. They own a grist and saw-mill, erected by the United States.

Some of the Delawares yet remain in the Lake country in the north. A few are in Texas; and a band of between 50 and 100 souls reside on the Choctaw lands on Red River, about 120 miles west of the State of Arkansas. These latter have acquired a knowledge of the languages of the Camanches, Kiaways, Pawnees, and other tribes to the Southwest, and are frequently employed as interpreters by traders from the Indian Territory.

Principal Chiefs.—Nah-ko-mund, Catch-him, Non-on-da-gon.

Maj. R. W. Cummins, Agent.

A blacksmith and assistant,   compensation $720 per. an.
A miller   "   500 " "

METHODIST MISSION.

Commenced in 1831.
Missionaries.—Rev. L. B. Stateler, Mrs. Stateler, Rev. Abraham Millice. Rev. Mr. Peery and Rev. Mr. Ellefrit, resigned.

School.—Fourteen scholars, twelve of whom are supported by the Mission, and board at the Mission house; and to the other two is given one meal a day.

Natives in society, 75
Whites, 2
In all 77.

BAPTIST MISSION.

Commenced in 1832. Under the superintendence of Rev. J. Lykins, of the Shawanoe mission.

School.—Mr. I. D. Blanchard and Mrs. Blanchard, teachers. Ten scholars instructed in English. Three of them are fed and clothed at the expense of the Mission, and the residue by their parents. Two of the latter reside in the Mission family.

Mr. Blanchard has also taught about 50 Delawares, chiefly adults, to read their own language. Has compiled and had printed three small books, embracing some hymns, and is revising a Harmony of the Gospels, which is nearly out of press; all upon the New System. The above prints he has introduced among his people, with good success.

Post Office for all among the Delawares, Westport, Jackson County, Missouri.

UNITED BRETHREN'S (MORAVIAN) MISSION.

Commenced in 1837.
Missionary.—Rev. Jesse Vaughler.

KAUZAUS.*

The country of this tribe lies on the Kauzau River, commencing 60 miles west of the State of Missouri; thence in a width of 30 miles, it extends west as far as the country can be inhabited.

About 1000 of them live on the south side of Kauzau River, six miles west of the eastern boundary of their country. About 150 on the north side, and about 600 also on the north side, about 25 miles west.

* Different persons have, at various times, written the name of this tribe differently, as suited the fancy of each. We have chosen to adhere to the pronunciation of the natives themselves, which is Kau-zau.

Their language, habits, and condition in life, are, in effect, the same as those of the Osages. In matters of peace and war, the interests of the two tribes are blended; and they are virtually one people.

Like the Osages, the Kauzaus are ignorant, poor, and wretched in the extreme; and are as uncommonly servile, and easily controlled by white men who mingle with them. Though we are happy to be able to state that civilization and improvement have commenced among them.

Almost all live in villages, where their huts are crowded closely, without order in their arrangement. Besides their houses of bark, and of flags, constructed like those of the Osages, they have a few of earth. These are circular, and in form of a cone, the wall of which is about two feet in thickness, and is sustained by wooden pillars within. Like their other huts, they have no floor except the earth. The fire is in the centre, and the smoke escapes directly above. The door is low and narrow, so that in entering, a person must half crawl. The door, as in their other huts, is closed by a skin of some animal suspended therein.

Their patches of corn are chiefly without enclosures, and cultivated with the hoe. Besides the small fields prepared by themselves, they cultivate about 300 acres of land fenced and ploughed by the Government, two years ago. The two principal chiefs occupy log dwellings, erected for them by the Government, some years since.

A few have been induced by their missionary to quit the villages, and to make separate settlements, and to erect log dwellings, &c. The natives own four yokes of oxen and one wagon. These have been furnished by the Government. They own a very few hogs, and no stock cattle.

Principal Chiefs.—1st Nam-pa-war-rah, (Fury.) 2d Kia-he-ga-wa-ta-in-ga, (Reckless-Chief.) 3d Kia-he-ga Wah-cha-ha, (Hard-Chief.) 4th Me-chu-shing-a, (Little White Bear.)

Maj. R. W. Cummins, Agent.
Cleremont Lessert, interpreter, Compensation $300 per an.
N. A. Warren, blacksmith, " 480 " "
Wm. Pichalker, (native) striker, " 240 " "
James Hays, farmer, " 600 " "

METHODIST MISSION.

Undertaken in 1835.
Missionaries.—Rev. Wm. Johnson, Mrs. Johnson.
School.—Three natives live in the Mission family, for the purpose of receiving instruction. Instruction in their own lan-

guage is also imparted, as occasions admit. A small book, in the Kauzau language, upon the New System, has been published and brought into use.

KICKAPOOS.

The country of the Kickapoos lies north of the Delawares, extending up Missouri River to a point 30 miles direct; thence westward, about 45 miles; and thence south 20 miles, to the Delaware line. Including 768,000 acres.

They live on the southeastern extremity of their lands, near Cantonment Leavenworth.

In regard to civilization, their condition is similar to that of the Peorias.

They have commenced a promising career of improvement. The amount of grain raised the last year exceeded that of any preceding. Several of them had more than enough for their own use. Sales were made of from $10 to $100 worth. They own cattle and hogs; their stock of which have recently been increased by the fulfilment of a treaty stipulation of the United States, by which they received 340 cattle, and about $700 worth of stock hogs. They have about 30 yokes of oxen; 14 yokes of these they have lately purchased, chiefly with the proceeds of their farms.

They own a saw and grist-mill, erected by the United States. These are in poor condition.

Nearly half of the Kickapoos are unsettled, and scattered in divers places. Some in Texas, and among the Southern tribes. These rovers are in bad credit.

Chiefs.—Pos-sa-che-haw, Ken-u-kuk.
Agent.—R. W. Cummins.
Mr. Potter, blacksmith,   Compensation $480 per an.
Charles Fish, (Shawanoe) striker,   "   240   "   "
T. B. Markham, miller, employed by the Indians.

METHODIST MISSION.

Commenced in 1833.
Missionaries.—Rev. J. C. Berryman, Mrs. Berryman, Rev. David Kinnear. The latter is U. States school teacher. Compensation $480.

Natives in society, 161 } In all 164.
Whites,   3   }

Post Office, Fort Leavenworth, Ind. Ter.

SAUKS.

The country of the Sauks contain 128,000 acres, adjoining the northern boundary of the Kickapoos, and bounded by the Missouri River on the northeast.

They are but little improved. According to treaty stipulations, they have had some improvements in houses and fields made for them by the United States, and are entitled to more. Some live stock furnished them, and more will be given them hereafter. Having but recently settled in their country, little has yet been done for their comfort, either by themselves or by the Government.

The main body of the Sauks, usually denominated the Sauks and Foxes, estimated at 6,400 souls, reside in the Ioway Territory, on the waters of the Mississippi. It is expected that they will, ere long, unite with the band already here. Unappropriated lands adjoin these, on which the whole can be accommodated.

Principal Chief.—Moless.
Maj. John Dougherty, Agent.   Comp. $1500 per an.
A blacksmith,   "   500   "   "
A farmer,   "   600   "   "
Post Office, Liberty, Clay County, Mo.

IOWAYS.

The country of the Ioways contains 128,000 acres, adjoining the northern boundaries of the Sauks, with the Missouri River on the northeast, and the Great Nemaha River on the north.

Their condition is similar to that of the Sauks. The aid which they have received, and are to receive from the Government about the same in proportion to numbers. The villages of the Sauks and Ioways are within two miles of each other.

Chiefs.—White Cloud, Nocheninga, Congee, Wautanaungquokoke, Watchamonga.

Maj. John Dougherty, Agent.
Jeffrey (colored man) interpreter,   Comp. $300 per an.
A blacksmith,   "   500   "   "
Mr. Wm. Duncan, farmer,   "   600   "   "
Mr. Aurey Ballard, teacher of U. S. school,   500   "   "

PRESBYTERIAN MISSION.

Commenced in 1837, by transfer from the northeast side of the Missouri, where it had been in operation a few years.

Missionaries.—Rev. William Hamilton, Mrs. Hamilton, Mr. Aurey Ballard, U. States school teacher, as above stated; Mrs. Ballard, Mr. Irwin, Mrs. Irwin, teachers.

School.—The school has not yet gone fully into operation. Mr. and Mrs. Ballard support, out of their own funds, six Indian children in their own family, to whom they impart instruction. Instruction has also been imparted by visits to the Indians; and among the learners, six or eight youths have made tolerable proficiency.

On these visits a few have been taught in the Ioway language. The Otoe and Ioway languages are nearly the same. An edition of a small book, published in the former language, by Mr. Merrill, is in use among the Ioways at this Mission.

Post Office, Liberty, Jackson County, Missouri.

OTOES.

This tribe claims a portion of land in the fork between Missouri and Platte Rivers. But their country is understood to extend southward from the Platte River, down Missouri to Little Nemaha River, a distance of about 40 miles; thence their southern boundary extends westward up Little Nehama to its source; and thence due west. Their western and northern boundaries are not particularly defined. Their southern boundary is about 25 miles north of the Ioway lands.

By treaty, such of their tribe as are related to the whites, have an interest in a tract adjoining the Missouri River, and extending from the Little Nemaha to the Great Nemaha, a distance of about twenty-eight miles, and ten miles wide. No Indians reside on this tract.

The condition of these people is similar to that of the Osages and Kauzaus. They take the buffalo with less difficulty than the former, and consequently suffer less with hunger.

Their villages are on both banks of the Great Platte River, about eight miles west of the Missouri. Most of their houses are made of earth, according to the description given of earthen houses among the Kauzaus. The United States Government has fenced and ploughed for them 130 acres of land. In 1838, they cultivated about 300 acres of corn, which is 100 acres more than they cultivated the preceding year. They own six ploughs, furnished by the Government. These they kept pretty constantly in use during the cropping season, most commonly by the chiefs and principal men.—The man would hold the plough, and his wife, or one of his children, lead the horse. This was their second year's effort at ploughing. The Missouri tribe of Indians is merged in that of the Otoes.

Chiefs.—1st. Shokapee, (Big Kauzau,) Meeh-hohungee, (Big Girl,) Wauronesaw, (a Surrounder) Ictan, the late principal chief, has been murdered. Missouri Chief Hajekathake, (Osage Killer.)

Major John Dougherty, Agent.

M. Dorion, interpreter,	Compensation	$300 per an.
S. Gilmore, blacksmith, with an asst.	"	720 "
Agriculturalists, J. L. Dougherty,	"	600 "
James Case,	"	600 "
Rev. Moses Merrill, U. S. school teacher,	"	500 "

BAPTIST MISSION.

Commenced October, 1833.

Missionaries.—Rev. Moses Merrill, United States school teacher, as stated above, Mrs. Merrill.

School.—The Otoes are absent from their villages hunting more than half of the year. In consequence of which regular attendance to instruction cannot be secured. Very little has been done in imparting instruction in English; 36 scholars attend during the season that they are about their villages, to receive instruction in the Otoe language. These are chiefly young men, and most of them belonging to influential families. About half of these read, and unite in singing hymns. Boarding in part is furnished them by Mr. Merrill, out of his own funds.

Much of Mr. Merrill's time is taken up in administering to the sick, in compliance with the pressing requests of the Otoes, and in encouraging industry among them.

Post Office for all connected with this tribe is, Fort Leavenworth, Indian Territory.

OMAHAS.

The country of the Omahas adjoins the Platte River on the south, and the Missouri River on the northeast; their northern and western boundaries are indefinite.

They have made a village on the southwest bank of Missouri, at a place chosen for them by the Government, about 120 miles above the Otoe village. There they have built houses of earth, similar to those of the Otoes.

Their condition is, in all respects, similar to that of the Otoes, who are their friends and allies.

Principal Chief.—Big Elk.
Agent.—J. Dougherty.
Blacksmith.—Compensation, $480 per annum.
Asst. " " 240 "

The United States school, which had been undertaken, has been discontinued.

Causes, unknown to us, have induced the smith to leave the Omaha country, and locate on the bank of the Missouri, eight or ten miles above the Great Platte.

BAPTIST MISSION.

Commenced in 1837, with Rev. Chandler Curtis, United States school teacher, as stated above, and Mrs. Curtis, has been discontinued, and the Mission buildings left unoccupied.

PAWNEES.

The country of the Pawnees is westward of the Otoes and Omahas. Their boundaries are not definite. Their villages are chiefly on the Great Platte, and its waters.

In their habits and condition they are further removed from those of civilized man than any tribe which we have noticed. Some of their huts are of earth, like those spoken of among the Kauzaus.

Agent.—John Dougherty.
Blacksmith.—Charles C. Rentz; comp. $480 per annum.

Hitherto the Pawnee smith has been located at the Otoe Agency.

BAPTIST MISSION.

The mission to the Otoes, which at first embraced the Omahas, was undertaken with reference to the Pawnees also; and this design is still maintained.

PRESBYTERIAN MISSION.

Under the direction of the American Board For. Miss.
Begun in 1834.

Missionaries.—Mr. Allis, Mrs. Allis, Rev. John Dunbar, Mrs. Dunbar. These have not yet formed a permanent settlement among the Pawnees. They reside on the Missouri, say ten miles above the Great Platte.

Doctor Benedict Saturlee, who had been connected with this mission, is dead. In the spring of 1837, he went on a journey of some hundreds of miles to one of the remoter tribes. As he was returning in the month of April, with two Pawnees as travelling companions, a season of greater cold and deeper snow occurred than is usual at that period. The horses of our travellers failed; their own provisions also failed. They were in a place where the Indians feared to lie by on account of enemies, had there been no other objection. They resolved to abandon their horses, and go home on foot. Doctor Saturlee, for reasons unknown, declined the adoption of that course. He was left behind, with his horse, in the bleak prairies, and never more seen. A company of trappers returning from the Rocky Mountains, a few months afterwards, discovered his gun, and some other articles on the prairie, by which it appeared that he had not been killed by a foe, but had perished with hunger and cold, though his body was not found.

PUNCAHS.

The Puncah is a small band, originally from the Omaha tribe, on the Missouri, in the northern extremity of the country spoken of as the Indian Territory. Their circumstances are similar to those of the Pawnees. They have no missionaries.

OTHER BAPTIST MISSIONARIES.

The author of this publication, and his wife, have been missionaries to the Indians ever since the year 1817. In August, 1828, they removed from among the tribes around Lake Michigan, to what is now termed the Indian Territory. Their circumstances differ from those of other missionaries, inasmuch as their labors have not been located to a particular tribe, especially since they left the tribes of the North; but they have extended their labors to places and matters generally; and they support themselves without cost to the Missionary Convention. Their Post Office is Westport, Jackson County, Mo.

MISSIONARIES IN GENERAL.

Excepting the missionaries noticed in the last article, and a few who have received appointments from Government as school teachers, all others, of every denomination of Christians, are supported by the societies which patronize them severally; but they receive no more than a bare support. The amount allowed varies according to the expensiveness of living at each station, and is fixed by the missionary societies, so as barely to cover the necessary current expenditures of the several missionaries. None of them, therefore, receive any compensation which they can lay up as their own personal property. By this means the voluntary surrender of the missionary to labors of benevolence for the benefit of the Indians, places him beyond the influence of temptation to acquire property. He does not receive even a promise of support for his family, should they out-live him; but he trusts all to Providence.

In the action of Government, missionaries are recognised as being in its service, and, like Agents, Sub-agents, and others authorized to reside in the Indian country, enjoy its protection. Should a missionary be convicted of a violation of the laws regulating intercourse with the Indian tribes, Government would expel him; but this circumstance would not be an obstacle to prevent the occupying of the station by an approved missionary.

By a regulation in the Department of Indian Affairs, missionaries are required to report to the United States Agent within whose agency they are, their establishments, and their operations, so far as schools are concerned; stating the cost of their buildings, their location, the names of the teachers, the number of scholars, their success, &c.

Rev. Johnston Lykins exercises a general agency, extending to the various tribes within the Territory, according to instructions given him from time to time, by the Baptist Board of Missions; and is duly authorized to fulfil this trust by authority from the proper officer of Government.

Rev. Thomas Johnson is superintendent of all the missionary stations of the Missionary Society of the Methodist Episcopal Church, north of the Cherokees.

Rev. Mr. Harral is superintendent of the Methodist stations among the Cherokees and Choctaws. Post Office, Vineyard, Washington County, Arkansas.

Missionary Societies are voluntary associations, composed of members of the several Christian Churches in the United States, which have embarked in the cause of missions.

The office of the American Board of Commissioners for Foreign Missions, is in Boston, Mass. Secretaries, Rev. Rufus Anderson, and Rev. David Green.

The office of the Board of Managers of the Baptist General Missionary Convention, is also in Boston, Massachusetts. Corresponding Secretary, Rev. Lucius Bolles, D. D. Treasurer, Hon. Heman Lincoln.

The office of the Western Foreign Missionary Society, is in New-York. Corresponding Secretary, Walter Lowrie, Esq.

The office of the Missionary Society of the Methodist Episcopal Church, is in New-York. Corresponding Secretary, Rev. N. Bangs, D. D. The immediate management of Indian missions, is by "The Mission Committee of the Conference," in connection with the President of the Conference.

WANT OF MISSIONARIES.

In twelve or eighteen months, the increase of missionaries, including those of all denominations, to wit: Presbyterians, Methodists, Baptists, Quakers, United Brethren, (Moravians,) and Catholics, equals about $11\frac{1}{2}$ per cent. The increase of the Indian population within the Indian Territory, during the same length of time, has been about $37\frac{3}{4}$ per cent. So far, therefore, as the wants of the Indians can be inferred from numbers, their wants have increased about three times as fast as the means of relieving them.

The last number of the Register showed a lamentable want of missionaries. Instead of improvement, or even keeping things as they then were, we have allowed them to become three-fold worse. Let those who profess to be the disciples of the Benevolent Saviour of man, prepare to settle the fearful account!!

TEMPERANCE SOCIETIES.

Within the Indian Territory are three Temperance Societies. The Fort Towson Temperance Society was organized in 1836. On the 1st January, 1838, its members were 6 officers of the garrison, 38 privates, and 3 citizens. The female branch of the Society numbered 14. In all 61.

The Cherokee Temperance Society was organized in 1836.

It embraces nearly 300 members. Its President and four of its Vice-Presidents are Cherokees.

The Otoe Temperance Society was formed in 1836. At our latest advices it embraced 36 Otoes, besides the white members.

All of the above Societies are constituted upon the plan of entire abstinence from intoxicating liquors.

Provisions of the Government of the United States, for the Education of the Indians within the Indian Territory, and for their improvement in civilization generally.

BESIDES the annual appropriation of $10,000 for the purposes of education, a portion of which is applied within the Indian Territory, and besides the schools which receive support from Government already mentioned, the following provisions have been made, viz: for the

KAUZAUS.

By treaty of 1825, thirty-six sections of *good* land were to be selected and sold, and the proceeds applied to the education of Kauzau children *within* their country.

The number of acres was 23,040. The value of which, at the minimum price of Government land, would be $28,800.

The cost of feeding, clothing, lodging, and instructing an Indian youth, if applied in conjunction with benevolent institutions, within the Indian country, may be kept within $50 per annum. At this rate, the proceeds of the Kauzau lands, had they been sold, as above calculated, would keep fifty children in school eleven years. Should the scholars be supported by their parents, the number which might be educated with the sum just stated, would be quadruple the above. A school-house, books, and teacher, for 40 scholars, could be furnished for $500 per annum. At this rate, their education fund, to wit, $28,800, would keep 200 children in school eleven years.

These lands have been selected; but unfortunately, the selection was not made by examination of the country, but upon the plats. The consequence is, that more than half the land is of little value.

The State of Missouri was allowed seminary lands, in the same district of country. The claims of the Kauzaus were entitled to precedence. Missouri fixed the minimum price of her lands at two dollars per acre, and it was not until the greater part was sold, that the price was reduced to $1 25 per acre.

Had the Kauzau lands been selected according to the provisions of the treaty, not an acre would have remained until this time unsold, and it could have been sold for two dollars per acre, which would have amounted to the sum of $46,080.

The difference between this sum and the calculation at $1 25 per acre is $17,280. This latter sum has been lost to this education fund. It would have kept 31 Kauzau children in school more than 11 years; and, if the youths had been supported by their parents, it would have kept 124 children in school the same length of time.

But the loss will more than double this calculation. The amount of Kauzau lands which have been sold is about 8000 acres, which would leave a balance unsold of 14,040 acres. This unsold land is of little value, and will scarcely sell for any thing. The loss to the Kauzaus has, therefore, been very great.

The proceeds of the sales which have been made of Kauzau lands amount to about $11,250—which sum has not yet been applied.

By the same treaty of 1825, provision was made for the application of $600 per annum, to aid them in agriculture.

OSAGES.

The treaty of 1825 provides " that the President of the United States shall employ such persons to aid the Osages in their agricultural pursuits as to him may seem expedient."

Under this provision, the sum of $1,200 a year, with the exception of a few years, has been expended by the Government. This has been done without rendering any substantial benefit to the tribe.

If the annuity of $1,200 per annum were expended in fencing and ploughing land, it would prepare for seed two fields of 75 acres each, or 150 acres each year, until they should need no more.

The same treaty of 1825 required that 54 sections of land be laid off under the direction of the President of the United States, and sold, and the proceeds applied to the support of schools for the education of the Osage children. The number of acres is 34,560.

Early in the present year, (1838,) the Department of Indian Affairs made an arrangement with the Osages, in which it was agreed that the latter should be paid at the rate of $2 an acre. This commutation has secured to the Osage tribe $69,120 for education purposes.

This sum, if applied according to our calculations for the Kauzaus, would support and instruct in school 100 children more than 13 years and a half. Should the children be supported by their parents, the above sum would afford instruction to 400 children thirteen and a half years.

DELAWARES.

The treaty with the Delawares of September, 1829, provides that 36 sections of the *best* land within the district which was at that time ceded to the United States, be selected and sold, and the proceeds applied to the support of schools for the education of Delaware children.

Within the current year (1838) the Delawares have agreed to a commutation of $2 per acre, which secures to them for the purposes of education the sum of $46,000.

According to our calculations for the Kauzaus, this sum would feed, clothe, and educate 100 youths 9 years, or if supported by their parents, it would keep 400 children in school 9 years.

PUTAWATOMIES.

By the treaty of 1833, the Putawatomies are allowed the sum of $70,000, "for purposes of education, and the encouragement of the domestic arts." They desire that, for the present, only the interest of this sum be expended. The interest of $70,000, at five per cent. per annum would be $3,500 a year. This would keep at a mission school in the Indian country, 70 Indian youths; or if the children should be fed and clothed by their parents, it would afford instruction to 280, kept perpetually in school.

Also, in the same treaty, is provided the sum of "$150,000 to be applied to the erection of mills, farm houses, Indian houses, and blacksmiths' shops; to agricultural improvements, to the purchase of agricultural implements, and [live] stock; and for the support of such physicians, millers, farmers, blacksmiths, and other mechanics, as the President of the United States shall think proper to appoint."

KICKAPOOS.

The treaty of October 24, 1832, provides that the United States shall pay $500 per annum, for ten successive years, for the support of a school, purchase of books, &c., for the benefit of the Kickapoo tribe, upon their own lands.

The school house and teacher which have been furnished them, have been in conformity with this stipulation.

The same treaty provides $4,000 for labor and improvements on the Kickapoo lands. If the sum of $4,000 should be applied in fencing and ploughing prairie land, it would prepare for receiving seed twelve fields, of forty acres each. But it is probable that, for the Kickapoos, it would be desirable to make some fields in wood lands, where the cost of preparing them would be greater than in prairie.

OTOES.

The treaty of 1830, secures to this tribe agricultural implements, to the amount of $500 annually, until the year 1840. The treaty of September, 1833, continues this annuity of $500 ten years longer, to be paid in the same articles.

The treaty of 1830, provides for a blacksmith, and an assistant blacksmith, for the term of ten years, and longer, if the President of the United States shall think proper. The smiths have been employed, and are at work for them.

The treaty of 1833, stipulates that a flouring mill, to operate by horse power, shall be erected for the benefit of the tribe.

Also, the value of $1,000, in live stock, will be given them; but it will remain so far under the control of the proper officers of Government, that the Otoes will not be allowed improvidently to waste it.

Two farmers are to reside in their country, to assist them, five years, and longer, by the direction of the President of the United States. These two farmers could fence and plough fifty acres of land each year, and thus furnish them with two hundred and fifty acres of land ready for seed, and enclosed in fields of convenient dimensions.

The two farmers have been employed, and have already fenced and ploughed one hundred and thirty acres of prairie land for them.

The treaty of July, 1830, secures to sundry tribes mentioned therein, $3,000 annually, for the term of ten years, for the education of their children. Of this sum, the Otoes are entitled to $500 yearly.

In the treaty of 1833, an additional annuity of $500 is provided for education, for the term of five years, or longer. While these annuities for education continue, they would support, in a boarding school, twenty Indian youths, or they would furnish instruction to eighty, who were fed and clothed by their parents.

OMAHAS.

The treaty of July, 1830, provides that an annuity of $500 shall be paid to the Omahas, in agricultural implements, for ten successive years, and longer, if the President of the United States shall think proper.

Also, a blacksmith, and the necessary tools, shall be furnished them the same length of time.

A treaty has been held with this tribe, by which their claims to a tract of country which has lately been attached to the State of Missouri have been extinguished. This treaty provides for fencing and ploughing one hundred acres of land.

The sum of $500, for the term of ten years, is to be applied to the education of their children. This sum would keep, in a boarding school, in the Omaha country, ten children, during the continuance of the allowance, or forty youths the same length of time, should they be supported by their parents.

PAWNEES.

The treaty of October, 1833, stipulates that the United States shall pay to the Pawnees, annually, for five years, $2,000 worth of agricultural implements, and this annuity is to be continued longer than five years, if the President deem it expedient.

Also, the value of $1,000, in oxen and other live stock, is to be delivered to the tribe, whenever the President of the United States shall believe that they are prepared to profit by them.—This stock, after being taken into the tribe, is to be placed in charge of the proper authorities of the United States, to prevent the Indians from prematurely destroying it, through improvidence. This is an excellent arrangement. The live stock which was paid to the Osages and the Kauzaus, was a disadvantage to them instead of a benefit. Their cultivated grounds were not enclosed with fences, and consequently they could not keep cattle and swine. In addition to this, their habitual improvidence was such, that they had not patience to wait for future advantages from stock. The stock was immediately consumed for food, and only served to indulge them awhile in indolence.

Further, a sum not exceeding $2,000 per annum, for ten years, is to be expended in support of two smitheries, with two blacksmiths in each, together with iron, steel, &c.

Four grist-mills are to be erected for them, to operate by horse power.

Four farmers are to be provided for them, for the term of five years. The country of the Pawnees being more remote from white settlements than that of the Osages, and others, the cost of enclosing and ploughing land would be increased. But if Government should thus employ their farmers, one hundred acres each year could conveniently be prepared for seed. This would give them five hundred acres of cultivated land, enclosed with fences.

The sum of $1,000 a year, for ten years, is to be allowed for the establishment of schools. This sum will support, in school, twenty children during the ten years; or if they should be supported by their parents, eighty children could be kept in school the same length of time.

CHEROKEES.

It is stipulated in the treaty of the 6th May, 1823, that "the United States will pay $2,000 annually, to the Cherokees, for ten years, to be expended under the direction of the President of the United States, in the education of their children *in their own country*, in letters and the mechanic arts. Also, $1,000, towards the purchase of a printing press and types."

By the treaty of December 29, 1835, the sum of $150,000 is provided for the support of common schools, and such a literary institution of a higher order, as may be established in the Indian country. The above sum is to be added to an education fund of $50,000, which previously existed, making the sum of $200,000, which is to remain a permanent school fund, only the interest of which shall be consumed. The application of this money will be directed by the Cherokee nation, under the supervision of the President of the United States. The interest of this fund, at five per cent., would be $10,000 per annum. This would keep in a boarding school two hundred children; or eight hundred could be kept in school, if supported by their parents.

CREEKS.

The treaty with the Creeks, of March 24, 1832, stipulates that "$3,000, to be expended as the President may direct, shall be allowed, for the term of twenty years, for teaching their children."

At a treaty on Arkansas, February 14, 1833, it was stipulated that $1,000 annually, during the pleasure of the President and Congress, should be applied, under the direction of the former, to the purposes of education.

These two annuities, amounting to $4,000, would support eighty scholars in a boarding school, or would instruct constantly three hundred and twenty scholars, who should be supported by their parents.

CHOCTAWS.

The treaty of September, 1830, provides for keeping forty Choctaw youths at school, under the direction of the President of the United States, twenty years. Also, the sum of $2,500 is to be applied to the support of three teachers of schools for the Choctaws, twenty years.

There is also an unexpended balance of former annuities, amounting to about $25,000, which is to be applied to the support of schools at twelve different places, at each of which a school house has been erected by the United States, and paid for out of this fund.

Also, by the treaty of 1825, they are entitled to an annuity of $6,000, for the support of schools within the Choctaw nation.

SAUKS.

Of an annuity provided for sundry tribes by the treaty of Prairie Du Chien, of 1830, the Sauks are entitled to $500 a year, for purposes of education.

By treaty of September, 1836, they are entitled to a schoolmaster, a farmer, and blacksmith, as long as the President of the United States may deem proper. They are to have three comfortable houses erected for them, and two hundred acres of prairie land fenced and ploughed; to be furnished such agricultural implements as may be necessary, for five years; one ferry boat, two hundred and five head of cattle, one hundred stock hogs, and a flouring mill. They have, therefore, the means of supporting two schools among them.

IOWAYS.

The Ioways are entitled to an annuity of $500, for purposes of education, by virtue of the treaty of Prairie Du Chien, of 1830. Also, a blacksmith, and instruments for agricultural purposes, to the amount of six hundred dollars.

By the treaty of September, 1836, it is stipulated that five comfortable houses shall be erected for them. Two hundred acres of prairie land shall be fenced and ploughed. They shall be furnished with a farmer, blacksmith, and schoolmaster, as long as the President of the United States may deem proper. They shall be furnished with such agricultural implements as may be necessary, for five years; one ferry-boat, two hundred and five head of cattle, one hundred stock hogs, and a flouring mill.— These may, therefore, have two schools among them.

CHICKASAWS.

The treaty of the 24th May, 1834, provides that $3,000 annually, for fifteen years, shall be applied, under the direction of the Secretary of War, for purposes of education.

By the peculiar manner by which they ceded their country east of the Mississippi to the United States, the Chickasaws have become very wealthy. They have a large fund applicable to various objects of civilization, including education. Of this fund, the sum of $10,000 has been made available, for the present, for purposes of education.

MILITARY POSTS,

Within the Indian Territory.

The United States' troops change places so frequently that little can be reported with certainty respecting the stations of particular persons. We are politely favored, by gentlemen of the Army, with statements in detail of the number of companies, names of officers, &c., at the different garrisons, but frequently before our account comes before the public, these troops have given place to others.

A new fort is being erected on the ground on which Fort Smith formerly stood, on the south bank of the Arkansas River, immediately on the line between the State of Arkansas and the Choctaws.

Also a fort has been commenced within the Cherokee country, about 40 or 50 miles north of Arkansas River, and not far from the State of Arkansas.

The necessity, at present, for some military posts within the Indian Territory, cannot be doubted, and that the number should be small, is equally plain. The organization of the Territory will secure peace on our border by means more pleasant than that of a suspended rod; and it should be a rule, from which there ought to be no departure, to throw no more white men into the country of the Indians than the circumstances of the latter positively require.

The inhabitants of the Indian Territory having a vast uninhabited prairie of four or five hundred miles, on their west and north, have nothing to fear from inroads of remote tribes from these quarters. On the southwest access is less difficult, and in that quarter a pretty constant intercourse has already been established between emigrant and remote tribes. It will, therefore, probably be deemed expedient to establish a military post upon that frontier of the Indian Territory, on the north bank of Red River, say 100 miles above Fort Towson.

FORT TOWSON.

In about north latitude 34°, and west longitude from Washington 19°. It is within the Choctaw country, six miles north of Red River, and six miles east of the Kiamishi River, about 50 miles west of the eastern boundary of the Choctaws; 238 miles from Little Rock, Arkansas State; 280 miles from Natchitoches, La.; and 120 miles from Fort Smith, on the Arkansas River.

The erection of the Fort, at present occupied, was begun in the autumn of 1831. The situation is pleasant, the water is good, and the place is esteemed healthy.

Lieut. Col. J. H. Vose, commanding. Recently the post was garrisoned by four companies of the 3d Infantry.

FORT GIBSON.

Fort Gibson is on the east bank of Neosho River, two miles north of Arkansas River, and two and a half miles below the junction of Arkansas and Verdigris Rivers. It is within the country of the Cherokees, and about 43 miles west of their Eastern boundary; about 55 miles on a direct course from Fort Smith, and about 140 miles north of Fort Towson.

It was established in 1823, by removal from Fort Smith.

Fort Gibson, or the mouth of Verdigris River, may be considered the head of steamboat navigation.

General M. Arbuckle, commanding. Both Infantry and Dragoons are stationed at this post.

FORT LEAVENWORTH.

Fort Leavenworth is on the S. W. bank of Missouri River, 25 miles above the mouth of Kauzau River. It was established in 1827. The post is head-quarters of the United States Dragoons. Six companies are stationed there; Col. R. W. Mason, commanding.

FORT COFFEE.

Fort Coffee is on the south bank of Arkansas, above Fort Smith, about 12 miles west of the State of Arkansas. It was established in 1825.

Fort Smith is unoccupied.

TRADING POSTS.

The number of white traders has greatly increased within a twelve month. Many of these establishments are transient. This business is so fluctuating, that its condition, and the places at which it is carried on, cannot be stated with accuracy.

AFFINITY OF LANGUAGES.

Chickasaw and Choctaw are dialects of one language.

Putawatomies, Ottawas and Chippewas speak the same language.

The language spoken by the Osages, Quapaws and Kauzaus is the same. That of the Otoes and Iowas is the same; and between these and the Osage, Quapaw, Kauzau, Omaha, Puncah, and Winnebago languages, there is a near affinity.

Weas, Piankashas, Peorias, Kaskaskias, and Miamies, severally speak dialects of the same language.

There is a near resemblance between the Pawnee and Arickara languages.

NAMES OF TRIBES.

Choctaw,	is properly pronounced	Chŏh'tau.
Cherokee,	"	Chĕl'o-kee.
Muscogee, (Creek,)	"	Mŭs-kógee.*
Shawanoe, -	"	Shaw'-aw-nó.†
Wea, - -	"	Wee'au.
Ottawa, - -	"	Ottaú-wau.
Delaware, -	"	Lĕn-nŏp'-pe.
Putawatomie, -	"	Put-a'-wŏt-o-me.‡
Osage, - -	"	Wŏs-sŏsh'-e.
Kauzau, - -	"	Kau'-zau.
Omaha, - -	"	Omaú'-hau.
Otoe, - -	"	O'tó.
Sauk, - -	"	Sauk'ee.
Ioway, - -	"	I'owă.
Camanche,	called by themselves	Pă-toh'-ka.
Seminole,	"	Sĭm'-a-lone, [wild.]

* G. hard.
† By themselves, Saú-wau-nó.
‡ By neighboring tribes, Waú-pun-uk'o.

WHOLE NUMBER OF INDIANS.

Tribes East of the Mississippi River.

Indians in N. England and New-York,	4,176
Indians from New-York at Green Bay,	725
Wyandots in Ohio and Michigan,	575
Miamies,	1,100
Winnebagoes,	4,500
Chippewas,	6,793
Ottawas and Chippewas of Lake Michigan,	5,300
Chippewas, Ottawas and Putawatomies,	5,000
Putawatomies,	1,400
Menominees,	4,200
Creeks,	753
Choctaws,	3,500
Seminoles,	1,000
Appalachicolas,	400
	39,422

Tribes West of the Mississippi River.

Sioux,	27,500	Camanches,	8,000
Sauks and Foxes,	6,400	Crows,	4,500
Assinaboines,	8,000	Arrepahas, Kia-	
Crees,	3,000	was, &c.	1,400
Grosventres,	3,000	Caddoes,	2,000
Arickaras.	3,000	Snake and other	
Cheyennes,	2,000	tribes within	
Minatarees,	1,500	the Rocky Mts.	20,000
Mandans,	500	Tribes west of the	
Black Feet,	30,000	R. Mountains,	80,000

Indians in Mexico,	3,600,000
Near the Northern boundary of the Government of the U. S. and within the territories claimed by other Governments,	1,464,918
Tribes within the Indian Territory,	94,860
In all,	5,400,000

This table is conjectural in regard to the remote tribes, and is probably very erroneous.

The population becomes more sparse as we proceed northward, to a clime less accommodated to the comforts of uncivilized man, and becomes more dense as we proceed southward to a more genial clime, where subsistence is more easily obtained.

PLEA FOR THE ABORIGINES.

Why should the aborigines perish? Is it possible that a race of men has been brought into existence, which possesses some innate self-destroying principle, which will produce its own extinction? If so, how did their numbers multiply, until they spread over a quarter of the globe? How did it happen that this baneful principle did not begin to develop itself until they came in contact with the white man? Why has not nature violated her laws in relation to some other animals? A nation of human beings, physically and mentally organized like all other human beings, multiplying to millions, and yet, *unlike* all other human beings, under the influence of a self-destructive principle, too inveterate to be remedied, and which will utterly destroy the whole race!!

They who have given little attention to Indian affairs, will hardly believe that such gross absurdities are propagated in these days, and in this country. They would ascribe them to a period a century before our time. Yet strange as it may appear, we are sorry to say it is true. When we exult in the wonderful march of mind in this favored period, we must not exhibit the above specimens of logic in justification of our joys. The reasoning of the most benighted of those aborigines would not involve equal absurdities.

The nature of the Register does not admit of controversy, nevertheless it is proper for us to satisfy our readers that the errors which we deprecate as having a pernicious tendency, do actually exist, and that, in opposing them by a reference to plain matters of fact, we are not "beating the air."

We have lately seen, in a periodical of considerable celebrity,* the following premises and conclusions assumed:—

"The North American Indians are a strongly marked race of men, constituting a distinct class, and maintaining their identity as such, and their peculiarities in every vicissitude of existence, which neither circumstances nor time have conquered.— Wasted by wars, consumed by want, driven by the iron arm of civilization from his native soil, and the places endeared to him by hallowed associations, the Indian is the same that he was when the white man first invaded his forests; unchanged and unchangeable in his nature, his habits, his physical constitution, and distinctive traits of intellect. We see to what a point the aboriginal intellect has advanced, and what have been apparently the stern boundaries fixed by nature to its progress. The narrow circle of Indian ideas has remained essentially the same,

* North American Review for July, 1838.

since their first intercourse with Europeans. * * * They have rejected the habits of civilized life, though, in some individual cases, they have proved themselves capable of adopting them. It seems as if they were born to be hunters, and hunters they were determined to die. The Christian religion has made a temporary progress among some of the tribes, but time has always removed the last traces of it from the savage mind."

If the sentiments we have quoted were limited to a few of our countrymen, we might have passed them unnoticed; but they prevail extensively. They intrude themselves into the halls of legislation, and by their hopelessness occasion indifference to the enactment of wholesome regulations. They accompany the execution of law, and too often occasion infidelity. They salve the conscience of the avaricious, who pleads that, since the Indians cannot profit by money appropriated for their use, he may apply it to his own; and they have a paralyzing effect upon every scheme of benevolence for their assistance, both in the Government and in the Church.

We are happy, however, in being able to meet the errors we deprecate, by plain and notorious matters of fact. Of this, unquestionable evidence is found in the forepart of this number, in the accounts given of improvements in civilization and religion, of different tribes. With peculiar satisfaction we refer to the account of the Choctaws. There we see that savage customs have been entirely abolished, and civil institutions adopted in their place; and this, too, has been done by themselves. It is true, there have long been laboring among them devoted missionaries, whose salutary influence has been felt, in moulding the character of society in general; but the direct operations of these men have been chiefly limited to religion and literature. And, moreover, the amount of missionary labor among the Choctaws has always been so small, that it can, at best, be esteemed only an auxiliary in improvement.

The Cherokees have been hindered in improvement by difficulties attending a change of place, otherwise it is fair to suppose they would not have been behind the Choctaws in any thing. Before the days of their late troubles on the east of the Mississippi, they were undoubtedly in advance of all other tribes. Then follow the Creeks, close in the rear of their neighbors.— Nearly by the side of the latter, in improvement, are the Shawanoes and Delawares, followed by Peorias, Senecas, Weas, Ottawas, Kickapoos, Sauks, and Ioways.

These are the people said to " have been born to be hunters, and hunters determined to die." A population of more than seventy-three thousand of these natural born hunters, now living by their industry at home, and having among them scarcely a greater proportion of individuals who neglect the field or the shop for the chase, than are found among the whites in the frontier settlements. Even the indigenous tribes, in the midst of all the disadvantages under which they have labored, have, almost from the moment that they were informed improvement was possible, been imbibing habits of civilization. When inspired with the first ray of hope, they arose and took hold of the plough. See the poor Otoe, who, a short time since, cultivated his maize with the shoulder-bone of the buffalo, unable to guide both plough and horse, holding the handles of the former, while his *wife* or *child* guides the latter.

This is the "race of men constituting a distinct class, and maintaining their identity as such, and their peculiarities under every vicissitude of existence!"

Next look into the schools, and into the classes which have been favored with a place in the schools, and you must remain silent on the subject of limited intellect. Go to the Choctaw Hall of Legislation, and hear men, with *true* eloquence, pleading and establishing the cause of civil liberty. Follow them, till in the ardor of friendly debate, you find the speakers enlarging beyond the limits of recollection, resorting for aid to written notes. Examine their constitution and their code of written laws, and then tell us " the narrow circle of Indian ideas has remained essentially the same since their first intercourse with Europeans." Lastly, approach the House of God, compared with the importance of which, all specimens of improvement sink into insignificance. Hear the native, with his bold and pious eloquence, telling his countrymen that the victim of Calvery extends his hands even to them, to wipe their tears and raise them to a better world. See hundreds surrounding the sacramental board, to commemorate the death of Him who lives to give them heavenly life. Follow these disciples of Jesus, and witness their consistency of profession, both in the closet and in their intercourse with their fellow-men. Mark the indications of grateful recollections of those white men who brought to them the " balm of Gilead." Then step to the brink of time, and see a Christian Indian die, and tell us that " time has always removed the last traces of the Christian religion from the savage mind!"

Further. Let it not be overlooked that these improvements, in their substantial form, commenced at the moment when, in the nature of things, they were enabled to hope for better condition. The hunter left the forest for the field, as soon as he knew that he could enjoy the fruits of cultivation. The barbarous council was dissolved, as soon as a secure home, and the prospect of enjoying civil freedom, suggested the propriety of a legislative assembly. Very few of the Choctaws had reached their present homes in 1828. About the same time the Cherokees, and Creeks, and Shawanoes, were making their first settlements.—The Delawares and others arrived at later dates. Here, then, as it were, with the fructifying influence of summer, the emigrant tribes, without a single exception, from the moment that they began to be relieved from dispair, and to feel the influence of hope, commenced improving, and are still advancing.

We admit that many formidable obstacles still oppose the national salvation of this lately broken-hearted people. But the hindrances are all in our own hand, and (with proper submission to Him who rules the destinies of man) we perceive that we have the power either to save or to destroy them. Upon us, therefore, rests the responsibility. We perceive that with opportunities which would enable any other people to improve their condition, the Indians will be prosperous.

One difficulty, among others, and not the least serious, is felt all over the Indian country. We refer to the lamentations of some among us for "the fate of the poor Indians, who are destined," they say, "to be driven still further West by our Government." The tribes have, for very good reasons, felt their removal to the West to be a great hardship. On this account, and many others, it cannot be expected that they will soon have entire confidence in the sincerity of our declarations, that they shall not again be disturbed. They are not yet fully prepared to appreciate the causes which have induced their removal, and hence, judging from the past, they look with suspicion on the future; and nothing so effectually checks the march of improvement as doubts concerning the permanency of their settlements. Their fears are ever on the alert, and they watch, with jealous anxiety, every movement of our Government in relation to them. While, therefore, public prints and public speakers, professedly mourning over the calamities of the Indians, predict that they will still be driven from place to place, and protest that the tribes are as insecure on the west, as they were on the east of the Mississippi, they are fostering the groundless jealousies of the Indians, and inflicting upon them positive and extensive injury.

For reasons to which we have referred, we can excuse the Indian for his fears, but not the citizen of the United States, who has an opportunity of contemplating the subject under circumstances very different from the former. He must be blind, indeed, who can perceive no difference in the tenure by which Indians hold lands now, and that by which they held lands within the chartered limits of States. It is beyond contradiction that the General Government never has had power, since its organization, to give to any of the tribes a perpetual residence on the east side of the Mississippi River. *Here it has power* to secure them in their homes forever.

"But the avarice of our citizens," you say, "is so strong that they will covet the Indian lands, and their cruelty is so great that they will wrest it from them." These assertions we deny, and justify the denial by the fact that emigrations to this Territory, since the Government conceived the design of making the Indians' residence permanent, have not been produced by the avarice and the cruelty presupposed. That our citizens have manifested avarice and cruelty, no one pretends to deny; but these passions have never acquired strength to remove one single tribe. The cause which produced removal, was, that the very existence of our Government was predicated upon the supposition that the Indian had no landed rights on the east of the Mississippi. By an European sovereign that country had all been conveyed to his subjects, and, in changing masters, these claimants never relinquished their claims. These claims were recognised in the formation of our Government, and have been confirmed by a continuous policy, in which every State in the Union concurred.

We admit that our citizens might become so corrupt that they would force the Indians from their homes without the sanction of law. At the same time we deny that any such instance of cruelty has occurred since the scheme of colonizing them has been conceived.

Again, we do not live in an age of increasing cruelty to the Indians. Public sympathy never was so much elicited in behalf of them as at present. Kindness of feeling in those who have managed the affairs of our Government, has been increasing for many years, particularly since the feasibility of rescuing the tribes from extinction has been perceived in the present plan. In proof of this, we need only compare latter with former treaties. In these we discover an increasing liberality towards the Indians. Now the Government will give half a million of dollars to a tribe for considerations which, twenty years ago, would have been thought dear at twenty thousand.

When, therefore, the Government has it in its power to secure the tribes in their settlements in the Territory, while it is pursuing measures for this purpose, and while it is endeavoring to make amends for past wrongs suffered by these people, by increasing kindness in future, it is exceedingly unfair, and, in regard to the Indians, cruelly unkind, to cherish their fears that they shall soon be driven from their homes.

Intimately connected with the views of precarious settlement which we have noticed, is that to which we have already referred, the tendency of which is similarly pernicious, to wit, the supposition that the Indians are perishing, and that their decline cannot be arrested. Lectures on the manners and customs of the Indians, whether consisting of encomium or censure, usually wind up with a prediction of the utter extinction of the race.

Speakers in benevolent associations, after telling of the wrongs the Indians have endured, and the sufferings to which they have been subjected, and giving, perhaps, a florid description of the noble traits of character which they fancy they have discovered in the man of nature, often leave last and uppermost on the minds of their audience the impression that these noble, but suffering people, are doomed to utter destruction, as a people. The effect of all this would be the less hurtful, were it not done under the profession of great regard for the Indians. Well might all the tribes adopt the prayer, " From the sympathies of such friends, good Lord deliver us." They have great sympathies for the *poor Indians*, and yet they can hinder them from making themselves comfortable, by telling them that they will soon be driven from their houses and fields. By discouraging improvement among them, they cherish ignorance and wretchedness, and thus increase their liability to be imposed upon. They check the ardor essential to improvement, by predicting their constant decline and ultimate extinction, and they discourage our citizens, whether statesmen or churchmen, from earnestly seeking the relief of the Indians—" for all efforts are to fail—they must be driven—they must disappear."

The rhetorical flourish, borrowed from Indian life, has become stale with time and use, that " the council fires of the tribes are about to be extinguished." Yes. The council fires of the Choctaws have already been extinguished, and those of other tribes are expiring, but the tribes are neither dead nor dying. They have exchanged the council fire for the legal institutions of a civilized community.

Nothing is better calculated to cherish in the Indians hostile feelings towards the United States than to persuade them that we design to drive them from their present residences. Confirm them in this belief, and war will be induced, and on their part it would be a war of desperation.

A word more concerning the professed friends of the Indians whom we have been noticing, and we will take our leave of them for the present. Dispassionate reflection will, we believe, admit the correctness of our opinion, that the calamities occasioned to the Indians by the war in Florida, during the period of its existence, have been light compared with the mischiefs fomented, and fomenting by the misnamed sympathies which we have been noticing, for the same length of time. For these two things we fervently pray that such men may at least "cease to do evil," whether they "learn to do well" or not; and that the Indians may have patience to contemplate fairly, their present condition, and may have judgment to appreciate the facilities for their improvement, with which they are favored above the generations which have preceded them.

Another error into which some good men have fallen is, that the Indians must necessarily perish, because they are "driven from the graves of their fathers." Or, if separation from the graves of their fathers should not be certainly destructive, it is necessarily cruel. Better let them remain at the "graves of their fathers" and *die*, than to go to a country of their own and *live*. Now, concerning the hardship of being compelled to leave a place to which they had become attached by a long residence, and to locate in one chosen for them by others, there can be but one opinion. We all agree, too, in admitting that the whites started wrong in Indian matters at first, and introduced an unjust policy, which is no credit to the whites, either as men or as Christians. Happy would it have been for us if our ancestors had corrected the evil. But they did it not—that work has been reserved for the present generation. The reform has been commenced, and it is progressing in the only possible way that has been suggested, and we rejoice that the deeply lamented evils—real, not imaginary evils, involved in the matter of emigration from the east to the west of the Mississippi, are being overruled for good. Evils, the force of which drove the pilgrim fathers from Europe to America, were real. The laws which allowed of their persecution were unjust. These good men might have remained by the "graves of their fathers," and have died under their oppressions, but they made a wiser choice, and soon discovered that the evil was made to them a blessing.

While we have much to lament in the case of the Indians, we have these substantial consolations, that their country is good; the latitudes they respectively inhabit nearly the same as those from which they came; that the causes which occasioned their removal from their former residences do not reach their present ones, and that notwithstanding it has been constantly reiterated in their hearing, that "they need not try to live, for the Indian race must become extinct—they need not improve their lands, for they would soon be driven from them." They have no sooner reached their country here, than they exchange the *hunter* for the *farmer*. So far from being naturally averse to improvement, as has been a thousand times reported, they as naturally commence improving as soon as they are placed in circumstances which render it possible, as a bird expands its wings for flight as soon as its cage is opened.

Here, then, we have the elements of that state of society which all who desire their happiness, wish to see established among the Indians. In regard to the propriety of some measures which have been employed to transfer these people to this country, there have been honest differences of opinion in the United States. These things are now matters of history. The Indians *are here*, and afford an opportunity for action. In acts of justice and humanity, all may unite. That it is our duty now to endeavor to afford assistance, none can doubt, and it is hardly possible for us to disagree in the choice of measures. Only suppose Indians to be like all other human beings—like ourselves, for instance, and all becomes plain and easy. We have only to apply for their relief such measures as our own citizens need when they locate in new and wilderness countries.

Suppose a population of ninety-four thousand of our citizens, suddenly thrown together on some part of our frontiers; that which would seem to claim first attention would be the establishment of rules of order; the adoption of measures of *law*, for mutual protection. It would not be sufficient for each prominent man to form a clan and adopt laws for themselves, in all respects distinct from others. Such local regulations might properly be made, but they would not supersede the necessity for laws of a more general nature, which would harmonize the whole community. In such a community as we have supposed, the institution of schools and of religious worship, would early claim attention. Industry, as well as literature and religion should be encouraged. All this would be *plain sailing* in regard to ourselves, and the whole would be equally appropriate for the Indians. Government, for various reasons, exercises over them a general superintendency and guardianship; it is therefore proper that it should take measures for uniting them harmoniously under the influence of regulations of intercourse. The tribes have never been in this manner united; it is not easy, therefore, for them to perform it without assistance.

But leave them to remain in their present incoherent condition, and the result will be what we would expect from ninety thousand of our own citizens, settled in a body without law—difficulties among themselves, and trouble to their neighbors, which would end in destruction. In no other way than this can the Indian be deprived of his country. Let quarrels arise between the tribes, and liability to lose their country will follow.

The favor shown to the bill, providing for the organization of the Indian Territory, in the United States Senate, at its last session, justifies the hope of a favorable issue. The objections made to the measure were barely sufficient to afford an opportunity for making some excellent speeches in its favor. Some of these have appeared in the public prints, others have not: on some of them we should draw large, by quotations for this work, if our limits would allow. We were deeply impressed with a compliment bestowed upon the framers of the bill, by a very respectable Senator from the West. It appeared that he had not previously given much attention to the subject of Indian affairs. When the provisions of the bill were explained, his discriminating judgment at once descried its propriety, and his gigantic mind reached around the happy consequences which might fairly be anticipated in its results; and in an ecstasy, declared it to be one of the most important measures ever brought before Congress, and one which redounded greatly to the credit of its projectors. With him, we may well say, that few measures of more importance have ever been before our nation. The original inhabitants, who have reluctantly been yielding their places to us for two or three centuries, and as they receded, diminished in numbers, and sunk deeper in accumulating woes, have at length found a resting place; and, like the bird of Noah, have found the flood of their afflictions retiring, and the olive emblem of peace and tranquillity accessible. Or, like the long imprisoned tenants of the ark, when they issued forth with pious hilarity to plough and plant, the Indian unstrings his bow, and gears his plough-horse.

The measures now contemplated by the Government will not be limited in their salutary effects to the few broken Indian nations near us. They combine the elements of a grand scheme of deliverance, embracing all the tribes. The vast region uninhabited by men of European descent, and lying westward and northward of their long line of settlements, is the sphere destined to be filled. Success in the present experiment will arouse benevolent enterprise to form Colonies elsewhere, and it will not be long in carrying messages of joy to the most distant and degraded hordes. Once fully establish in practice the design under consideration, and, like the Prophet's rock from the mountain, imperishable in its nature, it will magnify commensurate to the sphere of wretchedness for which it is adapted. Who would not co-operate in a work so magnificent! Shall we call it a revolution? It deserves a better name than one implying only a change of one form of Government for another, or one corps of rulers for another. Here is to be the establishment of Government among men who never before enjoyed it.—It is not a mere improvement in condition, but a rescue from extinction. The events of our own American Revolution acquire interest as time develops their importance to the world; and the hand which but tremblingly signed our Declaration of Independence, is now looked back upon with a kind of veneration, as if it had been guided by some influence from Heaven. The excellence of our institutions then introduced, acquires brilliancy by having led us to feel, and act, for others, far more distressed than we were then—to make them free and happy as we are now.

ERRATA.

Page 24, line 25, from top,—for, in Missouri, read *on the* Missouri.
Page 40, line 14, from bottom,—for Choctaws, read Choctaw.
Page 52, line 11, from bottom,—read, deposited therein.
Page 68, 1st line,—for contain, read contains.
Page 69, line 16 from top, for Jackson County, read *Clay* County.

Christiana McCoy
Courtesy of Kansas State Historical Society
Topeka, Kansas

APPENDIX A

Articles of Faith of the Baptist Mission at Fort Wayne, Indiana Territory

The following is the summary of doctrines which were subscribed, viz:

"We, whose names follow, being convinced of the propriety and utility of a church state, and having due knowledge of each other in respect to experimental and practical religion, by consent and with the assistance of Elder Benjamin Sears, of Meredith, New-York, and Elder Corbly Martin, of Staunton, Ohio, do agree to unite in a church compact, upon the firm basis of the Scriptures of the Old and New Testaments, as being of divine authority, and the only infallible rule of faith and practice. And whereas there are different opinions among professed Christians in relation to the true meaning of Scripture, therefore, in order to prevent unpleasant disputation, and to cherish harmony of sentiment, we deem it indispensable to subjoin the following expression of the leading features of those doctrines of the Gospel most liable to be disputed, which shall always be considered as the sentiments of this church.

"**ART. I.** We believe in one only true and living God, who is infinite and unchangeable in all his divine perfections or attributes, such as wisdom, power, justice, love, &c., the Creator and Preserver of all things; and that he cannot be brought under the least obligations to any of his creatures.

"**ART. II.** We believe that in Deity there is a Trinity, of Father, Son, and Holy Ghost, in all respects equal, and unlike the subordination between father and son among men.

"**ART. III.** We believe that God is not liable to the least disappointment, but that eternity is at all times fully comprehended by him, so that neither the malice of hell, nor the wickedness of men on earth, can any way frustrate his eternal purposes.

"**ART. IV.** We believe that God made man upright, but he has voluntarily fallen from his uprightness; that in his fall he lost all traces of virtue, (moral goodness,) and became wholly averse to godliness; yet he is, on that account, under no less obligations to his God.

"**ART. V.** We believe that as there is nothing *new* with God, it is his eternal purpose to save those who ultimately will be received into heaven, not upon the supposition of any condition to be performed by them, but wholly in consequence of what Jesus Christ has done in their behalf.

"**ART. VI.** We believe the Son of God united himself to humanity, and in that state fulfilled in his life the law of God, which was binding on man, and suffered in his death the penal requisitions of the same.

"ART. VII. We believe, agreeably to the inevitable consequences of articles first, third, and fifth, that Christ's life, death, resurrection, and intercession, were, and are, in behalf of those, and those only, who shall enjoy the benefits thereof.

"ART. VIII. We believe that regeneration is effected by the operations of the Spirit of God only, and is an essential preparation for the enjoyment of God in heaven, and an assurance of title thereto.

"ART. IX. We believe that, through grace, all who are regenerated will be preserved in a gracious state, and will certainly go to heaven.

"ART. X. We believe it to be perfectly congenial to the Scriptures, and to the spirit of the foregoing articles, for ministers of the Gospel to command all men indiscriminately to repent, and to exhort them to believe the Gospel.

"ART. XI. We believe that God hath appointed a day in which he will judge all men by Jesus Christ.

"ART. XII. We believe that the joys of the righteous will be eternal, and that the sufferings of the wicked will be of endless duration.

"ART. XIII. We believe that the sufferings of the wicked is the spontaneous consequence of their own wickedness, and not the effect of any thing in or done by Deity, hostile to their happiness.

"ART. XIV. We believe that none but believers in Christ ought to be baptized, and that immersion is the only scriptural mode of baptism.

"ART. XV. We believe that none but baptized believers in Christ, united in Gospel order, have a right to communion at the Lord's table.

"ART. XVI. We believe that God hath set apart one day in seven, for rest and religious worship, and that the first day of the week ought to be observed as such, in resting from our temporal concerns, excepting works of necessity.

"And being united together upon the foregoing plan, we deem it our duty to walk in all the commandments and ordinances of the Lord blameless, which, that God may enable us to do, let every member, at all times, fervently pray.

"ISAAC McCOY, JOHN SEARS,
"CHRISTIAN McCOY, MARY SEARS,
"GILES JACKSON, JOHNSTON LYKINS,
"MARY JACKSON, BENJAMIN SEARS, JUN.
Missionaries.
"WISKEHELAEHQUA, *a Delaware woman.*
"ANN TURNER, *a Miamie woman.*
"JESSE COX, *a black man.*"

McCoy, Isaac. *History of Baptist Indian Missions.* Washington, D.C., William M. Morrison. 1840, pp. 154-156.

APPENDIX B

Early Particular Baptist Churches of Oklahoma

The Muscogee Baptist church was constituted on September 9, 1832 by Isaac McCoy, John Davis, a Creek Indian preacher, and David Lewis, a missionary from New York. It was located north of the Arkansas River and four miles west of the Verdigris river, in the Creek Country, where Davis and Lewis had established a mission site called Ebenezer Station in 1829.[1] In the following extract from a letter written by McCoy, in September of 1832, one is given an eyewitness account of the beginning of the first Baptist church constituted in Oklahoma:

> "I enjoyed a blessed season in Arkansas[2] with our excellent missionary brethren, Davis and Lewis. They are both men of good sense, and ardent piety; and are devoted to their labors of love, in teaching sinners the way to heaven. I had written Mr. Lewis twice, but neither of my communications had reached him. He was in a land of strangers, and pennyless, without knowing when I would arrive to afford him relief. Nevertheless, he went to work with Mr. Davis. They preached among the Creeks, and visited from house to house; and before I reached them, they had fixed upon a day for the constitution of a Baptist church. In this constitution, I had the happiness of assisting, on the 9th inst[ant]. The church consisted of Rev. Mr. Lewis and wife, missionaries, John Davis, Creek Indian, and missionary, and three black men, (Quash, Bob, and Ned,) slaves to the Creeks, who had been baptized on the east of Mississippi. The church took the name of the Muscogee Baptist church. Mr. Lewis preached in the forenoon, and I preached at another place in the afternoon; and bro. Davis, besides interpreting, prayed, and exhorted, in both Indian and English. This was a good day to us all. We had no artifice employed to occasion excitement of feelings; nevertheless, we retired from our meeting place, not only with solemn countenances, but many faces, both black and red, were suffused with tears, and every heart seemed to be filled. For myself, I felt like seeking a place to weep tears of gratitude to God, for allowing me to witness a gospel-church

---

[1] Ebenezer Station was located about 15 miles west of Fort Gibson, and 3 miles north of the Arkansas River.

[2] Arkansas Territory, which at that time included portions of eastern Oklahoma. This church was actually located north of Muskogee in what is now Wagoner County, Oklahoma.

formed, under such auspicious circumstances, in the *Indian Territory*, towards which we have so long directed our chief attention with deep solicitude.³

The Tinsawattee Baptist Church was constituted late in 1825 among the Cherokees in what is now Dawson County, Georgia. Members of this church were dismissed on October 13, 1832, to remove to the west. These were reconstituted as Liberty Baptist Church on November 10, 1832, by pastor Duncan O'Bryant. The church was located in the Cherokee country near modern Piney in Adair County. (See: Gardner, Robert G. *Cherokees and Baptists in Georgia.* Atlanta; Georgia Baptist Historical Society, 1989).

On October 28, 1837, McCoy wrote to John Davis requesting him to organize a church among the Choctaws and ordain Ramsay D. Potts, who was a missionary there.⁴ Potts and his wife were in what was called the Red River District in southeastern Oklahoma. Mr. Potts "was under appointment and pay of the United States as [a] teacher, according to treaty provisions."⁵ The next day, on October 29, 1837, McCoy wrote to Potts about establishing a permanent work among the Choctaws, and suggesting that Potts be ordained.⁶ Sometime in November or December of 1837 a Baptist church was constituted by Potts in the Choctaw-Chickasaw country. It was located about 12 miles west of Fort Towson and 6 miles north of the Red River, in what is now Choctaw County.⁷

---

³ *The American Baptist Magazine*, Vol. 12, 1832. Boston: Lincoln and Edmands, pp. 396-397. The above is only a portion of the account given in this source. See also: Thoburn, Joseph B. *History of Oklahoma.* Chicago and New York: The American Historical Society. 1916. Vol. 1, p. 209; Marks, L. W. *The Story of Oklahoma Baptists.* (Unpublished MS, c. 1912), pp. 29-34; Gaskin, J. M. *Baptist Milestones in Oklahoma.* Oklahoma City: Baptist Messenger Press. 1966, pp. 11-22; McCoy, Isaac. *A History of Baptist Indian Missions.* New York: H. and S. Raynor, 1840, pp. 451-452, for more details on the founding of Muscogee Baptist church.

⁴*Isaac McCoy Papers*, Manuscript Collections, Kansas Historical Society, Topeka, Kansas.

⁵McCoy, Isaac. *The Annual Register of Indian Affairs*, Number 3, 1837, p. 13.

⁶*Isaac McCoy Papers,* Op.cit.

⁷McCoy, Isaac. *Annual Register of Indian Affairs*, Number 4, p. 45.

APPENDIX C

General Rules for the Fort Wayne Mission Family

In February of the present year, "Family Rules," so called, were framed, in imitation of the Baptist missionaries at Serampore. In consequence of Mr. Clyde's retiring from missionary service, the subject slept until after the departure of Mr. Jackson, when those rules were adopted and subscribed; but Mr. and Mrs. Sears, being at that time inclined also to leave the mission, declined subscribing.

"General Rules for the Fort Wayne Mission Family.

"We, whose names follow, being appointed missionaries to the Indians by the General Convention of the Baptist denomination for missions, deem it expedient for our comfort and usefulness to adopt, in the fear of the Lord, the following general rules for the regulation of the mission family, viz:

"**1st.** We agree that our object in becoming missionaries is to meliorate the condition of the Indians, and not to serve ourselves. Therefore,

"**2d.** We agree that our whole time, talents, and labours, shall be dedicated to the obtaining of this object, and shall all be bestowed gratis, so that the mission cannot become indebted to any missionary for his or her services.

"**3d.** We agree that all remittances from the board of missions, and all money and property accruing to any of us, by salaries from Government, by smith shops, by schools, by donations, or from whatever quarter it may arise, shall be thrown into the common missionary fund, and be sacredly applied to the cause of *this* mission; and that no part of the property held by us at our stations is ours, or belongs to any of us, but it belongs to the General Convention which we serve, and is held in trust by us, so long as said society shall continue us in their employment: Provided that nothing herein contained shall affect the right of any to private inheritance, &c.

"**4th.** We agree to obey the instructions of our patrons, and that the superintendent shall render to them, from time to time, accounts of our plans, proceedings, prospects, receipts, and expenditures; and that the accounts of the mission, together with the mission records, shall at all times be open for the inspection of any of the missionaries.

"**5th.** We agree that all members of the mission family have equal claims upon the mission for equal support in similar circumstances; the claims of widows and orphans not to be in the least affected by the death of the head of the family.

"**6th.** We agree that when any missionary shall not find employment

branch of business, as circumstances shall dictate.

"**7th.** We agree that, agreeably to their strength and ability, all the female missionaries should bear an equal part of the burden of domestic labors and cares, lest some should sink under the weight of severe and unremitted exertions; making the necessary allowances for the school mistress.

"**8th.** We agree to be industrious, frugal, and economical, at all times, to the utmost extent of our abilities.

"**9th.** We agree that missionaries laboring at the different stations belonging to this mission are under the same obligations to each other, as though resident in the same establishment.

"**10th.** We agree that it is the duty of missionaries to meet statedly at their respective stations, for the purposes of preserving peace and harmony among themselves, of cherishing kindness and love for each other, love to God, and zeal in the cause of missions.

"**11th.** We agree to feel one general concern for the success of every department of the mission, for the happiness of every member of the mission family, and to feed at one common table, except in cases of bad health, &c., in which cases the persons thus indisposed shall receive special attention, and shall be made as comfortable as our situation will admit.

"**12th.** We agree to cherish a spirit of kindness and forbearance for each other, and, as the success of our labors depends on the good providence of God, it is our duty to live near to him in public and private devotion, and to walk before him with fear, and in the integrity of our hearts, conscious that he ever sees us, and that by him actions are weighed; realizing that we are, at best, only instruments in his hand, and hoping that when we shall have finished the work given us to do, we shall dwell together in heaven, in company with fellow-laborers from other parts of the vineyard, and with those for whom we are now strangers and sufferers in this wilderness, and, to crown our happiness, shall gaze eternally on Him whose religion we are now endeavouring to propagate, to whom shall be ascribed *all* the glory of the accomplishment of our present undertaking.

"ISAAC McCOY,
"CHRISTIANA McCOY,
"JOHNSTON LYKINS,
"DANIEL DUSENBURY.

"*February* 15, 1822."*

---

* McCoy, Isaac. *History of Baptist Indian Missions.* Washington, D. C., William M. Morrison. 1840, pp. 170-171.

Index

Abel (Bible Character) - 135
Adair County, Oklahoma - 2
Adam (Bible Character) - 135
Adams, John Quincy - 63,155
Adams, Mr. - 237
Adjuton, Mr. - 159,274
Advertisement - 10,147,148,229-231
Affinity of Languages-50,102,193,310
Ah-Kau-Zau -36
Aldridge, Reuben - 286
Aldrich, Rev. S. - 21,69,161
Alexander, 1st Lt. E. P. - 47, 101
Alleghanies - 248
Allen, 1st Lt. James - 102
Allen, Dr. Alanson - 154,157,267,271
Allen, Mr. - 175
Allen, Mrs. - 270
Allen, Rev. - 270
Allis Mrs. - 183,298
Allis, Mr - 41,92,183,298
American Baptist Magazine - 326
American Bible Society - 24,73,165, 268-270,275,295
American Board of Commissioners for Foreign Missions -(Presbyterian) 14,18,22,27,41,42,63,67,71,75,92,93, 155,156,159,160,163,183, 184,268-270,274,275,295,298,300
American Fur Company -50,102, 193
American Revolution - 225,321
Amusement - 125
Anderson, Rev. Rufus - 93,184,300
Annual Register of Indian Affairs - 289,326
Appalachicolas -54,108,200,311
Arapahoes (See Arrepahas) - 103
Arbuckle, Col.(Gen.) Matthew - 48, 101, 104,309
Archer, 1st Lt. John - 47
Ardent Spirits - 254-257
Arickara - 194,201,310,311
Arickaree - 103
Arkansas - 14,15,19,69,100,131,149, 150,152,157,159,161,193,216,235, 238,244,248,253,257,262,263,271, 274,275,290,308
Arkansas, Little Rock - 47,100,192, 309

Arkansas, Vineyard (Washington County) - 19,69,299,321
Arkansas Conference (Methodist) - 161,163
Arkansas District - 61,62,65
Arkansas River - 13,15-18,20,21,36, 47,48,61,62,65,67,69,70,100,101, 103,131,154,157,159,161-163,193, 256,262,267,271,272,277,308,309, 325
Arkansas Territory - 2,11,13,16, 18, 48,59,61,64,65,67,68,75,160,167, 210,283,325
Arkansas, Fort Smith - 47, 309
Arms - 118
Armstrong, Capt. William - 60,62, 150, 154,239,260,267
Armstrong, Col. F. W. - 12,14,21,60, 104
Arrekaras - 54,108
Arrepahas - 54,108,201,311
Asia - 113
Assinaboines -54,108,201,311
Atlantic Coast - 205, 235
Audrain, Francis - 163
Autin, Mrs. Peter. - 269
Autin, Peter - 268,269
Axes and other Mechanic Tools - 117,118

Babbitt, 1st Lt. E. B. - 101
Bad Boy, Chief - 77,168
Baffin's Bay - 117
Baily, Dr. Joseph H. - 101
Baldwin, 2nd Lt. A.G. - 47,101
Ballard, Aurey - 294,295
Ballard, Mrs. - 295
Bangs, Rev. Nathan - 93,185,300
Baptist Board of Missions - 93,184, 282,299
Baptist General Missionary Convention - 15,19,21,28,30,32,34, 40-42,65,69,70,77,81,85,90-93,156, 157,161,163,168,172,175,181,182, 185,289,300
Baptist Milestones in Oklahoma - 326
Baptist Missions - 15,19,21,28,30,32, 34,40,65,69,70,77,79,81,85,90-92,156, 157,161,163,168,170,172,175,181, 182,270,271,277,282,285,287,289, 291,296,297

329

Index

Baptists - 81,185,275,289,300
Barbour, 2nd Lt. P.N. - 101
Barnwell, 2nd Lt. J. O. - 101
Bean, Capt. Jesse - 49
Bean, Mr. - 67
Benton, J. B. - 154
Berryhill, P. - 22
Berryman, Mrs. J. C. - 37,178,293
Berryman, Rev. J. C. - 37,87,178,293
Bethabara Station (Presbyterian) - 14,63,64,155,156,268
Bethel Station (Presbyterian) -64, 155,269
Big Elk, Chief - 39,91,182,297
Big John - 154,268
Birch, Maj. George - 101
Black Coat, Chief - 16
Black Dog, Chief - 283
Black Feather, Chief - 31,80,171,288
Black Feet - 54,103,108,201,311
Black River - 241
Blackhawk - 105
Blackhoof, Chief - 80,171,288
Blair, Joseph - 163
Blanchard, Mrs. Ira D. - 85,175,291
Blanchard, Ira D. - 35,85,175,291
Boats (Canoes) - 120,121
Bok Tuklo Church (Presbyterian) - 64,156
Boston (native preacher) - 275
Boudinot Station (Presbyterian) - 27,75
Bolles, Rev. Lucius (1779-1844) - 93, 185,300
Bowles, Capt. - 24,73,165
Bowman, 2nd Lt. James W. - 49,102
Bradley, Henry - 29,78,169,286
Bradley, Mrs. Henry - 169,286
Bradshaw, Miss - 159,274
Brainerd, David (1718-1747) - 1
Brainbridge, 1st Lt. H. - 47,101
Brant, Capt. Joseph - 24,73,165
Brant, Chief Thomas - 23,72,164,279
Brasos River - 263
Bretton, 2nd Lt. F. - 101
Bright, Dr. J. J. B. - 48
Bright, S. B. - 76,167
British - 105
British Fur Co. - 249
Brown, A. - 66,159
Brown, Capt. Jacob - 63,67

Brown, Chief John - 273
Brown, Cynthia - 40,90
Brown, John - 17,24,72,164
Brown, The book of Catherine - 160
Bryan, Joel M. - 102,193
Bull, Chief - 285
Burbank, Lt. Col. - 48,101
Burch, Rev. Sampson - 15
Burgoyne, 2nd Lt. J. H. K. - 49
Burmah - 110
Burnham, Miss Ann - 14,63,155,156, 270
Butler. Hon. C.F. - 218
Burtolph (Butolf or Buttolf), Mr. - 68,161,275
Burtolph, (Butolf or Buttolf), Mrs. - 275
Byington, Mrs. - 156,268
Byington, Rev. Cyrus - 156,268

Caddoes - 54,108,201,311
Cain (Bible Character) - 135
California - 116,136
Calloway (Caloway), R.A. - 279,282, 284
Camanches (Comanches) - 50,54,103, 108,131,132,194,201,204,251,252, 290,310,311
Campbell, Gen. John - 21
Canadian River - 13,16,19,20,21,61,65, 69,70,152,156,157,161-163,193, 244, 262, 270-272,275,277,278
Cannibalism - 124,125
Cantonment Leavenworth - 33,37,84, 87,174,178,290,293
Carey Mission Station (Baptist) - 28,77, 168,285
Carlisle, William - 29,78,169
Carney, Allen - 64
Carney, Rev. Charles J. - 64
Carter, 2nd Lt. L.F. - 48,101
Case, James - 181,296
Cass 2nd Lt. G. W. - 101
Catch 'im (Catch Him), Chief Capt. - 34,84,175,290
Catholic Mission - 285
Catholics - 300
Cause of Indian Degeneracy - 138-144
Charley, Chief - 285

330

Index

Cherokees -12,13,15-20,23-25,32,46, 48,54,60,65-69,72,73,76,91,93,99, 100-102,108,151,157-161,164,165, 184,191,193,198,200,218,222,239, 240,244,246,249,251,255,257,258, 262,271-275,277,279,280,299,306, 308-310,313,315,326
Cherokee Agency - 164
Cherokee Almanac - 160
Cherokee Mission (Baptist) - 182
Cherokee Mission Church (Presbyterian) - 18,160,274
Cherokee Mission Station (Baptist)- 19,68
Cherokee Temperance Society - 300,301
Cherokees & Baptists in Georgia - 326
Cheyenne -54,103,108,201,250,251,311
Chicago, Treaty of (1833) - 27,76,167
Chickasaws - 13,50,54,61,102,108, 153,154,193,200,240,242,249,253, 262,266-271,308,310
Chippewas - 32,50,54,81,82,102,108, 111,129,193,200,241,242,260,310,311
Chippeway - 108
Choctaws - 12-15,19,21,47,48,50,54, 60-65,69,81,100,102,108,150-157, 160,161,172,192,193,198, 200,218, 222,239,240,242,244,245,249,253, 255,257,260,262-273,275,277,284, 289,290,299,307-311,313-315,326
Choctaw Agency - 271
Choteau, A.P. - 50,102,193
Choteau, P.S. - 27,75,167
Christian - 113
Christianity - 111,179
Civil Government & Improvement in the Arts of Life - 136-138
Civil John, Chief - 23,164
Clark, Capt. J. B. - 47,101
Clark, G. W. - 29,154
Clark, Gen. William - 12,60, 105, 150,261
Clark, M.G. - 30,31
Clay, Chief Henry - 31
Clear Creek Station (Presbyterian) 63,155,269
Cleremont, Chief - 26,75,167,272
Clough, Miss - 14,63,269
Clyde, Mr. - 327
Cobb, 2nd Lt. S. K. - 47

Colbert, Chief George - 267
Colbourn, Miss Mary Ann (Mrs. C. Curtis) - 19,71,182
Colcock, 1st Lt. W. - 101
Cole, Jesse - 156
Columbia River - 117, 249
Comanches, (See Camanches)
Commissioner of Indian Affairs - 168,217,219,238,260,261,280
Committee on Indian Affairs - 215
Comstick, Chief - 23,72,164,279
Condition of the Indians - 114,115
Congee, Chief - 294
Conner, James - 34
Contents, Table of - 3,228
Cook, 1st Lt. Philip St. George - 49
Cookery - 123,124
Copeland, Austin - 67
Copeland, H. K. - 154,155,268
Corn Stock, Chief - 80
Cox, Jesse - 324
Crawford, T. Hartley -260
Cree - 54,108,201,311
Creeks - 12,13,16,18-22,46,50,54,60, 65,69-71,93,100,102,108,151,157, 161-163,184,192,193,195,196,198- 200,222,239,240,242,245,249,253, 255,262,271,275-278,306,307,310, 311,313,315,325
Creek Mission (Baptist) - 182
Crosland, Samuel - 67
Crows- 54,108,201,311
Cummins, (Maj.) Richard W. - 34,37, 78,79,84,86,87,171,175,177,178, 288,290,292,293
Curley Eye, Chief George - 23,72, 164,279
Curtis, Mrs. Chandler - 297
Curtis, (Rev.) Chandler - 69,91,161, 182,297

Davies, 1st Lt. Jefferson - 49
Davis, John - 21,70,163,278,325,326
Davis, Rev. John (-1839) - 22,71, 163
Davis, Mrs, John - 22,71,163,278
Davis, Anthony L. - 28,168-170,284- 287
Davis, 2nd Lt. I. P. - 48
Dawson, Capt. J. L. - 48,101
Dean, J. - 101

Index

DeCamp, Dr. Samuel - 101
Declaration of Rights - 263
Delawares - 12,13,32-35,37,44,45,51, 60,81-87,97,103,127,151,172-175, 177,178,188,194,195,198,210,222, 237,240,242,244,253,262,282,289-291,293,303,310,313,315
Department of Indian Affairs - 184, 237,244,281,282,299,302
Derrisaw, Judge Jacob - 20,70,162,277
Division of Labor - 115
Dix, 2nd Lt. R. S. - 48,101
Doaksville - 262
Dodge, Mrs. - 27,75
Dodge, Rev. - 27,75
Dodge, Col. H. - 49,102,103
Dodge, Israel - 62
Donelson, William - 80,171,288
Dorion, Martin - 181,296
Dougherty, Maj. John - 39,90,181, 294,296
Dougherty, John - 40,91,182,297,
Dougherty, Joseph L. - 181,296
Dougherty - 90
Dougherty, J. - 91,182,297
Dress - 115,116
Drew, John - 17,66,159
Dunbar, Mrs. John - 298
Dunbar, Rev. John - 41,92,183,298
Duncan, William - 294
Duncan, Mr. - 169
Duncan, John - 275
Duncan, Capt. M. - 49,102,103
Dunlap, Robert - 34,84,288
Dusenbury, Daniel - 328
Dwight Mission Station (Presbyterian) - 4,18,67,159,274

Eagletown - 64,155,257,262,269
Eaton, Secretary - 244
Ebenezer Station (Baptist) - 325
Eliot, John (1604-1690) - 1
Ellefrit, Rev. W.C. - 175,291
Emigrants - 13,60,151,262
England - 140
Episcopalians - 24,73,165
Error of supposing that Indians possess peculiar propensities - 134-136
Essex, Rev. -275

European - 118,130,131,136,139, 140,142,143,149,210,219,224,233, 234,246,313,314,316,318
Eustis, 2nd Lt. William - 49,102
Evans, Dr. - 160
Everitt, Hon. Horace - 215
Evil Spirit - 55

Fairfield Station (Presbyterian) -18, 68,160,274
Fellows, Dr. B. F. -49,102
Few-hat-che-mi-co, Gen. - 20
Fields, John - 275
Findlay, Thomas N. - 159,273
Fish, Charles - 293
Fleming, Mrs. John - 22,71
Fleming, Rev. John - 22,71
Flint District - 16,66,158
Florida - 253,317
Force, Peter - 227
Ford, Capt. Z - 49
Ford, Capt. Lemuel - 102,103
Forks of Illinois Station (Presbyterian) - 68,160,274,275
Fort Coffee - 4,193,257,309
Fort Gibson - 4,17,22,48,49,66-68,71, 93,101,102,104,159,160,163,184, 193,257,273,277,278,309,325
Fort Leavenworth - 38,49,87,90,102, 103,178,181-183,193,252,257,293, 296,309
Fort Smith - 4,14,48,100,101,193, 308,309
Fort Towson - 4,15,47,48,64,65,100, 101,156,157,192,257,263,268-271, 273,309,326
Fort Wayne Mission (Baptist) - 327
Foxe - 105,108,201,242,243,294
Fort Towson Temperance Society - 300
Frayiuse, Harris - 154
French Government - 235
Freshhour, Henry - 159,273
Freshhown, Henry - 67
Friends (Quaker) Mission - 290
Fry, 2nd Lt. Carey H.- 101
Fushatchemeko, Chief - 162,277

Garland, J. - 101
Gatlin, Lt. R. C. - 49,101
Gemasah, Chief - 30,78,169,286

Index

General Description of the Country- 248
General Council of the Cherokee Nation - 273
Genry, Jacob - 159,273
Georgia - 19,69,161
Georgia, Dawson County - 326
Ghent, Treaty of - 140
Gilmore, Mr. - 90
Good Hunter, Capt.(Chief) - 23,72, 164,279
Gooding, 2nd Lt. George C. - 101
Good Spirit - 55
Gordon, Mr. - 76
Gotokapooh, Chief - 285
Government, Indian - 51,104
Graham, Rev. - 275
Grapevine, Titus - 68,161
Grayson, Daniel - 276
Grayson, George - 276
Grayson, Richard - 276
Great Britain - 140
Great Nemaha River - 39,90,180, 242,294,295
Great Platte River - 39,40,91,181, 182,243,257,297,298
Green, Rev. David - 93,300
Green Bay - 54,108,112,200
Greenfield Station (Lukfoata Station - Presbyterian) - 269
Gregory, Rev. David G. - 80,171
Gregory, Mrs. David G. - 80
Grey (Gray), Aaron - 18,67,159,274
Gros Ventre - 54,103,108,311
Groves, Mr. [George] (Sequoyah)-79
Guess, Mr. - 32,68,160,258,275
Guess' System - 160

Hagen, B. R. - 47
Hajekathake (Osage Killer), Chief - 296
Halcyon Era - 225
Hamil, Rev. J. N. - 22,71
Hamilton, Mrs. William - 295
Hamilton, 1st Lt. James - 50
Hamilton, Rev. William - 295
Hardrich, Mr. - 276
Harmam, Lewis - 154
Harrall, (Rev.) John - 19,71,299
Harris, Hon. C. A. - 150,217,219, 238,260

Harris, 2nd Lt. A. - 101
Harris, Mr. - 267
Harris, Ass't. Qr. N. S. - 47
Hart, James A. - 67,159,273
Hatch, Rev. Charles G. - 268,271
Havett, 2nd Lt. H. M. - 101
Hawkins, Capt. E. S. - 48,101
Hayes, James - 292
Henderson, Nancy - 29,78,169
Heron, Chief George - 23,72,164,279
Hill, Seaborn - 50,102,193
Hill, H. A. - 24,73,165
History of Oklahoma - 326
History of Baptist Indian Missions - 324,326,328
Hitchcock, Mrs. Asa - 18,67,159,274
Hitchcock, Jacob - 18,67,159,274
Hitchcock, Asa - 18,67,159,274
Hitchcok, Mrs. Jacob - 159,274
Holcomb, (Halcomb) A. - 23,164
Holdridge, A. - 67
Holland, Mr. - 171
Holmes, 2nd Lt. Stephen - 48
Holmes, 1st Lt. J. H. - 101
Holt, Dr. Henry - 101
Hopefield Station - 27,75
Hopoelhyoholo, Chief - 277
Horn, Jeremiah - 68
Horses - 117
Hostilities - 249
Hotchkin, Rev. Ebenezer - 15,63, 155,268,270
Hotchkin, Mrs. Ebenezer - 15,63, 155,270
Houses (Indian) - 115
Hudson's Bay - 116
Hunter, Capt. D. - 49,102,104
Hunting - 128-134
Hunton, Rev. John W. - 19,68,161
Huss, Mrs. John - 275
Huss, Rev. John - 275

Ietan, Chief - 39,90,296
Illinois, Chicago - 326
Illinois District - 16,66,158
Illinois River - 67
Illinois Station - See Forks of Illinois Station.
Indiana, Fort Wayne - 323,327
Indian Advocate - 7,9
Indian Agencies - 12

Index

Indiana, Fort Wayne - 323,327
Indians not within Indian Territory- 54,108
Indians of Mexico - 201
Indigenous Tribes - 13,60,150,262
Infantry, Seventh - 48,101
Infantry, Third - 47,100
Internal Government of the Respective Tribes - 240
Iowa (Ioway), Governor of [Robert Lucas] - 261
Iowas or Ioways - 54,81,103,105,108, 172,193,201,237,242,243,250,262, 289,294,295,307,308,310,313
Irwin, Mr. - 295
Irwin, Mrs. 295
Irwin, Thomas - 267
Israelites - 55
Izard, 1st Lt. James F. - 49,102

Jackson County, Missouri - 29,78, 79,83,85,92,93,144,168-170,174, 175,177,183,285-287,290,291
Jackson, Giles - 324,327
Jackson, Mary - 324
Jackson, President (Gen.) Andrew - 217,237
James, Dr. E. - 282
James, Joseph - 37,86,177
Jacob's Seed - 55
Jefferson Barracks - 49
Jeffrey - 294
John, Gospel of- 71,81,163,172,289
Johnson, James - 277
Johnson, Jerusha - 18,68,160
Johnson, Mr. - 163
Johnson, 1st Lt. Thomas - 48
Johnson, Rev. Thomas - 31,93,171, 184,288,299
Johnson, Mrs. Thomas - 31,86,171,288
Johnson, Rev. William - 31,86,177,292
Johnson, Mrs. William - 177,292
Jolly, Chief (Maj.) John - 16,66,159,273
Jonah, Book of - 160
Jones, Abner D. - 268
Jones, Mrs. Abner D. - 268
Jones, John - 284
Jones, Lewis - 31,80
Jones, R. W. - 14,62
Joslyn, Sophia M.- 18
Juzan, Chief Pierre - 267

Ka-he-ga-shing-a, Chief - 86,177
Ka-he-ga-wa-ta-ne-ga, Chief - 86
Ka-he-ge-wa-chi-chi, Chief - 86,177
Ka-hi-ga-shing-ga, Chief - 36
Ka-hi-ga-wa-ta-ni-ga, Chief - 36
Ka-hi-ge-wa-chi-chi, Chief - 36
Kaji - 253
Kaketoh, Chief - 284
Ka-luk-uk (Kel-u-kuk), Chief -37,38, 87,89
Kansas - 2
Kansas Indians - See Kauzaus
Kansas, Kansas City - 2
Kansas, Topeka - 326
Kaskaskia - 13,29,30,31,60,77-79, 103,151,169-171,194,198,199,222, 237,245, 262,285-287,310
Kauchehtustunege, Chief - 277
Kauzau River - 7,13,31,33,35,36,40, 49,60,80,83-85,90,102,132,151,171, 174,176,181,193,287,290,291,309
Kauzaus - 12,33,35-37,39,40,44,45, 50,51,60,78,80,83-86,90,91,94-97, 99,102,103,132,151,171,174,176, 177,180-182,186-188,190,193-195, 199,222,237,243,244,250,262,287, 289-293,295,297,301,302,305,310
Kellam, Rev. - 163,277,278
Kellam, Mrs. - 278
Kello, 2nd Lt. W. O. - 101
Kentucky, - 155,268
Ken-u-kuk, Chief - 178,293
Kerney, Allen - 156,269
Kerr, Rev. Joseph - 29,78,93,184
Kerr, Mrs. Joseph - 29,78
Ketron, Rev. William - 80
Kiahega Teday, Chief - 284
Kia-he-ga Wah-cha-ha (Hard Chief), Chief - 292
Kia-he-ga-wa-ta-in-ga (Reckless Chief), Chief - 292
Kiahegetungee, Chief - 283
Kiamisha (Kiamishi) River - 47,100, 192,309
Kiamishi Station (Presbyterian) - 270
Kiawas - 54,108,201,251,290,311
Kickapoos - 13,28,37-39,45,46,50,60, 76,77,86-90,97,102,151,167,178- 180,189,193,198,199,222,237,245, 262,293,294,303,304,313
Kickapoo, Chief - 87,178

Index

Kickapoo, Prophet - 38,87,178
Kickapoo Religious Society - 38,87,178
Kidron - 274
Kincaid, Chief Joseph - 62,154
Kingsbury, Lt. G. B. - 50,102
Kingsbury, Rev. Cyrus - 156,270
Kingsbury, Mrs. Cyrus - 156,270
Kinney, 2nd Lt. Samuel - 49,101
Kinnear, Rev. David - 293
Kiowas - See Kiawas
Kompehau, Chief - 287

Lake Michigan - 54,92,108,117,200,210, 298,311
Lake Superior - 112
Land Titles - 246,247
Leavenworth, M. C. - 101
Lee, Capt. Francis 101
Lee, Rev. Burnell - 19,68
Lee's Creek District - 16,66,158
Leflore, Chief Thomas - 62,154
Legate, 2nd Lt. S. B. - 101
Lessert, Cleremont - 292
Letho, Chief - 31,80,171,288
Lewis, John T. - 268
Lewis, Rev. David - 21,325
Lewis, Mrs. David - 325
Liberty Baptist Church - 4,19,326
Light-Horse-men - 70,162
Lincoln, Hon. Heman (1821-1887)- 93,185,300
Lindsey, Mr. - 78
Lindsey, Mrs. - 78
Lin-nop-e - 33,83,174
Little Doctor, Chief - 277
Little Fox, Chief - 31,80,171,288
Little Nemaha River - 39,89,90,180, 242,295
Little River - 14,63,64,155,156,269
Lockwood, Mrs. - 18
Logan, Col. James - 277
Louisiana - 225
Louisiana, Natchitoches - 47,100, 192,309
Lowrie, Walter - 185,300
Lowther, Robert - 164
Luke, Gospel of - 24,73,165
Lukfoata Station (Presbyterian) - 64,156,269
Luna, Chief John - 273
Lupton, 1st Lt. L. P. - 49,102,103

Lura, Price & Paine - 67,159
Lykins, Rev. Johnston (1800-1876) - 32,34,81,85,93,172,175,184,288, 291,299,324,328
Lykins, Mrs. Johnston - 32,81,172,288

Macabe, R. A. - 70
Magaukwok, Chief - 284
Mails - 257
Maine - 225
Management of Indians - 260,261
Mandans - 54,108,201,311
March, Col. - 102
Mark, Gospel of - 24,73,165
Markham, T. B. 293
Marks, L. W. - 326
Martin, Elder Colby - 323
Mash-e-na, Chief - 87,178
Mason, Col. R. W. - 309
Mason, Maj. R. B. - 49,102,104
Mason, Rev. - 278
Mason, Mrs. - 278
Massachusetts, Boston - 42,93,184, 185,229,300,326
Mather, 1st Lt. V. V. - 101
Matson, Gen. - 29
Matthew, Gospel of - 289
Mau-shau-ke-tau, Chief - 27,75,167, 283
M'Causland, Thomas - 72
McCoy, Christian[a] - 324,328
McCoy, Isaac (1784-1846) - 1,2,5,57, 92,145,227,238,298,324-326,328
McCoy, Isaac - Papers - 326
McCurtain, Daniel - 154
McCurtain, Samuel - 267
McCustain, Thomas - 154
McIntosh, Mrs. J. - 276
McKenzie, Rev. J. W. P. - 270
McKenzie, Mrs. J. W. P. - 270
M'Clelland, David - 14
M'Comb, Lt. - 102
Means of obtaining subsistence - 118-120
Me-chu-shing-a, (Little White Bear) Chief - 292
Meeh-hohungee, (Big Girl) Chief - 296
Meeker, Jotham (1804-1855) - 2,5,30,32, 35,57,79,81,170,258,287
Meeker, Mrs. Jotham - 30, 32,79,81, 170,287

335

Index

Menominees - 54,108,200,242,243, 311
Merrill, Miss - 156,268
Merrill, Rev. Moses (1803-1840) -40, 90,181,250,296
Merrill, Mrs. Moses - 40,90,181,296
Mestizoe - 113
Methodists - 81,170,172,185,275, 289,300
Methodist Mission - 15,22,30,31,34, 38,64,68,71,79,80,84,86,87,156,161, 163,170-172,175,177,178,270,271, 275,280,285,286,288,291-293
Method of obtaining fire - 122
Methods of reckoning - 128
Mexican - 11,59,106,137,202,244,275
Mexican Dominion - 112
Mexico - 113,136,140,141,202-204, 222,262,311
M'Gowan, Rev. Peter M. - 93,184
Miamies - 28,54,77,78,103,108,168, 169,194,200,285,286,310,311
Mich-e-ke-kau-ba (Miche Kekaubee) Chief - 77,168,284
Michigan - 54,108,168,285,287,311
Michigan Territory - 28,77,168,170
Miles, 1st Lt. D. I. (S) - 48,101
Military Posts - 47-50,100-102,192, 193,308,309
Milliee, Rev. Abraham - 291
Miller, Mrs. - 80
Milton, David - 66,158
Minataree - 54,108,201,311
Min-gar-na-chi, Chief - 36,177
M'Intosh, Chief Rolly - 20,70,162,277
M'Intosh, Judge Chilly - 20,70,162,195, 196,277
M'Intosh Party - 195,277
M'Intosh, William - 68,161
Missionary Society for the M. E. (Methodist Episcopal) Church - 79,80,84,86,87,93,170-172,175,177, 178,184,185,288,299
Mississippi River - 12,28,37,59,70, 77,117,154,174,195,200,201,206, 210,215,218,233-235,241,246-248, 253,254,263,277,284,296,311,313, 315,316,318,325
Missouri - 7,11,16,23,24,27,29,31,33, 35,39,49,54,59,65,72,73,75,76,78-80,84,85,95,102,149,157,158,164, 165,167-171,174,176,186,190,197, 198,210,216,235,238,242,248,250-252,271,272,279,280,283-288,290, 291,301
Missouria - 60,151,262
Missouri Conference (Methodist) - 19,22,30,31,34,38,42,68,71,87,178
Missouri, Liberty (Clay Co.) - 294,295
Missouri River - 11,27,33,39,41,49, 50,54,59,76,78,79,83,84,86,89-92, 102,103,108,117,149,167168,171, 178,180,181,183,193,210,238,242, 248,253,256,257,284,287,288,290, 293-295,297,309
Missouri, St. Louis - 7,12,60,105,150, 260
Missouri, Westport - 9,10,29,30,33,35, 78,79,83,85,92,93,144,168-170,174, 175, 177,183,285,287,290,291,299
MacKenzie, Sir Alexander (c.1764-1820) - 113,122
Mackenzie's River - 116
M'Kinney, Chief Col. John - 267
M'Kinney, Thompson - 267
Mohawks - 23,24,72,73,164,165,279
Moless, Chief - 294
Mo-ne-push-ee (Monepushe), Chief - 27,75,167,283
Monroe, Mr. - 210,237
Monroe, Rev. - 38
Montgomery, 2nd Lt. A. - 101
Moore, Dr. - 102
Moore, 2nd (1st) Lt. Stephen (W.) - 48,101
Morris, Capt. L. N. - 47,101
Morrison, William M. - 1,324,328
Moulton, Mrs. Samuel - 14,64,155
Moulton, Samuel - 14,64,155
Mountain Fork - 14
M'Phail, Lemuel C. M. - 102
Muskogee - 19,21,69-71,81, 160-163, 172,275,277,289,310,325
Muskogee Baptist Church - 4,22,71, 163,325,326
Mushulatubbee District - 152,154, 156,267
Musk-o-ma, Chief - 87,178
Myers, Rev. - 15
Myers, Mrs. - 15

336

Index

Nah-ko-mul, Chief Capt. - 34,84
Nah-ko-muno, Chief - 175,290
Nam-pa-war-rah (Fury), Chief - 36,86, 177,292
Naswaugee, Chief - 284
Native Merchants - 67
Native Missionary Society - 269
Neamabtla, Chief - 162
Neameeko, Chief - 162
Neglected Garden, (book) - 160
Negroes - 113,202,262,263
Negro Legs, Chief - 29,78
Nekitchewa, Chief - 287
Nelson, Capt. J. S. - 47
Nelson, George - 268
Nelson, Isaac - 268
Neosho - 13,60,151,222
Neosho District - 16,66,158
Neosho, Lower - 75
Neosho River - 16,23,25,27,48,65,72, 73,75,101,157,164,165,167,193,271, 279,283,284,288,309
Neosho, Upper - 75
Ne-she-mo-ne, Chief - 27,75,167
New England - 129,139,140
New England Indians - 54,108,200,311
New Holland - 126
New System of Writing - 257-260
Newton, Mr. - 175
Newton, Mrs. Samuel - 68,275
Newton, Samuel - 68,160,275
New York - 93,163,229,241,242,300, 326
New York Indians - 54,108,168,200, 311
New York, Meredith - 323
New York, Rochester - 2
Nitahachi, Chief - 62,154
Noah - 135
Nocheninga, Chief - 294
Non-non-da-gon (Non-on-da-gon), Chief - 84,175,290
North American Review - 312
Northern Indian Agency - 78
North Fork River - 16,161,162
Northrup, Lt. - 251
Northrup, 2nd Lt. L. B. - 49,102
Nosha-kum, Chief - 77,168,284
Nowland, E. W. B. - 102
Nowland, 1st Lt. C. F. M. - 102

Nung-e-wash-e, Chief - 27,75,167,283
Nutting, George - 284

Oakehiah, Chief - 267
O'Briant, Mrs. Duncan - 19
O'Briant (O'Bryant), Rev. Duncan (1785? -1834) - 19,326
O'Brien, Lucius - 101
Officers - 102
Oglafliah - 61
Ohio - 54,106,108,160,241,242,290,311
Ohio, Staunton - 323
Oklahoma - 2,4,325,326
Oklahoma, Choctaw County - 326
Oklahoma, Oklahoma City - 1,326
Oklahoma, Piney (Adair County) - 2,326
Oklahoma, Wagoner County - 325
Ok-wun-ox-e, Chief - 30,79,170,287
Old Dwight Mission (Arkansas) - 68, 160,274
Olmstead, Jared - 269
Omahas - 13,39,40,46,50,60,91,92,98, 102,103,151,161,168,181-183,190,193- 195,199,222,243,262,296-298,310
Onondaqua, Chief Isaac - 23,72,164,279
Opukshenube District - 267,268
Ouisconsin (Wisconsin) Territory - 210,242
Orr, James - 18,67,159,274
Orr, Mrs. James - 18,67,159,274
Osages - 12,13,16,18,24-27,29,32,36, 39,43-45,51,60,65,73-75,77,81,85, 86,90,96,99,102,103,111,127,128, 131,150,151,157,165-167,169,172, 176,180,187,188,190,191,193,194, 199,222,243-245,250-252,254,255, 260-262,271,272,280-283,292,295, 302,303,305,310
Osage Agency - 50,193
Osage River - 76,168,244,284
Otoes - 13,32,39,40,46,50,60,81,89- 92,98,102,103,151,172,180-182, 189,190,193,194,199,222,243,250, 262,289,295-297,304,310,314
Otoe Temperance Society - 301
Ottawas - 13,27,29-32,54,60,76,78, 79,81,105,108,128,151,168-171, 193,198,199,222,237,241,242,244, 245,262,286,287,289,310,311,313
O-wau-sau-be, Chief - 27,75,167,283

Index

Pacific Ocean - 116,117,249
Palmer, Rev.(M.D.) Marcus - 18,68, 160,274
Palmer, Mrs. Marcus - 18,68,160,274
Palmer, Sarah Ann - 275
Park Hill Station (Presbyterian) - 274,275
Parks, Joseph - 78
Particular Baptist Churches - 4,325
Paschal, Chief - 78,169,286
Patterson, Chief Capt. - 34,84
Paul, 2nd Lt. G. R. - 101
Pawnees - 13,40,41,46,50,51,60,76, 91,92,99,102-104,131,132,151,182, 183,190,191,193-195,199,204,222, 243,249,250,262,290,297,298,305, 306,310
Pearson, Moses - 290
Pearson, Mrs. Moses - 290
Peery, Rev. E. T. - 34,84,175,285,291
Perry, Mrs. E. T. - 34,84,175,285
Peet, Pere - 284
Pennsylvania, Philadelphia - 63,155
Pennsylvania, Pittsburgh - 42,93,185
Peorias - 13,27,29-31,60,76-79,103, 151,168-171,178,194,198,199,222, 237,245,262,285-287,293,310,313
Peoria Jim, Chief - 30,78,169,286
Pepper, Col. - 27,28,76
Perkins, Capt. David - 49,102
Perry, Chief John - 31,80,171,288
Perry, Chief William - 31,80
Perry, Moses - 154
Perry, Rev. Moses - 64,156,268,270
Perryman, Chief Benjamin - 20,70
Perryman, Lewis - 276
Petit, Rev. - 285
Pe-Wy-ha, Chief - 23,72,164,279
Pheasant Bluff - 262
Phillips, Capt. J. A. - 101
Phillips, Ellis F. - 17
Physicians - 128
Piankeshas - 13,28,29,31,60,77-79, 103,151,169,171,194,198,199,222, 237,245,262,285-287,310
Pickerings' Orthography - 160
Pine Ridge Station (Presbyterian) - 64,156,270
Pitcher, Dr. Zina - 48

Platte, River (also Great Platte River) - 37,50,89-91,102,103,180, 181,193,242,295,296
Plea for the Aborigines of North America - 109-112,201-225,312-321
Pollock, P. G. - 277
Polygamy - 89
Pool, James - 23,72,164
Poshemataha District - 61-64,152, 154,155
Pos-sa-che-haw, Chief - 37,178,293
Pottawatomies, see Putawatomies
Potter, Mr. 293
Potts, Rev. Ramsay D. - 4,65,154, 157,268,271,326
Potts, Mrs. Ramsay D. - 65,157,271. 326
Prairie Du Chien - 242,307
Pratt, John Gill - (1814-1900) 2,145, 172,289
Pratt, Mrs. John Gill - 172,289
Prayer, Book of Common - 165
Presbyterian, Cumberland - 34,84
Presbyterian Missions - See American Board of Commissioners for Foreign Missions and Western Foreign Missionary Society.
Presbyterians - 81,172,185,275,300
Provisions for the Indigent - 254
Puncah - 13,41,60,92,103,149,151,183, 194,222,243,262,298,299,310
Puncah River - 11,59,238
Pushmetahau District - 267,268
Putawatomie - 13,27-29,32,45,50, 54,76,77,81,82,87,97,102,105,108, 151,167-169,173,178,188,189,193, 198-200,237,241,244,245,262,284, 285,289,303,310,311

Quakers - 300
Quapau - 60
Quapaw - 50,54,75,76,102,103,151,167, 193,194,222,244,262,282-284,310
Qua-qua-taw (Quaquata), Chief - 28, 77,168,284

Rains, 1st Lt. G. I. - 101
Raynor, H and S - 326
Read, 2nd Lt. J. G. - 101

Index

Red Fork - 20,69
Red River - 4,11,13,15,47,51,59,61, 62,65,100,103,104,149,150,152-157,192,194,238,243,244,248,253, 262,263,269,273,290,309
Red River District - 326
Reed (Read?), Chief Capt. - 23,72, 164,279
Regular Baptist Communion - 9
Relative Proportion of Improved Indians - 114
Religion - 125-128
Religious Festivals - 55
Rennick, Rev. Henry - 34,84
Rentz, Charles C. - 182,297
Requa, William C. - 27,75
Rhind, Rev. H. G. - 270
Rhode Island - 51
Rice, Mary - 22,70
Richmond, John - 159,273
Riddle, William - 267
Riley, Maj. Bennet - 49
Rind, H. G. - 154
Robinson's History of America - 121
Roche De Boueff - 241,244
Rocky Mountains - 12,54,59,60,103, 108,116,150,201,211,256,260,298
Rogers, Charles - 66,158
Rogers, Chief James - 66,159
Rogers, Lewis - 67,159
Rollin, Rev. D. B. - 19,70,163,172,289
Rollin, Mrs. D. B. - 19,70,163,172,289
Roman Catholic - 179
Ross, 2nd (1st) Lt. R. H. (W.) - 49,101
Routh, Eugene Coke - 1
Roving Habits - 115
Russia - 141

Saginaw - 241
Salisaw Creek - 18,68,160
Salison Station (Methodist) - 275
Sa-mau-kau, Chief - 80,171,288
Sandwich Islands - 110
Santa Fe - 50,103,132,194,253,257
Santie Band - 242
Saturlee, Dr. Benedict - 183,298
Sauks - 54,105,108,201,242,244,250, 262,284,294,307,310,311,313
Sault De St. Marie - 112,258
Sau-wau-no -171
Sauwaunowe Kesauthwau - 81,289

Schoolcraft, H. R. - 260
Scripture Tracts - 160
Seaman, Rev. - 270
Sears, Benjamin Jr. - 324
Sears, Elder Benjamin - 323
Sears, John - 324,327
Sears, Mary - 324,327
Seaton, 2nd Lt. A. F. - 101
Seawell, 1st Lt. W. - 101
Secretary of War - 218
Seminole - 54,108,196,200,240,242, 249,253,278,279,310,311
Seneca - 13,16,23,24,60,72,73,75, 151,157,164,165,167,198,222,244, 262,271,279,280,282,283,313
Seneca River - 16,65,157,271
Seneca Steel, Chief - 23,72,164,279
Serampore (India) - 327
Shaler, Rev. N. T. - 171
Shane, Charles - 29,31
Shau-wau-no - 171
Shaw, W. A. - 67
Shawnees, see Shawanoes
Shawanoes - 13,23,27,29-35,50,60, 72,75,77-83,85,102,107,111,127, 132,151,164,167,169-175,193,198, 199,222,238,242,244,245,253,262, 279,283,285-291,293,310,313,315
Shawanoe Baptist Mission House - 5,30,57,71,79,145,157,168,227,258, 271,286
Shawanoe Council House - 238
Shawanoe Mission (Baptist) - 2,5, 65,77,84,157,182
Shawanoe Sun - 172,289
She-kauk, Chief - 30,170
Sho-ba-shing-a (Shobshinga), Chief- 27,75,167,283
Shokapee (Big Kauzau), Chief - 269
Simerwell, Robert (1796-1866) - 28, 32,77,81,168,172,285
Simerwell, Mrs. Robert - 28,32,77, 81,168,172,285
Simonton, 1st Lt. - 49
Sioux - 54,76,103,108,129,201,242, 253,311
Skillowa, Chief - 72,164,279
Small Cloud Spicer, Chief - 23,72, 164,279
Small Pox - 248,249

339

Index

Smedley, Rev. Joseph - 65,154,157, 267,271
Smedley, Mrs. Joseph - 65,157
Smith, Esther - 67,68,159,274
Smith, John P. - 87,178
Smyth, Rev. - 280
Smyth, Mrs. - 280
Snake - 54,108,201,311
Spaniards - 139,202
Spanish - 223,257
Spanish Dominions - 140
Spear, Jack - 67,159,273
Spring, Christian - 62,154,268
Stateler, Rev. L. B. - 22,291
Stateler Mrs. L. B. - 291
St. Cook, Capt. P. H. - 102
Steen, 2nd Lt. E. - 50,102
Stetson, Miss - 67,159,274
Stevenson, Capt. J. R. - 101
Stewart, Capt. - 48
St. Joseph River - 117
St. Lawrence River - 117
Stokes, Gov. Montfort - 104,159,167, 273
Surveys - 244,245
Swan, Chief - 29,78,169,285
Swords, 1st Lt. Thomas - 49,102

Talbot, Rev. N. M. - 30,79,169,286
Talbot, Mrs. N. M. - 30,79,169,286
Tall Chief, Chief - 23,72,164,279
Tally, Rev. M. D. - 15
Tally, Mrs. M. D. - 15
Tauweash - 253
Tawareka - 253
Taylor, Miss [Lucy H.] - 271
Taylor, 2nd Lt. J. H. - 47,101
Tellinghast, Capt. N. 101
Temperance Societies - 300,301
Tennessee Conference (Methodist) - 18,19
Terret, Lt. A. - 102
Terret, 2nd Lt. Burdet - 50
Texas - 13,61,152,211,248,250,262, 263,273,276,284,288,290,293
Thomas, Capt. Charles - 101
Thornton, Dr. John - 66,67,159
Thrall, Cynthya - 18
Tinsawattee Baptist Church -4,326
Tipton, Mr. 206
Tishetau Waukonta, Chief - 284

Topinepee, Chief - 284
Tow-un-ma-kee, Chief - 27,167,283
Trading Posts - 50,102,193,310
Trayner, Capt. E. - 49
Trenon, Capt. E. - 102
Tribes More Wretched - 116
Trinity River - 263,288
Triplin, C. S. - 47
Tubbs, Alvin - 277
Tuckebachemeko, Chief - 277
Tucker, Rev. Eber - 154,157,271
Turner, Ann - 324
Tus-hat-che-me-ko, Chief - 70

U-fa-la-ha-cho (Ufalahache), Chief - 70,277
Unexplored Country - 117
Union - 141
Union Mission Station (Presbyterian) - 18,160
United Brethren (Moravian) Mission - 291,300
United States - 8,18,21,24,26,27,34, 44-47,51-54,58,63,65,67,68,70,72, 74,84,90,93,97,99,100,104-106,108, 110,114,127,137,140-143,154,157, 159,162,164,174,175,178,188-193, 195-203,206,210-213,216-219,222, 224,230,237-240,242,246,250,253, 257,262,264,266,268,290,293,294
United States Army - 253
United States Congress - 149,215
United States Dragoons - 49,102, 193,309
United States Government - 29,37, 45,76,77,86,94,158,176,181,186, 196,200,276,295
United States President - 96,97,99, 100,187,189-192,212,213,217,237-239,302-307
United States Treasury - 95,187
United States Territories - 12,16,60, 65
Upolhlohola, Chief - 162
Ury, Lt. Asbury - 50,102

Van Buren, Mr. [Martin] - 237
Van Deveer, 2nd Lt. John - 50,102
Van Horn, Lt. J. - 67
Vann, Chief Joseph - 66,159
Vashon, Capt. George - 17,67,76

Index

Vaughler, Rev. Jesse - 291
Verdigris River - 16,21,25,48,65,70, 73,101,157,162,163,165,193,271, 280,309,325
Vessels to Hold Water & c. - 122,123
Villages - 254
Virginia - 139
Vose, Lt. Col J. H. - 47,101,309

Wako - 253
Wallace, Jefferson - 62,154
War - 50,103,104,128-134,194-196
Warren, N. A. - 292
Waseun, Chief - 287
Washington, D. C. - 1,2,47,100,150, 227,238,324,328
Washburn, Rev. Cephas - 18,67,159, 274
Washburn, Mrs. Cephas - 18,67,159, 274
Watchamonga, Chief - 294
Watson, 2nd Lt. John - 50
Watson, John - 268
Waugh, Lorenzo - 288
Wau-pu-nim (Waupenim), Chief - 77,168,284
Wauronesaw (A Surrounder), Chief- 296
Wautanaungquokoke, Chief - 294
Waweeshqua, Chief - 287
Weas - 13,27-31,37,50,60,76-79,81, 102,103,169,171,172,193,194,199, 222,245,262,285-287,289,310,313
Webber, David - 67,159
Webber, Col. Walter - 16
West, 2nd Lt. James - 49
Western Cherokee Country - 2
Western Foreign Missionary Society (Presbyterian) 29,42,78,93,169, 184,185,286,300
Western Territory - 12,38,57,58,64, 65,67,87,90,102,145,156,157,178, 181,182,216
Wharton, Capt. C. - 49
Wheeler, John F. - 160,275
Wheelock Station - 14,15,63,155,269
Whelock, 1st Lt. T. B. - 50
Whin-ra-shu-ga, Chief - 36,86,177
Whistler, Lt. Col. William - 101
White, Chief Isaac - 23,72,164,279
White Cloud, Chief - 294

White Dog, Chief - 77,168
White Feather, Chief - 86,177
White Plum, Chief - 36
White Skin, Chief - 30,78,169,286
Whiting, 2nd Lt. A. P. - 101
Williams, Miss L. M. - 63,155
Williams, Rev. Loring S. - 14,15,63, 64,155,268
Williams, Mrs. Loring S. - 14,63,155, 268
Williams, Roger - 51
Wilson, Rev. Charles E. - 15,64
Wilson, Rev. Henry P. - 15,64
Wilson, Thomas E. - 102
Wilson, William - 267
Winebagoes - 50,54,103,108,194,200, 242,243,311
Wisconsin (Quisconsin) Territory - 210,242
Wiskehelaehqua -324
Withchetau - 253
Wohkonda - 128
Wolf Rapids - 241,244
Wolf, Samuel - 68,161
Wood, Rev. Joel - 64,156,269
Wood, Mrs. Joel - 64,156,269
Worcester, Rev. Samuel Austin (1798- 1859) - 67,160,274
Worcester, Mrs. Samuel Austin (Ann Orr) - 67,160,274
Worth of a Dollar, (book) - 160
Wosseoneguet, Chief - 287
Wos-shosh-e - 24,73,165-167
Wright, Rev. Alfred - 14,63,155,269
Wright, Mrs. Alfred - 14,63,155,269
Wyandots (Wyandauts) - 54,108,168, 242,311
Wyatt, Harvey - 159,273

Yancton Band - 242
Young, Maj. Nathaniel - 101
Young Wolf - 68,161,275
Youth's Missionary Society - 63

Zambos - 113

Other Publications

The Life and Works of Joseph Kinghorn
(in four volumes)

The Life and Ministry of John Gano
(in two volumes)

The British Particular Baptists,
1639 - 1910
(in three volumes)

The Three Mrs. Judsons

Early Indian Missions

Available from:

Particular Baptist Press
2766 W. FR 178 (Weaver Road)
Springfield, Missouri 65810

NOTES

NOTES

NOTES

NOTES

BELMONT UNIVERSITY LIBRARY
BELMONT UNIVERSITY
1900 BELMONT BLVD.
NASHVILLE, TN 37212